PRAISE FOR

TRUE
HUMAN

"Some writers know how to craft pathways of permission that ignite the latent potential held within us. They offer mirrors to the deeper genius and capacity of the human heart, to remind us who and what we are, *exactly as the crisis we face provides the tension needed for a quantum leap*. True Human is a map, a path, a key and a companion for those who want to leap."

CLARE DUBOIS, founder of TreeSisters.org

"*True Human* is a highly coherent, insightful, and important work; full of wisdom, beauty, and post-tragic inspiration for how to live with meaning in this time. Specifically, In our relationship to sacredness, Samantha's focus on making immanence more fundamental than transcendence is essential to shifting our path from ecocide to stewardship. A Creator or creative force that is not beyond creation but indwelling within all of creation makes all life sacred— and any avoidable harm caused sin. This book offers the deeply engaged reader a reattunement of senses and mind to the miracle and incomprehensible sacredness of this Earth and biosphere, giving rise to a love affair with reality and an attendant obligation to its protection and care."

DANIEL SCHMACHTENBERGER, founder of the Civilization Research Institute

"We must escape the deadly game-theoretic traps of our world, and *True Human* is our way out."

LIV BOEREE, international poker champion and creator of the *Win-Win Podcast*

"Plato said that true transformation enlarges the soul. This is what *True Human* does. Samantha Sweetwater has created a mosaic of truth drawn from deep memory of the ancestors to illuminate how we can become more fully human. At a time when we teeter on the brink of self destruction, this book offers a pathway to our redemption."

JIM GARRISON, PhD, founder and president of Ubiquity University

"Samantha Sweetwater's *True Human* is not only an extraordinary philosophical achievement but a quintessential roadmap for the future of human civilization. This brilliant masterclass of a book gifts us a rare transmission of *gnosis* (γνῶσις) allied with a deeply researched, well-footnoted thesis and pathway for a protopian future. My hope is that a hundred years from now, *True Human* will be considered a twenty-first-century historical threshold, a catalyst for our collective global healing and awakening, and an essential ontological building block for the higher potential of Homo sapiens living in harmony and consideration of all sentient life."

SARAH DREW, author of *Gaia Codex*

"I knew Samantha's words before they were ever written on a page. They were the words that held me through my dark night, my lifeline in the storm, the eloquent articulations that lit the way back to life. It is a gift to the world, to now see those same words woven into the pages of this sacred book. My prayer is that Samantha's poetic and profound insights on the nature of spiritual awakening resonate in the deepest chambers of the soul for all who open these pages. Once in a great while, humanity receives a timeless gift of assurance and guidance. This book is such a gift."

WES CARTER, president of Atlantic Packaging and founder of A New Earth Project

"In *True Human: Reimagining Ourselves at the End of Our World*, Samantha Sweetwater frames this tumultuous time as a planetary rite of passage requiring both personal and collective transformation. Drawing on personal stories, spiritual practice, and ecological insight, she guides readers to heal the wounds of separation, remember and embrace our deep kinship with all life, and find their unique place and purpose in co-creating culture, technology and governance aligned with the flourishing of Earth. This courageous work is ultimately an invitation to mature spiritually, embrace interbeing, and choose love over indifference in shaping our shared future."

RANDY HAYES, founder of Rainforest Action Network
and executive director of Foundation Earth

"Systemic change has long been plagued by debates between the importance of inner vs. outer work. This essential read moves us past this false dichotomy; reminding us that the notion of an individual is an illusion that has led us astray for centuries. We are in fact relational beings, inseparable from the world around us. Samantha's wisdom ensures we understand that returning to this truth is an essential step in the path forward."

JENNY STEFANOTTI, founder and steward of Denizen
and host of the *Denizen* podcast

"*True Human* is an empowering work that makes transformation deeply personal. Drawing from inspiring accounts of leaders and organizations who have done the hard work, Samantha Sweetwater distills timeless wisdom and practical guidance that can reshape the path of individuals and institutions alike. This book changed how I think about personal and organizational evolution."

DAVE LOGAN, New York Times #1 bestselling coauthor
of *Tribal Leadership* and co-CEO of Care4th

"*True Human* is a masterwork of integration—weaving personal healing with civilizational transformation in ways that feel both urgent and deeply moving. Samantha Sweetwater has created something crucial: a framework that honors both the metacrisis we face and the profound remembering required to navigate it. Her concept of 'enlifenment' offers a grounded spirituality for our planetary moment, while her detailed maps of healing and initiation provide practical pathways through the chrysalis of change. This is imagination activism at its most sophisticated—not wishful thinking, but rigorous imagining that dares to envision humans as 'harmonizers of the forces of nature.' Essential reading for anyone called to participate in the Great Remembering."

PHOEBE TICKELL, founder of Moral Imaginations

"*True Human* is a masterfully crafted invitation to come home to life and our true self as human expressions of a living planet. Samantha maps out patterns, pathways, and habits of paying attention that can help people to step back into aware and embodied participation in life as a planetary process. This is a crucial individual and collective step if we are to re-align with life's regenerative impulse everywhere, fanning the embers of regeneration, which are present in all communities, and acts of sharing, healing, nurturing and being 'in right relationship.' Samantha's invitation into the body as our vehicle for 'being in relationship,' her reminding us of 'nowness' and 'hereness' as portals into the immediacy of relating, and her invitation to live live as a sacred practice of relating and manifesting through the power of our attention, could not be more timely as collapse awareness spreads. Treat yourself to this eloquent distillation of alchemical wisdom for a time where the end of the world as we know it, opens the potential of a vibrant pluriverse of place-sourced regeneration in bioregions around the world. This is an important work that works!"

DANIEL CHRISTIAN WAHL, author of *Designing Regenerative Cultures*

"SHE—A Prayer of Blessing

The first moment we met—She, Samantha, was dancing in concert, in ceremony.

Now, decades later, her song is as clear as that first moment.

From this perception of 'Living Ceremony'—there is a prophecy that sings of Medicine Women traveling between lodges at this timing in our evolutionary cycle.

Etched on far away Kiva walls, echoed through great canyons, felt in the currents of moving waters and winds, awakened in the spirit fire of beauty, dancing remembrance from Star Nations . . .

It is understood—She is one, of a clan, of Ceremonial Medicine Women that have come to cultivate, to sustain:

This Indigenous Soul,
This Ancient/Now Dream,
Some call the 'NEW WORLD.'

Her perseverance through time and space is a gift—as is this offering of her resilient words which carry a sound, a reverberation, a TRUTH.

THIS TRUTH: All Nations, All Creation, Ho'zhoni, Lila Wopila Tanka. Ho'a . . ."

SAHN NICOLE HILL, author of *Sacred, A Discreet Medicine Story* and senior designer at the Centre' of Indigenous Arts

TRUE
HUMAN

REIMAGINING OURSELVES
AT THE END OF OUR WORLD

SAMANTHA SWEETWATER
foreword by Lynne Twist

Published by

MANDALA
TREE PRESS
mandalatreepress.com

Paperback ISBN (KDP): 979-8-9999657-0-7
Paperback ISBN (LSI): 979-8-9999657-2-1
eBook ISBN: 979-8-9999657-1-4
Audiobook ISBN: 979-8-9999657-3-8

SEL032000 Self-Help / Spiritual
NAT010000 Nature / Ecology
OCC033000 Body, Mind & Spirit / Gaia & Earth Energies

Cover image composited using Midjourney, inspired by the art of ju sting
Edited and designed by Kaitlin Barwick

SamanthaSweetwater.com

To C.G.
for initiating me into motherhood.

To all indigenous and original peoples
who have listened in a way that is true.

To my more-than-human kin
and all your future children.

To the future ancestors—
You are my North Star.

And, to Life.
I love you.

CONTENTS

FOREWORD
LYNNE TWIST

For many decades, my life's work has been devoted to ending world hunger, empowering women and girls, preserving the precious ecosystems and cultures of the Amazon rainforest, and awakening people in the industrialized world to change the "dream" that is desecrating our planet. At its essence, my commitment has been to call forth a human presence on this planet that is environmentally sustainable, spiritually fulfilling, and socially just. And this is the work, I believe, of the true human—a human being who is dedicated to the flourishing of all life on Planet Earth.

Each of us has the capacity to become such a human. And in doing so, we have the opportunity to live the most meaningful lives that any generation has ever lived. Spiritual teachers, Indigenous elders, and wisdom keepers from many traditions remind us that we were born for these times: that the very magnitude of our global challenges is what can awaken the courage, wisdom and love required to shape a new future for Earth and for humanity.

True Human is a guide for this great passage. It is both map and companion for the journey we are all called to make—from fragmentation to wholeness, from separation to belonging, from fear to love. For anyone seeking to realize their fullest humanity while contributing to the healing of the world, this book is a wellspring of wisdom to which you will return again and again.

Samantha Sweetwater is, in my view, a true prophet of our time— rooted, trustworthy, and radiant with vision. Drawing from evolutionary biology, systems theory, theology, psychology, economics, regenerative design, and the deep wells of philosophy, she illuminates both the causes of our current meta-crisis and the possibilities for transformation. With the rigor of a scholar and the heart of a healer, she reveals how the story of separation has entrapped us—and how we might step into a new story that is whole, life-giving, and aligned with the intelligence of Earth herself.

At the center of this book is a process Samantha calls "the kinship journey"—a profound initiation into self-knowledge, sacred reciprocity, and planetary maturity. She writes not only as a thinker, but as a dancer, a spiritual teacher, a transformation guide, and a medicine woman who has walked her talk across continents and cultures. Her journey through embodiment, plant medicine, and apprenticeship with Indigenous wisdom teachers and traditions has shaped her into a voice both ancient and utterly fresh. She has been called a "living systems oracle," and indeed, she seems attuned to the subtle intelligence of life in ways that remind us of what we have forgotten—and what we long to remember.

Throughout True Human, she channels the wisdom of Sophia, offering a sweeping vision of what our world might become if we dare to create a life-centered economy and an ecological civilization. And yet, Samantha does not bypass the darkness. She understands that only by facing the shadow of our human journey can we participate fully in the birth of something new. Her courage, curiosity, and fierce compassion shine through every page.

This book is dense with insight and alive with possibility. It invites us to linger, to pause, to circle back. You may find yourself reading slowly, savoring a section, or opening it at random when seeking guidance. However you engage, you will discover yourself accompanied by one of the most important new voices of our time—someone who speaks not only from wisdom but from Love.

In these entangled times, Samantha Sweetwater offers us clarity, depth, and the luminous reminder that another future is possible—and that we ourselves are the ones who will bring it forth.

Lynne Twist is a global visionary and proactivist committed to creating a thriving, just and sustainable world and a flourishing future for all of life. She is the co-founder of the Pachamama Alliance, the founder of the Soul of Money Institute, and author of The Soul of Money and Living a Committed Life. Her website is soulofmoney.org.

INTRODUCTION

Sapience exists to serve sentience.

THE POWER OF LIFE

This book is as unfinished as I am, as unfinished as our collective story. It flowed from me like a river whose source I do not own. If it says anything useful or true, it is not because it is perfect or complete but because it belongs to Life's Song.

Our species seems to be having an identity crisis; sandwiched between climate chaos, geopolitical and social meltdown, and the rising intelligence of AI, we are unmoored, confused, and anxious. We are becoming increasingly aware that our dreams and desires are bound to systems that are rapidly consuming the planet on which we depend. The social fabric frays as people seek security and control in fundamentalism, fascism . . . any -ism. If the "we" of the human collective were a single person, we might pathologize our current situation as psychosis or schizophrenia. We might even call it a spiritual emergency. Personally, I feel a bit more sane when I acknowledge this. It validates the vertigo I feel.

✍ **What does it mean to be human when our way of being is unraveling the biosphere we depend upon?**

If we want a future worth living in, then we need to address *power*. There are two kinds of power in the world: power *over* Life and the power *of* Life. The first is a zero-sum game of domination. It's the kind of power most people speak of, hoard, or fight for. It's a human thing—a game no one ultimately wins because win-lose games (scaled by global economy, then multiplied by existential tech) ultimately become all-lose.

Modern civilization has been built on the game of power over Life. This kind of power emerges from abstraction, self-interest, and narrow goals. It scaffolds economy, technology, and science. It railroads complexity, community, and ecology. If you don't play the game—if you offer succor or breadth or subtlety—then you lose the game. This is an old story enacted through countless cycles of enslavement, colonization, and degradation. But this is a brittle, *immature* kind of power. It requires control and closure. It makes us lonely and helpless and bored, obscuring what we can be and create together. It is a game of people who do not feel or trust love as the greater power. Of the two types of power, power *over* Life is the lesser power, a subset of Life's infinite game. This is a critical distinction.

In contrast, the power *of* Life pulses in, as, and through everything. It courses through our veins. We breathe it with every breath. It's the power of interdependence, entanglement, and co-emergence; of birth, growth, death, decay, and rebirth—over and over again. This power has always been here. Indomitable. We humans get fixated on bright, shiny, dopaminergic games that hijack our brains into believing we have achieved something. Yet there are expressions of agency far more beautiful and symbiogenic, ways of being that carry ethical gravity. Envision the peace and fulfillment of an honest, co-regulated apology; or a garden watered, tended, then harvested; or a call to your senator; or the slow reestablishment of secure attachment; or a good orgasm.

Life wins. No matter how hard anyone tries to control it.

✒ **What if our current story of power is only just a beginning? What if we are starting to discover the joy and discipline of mature collaboration with the greater power of Life?**

Having mastered subject–object power over things, land, and other people, we have an opportunity to *own* our power and learn how to better shape it in service to a larger whole—to mature into a species who enacts power as a subject–subject dance of relational reciprocity in all domains and at all orders of scale.

I am cautiously optimistic about an excruciatingly narrow, sublimely lovely possibility of *wise humans* partnering with each other, nature, and emergent technologies to nurture the continuity and emergence of Life's Song at a planetary scale. This could flip the entire civilizational game from the finite to the infinite—from extractive, colonizing dominion over all we humans have seen as lesser intelligences to ecocultural symbiosis with

Earth at levels of granularity and grandeur we've never imagined. It would necessitate the right incentives. Picture it: complex flows of atoms, energy, and information, metabolically aligned with the mind and body of nature, co-creating biocompatible abundance for all. Imagine the lowest possible entropy and the greatest possible diversity and beauty for generations to come, co-orchestrated by an attuned technosphere working synergistically with humanity and nature.

This is a potential doorway to *planetary relational maturity*—that is, an emergent age of Gaian and human coevolution that can only come about when we grow up and become responsible with our power. Imagine with me the possibility of a human world (culture, technology, economy, and governance) that hums in harmony with Life's Song. This is a *protopic vision*—a possibility, not a fantasy—of who and what we humans might become if we choose to embrace the great initiation of our time. Our opportunity is to restore embodied intimacy with Life and realign *our* world with the rest of *the* World. This is about remembered aliveness in beauty and pain, grace and shit—welcoming the whole messy bundle of shared reality.

This is where things get *very* personal. The transformational work you do means nothing if it does not draw you back into your body in kinship and communion with the animate world. Here, you enter a collective rite of passage; a planet-wide ceremony of persistence and emergence that demands a Big Cleanup; a reckoning, repair, and maturation for each of us and all of us where we wrestle with rupture, trauma, and hubris. As you do this, you will recover the inborn ability to heal, to compost fragmentation, and to know the sovereignty of your soul. You will realize that the basic assumptions of modernity (human exceptionalism, hyperindividualism, and progress as unending growth) no longer work. You can break these spells to recover belonging—not free of pain or imperfection, not without remorse or contrition—but as a lover, steward, and collaborator whose care and contrition dignifies your membership in the Earth community.

This book is an invitation to align your power with flourishing Life. It cozies up to power indirectly, calling not for head-on confrontation but for a sea change in the flow and cadence of time, energy, attention, agency, and action. It offers stories, praxis, design principles, and common directionality. It invites you to notice and share power differently, not as a player in a game you either win or lose but as a listener, participant, and co-weaver in a game of symbiosis that will go on far beyond your lifetime. It invites you to look at how you show up as a teenager and to do your work to become a spiritually mature adult. As you learn to feel and share in sacred reciprocity, you will also know when to speak truth to power, stand up, and set critical boundaries.

An adjacent possible *world* can come into being when many healed and healing humans join in interdependent devotion to Life. I don't have all the answers. But I did not write this book on a promise of solutions. I wrote it to generate conversations, to plant seeds we can only water together.

Some might judge it as the rantings of a naive dreamer. Fair enough. I am a dreamer. But people and cultures die without dreams. We cannot embody what we cannot imagine, nor can we create what we believe to be impossible. Agency hinges on story. So I offer this spell of Gaian dreaming—an incantation of an Ancient Future that wants to happen.

SLOW COOKING

This book has been gestating within me since childhood. As a small girl, I felt the underlying insanity of a human operating system fundamentally at odds with nature and the human soul. Even in my youth I could see the multipolar traps embedded in capitalism's logic of profit, limitless progress, and externalized costs. If my dolphin friends were more valuable as canned tuna than as free beings, what hope was there for a flourishing ocean? If forests were accounted for in dollars and two-by-fours rather than as cathedrals of biodiversity, how could I possibly trust the people doing the accounting? Born in 1972, I was excruciatingly aware that a handful of people could instantly extinguish humanity with the push of a nuclear button. It was abundantly clear to me that the future of life on Earth was tethered to human activity and desire and that we could easily botch the whole project due to nuclear irresponsibility, economic greed, technological overdependence . . . or even a simple inability to talk to each other and resolve conflict. I intuitively understood the toxic organizing force I now call *separation*: humanity's ancient disconnect with the underlying interbeing that makes all of Life, all of reality, possible. I knew that we were headed into an existential eye of the needle—within my lifetime.

Because of this clarity, I took a path less traveled. Instead of becoming a doctor, lawyer, or cog in the corporate machine, I stumbled onto the path of embodiment. I decided that experience and relationship were more interesting than knowledge, control, or wealth. I became a dancer, choreographer, community organizer, and permaculturalist, then a yoga teacher and teacher trainer. Then I created a transformational movement practice called Dancing Freedom and took it all over the world, working with diverse people on five continents and training hundreds of facilitators. The genetics of the explorations contained in this book were tried, tested, and proven in experiential processes with tens of thousands of people over decades.

I wrote the bones of this book between 2020 and 2021. With the pandemic as my backdrop, I installed myself at my kitchen counter to coalesce the insights I'd gained in over thirty years of working around the globe with the body, community, nature, soul purpose, and leadership for systemic change. As I wrote, I found myself traversing the interweave between personal transformation and civilization transition that has been the background for and a subject of my life's work.

Some of the writings began as impassioned responses to current events including the COVID-19 lockdowns, George Floyd's murder, the January 6, 2021 Insurrection, and the subsequent meltdown of the American mind. Other pieces were written for much-loved clients as they struggled with intense awakening experiences, conundrums of purpose, heartbreak, addiction, suicidal ideation, existential angst, and the natural twists and turns of their healing journeys. Some were written for those same clients to empower self-trust and sacred leadership. Others were written more generally for readers and friends as sensemaking and soul-salve for these troubled and magical times. Some emerged out of meditations, ceremonies, and lucid dreams. While many of these writings are personal, all of them deal in some way with the dialectics between personal work and world work and between the individual and the collective. All of them grapple with the question, *What does it mean to be human when the future of life on Earth hangs in the balance of our collective choices?*

It's clear to me that *personal transformation is no longer just personal. None of us are here alone.* As a transformational facilitator with decades of experience, I have seen with saddening predictability that, if we do not deconstruct separation as part of our personal transformational journeys, we tend to unconsciously align increased capacity with the incentive structures of the larger (still toxic) system. We are called to evolve, not just as solo players but as members of the human collective bootstrapping our way toward a world where better-healed, earth-rooted people co-create a life-centric civilization. We don't need more heroes. We need kindred collaborators willing to move beyond rigid polarities and side-taking into higher synthesis and genuine compassion. We'll need all our tools on this journey: artistic, intellectual, neurological, relational, somatic, psychological, memetic, ecological, economic, governmental, technological, and psychedelic. And we'll need to consciously traverse the interstices between inner and outer, personal and collective, and subjective and objective aspects of experience. By doing this, we may co-create systemic healing and regenesis—for humanity and for all the other beings we share this world with.

And . . . I wrote this book because it is my story—the story of a kid who was born knowing that this would be a volatile, make-or-break lifetime for our species. It's the story of a human being who has been slowly cooking her childhood insights, studying Life, weaving community, and whispering souls. It's the offering of a woman whose heroine's journey has been to become worthy of the medicine she's gathered as a gift of wholeness for a world at odds with itself.

WHO IS THIS BOOK FOR?

This book is addressed to the part of you who instinctively knows you love Life. You are part of a larger wholeness.

It's designed to trigger a remembering of the sacred as it supports healing and authentic soul expression. It carries a prayer for freedom from separation and inspired life-centric imagination. It's a little nudge to help you find your seat at the table of mature human beings who are responsive to the evolutionary moment we find ourselves in. If you're at a crossroads, facing a choice between the deadness of business as usual or the mysterious calling of a more meaningful, healed, and impactful life, this book meets you with a strong invitation to risk saying yes. It's a risk worth taking. The road less traveled promises no certainty or security, but it will redeem pain and hope and shape you into who and what you truly are.

If you're aware that we've entered a wholesale transition in the very nature of self and civilization and that only a miracle (or billions of small, medium, and massive miracles) will get us to the other side, then you've just opened a book that will dignify your innate instinct. If you're already working to embrace, metabolize, and respond to grief, despair, and death; to bring new systems into being; and to tell effective, loving stories that are both grounding and generative for yourself, others and our world, then the writings contained in these pages will meet you well. If you have a prayer for healing—for your own health and happiness and the well-being of other human and more-than-human beings—then this book can support you in your prayer.

This book is for those with the courage to face our current world context authentically as an opportunity for personal and collective transformation and to live a better story. In these pages, you will find a no-BS approach to spirituality, healing, work, and relationship that can resuscitate meaning, purpose, and sanity and guide you toward the life your soul is designed to live—even in turbulence. We dance on the verge of annihilation or miracle. Let's choose Life.

HOW TO USE THIS BOOK

This book is a companion, a confrontation, and an invitation to come home. It carries you through a kinship journey that meets the sickening pain of disconnection as your doorway to soul initiation, maturation, and the possibility of a more connected and fulfilling life that finally makes sense, even in the context of major world upheaval.

It invites you to be your own best storyteller, calling you to discern between stories that reify disconnection and those that nurture intimacy with Life, then to deconstruct and recraft the stories you live by. We live in a time of narrative warfare. But you will find that some truths are more true, more contextually relevant and vital. We are all here on this small planet together. No matter how you "create your own reality," we also share a dependently co-arising world. This book invites you to ground the stories you live by in care for shared reality.

It calls you to play in the dialectic between remembering and reimagining. Think of remembering according to its etymological meaning: putting the "members," or the parts of a body, back together. Remembering is an embodied process of reconnecting or reweaving physical, intellectual, emotional, energetic, and spiritual parts. It means aligning your life force and agency with the underlying wholeness of Life. Reimagining, on the other hand, is a process of mind, of using your visionary faculty to construct an image of a possible thing or world. When you soften your grip on existing assumptions and beliefs, imagination gives you access to what might be and thus helps you bring what does not yet exist into being. Where imagination conceives of possible realities, remembering enacts them within a shared world. In holding both remembering and reimagining, we become capable of profound co-creation. We gain the capacity to meet the constraints, affordances, and complexities of our deeply fractured yet wondrously fecund world with all the life-centric genius of our bodies and souls.

The four sections of this book (The Metacrisis, The Great Remembering, Initiation, and Reimagining Ourselves at the End of Our World) take you through an initiatory journey from unconscious separation to conscious communion, a journey that begins in the collective and transpersonal, then zooms in on the personal, then telescopes out again. We begin with a deep dive into the meta-mess of our world. Then we explore *enlifenment*, a relational path for finding our way through it. After that, we dive into the personal, initiatory journey of meeting trauma and dissociation to reclaim the aliveness at the heart of humanness. We then conclude by restitching the personal into collective, planetary maturity. Each chapter begins with a framing story, explores themes related to that story, then ends with a short, guided meditation, decree, prayer, or poem. You can read these experiential sections in first person (as though in your own words) or as though I, as a facilitator, am speaking to you.

You will find four distinct voices in these pages. As a storyteller and narrator, I braid personal and client stories, psychedelic visions, and historical, philosophical, and metaphysical inquiry. Most of the book is written in this voice. I end each chapter as a facilitator or poet. This begins with "This Reality We Share" at the end of chapter 1. The third voice is Sophia, a teacher from a planet where they have transcended technological adolescence and achieved technological maturity without breaking Life. You'll meet her for the first time in chapter 4. The fourth voice is that of my future self speaking as an ancestor from three hundred years hence. You'll only find this voice in chapter 1. I include all these perspectives so that you can explore what it might mean to be a true human from many angles. These voices will speak to different parts of you: your intellect, your mystic, your cynic, the part of you that is healing and seeking, and the part who knows you are already whole. They speak to body, mind, and soul, because there is no intellectual substitute for an embodied experience.

As you read, I invite you to take multiple perspectives, surfing between personal and collective, internal and external, imaginal and factual. I ask you to explore the subjective interiority of your own experience, the objective exteriorities of shared reality, and the intersubjective and interobjective relationships between these domains. This will support you to sensemake and engage with your life in a more embodied and connected way.

I suggest reading intuitively—cover to cover, or one chapter or section at a time. Choose a title that piques your curiosity and just read that. Or engage in bibliomancy, letting chance to guide your selection, trusting that it will offer what is "for you."

Lastly, enter with a sprinkle of curiosity, a handful of humility, and a healthy pinch of sobriety. If you read with an open mind and heart and are willing to try on the explorations and practices contained here in your day-to-day life, then some alchemy—some remembering of who and what you are—just might arise as an emergent texture of your life force, your leadership, and your love for Life.

PART I

METACRISIS

The Conundrum

Civilization as we know it is eating the planet.
How the fuck did we get here?
And where might we go now?

CHAPTER I

A COLLECTIVE RITE OF PASSAGE

Oneness excludes nothing. No exceptions.

BORN KNOWING

Some truths chase you. No matter where you turn, they whisper peripherally, bleeding through the hidden architectures of your perception, feelings, and choices. For me, there have always been these three truths:

One: I am nature. I am part of nature. I dependently co-arise with Life. I am a living body made of and by other living bodies. This body is a vehicle for feeling what is relevant, authentic, and true relative to the living world I am part of.

Two: We live in end times—endings for species, ecosystems, ways of living, languages, ways of knowing, whole peoples, and possibly the integrity of the biosphere itself. I was born during the Cold War, raised in a community of OG environmentalists, and educated in the school of mutually assured destruction. My earliest memories are shaped by my young self's assessment that the game of human politics, economy, and technological progress could cause the extinction of most of Life on Earth within my lifetime. I have never not been able to hear the Earth groaning under the weight of our unconscious and ever-growing expectation that She feed our insatiable appetite for more of ourselves.

Three: Each soul brings unique intelligence to Life. I cannot remember a time when I didn't have a subtle sense of the specificity of my soul as a continuity that came from a great beyond, transcending this lifetime, body, and earthly identity, yet also choosing it fully. I have always known how to attune to myself through intricate, quirky, curious communion with nature and the subtle realms. I did not grow up thinking about soul, but I *knew* who I was.

I was the kid who tucked herself under the kitchen sink to listen to everything the adults had to say. I was absorptive, my eyes constantly dilated. I wanted to understand *all of it*. Art and science formed the warp and woof of my developmental fabric. Abandoned barns and urban wilds were my playgrounds. I was raised to ask questions (probably too many questions) and to trust wonder.

As I matured, I struggled to understand the "grown-up" human world. It didn't seem particularly grown-up. It felt like a strange, violent play. The pain of *separation*—the acculturated disconnect between humans and nature, between bodies and minds, between men and women, between the supposedly sacred and the supposedly profane—was glaringly obvious.

At fourteen, I found dance. Locked in the sweat-reeking wrestling room of my high school gym, I made dances about war, love, home, and states of consciousness beyond name or form. Dance was my first true *medicine*, an antidote to the insults of standardized education and vacuous suburban culture, a refuge of soul expression and emotional safety, and a source of endless fascination where I could marry mind and body in a living exploration of the architecture of experience. I spent hours in holotropic[1] trance states surfing the repetitive waves of Keith Jarett, Steve Reich, and Philip Glass. No one knows what drove me to dance. My passion for movement emerged unbidden as a dialogue between my body and soul, nature, humanness, and subtle energy. I enrolled other kids in my experiment. I asked them life's biggest questions, then had them close their eyes and move. Our bodies answered. Voluminous choreographies emerged, evoking tears, laughter, and thoughtful dialogue. I've been a student and teacher of the experiential core of meaning ever since.

Entering college, I faced a choice between my love of science or diving deeper into legal philosophy and dance. I chose the latter, because I had a soul-sense that I would need to understand humans, ideas, beauty, and power to do whatever it was I would be doing with my life. I was a solid "fuck you" to anyone who said I couldn't change the world.

On graduation, despite pressure to take a more conventional path, I followed my theory of change to San Francisco. Dance, choreography, and embodied education were my mediums. Community and culture were my chosen zones of impact. I formed multiple multidisciplinary performance collaboratives and cofounded a 7,500-square-foot arts warehouse. I became

---

1. The word *holotropic* means "moving toward wholeness." It was coined by psychiatrist Stanislav Grof in the 1980s. In the context of dance, holotropic processes involve rhythm, breath and focus on sensation, aided by music, that invoke visionary trance states.

a devotee of Ashtanga and Raj Yoga. I took *kriya* initiation with the "silent saint" Baba Hari Dass, studied Sanskrit, and practiced yoga, meditation, and pranayama two or three hours a day. I began training yoga teachers and helped open a few yoga studios. I picked up a passion for permaculture, the design science of crafting human systems in harmony with living systems. A major knee injury stole my virtuosity at twenty-four. Rather than walking away from movement, I went deeper into embodied experience, recognizing it as the foundation of cognition, meaning, and change.

On All Hallows Eve of my twentyninth year, my recently "ex" lover, a highly skilled meditator obsessed with transcending the mess of human experience, meditated himself into a violent psychotic break. Over the next ten days, I cared for him in intensely regressed and split states. At one point, he tried to convince me to kill him with a twelve-inch kitchen knife his father had given him. I buried the knife. On the tenth day, he walked across rush-hour traffic on the Golden Gate Bridge and was summarily arrested and taken to psychiatric services. Our community devolved into arguments about how to help him. I was left alone in our barren house with the rain and an empty hearth.

I had experienced a rude awakening to the shortcomings of the path of enlightenment. While my yogi ex was adept at the bliss of high level *samadhi* (nonsymbolic states that transcend normal consciousness), he had used his practice to bypass unresolved hatred, rage, disgust, entitlement, and ambivalence. He had sought limitlessness and turned away from love and his own humanity. It turns out, you can't meditate away unintegrated developmental trauma, fear, alienation, shame, anger, or disorganized attachment. *You can't transcend yourself into an integrated human.*

That experience, and the wake it left in my heart and community, shattered my trust in Life. It was obvious to me that dominant culture had failed him. Enlightenment was his "out" from a default culture that offered no more imaginative path to engage his spirituality or his voluminous creative gifts. In some ways, he was a victim of his own deeply incisive critique of our civilization. He hadn't considered the possibility of being fully awake *and* fully human. But I knew: *Life can't be bypassed.* Nondual awareness that denies the primacy of embodied relationships isn't really nondual. It was at that point that I made a commitment to humanness, both for myself and my students. Everything—including rage, fear and the need for healthy attachment—has to be welcomed and loved if we want to serve Life, even when choosing to do so is painful or scary. My mantra for that decade became this: *Oneness excludes nothing, no exceptions.*

I moved to Australia after that, planning to immerse myself in permaculture. But, quite despite myself, both land and people called for my dance medicine. In drum circles at the local market, African choreographies rippled through me. The community clamored for my skills in embodiment and organizing. So I created Dancing Freedom: The Path of Embodied Awakening, expanding the toolkit for somatic transformation I had developed as a choreographer. The practice gave me wings. It carried me to conferences and festivals around the globe. Over the next ten years, I worked with thousands of people and trained over two hundred facilitators to seed other communities. Then I created The Peace Body School to bring embodied spirituality to the people of Japan.[2]

Eventually, life brought me back to the US. In 2009, soul-crushed by another violent breakup, I dragged myself to a traditional plant medicine ceremony. I had thought my spiritual and psychosomatic tools could heal my scrambled attachment system. But I was stuck. Prayer, community, and the healing genius of the man who was to become my adopted spiritual father, George Grey Eagle Bertelstein, were the help I needed to heal. I spent those years absorbing every possible nuance I could from George and spreading Dancing Freedom around the world.

By 2013, having driven myself ragged building a global community on a shoestring, I hit a wall of chronic fatigue. City life was making me sick. I felt complete with dance and desperately wanted to find new ways to put my creative gifts to work. And the dissonance between my regenerative values and my lifestyle was grating on me. So I followed the dream of returning to the land (and a roguish farmer) and moved to a biodynamic seed farm at the literal end of a road in Southern Oregon. On those forty acres nestled against the north slope of a forested mountain, I tended sheep, ducks, chickens, goats, seed crops, and raspberries; ran the permaculture education program; and helped raise two beautiful boys. I butchered our meat, chopped our wood, and ground our corn. I hosted ayahuasca ceremonies for the community guided by a local elder. We rebuilt the sweat lodge. I learned to tend sacred fire. I guided soul quests and hosted my final Dancing Freedom training. Eating homegrown food, drinking live water, and working with my hands, my energy returned. Tending to that land, family, community, and medicine, I finally found

---

2. Thirty years later, I've facilitated tens of thousands of people in dance, yoga, meditation, authentic communication, vision questing, permaculture education, purpose-driven leadership, and ceremony. I've spent somewhere between 35,000 and 40,000 hours in some kind of embodied practice or teaching. I believe that embodied experience is the single most critical ingredient for integral healing, growth, or worldview transformation.

my elusive dream of *home*. Those years taught me what it is to be a person of place. (We must work for it.) But my romantic relationship was painfully dysfunctional. The charming farmer, as it turned out, was also an unfaithful womanizer who wouldn't make time for therapy. For my own sanity, I had to move on.

INITIATED BY FIRE

In May of 2015, grieving my lost home but remaining stalwart, I resettled in Ashland, Oregon. At least I would be close to my most beloved waters, farm food, and friends.

In mid-July, heat lightning ignited fires throughout Southern Oregon's endless tracts of roadless forest. The Cyamopsis Wilderness, the nation's second-largest roadless wilderness, burned uncontrolled for months. Smoke filled the Rogue River Basin and shut everyone indoors. The air was palpably thick and unceasingly toxic. I counted sixty straight days with no sight of the sun.

On September 12, 2015, the Valley Fire engulfed Harbin Hot Springs, the sacred place that gave me the name Sweetwater. I screamed inside as another home went up in smoke. This was followed by numb shock, then aimless anger that could find no object. Some part of me died with that fire—the part of me that was dancing with denial about climate derangement ever touching me. It was an unwanted and unwelcome initiation by a conflagration caused by a century of human mismanagement compounded by rising average temperatures. I wanted to see the wreckage, honor the land, and help the community, but I couldn't make my body get in the car. Instead, I grieved silently and committed to loving the land beneath my feet.

At home in Ashland, the smoke finally cleared. One afternoon, I was hiking the hills while on call with two colleagues who specialized in storytelling. We were having a casual conversation about how each of us embodied a particular archetype that, when woven together in a shared story, could support each of us to show up in full power and purpose. They asked me to tell the story of my origin. A strange clarity came into me, and this story poured forth:

My name is Samaya Storm. I am an ancestor from the Ancient Future. I have come to you in the Summer of your world burning to awaken your potential. I come from a future when humans have shaped their creative capacities in conscious service to peace, symbiosis, and the ongoing evolution of all of Life. I come from a time of great harmony when technology has been placed in service to humanity and natural living systems, a time when creativity and beauty flourish for humans and for all other beings, together. We know no poverty, no war, no separation. We live in communion with the divine in Life, organizing our consciousness and human systems in integrity with the health and full expression of all souls.

In the future I come from, the world story and system you currently take as normal has become a precautionary mythology. You are at the end of an Age of Separation that has allowed you to differentiate from your planetary Mother. In my time, we honor the stage of separation as an adolescent phase of human development that brought about the advancement of our sciences, technologies, global capabilities, and consciousness and which ultimately forced us to turn our attention back toward biological and ecological processes as the primary locus for the evolution of consciousness itself. The mess we made during the Age of Separation obviated the necessity for us to align our vast creative capacities with the Song of Life at a planetary scale. Separation initiated our maturation.

In our time, we have developed life-centric and soul-centric constructs of self and civilization. We live by a radically different metastory than you. Our World Story assumes that humanity is part of a larger ecological and cosmic Wholeness. You see, we humans are beings uniquely designed to tend the beauty, abundance, diversity, and continuity of the World. This story collectively harmonizes the Human Project with the Earth Project and makes us worthy of the galactic status you are currently reaching toward. We call this the Ancient Future because it recapitulates what indigenous people have always known, yet integrates planetary identity, governance, technology, and economy in ways none of us had experienced before.

I have traveled down the living memories of water, bringing myself through a wormhole in Her transdimensional memory. I come to help you find the timeline to the future I come from. I am here to keep that doorway open.

My birth into this world was a maelstrom of smoke and improbability. I rose, gasping and fully grown, from a lake surrounded by flames. I swam to shore, bedraggled, and lost. I knew I had to find my way in this inhospitable time and place. My heroine's journey, my sacred task, has been to sustain the memory of who I am and to shape myself as a woman who can effectively share the stories, meta-physics, and sacred practices that can steer us toward the future I come from. I have had to discover how, within the context of your current world system, to be a friend, a leader, a guide, and a teacher. I had to restore trust in myself to become a trustworthy voice that you can receive.

I come to you now, in this Burning Summer, to help you remember yourself to Life.

In the future I come from, we know ourselves as "the ones who came home."

We were all silent for a few beats. We knew this wasn't a random story. I had constellated the threads of a memory of my Ancient Future self. There, in the space between us, hovered the etchings of a gorgeous possibility.

We ended the call. The story stayed. Like a seed, it lodged itself in a fertile crevice of my bodymind.

I didn't quite know where the story came from. At the very least, I had happened upon a thought experiment to inform a central question: what ways of being can redeem the strange accident of being born into a time when human endeavor is extinguishing most complex life on planet Earth? Thinking like an ancestor from a future worth living gives a clear shape to things. The future Samaya spoke of would take us fifty, one hundred, three hundred, one thousand years to get to. Could it be that I, Samantha, am here to keep the doorway to that future open?

I moved back to the Bay Area in the spring of 2017. In October, two years after Harbin burned, the Tubbs Fire consumed huge swaths of Napa, Sonoma, and Lake Counties. All of California was engulfed in smoke. Whole neighborhoods of Santa Rosa were immolated: 5,643 structures, 36,807 acres. Untold damage to wildlife and watersheds. It was the most destructive fire in California history and the most expensive national disaster on record to date.

A few days later, an eerily familiar picture appeared online: a lake surrounded by flames. It showed water flickering orange-black as the forest around it exploded in violent red. The image was precisely the vision I had of the lake where I, Samaya Storm, emerged through water's memory.

I gasped.

It was my lake!

My future ancestor self had arrived.

That image was my second initiation by fire, the opening of a doorway of memory that has never closed.

Looking back at that sequence of events, it's impossible to know if the story represents an actual memory, something archetypal, or pure imagination. I believe, and my elders tell me, and physics confirms, that time is nonlinear, but rigor says to maintain skepticism. One way or the other, Samaya's story provides a fruitful thought experiment. She gave me roots in a future worth living toward.

THE END OF OUR WORLD

In September of 2018, one year after Santa Rosa burned, I drove north to Oregon for an ayahuasca ceremony with my rootsy, rural community.

We began the second night of work as the sun set red on a hazy horizon. Fires raged to the north. Air quality had decreased significantly, but we felt confident we'd be okay indoors. So we gathered into the little temple, closed the doors, and began our prayers.

Sometime around three a.m., the smoke became unbearable. So thick, we could barely breathe. I was five cups into the medicine and could *see and feel everything.*

The night came alive with terror. We tumbled out of the temple into the dense air. All around, in the heavy dark, animals screeched and chirped with alarm. Wings flapped. Bees swarmed. We had to bury our noses in the grass next to the cool earth to breathe. We prayed hard, visualizing all beings safe, begging for rain, for the fire to calm itself and for the smoke to clear.

Through the eyes of the medicine, I could sense the millions of living beings who make up the forest, from the tallest tree to the smallest beetle, all vibrating with us in prayer and terror. I lay there, face down, focusing every ounce of my extremely expanded attention on respiration.

Then I realized no one had checked the emergency channel to see if the fires were coming our way! This was a very real danger that could lead to being trapped on the single-lane mountain road. I crawled to my car—still high on the five cups of ayahuasca—and managed to turn on my phone, focus my eyes on the screen, and check emergency signals.

Safe.

I crawled back to my spot in the grass and buried my nose again in the moist darkness next to the soil. Mercifully, the smoke began to clear.

As my body relaxed and breathing became easier, I rolled over on my back and *opened*. My being expanded to meet and embrace the greater field of that vast night. I moved my mind to commune with the fires—not just the one close to us but the fires burning hundreds of thousands of acres in Canada and in Siberia. As I opened, I became a sacred witness, a vessel of presence for a living process infinitely larger than myself. The fires showed themselves as raging, voracious dragons, consuming all in their path, devouring parched biomass by the ton in their whirling, uncontrolled conflagration, yet revealing an indomitable logic. They showed themselves as master teachers, reflecting the magnitude of human insensitivity, hoarding, and greed and the debt of our disowned responsibility to tend the commons.

Then my inner vision shifted. I became attuned to countless living beings dying as their bodies were consumed in the flames. *Literally billions of lifeforms leaving all at once.* This was no small magnitude of destruction and suffering. While news reports had been focused on human injuries, deaths, and loss of property, there was an even bigger apocalypse going on for the more-than-human world. I saw and felt the dissolution of the structured patterns of energy and information that were held in their bodies. I lay there, heart pounding, bearing witness to billions of souls disincarnating in smoke. Billions of animals: mammals large and small, reptiles, amphibians, birds, insects. Billions of trees, bushes, ferns. Trillions of fungi, lichens, microbes, and other microscopic beings.

As I expanded in awe and grief, I realized the holiness of my witnessing. My undivided attention, filled as it was with love, became a currency of grace meeting and ennobling the intelligence of all that was being lost. In giving my concentrated witness, I had become a reciprocal space for the recirculation of the dissipating intelligences of these dying lifeforms back into Life. I had become a conductor for the conservation of consciousness—a conduit amplifying the potential of one form seeding future forms. *I could see the circularity of consciousness.* As I attended to one world dying, I was tending the bare threads of an emergent, possible future that can only rise through my (and our) heart-shattered witness of what is being lost.

As the early light of dawn broke through the gray-pink, smoke-laden air, I had a vision of startling clarity:

> *The world we were born into no longer exists. The one that will be will arise as we live, love, narrate and create it.*
>
> *The end is the beginning. The world that will become our future is a function of our love and courage or our indifference and greed.*

It will rise on the basis of what we choose to attend to and how we attend to it.

It is up to you to birth it with your love. It is up to us.

For the third time, I had been initiated by Fire.

That ceremony was a gnostic confirmation of what I already knew. The end began long ago. It has now gone exponential. We live in the basin of a great unraveling. It's up to us to grasp the threads of the possible future and to tend them with love, witness, willforce, and story.

A COLLECTIVE RITE OF PASSAGE

So, here we are. Ours is the hottest, fastest, most insecure and complex time any humans have ever experienced. The seventy years after the post-WWII signing of the Bretton Woods Agreements were both the most stable and the most accelerated in history, catalyzing the "Green Revolution" in factory industrial agriculture, exponential growth in global "free trade," the tech revolution, and the current explosion of AI and other exponential tech. They defined what most of us know as "normal." Now, growth continues at a fever pitch, but stability has decidedly ended.

We are in a metacrisis[3] of compounding, mutually reinforcing megacrises on ecological, economic, technological, geopolitical, and public health fronts, with significant short-, mid- and long-term existential risks[4] posed by nuclear war, AI misalignment, synthetic biology, toxicity, ecological collapse, and epistemic meltdown, all of them predicated on and potentiated by the game dynamics of a system that requires continuous growth for its survival. We are increasingly, anxiously aware of the root misalignment between the incentives and structures of our civilizational operating system and the well-being of the biosphere. We face what Nate Hagens, director of The Institute for the Study of Energy and Our Future, calls "The Great Simplification," or the beginning of the end of the radical expansion afforded by the *carbon pulse,* the one-time metabolic endowment of ancient

---

3. I use the word *metacrisis* rather than the more common *polycrisis* because "meta" implies a shared root cause. (See Rufus Pollock and Rosie Bell, "From Polycrisis to Metacrisis: A Short Introduction," *Life Itself,* April 24, 2025, https://news.lifeitself.org/p/from-polycrisis-to-metacrisis-a-short; see also https://www.sloww.co/meta-crisis-101/ for an excellent comparative overview of the metacrisis through multiple lenses.)

4. Nick Bostrom is credited with coining the term "existential risk" as it pertains to the possibility of human extinction or the cessation of technological progression ("Existential Risks: Analyzing Human Extinction Scenarios and Related Hazards," *Journal of Evolution and Technology* 9, no. 1 [March 2020], https://nickbostrom.com/existential/risks.pdf). But indigenous people have understood existential risk relative to the operation of the economic superorganism for thousands of years. The early environmental movement also understood existential horizons.

fossil fuels that we have used to exponentiate ourselves. Our systemic challenges are too big to touch. They are hyper-objects, gorgonian knots of wicked complexity that thwart the mind and intimidate the heart.

We've entered a liminal time between worlds. *Liminality* refers to a state of ambiguity and disorientation, typically in the middle of a rite of passage, a big life transition, or a psychedelic journey, where certainty about *what was* has broken down, but the end state is not yet known.

The very behaviors and stories that have enabled us (a relatively innocuous bipedal creature seeking power and knowledge) to reach a population of eight billion and growing, have reached the end of their effectiveness for our psychological and physical health and our long-term survival and flourishing. The ways in which we have solved problems and manifested dreams have themselves created greater problems. Our concept of progress as endless growth is naively cancerous.[5] Our meaning-making apparatus is disconnected from Life itself. In Einstein's familiar words, "We cannot solve our problems with the same thinking we used when we created them."

This can be scary and scrambling. The magnitude and complexity of our personal and collective challenges, compounded by fake information and communication oversaturation and multiplied by an increasingly prevalent sense that we don't really know where we're going, create a cognitive and emotional recipe for dissociation and overwhelm.

If you ask experts in complexity, climate, or AI risk about our midterm future, they are likely to say something like this: We face long odds; we'll be lucky to get through the next few decades without falling into abysmal collapse. Existential risk expert Toby Ord says our long-term future could be beyond amazing, but we're putting it at grave risk. He gives us a one in six chance of extincting ourselves by the end of this century.[6] Geoffrey Hinton, "the Godfather of AI," has said there is a "10% to 20% chance AI will lead to human extinction in three decades."[7]

---

5. "Our current idea of progress is *immature*: it is developmentally incomplete. Progress, as we define it now, ignores or downplays the scale of its side effects. Our typical approach to technological innovation today harms much that is not only beautiful and inspiring, but also fundamentally necessary for the health and well-being of all life on Earth. Developing a more mature approach to our idea of progress holds the key to a viable, long-term future for humanity." ("Development in Progress," The Consilience Project, July 16, 2024, https://consilienceproject.org/development-in-progress/.)

6. Toby Ord in Robert Wiblin, Arden Koehler, and Keiran Harris, "#72 – Toby Ord on the Precipice and Humanity's Potential Futures," 80,000 Hours, March 7, 2020, https://80000hours.org/podcast/episodes/toby-ord-the-precipice-existential-risk-future-humanity/.

7. Geoffrey Hinton in Dan Milmo, "'Godfather of AI' Shortens Odds of the Technology Wiping Out Humanity Over Next 30 Years," The Guardian, December 27, 2024, https://www.theguardian.com/technology/2024/dec/27/godfather-of-ai-raises-odds-of-the-technology-wiping-out-humanity-over-next-30-years.

The UN Intergovernmental Science-Policy Platform on Biodiversity and Ecosystem Services (IPBES) reports nature's "unprecedented" decline and estimates that up to one million species are threatened with extinction.[8] Philosopher Nick Bostrom writes:

> *Our species is introducing entirely new kinds of existential risk— threats we have no track record of surviving. Our longevity as a species therefore offers no strong prior grounds for confident optimism. Consideration of specific existential-risk scenarios bears out the suspicion that the great bulk of existential risk in the foreseeable future consists of anthropogenic existential risks—that is, those arising from human activity. In particular, most of the biggest existential risks seem to be linked to potential future technological breakthroughs that may radically expand our ability to manipulate the external world or our own biology. As our powers expand, so will the scale of their potential consequences—intended and unintended, positive and negative.[9]*

Civilization researcher Daniel Schmachtenberger describes the potential future horizons of the metacrisis as follows. Societal unravelling could take two different directions: techno-surveillance control (e.g., *Black Mirror*), or anarchic total chaos (e.g., *Mad Max*), or some ghettoized, unequally distributed version of both (e.g., *Blade Runner*). But somewhere situated delicately between these dystopian paths is another possibility, which he calls the Third Attractor.[10] The Third Attractor is a win-win way forward that nourishes the beauty, abundance, continuity, and emergence of Life for all of humanity and our biosphere. The Third Attractor implies a life-centric phase shift in our constructs of self and civilization, and everything that follows from them. It can only come about through radical reckoning, composting, and reconnection with Life. It is characterized by collaboration, reciprocity, regeneration, diverse unity, trust, and stable peace. It offers a path beyond multipolar traps and zero-sum games. It's a shift from the finite to the infinite game and from hubris to wisdom. And

8. "UN Report: Nature's Dangerous Decline 'Unprecedented'; Species Extinction Rates 'Accelerating'," UN.org, May 6, 2019, https://www.un.org/sustainabledevelopment/blog/2019/05/nature-decline -unprecedented-report/.
9. Nick Bostrom, "Existential Risk Prevention as Global Priority," *Global Policy* 4, iss. 1 (2013): 15-31, https:// existential-risk.com/concept.
10. Daniel Schmachtenberger in conversation with Rebel Wisdom, "In Search of the Third Attractor Part 1," The Consilience Project, August 16, 2022, https://consilienceproject.org/media/daniel-schmachtenberger -in-search-of-the-third-attractor-part-1/.

it's a mystery. Indeed, our greatest possibility lies in an "unknown of the unknown" set of solutions—in what we might call miracle. *And we will need to choose our stories wisely if we are to get there.* Why? Because we shape reality according to the stories we believe to be true.

Given all of this, most of us experience some level of existential angst, whether consciously or unconsciously. We feel the unbearable lightness— or untouchable heaviness—of being. We feel anxiety, grief, dread, paralysis, and the maddening itch of cognitive dissonance. This pervasive emotional energy sits like a cold stone in the belly of our collective soul. Some metabolize these feelings consciously. Others persist in denial.

Existential angst isn't a minor emotional disturbance to be meditated away. Existential unrest holds immense evolutionary potential, both creative and degenerative. On one hand, it can drive radical awakening, healing, innovation, collaboration, and effective action. It can catalyze a new and ancient story of human co-creation with Life itself, igniting millions of uniquely attuned responses to the calling of the world. One could even think of these responses as the inception point of miracle. On the other hand, it drives an ever-deepening malaise of nihilism, narcissism, addiction, apathy, overconsumption, and self-protection. In overwhelm, fear, and isolation, many would rather numb out, party, or double down on personal gain than be fully present with hard, complex truths. Some take refuge in technoutopianism. Many choose self-interest over empathy.

But being dissociated and lonely sucks. And the effort to persistently ignore a planet-sized elephant in the room can be both exhausting and scrambling.

Our choices in how we respond to our personal experience of this collective journey are somewhat binary: we can wall off, anesthetize, self-protect, and keep doing the same old things, or we can expand in grief, awe, healing, and compassion to show up as conscious collaborators with the pain and potential inherent in this moment.

As our perceived stability crumbles, jumbled psychosocial responses emerge. Sometimes, we contract into self-interest and tribalism. Defensive, dysregulated, amygdala triggered, we fixate on wounded identities, side-taking, and simplistic sensemaking to generate security. We silo ourselves in imaginary worlds, staking small, curated islands of comfort, uncaring for the social and ecological costs our dreams externalize. But sometimes, we respond to insecurity by rooting into the reality of our interdependence. We open in rigorous mutuality and care and take responsibility for our shit, our complicity, and our healing. We respond to others' pain, need, and indifference with kindness, honesty, and respect. We become more self-aware, attuned to others, and situationally responsive, and less attached to being special or being right. We choose sacred reciprocity.

These disparate tendencies in human nature form the axis around which our shared future turns. We will be tested everywhere that coherence breaks down. In every instance of challenge or privilege, there will be choices to face. Do you choose numbness or availability? Do you choose to be small, weak, fearful, and angry, or do you choose to be courageous, open, and collaborative? Do you choose to be the victim, perpetrator, or rigid savior, or do you choose authenticity, intimacy, and forgiveness? Do you choose indifference or love?

In this time of disruption and possible collective transformation, the stories that have guided us thus far are no longer sufficient to steer our way through the coming storms. We're experiencing a collective identity crisis. This is where any good rite of passage begins—with the crossing of a threshold from one way of being into the abyss of the unknown. But this time, rather than crossing that threshold as a single being (a hero heading into a hero's journey) we are crossing it together in a kinship journey that just might transform what we know to be true about us—whether we like it or not.

The kinship journey, as a narrative structure, offers an alternative transformational arc to the hero's journey. Where the hero's journey is a seeking to find oneself, the kinship journey reaches for reconnection, recontextualizing identity development within the meaning-rich web of relations that encircle our lives. The story begins when the protagonist recognizes that the source of their suffering is disconnection or disenfranchisement. They then embark on a journey where they must confront separation to reenter the web of Life. Through direct encounter with their greatest fears and the healing help of human and more-than-human allies and guides, they are able to sublimate the calcified armors that previously blocked connection, reclaim *both* sovereignty and interbeing, develop humility and stamina, and restore balance through acts of reconciliation, service, and reciprocity. This initiation matures the soul and shapes the person as a trustworthy partner with the greater Whole. Very little has been written about the kinship journey, yet this narrative is latent in works such as Thomas Berry's *The Great Work*, Robin Wall Kimmerer's *Braiding Sweetgrass*, Tyson Yunkaporta's *Sand Talk*, and Joanna Macy's *Coming Back to Life*. I have observed (and facilitated) this narrative arc in the healing journeys of countless clients and students.

As we navigate this kinship journey individually and collectively, everything comes up for review: identity, inner motivation, outer incentive, and the story and structure of civilization itself. Epidemics of depression, anxiety, addiction, and existential angst are all expressions of civilization-wide disconnection. Whether you know it or not, your personal struggles and transformations are also part of this collective sojourn of remembering.

But just because *our* world is breaking apart doesn't mean it's the end of *the* world. Our planetary crucible offers a real-time, whole-planet rite of passage or trial by ordeal. It's an initiation for each of us and for the collective human soul. This liminal ceremony for a small planet—a ceremony you can't not be in—demands a remembering of our place in the larger ecology of things and a reimagining of the meaning of humanness.

A PRACTICE: TOUCH THE SACRED

To what or whom do you owe the blessing of your life? Have you ever considered the web of relations that made you who you are? How wide and deep (ancestrally, ecologically, culturally, temporally, and geographically) can you extend the felt sense of all that makes you possible? If you don't feel that your life is a blessing, then get very simple. Notice the basic ways in which each breath pulses through your body, the way water quenches thirst, how food feeds you. Can you find a glimmer of gratitude for this One Life we all share? What basic things are already supporting you, even if you almost never give them notice?

A POEM: THIS REALITY WE SHARE

I will not help you to "create your own reality."

But if you want my help to create your part in the reality we share, I am here.

If you want to revive the organic intelligence of your body, mind, and soul, restore the empathic capacity of your heart, retrieve the majesty of your senses, and reclaim awe in this One Blessed Life . . . then I am here.

If you want me to mirror your sovereignty, to support you in becoming your unique soul essence, disabused of trauma and armors, secure in your belonging, and free to respond to the calling of this world, I am here.

If you want a kind friend with whom to let down your walls as you feel your way back into interbeing with the living web of Life, I am here. I will be the resonant voice and body who invites you to soften, to open, to consider the possibility of truly coming home. I will remind you of your nonseparation with all other selves and things. We are here.

I am here—praising the same sun, breathing the same air, subject equally to gravity and time, grounded on this same planet's skin.

I am here in devotion to what we can only do co-creatively.

To tend the beauty of the One Life we all share.

I am with you singing my part in the symphony of soul.

There's a part for you in this reality we share.

Join me here.

CHAPTER II

WHAT ARE HUMANS FOR?

Incarnation is nonaccidental and nonarbitrary.

THE COVENANT[1]

In a time before the marking of time, saber-toothed cats roamed Africa, Eurasia, and the Americas. As apex predators, they ruled the land, their predation defining the trophic cascade of relations between all other creatures below them on the food chain. Alongside these huge felines, an unassuming (seemingly helpless) two-legged creature with opposable thumbs and strong social tendencies was finding its way into the world. Our progenitors lived as contemporaries with these big cats. Fossil records indicate that during the last ice age, they cohabited caves, likely seeking shelter from extreme cold.

Bone fragments found in historically distinct layers in Sterkfontein and other caves in South Africa tell a story of human–cat coevolution. In the earlier layer of the fossil record, it appears the cats preyed upon the hominids. Forensic examination of bone fragments indicate that we were a tasty lunch for the tigers. In the later layer of the fossil record in these same caves, as we became anatomically modern humans, we see the balance of power shift. Analysis of these bones indicate that we lived side by side with the cats, cohabiting in a mutual arrangement that may have been mediated by our fires.[2] Still later remains, dated around 16,000 years ago, found

---

1. In May 2016, I made my first pilgrimage to meet the white lions of Timbavati, South Africa. I had been invited by their remarkable steward, Linda Tucker, to visit their sacred homeland at the heart of the Kruger to Canyons bioregion. The white lions are a rare subspecies of *panthera leo*. They are not albinos. Rather, they carry a genetic inclusion that makes them white and larger than their tawny sisters and brothers. In African indigenous prophecy, they are harbingers of the Golden Age. I returned home from that life-changing journey carrying this story.
2. Linda Tucker, *Mystery of the White Lions* (Npenvu Press, 2004), 57-60; citing South African paleoanthropologist Dr. C.K. Brain's ongoing research in the Sterkfontein Caves.

in caves in La Garma, Spain, indicate that we likely hunted and killed the cats. We may have even used their pelts as ornamentation or as ceremonial regalia.[3] Many scientists now believe that we hunted them to extinction.

Meanwhile, Ancient African stories are filled with meaningful interactions between big cats and humans. The stories correlate prehistoric saber toothed cats with contemporary lions.[4] They tell us of a prophetic and sacred meeting between the cats and early man. Recognizing the rising star of humanity's power, big-cat ancestors to our present-day lions ceremonially handed their leadership responsibilities for stewardship of all of Life to the humans, thus entrusting us with the mantle of "kings and queens of the kingdom."[5] Here is the story of that meeting:

The huge cat slowly padded to the entrance to the cave, settling her lithe body next to the little man. This wasn't a casual meeting; it was a Council. There were important things to discuss. The Sacred Covenant was getting wobbly. The saber-toothed tigers and their ancestors had called this meeting with the humans to ensure the harmonics of power in the World.

For the last few generations, the cats had noticed a significant uptick in human activity. For as long as anyone could remember, the humans and their hominid relatives had lived relatively peacefully within the ecologies they occupied. As gatherers, hunters, and scavengers, they lived and ate at multiple levels of the food chain. Occasionally using fire and spears to defend themselves or kill prey, they were aggressive and intelligent. They had even learned to kill the tigers and had taken over as the principal occupants of the big caves. The cats accepted all this. But in recent years, the humans had become more organized and more ubiquitous. They were overtaking the big cats in their place in the ecosystem and unconsciously upsetting the balance. The tigers, ancestors to present-day lions,[6] had decided it was time to mark these changes with a responsible transition.

---

3. Rachel Nuwer, "Humans May Have Hunted Cave Lions to Extinction—For Throw Rugs," Smithsonian, October 26, 2016, https://www.smithsonianmag.com/science-nature/humans-may-have-hunted-cave-lions-extinction-throw-rugs-180960915/.

4. Contemporary lions, *panthera leo*, are not direct genetic descendants of saber-toothed tigers (of which there were many different specific species). But from an ecological perspective, they obviously fulfill the same niche. And from the perspective of an indigenous worldview, one might consider that they come from the same ancestors, or even that the ancestors who were once the saber-toothed tigers have now reincarnated as lions.

5. Tucker, *Mystery of the White Lions*. Note: Linda shares part of this story in her book, recounting her meetings with the late Credo Mutwa. However, I received the deeper transmission of this story orally when visiting her and the White Lions in their homeland in Timbavati, South Africa, in 2018.

6. To be clear, modern lions are not genetic descendants of saber-toothed tigers. However, in the telling of these tales by indigenous wisdom stewards, it is implied that there is a soul continuity (i.e., an ancestral continuity) between the saber-toothed tigers and present-day lions.

Sitting side by side in the mouth of the cave, the two beings, leaders of their people respectively, surveyed the verdant valley before them. Down below, a serpentine river sparkled as it meandered lazily to the horizon. Here and there, the waving grasslands, dotted by trees, were obscured by darkly pulsating herds of hooved ones moving across the earth. Murmurations of colorful birds played among the clouds.

This was no council of words but a transmission of minds received body and soul.

The tiger began, "For untold generations, we have carried a sacred responsibility for harmony in this kingdom. We have been the masters, the queens and kings, partnering with the waters, the winds, the seasons, and the ancestors to tend abundance for all. We have hunted the weak, the infirm, and the maladapted, keeping the herds strong and the waterways flowing. We have been patient and observant, taking only what we need and giving back in reciprocity. We have watched over the sacred balance. We come to you now to acknowledge that you are overtaking us in the distribution of power."

The man quietly nodded, absorbing every word.

She continued, "We come to you now to tell you that your time has come. It is your time to lead. Our time is ending. Our reign is receding. This is the nature of succession. You must take up the Mantle now. You must lead on behalf of all of Life. This is the Way, the Sacred Covenant makes it so."

The man responded, "Yes. It is true what you say. We see this too. We are ready. We are able. We are willing."

"But my friend, you must know that this role comes at the cost of great responsibility. Your sovereignty as kings and queens is predicated on your care for the well-being of the whole. You must organize your power according to Life's Way for all of Life. To live and die and consciously participate in the miracle of Life is the ultimate Gift. The central responsibility of those who bear the mantle of leadership is to perpetuate this Gift. Those who lead cannot be selfish. Those who lead must care for all. You are students and participants, custodians and celebrants. You must initiate your young people and harmonize your powers. You must lead from love. This is how you will keep the balance. Through this, you and all of Life will flourish."

The man took a deep breath, receiving the lion's transmission. "We hear you. We, too, have seen how our uninitiated pride members disrupt the balance. We have been learning how to shape ourselves wisely to ensure the well-being of future generations. We have learned to honor seasons, stars, and cycles and to know and celebrate our place in the Circle of things. We have discovered the currencies of consciousness: presence, gratitude, praise, naming, grief, and restraint. We carry the original stories of Life's way for us. We take responsibility for the continuity and emergence of the Gift. This we will do. We commit to this Sacred Covenant."

As the apex predators of those ancient plains, the tigers had formally transferred custodial responsibility to the humans. It was done.

The two sat silently for a few minutes. Then the man stood. He leaned forward in a gesture like a bow, but also like a kiss, offering his brow to gently touch the tiger's softly vibrating forehead.

He sat again. They remained for a long time, absorbing the peace and togetherness of a fellowship grounded in shared reality.

Then the two beings walked their separate ways. They would never see each other again. The echoes of their meeting would live forever.

Thus was born the original Covenant humans agreed to uphold in their ascension to the apex position in the food chain—a contract with all of Life to sustain harmony in the kingdom.

A GAIAN THOUGHT EXPERIMENT

Does evolution create unfit organisms? Does the Earth make creatures that don't serve a role within Her ecologies? Would She manifest an organism simply to destroy Her? Of what use is a bipedal, prehensile, visually biased, tool-making, storytelling, hyper-creative, culturally adaptive species to the greater Earth community? What is our unique class of organisms for?

You and I are Gaians. We are denizens of this biosphere. And I believe we are a vital element of Gaia. Like all other organisms, *homo sapiens* fill a unique niche in the ecology of our living biosphere. We are radically creative beings with the power to shape or destroy worlds.

The ancient Greeks conceived of our planet as a goddess with infinite life-giving powers and gave Her the name Gaia. More recently, chemist and inventor James Lovelock and biologist Lynn Margolis posited the Gaia Hypothesis, a theory that describes the interwoven biotic and abiotic features of the biosphere as a single self-regulating, self-perpetuating superorganism. This planet-sized living entity exists, persists, and evolves through delicately harmonized positive and negative feedback loops that keep the conditions of the biosphere within boundaries favorable to Life. Gaia gave birth to humans. We birthed civilization, which now functions as a second, unconsciously parasitic, technologically mediated, economic superorganism. The survival of the economic superorganism depends upon the continuity of the more primary superorganism of the living Earth.

Within this context, let's consider *what we are*, not just as a projection of our own ideas, fantasies, and impulses but contextually, as organisms who occupy a niche within the larger planetary ecology. Humanity is a holon (a part of a greater whole) within the very real, continuously evolving, living process of Gaia. Could it be that our consciousness and creativity provide invaluable resources within planetary ecology? Who might we get to be and become if we align the Human Project with the flourishing of the Earth Project? How might we experience health, happiness, and meaning if we ground our individual lives and the collective project of civilization in a greater-than-human sense of reciprocal interdependence? How would we think about technological maturity if it were bound to the health of Gaian processes? How would this shift our relationships with ourselves, each other, nature, creativity, and time?

To think like a Gaian, begin from the view of *immanence*—the understanding that divinity or sacredness is inherent to the world.[7] This is not the perspective of a rational, uninvolved observer but the perspective of a participant and co-creator who is bodily, relationally embedded within the pulsating processes of Life. This view is a more accurate representation of what's happening in, as, and through you than the fictionalized stance of the impartial observer. The persistence of this world is cyclical and rhythmic; it moves and breathes according to the harmonics of greater tides. Every object carries its history within it.[8] You are here because others have been. This is nonarbitrary. You are in a body among other more-than-human bodies that co-evolve together. The phrase "more-than-human" was coined by philosopher David Abrams in the early 1990s to point us in this direction. It describes nature as a realm that thoroughly *includes* yet also necessarily *exceeds* humans, invoking fidelity to a web or relations greater than ourselves. You are a participant in the ever emergent *here* that you occupy.

You are a member of an adolescent creator species who has differentiated from its planetary mother, created technology and economy, learned to harvest exponential quantities of materials and energy to build unique ecologies, globally scaled itself, and is now navigating the phase where that species must either learn to effectively coordinate its own actions and

---

7. *Immanence* means "being entirely within something." Theologically, it describes God as "existing in and throughout the created world"—as opposed to deism, which describes God as a separate, transcended being. See *Britannica*, s.v. "immanence," https://www.britannica.com/topic/immanence-divine-attribute.
8. Lee Cronin in "#269 - Lee Cronin: Origin of Life, Aliens, Complexity, and Consciousness," *Lex Fridman Podcast*, March 11, 2022, https://lexfridman.com/lee-cronin.

technologies in alignment with itself and its home biosphere or crash both civilization and the planetary project. This juncture in collective evolution necessitates both a leap in consciousness and radical behavioral and systemic evolution. If we want to succeed, we will need to grow up and get very real about the second, third, and nth-order consequences of all the costs we've externalized, ignored, or sent downstream of our actions. And we will need to cultivate a maturity that owns our unique ecological station within the biosphere.

What are humans for? We are problematic creatures. We are complex, voracious, awkwardly self-conscious beings who are far less rational than we like to believe we are. The world as we know it is an outgrowth of our creativity, desire, trauma, and fear. We are challenged to get along with each other. We dominate and abuse nature. In the privacy of our own heads, we scarcely get along with ourselves! We built transglobal civilization through a collective story of separation from the natural world that made us. Thus, we have driven ourselves into a collective mental and physical health crisis and stretched far beyond our Earth's ecological bounds.

Can we realign ourselves and our technologies with each other, our biosphere, and our souls in time to turn the tides toward regenesis?

Maybe.

I think we can.

Here is our choice: hold tight to the constructs of separation and go down with the sinking ship of civilization as we have known it, or rise in remembrance to co-create an emergence unlike any our species or our planet have yet experienced.

WHY DID WE BREAK THE COVENANT?

But why did we forget? Why did we pull God out of the world? Why did we divorce spirit from matter, tear souls from bodies, and declare the world a profane place? Why do we unconsciously continue to enable a global system that eats Life?

Perhaps we could not help ourselves? Maybe we, as creator, preserver, destroyer beings, needed to desecrate our home just to discover how precious home really is. Perhaps, in our curiosity, desire for novelty, greed, and immaturity, we could not help but enact recursive cycles of genocide, colonization, and ecocide. Or perhaps we required a teenage stage to come to a deeper understanding of power. Naive progress at any cost is one the strongest attributes of modern societies.[9] It is also juvenile. Our progress-narrative structures desire according to the logic of narrowly defined goals and incentives. This enables individual wants, yet slowly subsumes and erases people, beings, lands, and cultures as opportunity costs of expansion. Everyone gets tangled in double binds between individual self-interest and care for the commons.[10] Whether we could help it or not, there is a toxic interweave between our expansionary impulse and the structural decimation, harm, and trauma it causes and continues to exponentiate. We live in the wake of wave after wave of desacralization.

We all come from somewhere that our peoples called home. But at some point back in everyone's ancestral memory lives a catastrophic rupture with place. Somewhere in the distant or recent past, lives were lost, lands were violated, sacred contracts with rivers and springs, mounds and caves, salmon and beavers, were ruptured. The continuity of intimate reciprocities that formed the very fabric of sacredness was torn asunder. We lost sisters, brothers, grandmothers, grandfathers, and children. We lost oak circles, death practices, harvest rituals, rites of moon blood, star maps, and navigation songs. We lost conversations with migrating fowl, rutting deer, grandfather bear, and trusted medicines. We were forced to leave the bones of our ancestors and the forests, savannahs, prairies, and coastlines that fed us as we tended them. We forgot binding stories and praise songs woven of love, loss, work, play, and time. Or they were taken from us. All this lives in us as buried trauma. We are now, quite literally and mostly unconsciously, afraid to set down roots or inhabit the ground we walk on as sacred ground.

When we were enslaved and persecuted, enclosed and denied, pummeled into submission, we had to make God portable. We could no longer feed our kindred relations, and therefore we could no longer locate the sacred in place, nor could we account for the level of pain and senselessness that overtook us and froze us, a rupture so primal it upset the harmonics of wholeness. So we put God up above and did our best to make home in a world stripped of divinity. To comfort unconsolable losses, we created a

---

9. For a full analysis of the dangers of naive or immature progress and a framework for authentic, systemic, and life-sustaining progress, see https://consilienceproject.org/development-in-progress/.

10. The double bind theory was introduced by Gregory Bateson and his colleagues in 1956. Now foundational in family therapy techniques, this theory describes the correlation between poor family communication patterns and the onset of schizophrenia and other emotional disorders. When an individual is constantly trapped in a paradox of contradictory messages, "the psychological toll can be profound." (See Padraic Gibson, "Speak Your Mind, But Not Like That: The Double Bind Theory," *Psychology Today*, February 20, 2024, https://www.psychologytoday.com/us/blog/escaping-our-mental-traps/202402/speak-your-mind-but-not-like-that-the-double-bind-theory.) Double binds also apply to societal issues like confronting racism versus exhibiting familial loyalty, or caring for an ecosystem versus building a new home.

distant, omnipotent image and called it God. And when we become the enslavers, we shaped this Sky God to justify our actions.

The removal of God from the world is a trauma response to annihilating circumstances. When people are torn from their homes, cast out of the living landscapes they, their ancestors, and their Gods were situated within, they must make Sky Gods so that they can carry a sense of power, truth, and direction with them. They break with the wholeness they have been tending so they, as a people, can survive. They become victims and perpetrators looking for scapegoats and saviors.

Once you take God out of the world, you can do whatever you want with it. You can extract, pollute, subjugate, commodify, redesign, or reassign in whatever ways desire and fear dictate. You can espouse eternal and transcendent truth even as you lose track of the relational fabric that generates intergenerational health and cohesion. The sprouting seed's genius, in collaboration with rain, soil, and sun, becomes a lesser intelligence than the Higher Authority that made the seed. The mountain that no longer speaks (because it is no longer heard) can be traded, denuded, and strip-mined. The river becomes a boundary rather than a gathering place. The seed can be patented, modified, commodified, and engineered to self-terminate.

When you take God out of the world, you change the architecture of power. You create separation. The power moving within and between things becomes subservient to the power that "made" those things. You learn to deny flows of meaning, value, and communion between subjects. As the power of the world is forgotten, people come to believe that the world has no inherent sacredness or power in it. You shift the collective story about what makes creation possible from the animate fabric of multitudinous intelligences to a single pinnacle of authorship and authority that manages, orchestrates, and manifests everything. You begin to forget the miracle of the acorn dreaming the oak and the lightning inseminating the soil. You set yourself apart from the river that brings you water and fish and messages from upstream, the river that used to be a goddess, a guide and a life-shaping force. Instead, you model yourself as a small god with dominion over it. Your God may be loving or wrathful or vengeful or favor bestowing, but one way or the other, that God is more powerful, more divine than the world around you.

Ruptures of intimate communion with homeland live in the collective body and the land itself, as primal, unconscious wounds. Because of this, we run from home to find home; we reach elsewhere to discover belonging; we are ungrounded tourists who don't trust the Garden. But it wasn't God who cast us out. Rather, the bluntness of our expansionary impulse justified the harms we did (and do) to others.

We were all Earth peoples once. We are something else now. Colonized. Settlers. Settled. Uncomfortable orphans. Comfortable creatures of a globalized culture bound to erasure of memory, claiming arbitrary human supremacy. Disembodied minds. We have forgotten that we have forgotten.

Meanwhile, the trees never stopped whispering. The streams kept singing. The birds kept speaking their praise. In some places, women still gather at the river's edge to fill their jugs and tell stories.

And our bones still remember:

We humans are part of Life's greater story. The lands we inhabit are holy lands. Tending the sacred in Life is how we make home in the world. The response to apex separation can't be more separation. Rather, what is called for is a remembering, a restitching of the currencies of our love and will force into the fabric of Life.

All Life wants is more of itself. Life is a divine relational continuity that never ceases its emergence. We are part of this tapestry, bound to its pain and beauty. We *become* together, and in this togetherness, in all flavors, we make or unmake the world a home.

Somewhere, in your recent or long-distant familial and epigenetic memory, the rupture with place lives as a searing absence and a longing, a trauma echo with an immensely long arc of homelessness that has carried us into our current world construct and blocked our ability to see, feel, hear, and collaborate with Gaia.

It is time to recover from these shattered intimacies, to break through the veil of fear, ignorance, and numbness that trauma has pulled over our souls, and remember our entanglement in the sacred web of things. Buckminster Fuller said, "Everyone is born a genius, but the process of living de-geniuses them." You can remember your natural genius as a collaborator with Life. Putting the parts together is intuitive, instinctive, and available to anyone who is willing to dedicate attention to the embodied, relational, constantly unfolding miracle you are embedded within. On a more challenging note, coming back to Life demands that you take responsibility for your participation in separation—for how you have benefitted from it, for your investments in it, for the ways in which you have consciously and unconsciously played the roles of the victim, perpetrator, or savior, and for the places where you are comfortably numb or shut down. But it's worth it. The effort to restore your natural intimacy with Life will bring you fully alive.

AN INVITATION: MEET YOURSELF IN THIS MIRROR

As temperatures soar, fires rage, crops fail, and storms swirl, we reckon with the hubris of our dreaming. In our fantasies of ceaseless progress, we collude in our own extinction. In our hyperindividualism, we are hopelessly lonely. In our adolescence, we absorb ourselves in algorithmic halls of mirrors. The truth is, we are all inseparably interdependent, all part of one human species that is but one part of the greater Circle of Life. We are not separate from that which makes us possible.

Have you met yourself in this mirror?

Have you tasted the madness of strip mining, or bottom trolling, or ethnic cleansing, or single-use plastics—even as you continue to participate in a world dependent on extraction?

Have you struggled with the why of your daily existence? How can you make a living without compromising your soul? Where's this all going? Does it have any meaning? Is it all going to shit?

Have you found your purpose? Do you hear the calling of the world? Does your life serve future generations?

But seriously . . . what are humans for? From an ecological perspective, we are a custodial species. We are ideally designed to tend and steward the beauty, biodiversity, and abundance of the natural world we occupy. Yet the constructs of self and culture that currently encircle our daily lives have very little, if anything, to do with our role in nature or our nature as nature.

It's worth asking: Is civilization even good for us?

When asked what he thought of Western Civilization, Gandhi famously replied, "I think it would be a good idea."[11]

In a talk delivered in the early 2000s, Steven Greer, founder of the Disclosure Project[12], offered this extraplanetary definition of civilization:

> *A planet has not reached civilization until its creator species has discovered how to organize itself in harmony with its biosphere and with all of its members.*[13]

---

11. The origins of this quote are contested. An alternate version, "What's your opinion of civilization?" "It's a good idea. Somebody ought to start it," is attributed to George Bernard Shaw, Albert Schweitzer, and a long list of parody writers, evidencing that this is not a novel thought. (See https://quoteinvestigator.com /2013/04/23/good-idea/)
12. The Disclosure Project is a research organization that pressures the US government to declassify information about UFOs, UAPs, and extraterrestrial life and technology.
13. Presentation at Northern California Harmony Festival.

Native American orator, activist, and artist John Trudell said:

> The great lie is that this is civilization. It is not civilized. It has literally
> been the most blood-thirsty, brutalizing system ever imposed upon
> this planet. That is not civilization. That's the great lie. Or if it does
> represent civilization, and that is truly what civilization is, then the
> great lie is that civilization is really what is good for us.[14]

The thing we currently call civilization has positioned you—a child of moder-nity—in hierarchical dominion over Life while decontextualizing, objectifying, and atomizing people, places, beings, and things, thus pulling the world apart. Civilization has obscured the deeper wholeness of which humans are a part, instituting a kind of collective dementia. Interbeing is the first Law of Life. Yet we've dilapidated our intimacies, abandoned our duties, and forgotten the stories that remember us to kinship and communion. The whisperings of the sacred have been veiled by separation and compounded by generation upon generation of complex, systemic trauma. Your unconscious scars have denatured your instinctive belonging to Life.

What does this have to do with your spirituality? With healing? With soul?

Everything.

Dominance denatures the soul's ability to feel itself in relation to all things. Your "win" is not really a win if it participates in toxic feedback loops of unrav-eling. Complicity in structural double binds generates a cognitive dissonance that makes us all slightly schizoid or numb. But we want to feel ourselves. We balk at the drab nihilism of a dead world. We crave congruence. We are tired of living in a system in which our day-to-day choices conspire to unravel the fabric of the Real.

In a time of such radical disenfranchisement and dissolution, things quicken. We enter an amplified window of volatility, turbulence, and systemic contrac-tion—which is simultaneously an opportunity for healing, and remembering, and rebirth. We begin to realize that freedom means nothing if not grounded in shared belonging.

A biospiritual process of human transformation is being facilitated by our groaning biosphere. Encroaching limits push us to rediscover our right place-ment in the ecology of the whole.

Gaia's dis-ease calls us to relearn how to collaborate with each other, the Earth, and technology with unprecedented nuance, granularity, and scale. These collaborations are tender and specific, informed by science yet rooted in supple, embodied singing of our love for Life. Our cells remember the songs of

14. John Trudell in Heather Rae Priest, dir., *Trudell* (2005).

mangrove forests, dolphins, and black tail deer. Our hands remember rhythmic gestures of gathering and the making of beautiful things. Our feet know how to walk the path. And our technologies can learn circularity and resonance. This remembering is literally a process of putting the body back together. Our Earth is a body; our bodies are part of Her larger body. Her health is our health. We can, and must, relearn the timeless arts of deep relationality.

We are part of Life, not separate from it. We are emanations of a wholeness that was never broken, but from which we have radically distanced ourselves. The violence of civilization is not your fault, but you can transform it as a co-creative agent.

This is our collective rite of passage. Will you remember who and what you are as an archetypal architect, engineer, artist, healer, and gardener—from within the Gaian Song? Will you join me as we reimagine self and civilization at the end of our world?

CHAPTER III

OUR PLANETARY CRUCIBLE

*Humans are organisms uniquely capable of
separation, maturation, and conscious return.*

THE SADDEST SOUND

In August 2019, I traveled to B.C., Canada, following a many years' calling
to sit with the African plant medicine Iboga. I was holding three intentions:
to clean up fragmentation and trauma in my nervous system, to uplevel my
personal and professional life, and to counsel with the medicine about Life,
love and reality. I had a prayer to refine insights into the big questions I'd
been exploring for decades. Nervous, excited, and already quite expanded, I
flew to British Columbia where I was able to work with the medicine legally
under the care of a traditionally trained guide.

Iboga is a psychoactive African root bark from the jungles of Gabon
and the Congo. It is debatably the strongest psychedelic known to man. It
tastes like battery acid and sawdust. Journeys last over twenty-four hours.
It takes the journeyer into heavily altered physical, mental, and emotional
states, which sometimes appear as lucid waking dreams. A person may
achieve an extraordinary state of omniscience, becoming an active witness
to one's own life, to ancestors and spirit guides, or to aspects of the physical
and metaphysical universe relevant to the practitioner's inquiry.

On my first journey with the sacred root, lying blindfolded in the dark,
many hours after time had dissolved, the medicine said to me:

What's the saddest sound in the universe??

(A pregnant pause . . . Ask yourself the question.)

The sound of a complex-life–bearing planet dying before it has reached its evolutionary potential.

The medicine then proceeded to show me, in vivid, fast-action, cartoon detail, what it looks like for a human being to be conceived, gestate, be born, grow to maturity, navigate adulthood and parenthood, then age naturally and beautifully and die in dignity. It then showed me a Gaian planet booting up *Life*—from the most basic, self-replicating molecules to the most complex lifeforms and living systems—then dying its own, roughly similar, natural, and beautiful death. It then showed me the equivalent birth, maturation, and death cycle of a universe. I watched as an entire universe bloomed out of the Void, becoming a toroidal form of truly infinite creative potential and actualization, which then, in its own natural, cosmic timing, folded back into itself, leaving only empty space and a whisper in God's memory.

The message: *Everything*, at every order of scale, exists as an expression of the divine mind that wants to be fully expressed (including cells, humans, planets, universes, and possibly even bigger things). Life generates diversity. Life is a process through which the Grand Organizing Design (shorthand: G.O.D.) constantly iterates new intelligences. Human adjectives are too small to point to the genius, majesty, and miracle of this living process.

All things have a natural lifecycle. Death is a gorgeous, glorious, welcome, and necessary part of the life process. Death empowers reciprocal and regenerative cycles in consciousness and matter. Birth, Life, Death, and Rebirth form a Circle of Life that never ends. Living systems seek to know the fullness of their lifespan. Through all of this, God learns. From the medicine's perspective, the lifecycle of a human, a planet, and a universe are similar processes of emergence and return.

When you (the human observer) zoom out to view the evolutionary process of an entire universe from a God's Eye perspective, you see something terrifying and profound relative to our own planetary existence: the most precious thing in an entire universe is the fullness of the lifecycle of a complex-life–bearing planet!

Why? Because the order of scale and complexity that occurs on a Gaian planet is an unparalleled generator of intelligent diversity and possibility. Gaias generate emergent textures of infinity. Our Earth is not the only Gaia. Gaias are sentient, water-bearing planets who boot up intelligent life in collaboration with matter and local suns over vast arcs of time. Gaian planets are playgrounds for ecologies of souls in bodies to co-evolve with each other. Gaias provide context for the emergence of new horizons of uniqueness, relationship, and agency.

Gaias birth organisms such as ourselves: a special class of social organisms able to differentiate from their planetary mothers and generate civilizations. This class of creator beings have a particularly high capacity for self-awareness separate from their ecologies. Their presence represents a distinctively volatile phase in the maturation of a Gaian system. Some races of creator beings are able to harmonize themselves and their technologies with their home planets; some flounder and crash the whole system.

Later that night, the medicine said to me:

Technology is a soul-sucking exoskeleton on the life force of the planet.

I recoiled viscerally as I received this unambiguous message.

Technological development that breaks ecology also denatures the soul. Our technologically adolescent civilization is literally eating the planet alive as it extracts energy, atoms, and attention and spews waste that can't be metabolized by living things. From the medicine's perspective, our human-created technosphere parasitizes the body and soul of Gaian Life.

Consider this. Perhaps we, the human species, and our anthropogenic activities are embedded within, part of, and participants in the most sublime and valuable thing in the entire universe: the evolutionary process of a complex-life–bearing planet, a superorganism of unparalleled intelligence, diversity, and potential. The birth, growth, maturation, and natural death cycle of a Gaia is a bioconscious process that contributes matchless learning to the divine mind. Complex life at the scale of a planet—the very substrate of all that makes you or me possible—is the ultimate miracle. Gaian planets, like our home, are the single most powerful and valuable potentiators of creative possibility in all of existence. Yet we are ever so close to causing the unthinkable: the infinite ripple of sorrowful silence that Iboga called *the saddest sound in the universe.*

I do not believe this is our destiny.

We are all co-creators of culture. We are, each one of us, powerful, responsive, creative. We are entangled with the Song that made us. We can learn how to sing.

A NOTE OF ENCOURAGEMENT

This chapter isn't fun, but it's necessary. Carl Jung said, "Until you make the unconscious conscious, it will direct your life and you will call it fate." In other words, unearthing the invisible architectures that shape consciousness is the beginning of real choice. This chapter deals with the unconscious mythopoetic, social, and physical architectures of separation that undergird our current constructs of self and civilization, architectures that are driving us crazy and pushing us toward the brink of collapse.

I take the view that separation is the root cause of our current epochal crisis. We are unconscious carriers of a meta-story that perpetuates disconnection from our own bodies, each other, and nature as it drives systemic violence, scarcity, fear, and trauma. Separation, I argue, is toxic to our physical, mental, emotional, and spiritual health and to the health of our biosphere.

Understanding is power. Einstein is credited with saying, "If I had an hour to solve a problem I'd spend fifty-five minutes thinking about the problem and five minutes thinking about solutions." The intention here is to get to know the invisible roots of our dis-ease so we can move toward greater wholeness.

Until we unearth our hidden assumptions and unconscious behaviors and remake them, the invisible architectures that shape awareness will become our fate. No matter how much personal healing we do, we will inevitably reproduce harm. By making unconscious norms, expectations, assumptions, and values conscious and repatterning them, we may live into a more beautiful and mature destiny. We may become Ilya Prigogine's proverbial "small islands of coherence in a sea of chaos [who] have the capacity to lift the entire system to a higher order."

SATURATED IN SEPARATION

We are saturated in separation: the strange, insidious illusion that anything exists separate from anything else. In this section, I will articulate five different views of separation, each of them a distinct way of understanding the causal processes by which it is created and perpetuated.

But first, where did it come from? Separation is the legacy of the last ten thousand years of human development that has abstracted culture[1] from the ecologies in which our bodies, brains, and minds evolved while moving toward ideological, economic, and technological systems that isolate us from nature and atomize us from each other. The beginning of "separation" can be mapped to the advent of agriculture when we first yoked oxen to plows to cut through virgin soil, thus beginning the long arc of human domination and subjugation of nature. Alternatively, it can be correlated to the advent of universal currencies around 3000 BC, which created symbolic (rather than literal) value and enabled debt.[2] Or it can be linked to the advent of axial religions, which pulled God out of the world and split spirit from matter, decontextualizing culture and meaning-making from place and the animate fabric of a kindred world. Separation gained full momentum with the Age of Enlightenment (or the "Age of Reason"), which hammered the final nail into the coffin of the sacred in the world, firmly establishing the secular foundations for modernity.

From the broadest possible view, separation can be seen as a developmental stage in a Gaian planet's evolution—both for the geophysical body of the Earth and for consciousness. It's the age within which a planet's keystone creator species (us) individuates from nature. This individuation generates self and civilization as something distinct from the planetary body that made those selves and that civilization possible. Separation coincides with the adolescent phase of a planet's creator species. It is characterized by egoic differentiation from and control over nature, radical innovation in subjective (first person) and objective (third person) ways of knowing, unprecedented focus on narrowly definite goals, abstraction and recursive development, the ascent of the individual at the expense of community, unlimited progress as a primary good, and fixation on anthropocentrically defined concepts of meaning, value, purpose, and progress. This stage brings snowballing developments in technology, economy, and science and

---

1. One way to think of the operation of culture is through Marvin Harris's framework of Cultural Materialism. He described culture as a process that emerges and is maintained through complex interrelations between superstructure (story, myth, ideology), social structure (family structures, legal and political systems, educational systems), and infrastructure (the technologies and techniques used to harness and distribute food, energy, and information). None of these alone cause culture. Shifts in any of these spheres causes change in the others. Separation exists in each of these three domains, which continuously feed back on each other to co-generate culture. (Marvin Harris, *Cultural Materialism: The Struggle for a Science of Culture* [New York: Random House, 1979]. See also Catherine Buzney and Jon Marcoux, "Cultural Materialism," *The University of Alabama*, https://anthropology.ua.edu/theory/cultural-materialism/.)

2. Chapurukha Kusimba, "When—and Why—Did People First Start Using Money?", *The Conversation*, June 19, 2017, https://theconversation.com/when-and-why-did-people-first-start-using-money-78887; "Commerce and Coins in the Ancient Near East," *The University of Chicago*, https://isac.uchicago.edu/museum-exhibits/special-exhibits/commerce-and-coins-ancient-near-east.

aggregation of power, which is accompanied by decreased care and connection and increasing fragmentation. This stage depends upon a collective devaluation of interbeing: the intersubjective second-person domain (of we) where collectivity, mutuality, and entanglement are felt and understood to be real. It culminates in the Anthropocene, a geologic age defined by human impact on the biosphere, which can either devolve into degradation, violence, and ultimately extinction or evolve toward increased harmony, abundance, biodiversity, and beauty. Seen from this perspective, the Age of Separation is implicitly neither good nor bad but rather a neutral evolutionary jump. It's simply a phase of development that, like all stages, brings gifts and challenges and has its own duration and logic.

From a second view, separation is an epochally defining meta-myth (or, in author Charles Eisenstein's words, a "Story of the World") that exists in the collective human mind as a bundle of chaotically interwoven narratives, symbolic systems, values, and agreements "that comprises the answers our culture offers to life's most basic questions."[3] The story of separation imagines humans as the apex of evolution, *at the top of the pyramid.*" It promises human supremacy, unending linear progress, and freedom unburdened by responsibility. It is founded on perceived splits between humans and nature, spirit (or consciousness) and matter, the body and the soul, and between some people and "other" people. The myth of separation sits in opposition to a story—and an experience—of wholeness, at-home-ness, kinship, and communion. As an anthropocentric narrative, it entrains human minds in our own mirror, withdrawing attention and care from the living world around us. It sees ego development as a primarily individual process and blocks us from feeling (and therefore living from) the underlying reality of interbeing. Its ideologies shape invisible architectures of perception, cognition, choice, and behavior. Thus, separation puppets individuals and entities as unconscious agents of its logic. It is reinforced by social and technological systems[4] which have themselves been founded on and are maintained through the myth of separation.

From a third view, separation is enabled by physical, institutional, procedural, and linguistic structures that facilitate disconnection between humans and the sacred continuity of Life. Our constructs of economy, design, science, education, design, law, religion, medicine, and even

---

3. Charles Eisenstein, "The More Beautiful World Our Hearts Know Is Possible: Chapter 1: Separation," Charles Eisenstein, https://charleseisenstein.org/books/the-more-beautiful-world-our-hearts-know-is-possible/eng/separation.

4. Cultural Materialism understands that story (superstructure) guides, binds, and directs social systems and infrastructures, even as infrastructures and social structures shape story.

grammar structurally insulate us from intimacy with our own bodies and emotions, other bodies, ecology, and the felt miracle of a living world. In other words, they systemically encourage dissociation in ways we generally fail to notice. Any epistemic framework that divides the mind from the body is a vehicle of dissociation. A building that shuts out birdsong, the breathing of trees, or contact with neighbors is a design of disconnection. A food system that renders invisible the violent deaths of the animals you eat and the social conditions of the person who picked your peach is a structure of alienation. An educational system that grooms you to "fit the workforce" devalues your authentic inspiration and soul gifts. A global financial system that necessitates continuous growth through extractive processes is a collective engine of fragmentation. As long as we fail to design social systems and infrastructures that visibilize the interdependencies between body, mind, and nature, these structures will unwittingly perpetuate separation.

From a fourth view, separation is the result of the finite game of our world system. It is simply an outcome of misaligned incentives. In *Finite & Infinite Games*, James P. Carse writes, "a finite game is played for the purpose of winning, an infinite game for the purpose of continuing the play." A finite or zero-sum or win-lose game is a situation where one party's win is equal to the other's loss. For every winner, there is a loser. To have power is to have it *over* another. Common examples include chess, football, options and futures trading, and polarized political parties. When you multiply a zero-sum game across multiple players, this creates what is known as a multipolar trap, also metaphorically referred to as *Moloch*, the destructive force of rivalrous incentives multiplied by narrowly defined goals within a multi-agent system.[5] Moloch incentivizes individuals, companies, or countries to prioritize short-term gains over long-term common good. Winning strategies generate immediate advantage for one while externalizing social and ecological costs onto others. This creates a *misalignment* where everyone's actions lead to negative outcomes for everyone.

We are intuitively familiar with Moloch. Our economy is a zero-sum game that you can't easily choose not to participate in. A tree is "worth" more (in dollars) in board feet than in ecosystem services or beauty or cultural value. If you don't cut the tree down, someone else will. They will then be able to buy more food, fuel, machines, and guns. If you don't play, you still lose your precious tree and likely your livelihood, your security,

---

5. "Meditations on Moloch" is an essay by Scott Alexander about competition, game theory, and multipolar traps: https://slatestarcodex.com/2014/07/30/meditations-on-moloch/.

and the beauty that made your place home. In an attention economy, platforms compete for user engagement, which is best achieved by hijacking the brain's reward system, so society pays the cost in addiction, body dysmorphia, polarization, and fragmentation. In the race to artificial general intelligence, every player must push for dominance, thus exponentiating the risks posed by the technology itself *and* all the other multipolar traps already embedded within the economic and geopolitical system. Power seeks more power, outsourcing harm without care. As this scales, win-lose becomes all-lose. In Daniel Schmachtenberger's words, *"Rivalrous (win-lose) games multiplied by exponential technology self-terminate."*[6]

From a fifth view, separation festers in the primal rift between the masculine and feminine, a rift between the archetypal earth-body-mother-chaos, Yin-Shakti-Creation, and the archetypal sky-mind-father-order-Yang-Shiva-Creator. We have a word for this: patriarchy, the blunt imposition of the masculine over the feminine. Patriarchy is an entrapment of both the masculine and feminine in a false dominance hierarchy. Matriarchy can fall into this same trap. It just so happens that the male bodymind is more prone to the left-brain dominant emphasis on control and abstraction, while female beings with wombs (who birth and raise children) are more attuned to emotional intelligence, relational harmony, and long-term resilience.[7] In addition to biological predispositions, in the last few thousand years, dominant culture has programmed men to be controlling and violent and women to be submissive and self-forgetting. This plays forward intergenerationally. Boys are told to be tough and emotionless, while girls are taught to be silent, caring, and conciliatory.

Patriarchy denies interbeing to justify enslaving ecosystems, animals, women, and people of color in service to persistent growth, efficiency, hierarchical power, and control. White supremacy is another instantiation of these same dynamics. Instead of gender, dominance hierarchies are defined by the social construct of race. Lightness and darkness are (falsely) constructed as measures of intelligence, moral capacity, and humanity. Importantly, the way beyond patriarchy and white supremacy isn't to smash them but to heal these lies by elevating the wholeness, uniqueness, and beauty of all people. The energies of the masculine and feminine were made for conjoinment and complementarity, not dominance and

6. Daniel Schmachtenberger, "Solving the Generator Functions of Existential Risk," *Civilization Merging*, October 11, 2017, https://civilizationemerging.com/solving-generator-function/.

7. See Bruce Goldman, "Two Minds: The Cognitive Difference between Men and Women," *Neurobiology* (May 22, 2017), https://stanmed.stanford.edu/how-mens-and-womens-brains-are-different/.

control. The intelligences of all nations were made to weave in a rainbow of diverse unity.

In everyday terms, saturation means to fill something or someone with something until no more can be held or absorbed. In chemistry, to saturate is to cause a substance, like water, to combine with, dissolve, or hold the greatest possible quantity of another substance, like salt. In economics, saturation means to supply a market beyond the point at which the demand for a product is satisfied. In terms of attention, saturation leads to overwhelm and analysis paralysis.

The living systems of the Earth are holding as much—and more— human activity, resource consumption, and waste as they can metabolize. We, too, are physically, mentally, emotionally, and spiritually saturated in less-than-life-full systems and structures. The mental health crisis, as well as growing epidemics of cancer, autoimmune disease, autism, infertility, and so many other health issues, indicates that our human bodies and minds are reaching saturation with living in ways that are out of alignment with the delicate co-regulatory balances our bodies and brains co-evolved with. We have reached apex individuation, enshrining the individual as the seat of power while undermining kinship, belonging, and community. We have pushed ourselves beyond safe and sane levels of aloneness, self-interest, and synthesized desire. We have "socially distanced" from each other and nature as far as we can and remain healthy and sane.

What happens to a system when it is saturated? A living system, like a cell, a person, or a society, will either lift to the next octave of coherence or collapse.[8]

INVISIBLE ARCHITECTURES

We are in a crisis of meaning—and a crisis of trust. Our well-worn stories and ways of being are insufficient to steer us through the eye of the needle of the next few decades. Separation has formed a crucible for the evolution of self and civilization. Its pressure has the potential to catalyze a new *way of being*, an emergent ontology for our species.

Ontology is one of those ephemeral ivory-tower words that can be quite hard to grasp. That's because the word points to the invisible architecture of being itself. Ontology as a domain of study is concerned with the nature of existence. Ontology explores what types of entities exist, how they are

---

8. See https://www.sciencedirect.com/topics/engineering/dissipative-structure.

grouped into categories, and how they are related to one another on the most fundamental level. In other words, ontology describes the subtlest structure and operation of being, doing, and becoming. The ontology of a bat is distinct from the ontology of a mountain is distinct from the ontology of a vacuuming robot. When applied to a culture's "way of being," you could also say that ontology is the meta-story that encircles and undergirds all other stories, shaping identity, motive, and meaning.

We are unconscious carriers of the ontological assumptions of separation. Like the fish in David Foster Wallace's story, we are under its spell:

There are these two young fish swimming along, and they happen to meet an older fish swimming the other way, who nods at them and says, "Morning, boys, how's the water?" And the two young fish swim on for a bit, and then eventually one of them looks over at the other and goes, "What the hell is water?"

Separation shapes how we think; how we construct identity; how we structure value and success; how we enact markets, governance, education, and medicine; how we conceive of and practice birth, maturation and death; and even how we think about thinking.

Separation suggests: Matter is inert and dead; nature and the material world exist to serve humans; soul, if there is such a thing, is separate from the body; God may or may not be real, but if "he" is, then he exists apart from the world. Power is hierarchical. Individuals and entities (companies, nations, etc.) compete for dominance in the context of scarcity. You win or you lose. It's a finite game in which only the "fittest" survive and thrive.

The geometries of separation are the line, the arrow, the mountain, the pyramid, the skyscraper, the rocket. We are at the top of its hierarchy. We are its builders, driving relentlessly toward the next frontier.

Separation cherishes the gods of Individuality, Rationality, Technology, Profit, Progress, and Scientific Materialism who feed on narrow goals. It trusts these gods for refuge, certainty, control, and solution.

Separation plays finite games. There must be losers for there to be winners. As this multiplies across many players, it fuels an exponential degradation of *everything*. This is also sometimes called the tragedy of the commons. All the things that are greater than the sum of their parts—like a viable atmosphere, a healthy ocean, or the fabric of trust that weaves society together—get dismantled, part by commodified part. Finite games guarantee fear, scarcity, insecurity, inequality, and comparison. Power equals power over. Deeper kinds of power—the power that flows within, between, and through things; the power that moves in circles and weaves the world together; the power of symbiosis between organisms and environments; the power of love itself—find themselves without voice or value. When push comes to shove, power over colonizes the power of the circle.

To succeed, you must get to the top, get ahead, ascend, transcend, dominate, maximize power over, "kill it." The personal dream is to achieve individual success, optionality, and self-actualization, regardless of how your dream impacts others or the environment. Social media super egos, representing these dreams, outcompete more humble dreams for likes, attention, and profit. The collective dream is to sustain progress, development, growth, and youth regardless of collateral damage or externalized costs.

You, as an individual, are the locus of meaning, purpose, and power that matters. You are number one. Your job is to optimize yourself. Time offered to others (friends, family, community), if not transactionally relevant to your own forward momentum, can easily become a disadvantage. Separation gives the individual rights but says nothing of shared belonging or responsibility.

Separation invented individualism, the relatively recent idea that the individual is the culturally and morally relevant unit of agency above family, tribe, community, place, or more-than-human kinship.[9] This construct emerged in the late eighteenth century as a central ideological pillar in a global wave of revolution. On July 4, 1776, the Continental Congress declared independence from Great Britain and enshrined individual rights and freedoms with these famous words, *"We hold these truths to be self-evident, that all men are created equal, that they are endowed by their Creator with certain unalienable Rights, that among these are Life, Liberty and the pursuit of Happiness."* This legal and ideological innovation carried great benefits. People (white men) were granted unprecedented freedoms, political power, and protections. The rights granted men have progressively been "granted" to women and people of color. Yet the primacy of the individual carries a long shadow; from that moment forward, care for communal well-being and the commons would be increasingly obscured. In the 1886 ruling *Santa Clara County v. Southern Pacific Railroad*, the Supreme Court determined that the Fourteenth Amendment applied to corporations, endowing them with the same privileges and immunities as citizens.[10] It's easy to see the cascading effects of this. The zero-sum competition between these

---

9. *Britannica*, s.v. "individualism," last updated July 5, 2025, https://www.britannica.com/topic/individualism.
10. *Wikipedia*, s.v. "corporate personhood," https://en.wikipedia.org/wiki/Corporate_personhood.

"individual" entities has led to inequality, extreme concentration of wealth, oligarchy, and autocracy.

Separation biases the masculine, preferencing structure, planning, measurability, linear progress, and the predictability of complicated systems over process, presence, pleasure, complexity, and mystery. Separation loves control. Rationality is its most sacred assumption, objective truth its goal. It privileges intellect above feeling, measurement above aesthetic sensing, and mind above body. Bodies and emotions are seen as inconstant, inaccurate, and inconvenient burdens rather than as the intelligent and truly miraculous vehicles they are for whole-being experience, expression, and co-regulation with each other and the world around us.

The feminine and her Gaian body are subjects under separation's reign. Her webs and cycles are too complex, her desire too unwieldy. Her wildness is to be tamed, othered, and feared or placed on hypersexualized, objectified pedestals tethered to the male gaze. Emotional intelligence, if not comfortably composed, is seen as a threat to rationality and reputation. Communal and mythopoetic processes of culture—domains of the feminine—are seen as impractical, inefficient, and less trustworthy. Shame is used to control and dull down the more chaotic, flamboyant, queer, or nonconforming dimensions of creativity, sexuality, and wisdom. Physical, sexual, emotional, and reputational violence subdues her power and voice. Aging is pushed to the shadows. And death becomes something to trump or transcend.

Separation fabricates otherness and obscures harm. It breaks people (and organisms) into castes, races, creeds, and classes that obscure the sentience, humanity, and entanglement of the "other." During the Age of Discovery (1400–1600), European seafarers and their royal backers constructed the notion of race to justify ruthless expansion, arguing that original peoples were "primitive," then characterizing these peoples and their complex societies and cosmologies as "savage," "uncivilized," "uncontrollable," "dangerous," and "dark." In a 1493 Papal Bull, Pope Alexander IV instantiated The Doctrine of Discovery, claiming that lands not inhabited by Christians were uninhabited.[11] Such ideas had been used for millennia to justify and propagate genocide, enslavement, land theft, and cultural erasure. But the construct of otherness was truly perfected by transatlantic slave traders, the merchants, bankers, and insurance companies who benefited from their dirty work, and the Papacy. Without a strong story to pacify

---

11. "The Doctrine of Discovery, 1493," *The Gilder Lehrman Institute of American History,* https://www.gilderlehrman.org/history-resources/spotlight-primary-source/doctrine-discovery-1493.

moral outrage, the good people of the world would not have allowed such barbarism. But people caved into self-interest above common humanity.

Following on this, nineteenth-century proponents of Manifest Destiny claimed it was God's will for the United States to expand its territory across the whole of North America—at the expense of millions of existing residents.[12] Again, greed (backed by superior force and a strong story) won. These largely unconscious biases congealed into the "Myth of Primitivism,"[13] which categorizes anyone who doesn't fit into standardized Western developmental models as "less evolved." This epistemic frame has justified a century of eugenics[14] projects and still permeates key areas of society including anthropology, art criticism, mainstream psychology, cutting-edge medicine, and world bank policy. Indigenous knowledge systems and alternative ways of knowing are still often cast as quaint, backward, immature, underdeveloped, pre-rational,[15] or "woo."

Separation divides mind from matter. The Age of Enlightenment[16] (seventeenth and eighteenth centuries) brought about huge advances in science, governance and consciousness, yet drove us further from inter-being. Descartes's dictum, "I think therefore I am," firmly enthroned the belief that mind is more primary than embodied belonging to an animate, interconnected world. The "rational" observer and actor's task became to objectively "know" the world by analyzing it from a comfortable distance. We gained "objectivity," precision, and measure but radically departed from feeling ourselves as intersubjective members and kin. Placing the mind above the body and relationality is a mental sleight of hand that cleaves the "rational observer" from the observed. This rigorously formalizes a kind of dissociation that collapses *the between*. The Enlightenment emphasis on rationality and disdain for the inconvenience of bodies, emotions, and ecological entanglements stunts the psychosomatic sense of mutual belonging. In some ways, this can be seen as the ultimate act of colonization. "I think

---

12. Research by some scholars provides population estimates of the pre-contact Americas as high as 112 million in 1492, while others estimate the population to have been as low as eight million. In any case, the native population declined to less than 5 million by 1650. (*The Native Population of the Americas in 1492*, edited by William M. Denevan, 2nd ed. [University of Wisconsin Press, 1992].)

13. Susan Hiller, *The Myth of Primitivism* (Routledge, 2004).

14. Meghan Kalomiris, "Unfit to Breed: America's Dark Tale of Eugenics," The NIH Catalyst, last updated February 3, 2022, https://irp.nih.gov/catalyst/29/4/unfit-to-breed-americas-dark-tale-of-eugenics.

15. The denotation "pre-rational" entirely fails in epistemic humility because it does not know what it does not know about the ontological, linguistic or cultural complexity of the societies it labels (and judges).

16. Also called the Age of Reason, the seventeenth and eighteenth centuries were a major turning point in Western civilization. Thinkers like John Locke, Isaac Newton, and Descartes advanced the idea that reason could improve society, which facilitated huge shifts, including the emergence of democracy and the codification of scientific methodology.

therefore I am" intellectually colonizes shared reality by making the mind more primary than *prima facie* existence.

Separation lives in the left hemisphere of the brain, the side of the brain that attends to parts rather than wholes. The left brain thinks in bullet points, narrowly defined goals and deliverables; it puts things into neatly defined categories, pulling them apart from context. This offers immense and obvious gifts, among them our current levels of scientific knowledge, medical acumen, and technological advancement. But left-brain dominance blocks the holistic and relational sensing of the right brain. It obscures both the felt sense of the whole and the relationships *between* parts. In doing so, it reifies a very particular orientation of power—power *over* rather than power *with*. Psychiatrist, neuroscientist, and philosopher Iain McGilchrist, author of *The Master and His Emissary* and *The Matter With Things*, writes,

> *Our dominant value—sometimes I fear our only value—has, very clearly, become that of power (over). This aligns us with a brain system, that of the left hemisphere, the raison d'être of which is to control and manipulate the world. But not to understand it: that, for evolutionary reasons that I explain, has come to be more the raison d'être of our—more intelligent, in every sense—right hemisphere. Unfortunately, the left hemisphere, knowing less, thinks it knows more. It is a good servant, but a ruinous—a peremptory—master. And the predictable outcome of assuming the role of master is the devastation of all that is important to us—or should be important, if we really know what we are about.*[17]

If we take his theories with any degree of seriousness, we could say that a world dominated by the left brain is a world precipitously organized to pull itself apart, a world that denies and defiles the sacred and that cannot help but fail to care for the well-being of the whole as it privileges parts. McGilchrist has suggested that left-brain dominance is a form of brain damage.[18]

Separation's most subtle and insidious Small God is the god of self-interest. Separation upholds individual freedom without care for community or kinship. Freedom means having the optionality to buy, do, create,

---

17. Iain McGilchrist, *Channel McGilchrist*, https://channelmcgilchrist.com/home/.
18. A cursory web search will reveal the many arguments against this, which themselves have been upregulated by the largely left-brain dominant world of tech businesses and developers. But recent psychedelic science strongly indicates that the healing effects of psychedelic brain states are correlated with upregulation of right brain activity, which would imply a vindication for McGilchrist. (See Ruben Herzog, et. al, "A Whole-Brain Model of the Neural Entropy Increase Elicited by Psychedelic Drugs," *Scientific Reports* 13, no. 6244 [2023], https://www.nature.com/articles/s41598-023-32649-7.)

go, or be whatever, whoever, wherever you want. This kind of freedom has its place in personal empowerment, but when held as a singular conception, without care for interdependence, it generates schismatic polarities between self-interest and the integrity of the whole. The American Dream, when untempered by loyalty to the Republic, is essentially a dream of self-interest. Freedom to (be, do, have) is untethered from implication or impact. Similarly, the idea of *homo economicus* or "economic man," a theoretical model proposed by John Stewart Mill in the nineteenth century, portrays humans as rational, self-interested, and motivated to maximize their own well-being and wealth. The combination of these two stories of individual freedom has, in many ways, become the default global dream. Expanded personal gain necessitates (invisible) incurred losses for other human and more-than-human stakeholders. Few notice that their dreams and desires are largely manufactured by engines of extraction that train everyone to be good consumers to feed growth. And since everyone wants to live their dreams, everyone becomes an apologist for the ways in which their self-interest undermines social and ecological commons. Your own best attempts to be a life-centric, infinite game player get captured by the moral vacuity of a system that wants you to feed it.

Finally, separation undergirds dominant concepts of technological progress, techno-optimism, and technological maturity. Popular (and well-funded) ideologies include transhumanism, the singularity, technoutopianism, and effective accelerationism. These pseudoreligious narratives position technology as humanity's savior. Yet they are naively optimistic additions to the unmitigated progress narrative that lack any critique of the zero-sum game or the devolutionary tendencies of power over Life. Exponential growth is good—or is God—the source of all hope and possibility. Such memetic frameworks are crafted by technologists who are themselves creatures of the left-brain, reductivist biases of separation. They are incomplete at best, maladaptive and immature at worst—a nihilistic fantasy of disembodied minds, uninitiated hearts, decontextualized values, and moral anemia. They may solve specific challenges, like cancer or fusion or getting to Mars, but will no doubt break the entangled majesty of our Earth. Rather than elevating or harmonizing Gaia's intelligence, they and their proponents drive us exponentially toward biospheric collapse.

It is worth noting that all these invisible architectures have been ethically justified over the past 160 years by Social Darwinism, philosopher Herbert Spencer's social theory loosely based on Darwin's biological concept of natural selection. Spencer (not Darwin) coined and superimposed the phrase "survival of the fittest" onto zero-sum social systems. He wrote, "Society advances where its fittest members are allowed to assert their fitness with the least hindrance."[19] This was then projected back onto Darwinian theory. But Darwin never said "fittest." He said, "survival of the fit." His concept described fitted-ness within the larger, ecological context, as being "fit-to-purpose." The word "fittest" was added to the fifth edition of *The Origin of Species* by editors seeking to match prevailing social ideology.[20]

While colonialism and capitalism function according to top-down, win-lose power, healthy ecological and human systems are more primarily collaborative than competitive. Social Darwinism, as a framework to justify these organizing patterns in society, is both ecologically and anthropologically inaccurate.[21] In ecologies, fitness can be expressed through a wide variety of traits—from the best camouflage to the most fecund to the cleverest to the most cooperative.[22] Furthermore, over the arc of many generations, fitness does not determine who survives in a diverse system.[23] In human societies, effective long-term collaboration emerges in local commons without regulation by central authorities or privatization. Economist Elinor Ostrom won the 2009 Nobel Prize for economic science for her groundbreaking research demonstrating this. The Nobel website shares,

> *It was long unanimously held among economists that natural resources that were collectively used by their users would be overexploited and destroyed in the long-term. Elinor Ostrom disproved this idea by conducting field studies on how people in small, local communities manage shared natural resources, such as pastures, fishing waters, and forests. She showed that when natural resources are jointly used by their users, in time, rules are established for how*

19. Michael Heeney, "'Survival of the Fittest': The Flaws and Dissemination of Social Darwinism," *Serendip,* Spring 2005, https://serendipstudio.org/sci_cult/evolit/s05/web1/mheeney.html.

20. Krista Tippet and Janine Benyus, "Biomimicry, an Operating Manual for Earthlings," *On Being with Krista Tippet,* March 23, 2023, https://onbeing.org/programs/janine-benyus-biomimicry-an-operating-manual-for-earthlings/.

21. "Misunderstanding Evolution: A Biologist's Perspective on Social Darwinism," Khan Academy, https://www.khanacademy.org/humanities/us-history/the-gilded-age/gilded-age/v/darwinism-vs-social-darwinism-part-1.

22. Michael Le Page, "Evolution Myths: 'Survival of the Fittest' Justifies 'Everyone for Themselves'," *New Scientist,* April 16, 2008, https://www.newscientist.com/article/dn13671-evolution-myths-survival-of-the-fittest-justifies-everyone-for-themselves/.

23. Fitness itself, as a fundamental determinant of survival over many generations, has been disproven. Stable diversity means that not only the fittest but also "the flattest" survive. (Robert E. Beardmore, et al., "Metabolic Trade-Offs and the Maintenance of the Fittest and the Flattest," *Nature* 472, 342–346 [2011], https://doi.org/10.1038/nature09905.)

these are to be cared for and used in a way that is both economically and ecologically sustainable.[24]

Social Darwinism was a sloppy misreading of Darwin that offered a convenient rationale for top-down control and systemic injustice while effectively obscuring the underlying prosociality and collaborative competency of both human and more-than-human living systems.

Separation, as a worldview and way of being, can be seen as the underlying cause and continuing catalyst of our most insidious personal and collective problems. It generates the stories and structures that perpetuate disconnection, dissociation, and win-lose gaming between humans and nature, between nations, between people, and even within ourselves.

A PRACTICE: GETTING HONEST ABOUT SEPARATION

Sit yourself down with a journal, or take a long walk, and ask yourself the following questions. How does your life experience intersect with separation? To what degree do you see yourself as a winner or a loser in the global win-lose game? To what extent are you working to climb the ladder or stay in place? How do you gain comfort or certainty or control in the context of separation? How is your professional, financial, or family life bound up in separation's norms?

OUR PLANETARY CRUCIBLE

We are under compression.

The zero-sum game of civilization is eating our planet. We are a ravenous economic superorganism[25] feeding on the body of the larger, organic superorganism of our living biosphere. As participants in a global economic system that requires continuous growth, we, as individual actors,

---

24. "Elinor Ostrom," The Nobel Prize, https://www.nobelprize.org/prizes/economic-sciences/2009/ostrom/facts/.
25. In his podcast *The Great Simplification*, energy expert Note Hagens describes humanity as an economic superorganism driven by the imperative for growth. While biological superorganisms, like ant colonies or bee hives, contribute ecosystems services (like recirculating waste into the surrounding ecology) that mutually benefit the whole, the economic superorganism extracts and generates anthropocentric waste that cannot be recirculated by living systems. (See https://www.thegreatsimplification.com.)

are economically bound up in systemic multipolar traps that are ultimately all-lose. Our technological world runs on materials, energy, and labor extracted from real places, ecologies, and marginalized peoples that are not renewable at the pace we consume them. Ironically, even as efficiencies increase, the speed and intensity of degradation also grows.[26]

We've surpassed the "safe operating space" of seven out of the nine planetary boundaries that have been identified as the biological commons within which human and other complex life can thrive.[27] Humans and our livestock comprise over 96 percent of the mammalian biomass on our planet.[28] Species are disappearing at a rate not seen in ten million years with over one million of our more-than-human relatives currently on the brink.[29] Insect biomass, the base of the food chain for all of Life, has decreased by 80 percent. We've destroyed, degraded, or polluted all original ecosystems. Increasingly fierce superstorms and floods remind us that we've radically dysregulated both the large hydrological cycle (the global flow of ocean currents and jet streams regulated by ocean temperatures) and the small hydrological cycle (the more localized "pump" facilitated by the evapotranspiration of healthy plants and soils that call rain down to earth).[30] We've exceeded safe zones for novel entities, including microplastics, heavy metals, nuclear waste, and PFAS (the so-called "forever") chemicals. And anthropomass (the aggregate mass of all human-created materials) exceeded biomass (the aggregate mass of all life-created materials) in 2020.[31]

AI, robotics, and quantum computing turbocharge already catastrophic misalignments between the economic superorganism and the base, ecological substrate we depend upon. The increased capacity afforded by AI is omniuse. While its gifts are extraordinary, it speeds development in all domains, amplifying cycles of extraction, habitat destruction,

26. The Jevons Paradox states, "In the long term, an increase in efficiency in resource use will generate an increase in resource consumption rather than a decrease." Creating more efficient technologies, counterintuitively, only increases resource extraction, deepening our conundrum. (Mario Giampietro and Kozo Mayumi, "Unraveling the Complexity of the Jevons Paradox: The Link Between Innovation, Efficiency, and Sustainability," *Frontiers in Energy Research* 6 [2018], https://www.frontiersin.org/articles/10.3389/fenrg.2018.00026/full.)

27. "Planetary Boundaries," Stockholm Resilience Centre, https://www.stockholmresilience.org/research/planetary-boundaries/the-nine-planetary-boundaries.html.

28. Olivia Rosane, "Humans and Big Ag Livestock Now Account for 96 Percent of Mammal Biomass," EcoWatch, May 23, 2018, https://www.ecowatch.com/biomass-humans-animals-2571413930.html.

29. Katy Daigle and Julia Janicki, "Extinction Crisis Puts 1 Million Species on the Brink," Reuters, December 23, 2022, https://www.reuters.com/lifestyle/science/extinction-crisis-puts-1-million-species-brink-2022-12-23/.

30. Disruption of the small hydrological cycle is largely unreported. Wherever we have covered the earth in concrete, left monocropped soils bare, or chemically denatured soil fungi and microbes, it breaks down.

31. Emily Elhacham, et al., "Global Human-Made Mass Exceeds All Living Biomass," *Nature* 588, 442–444 (2020), https://doi.org/10.1038/s41586-020-3010-5.

consumption, and pollution, magnifying epistemic meltdown, and democratizing access to a host of other existential (potentially life-terminating) technologies, including CRISPR gene editing, bioweapons, nanotech, and nuclear weapons.

Our relationships are mediated by devices and user interfaces designed to maximize addiction. We've plugged ourselves into technologies that divert our attention from each other and base reality and amplify ideological divides while deeply altering our neural and embodied capacities of connection, communication, and concentration.

Our existing political structures are insufficient to meet current challenges. We hover at the brink of a nuclear-fueled World War III. A handful of tech companies race for dominance, further speeding development and disincentivizing coordination. We are inundated with change, overwhelmed by volumes of meaningless, deeply biased, or fake information generated by bad actors and AI bots that never sleep, and underwhelmed by the future prospects for our lives. This marks an evolutionary inflection point that sandwiches us, as a species and as a civilization, between our biological origins and our technological creations.

Health issues causally linked to environmental factors are steeply on the rise. About one in four people struggle with mental health disorders including depression, addiction, anxiety, and obsessive-compulsive disorder.[32] Our tendencies toward nihilism, narcissism, and sociopathy are radically amplified by all the above. The social fabric is tattered.

Could all these things, multiplied together, cause an alchemical reaction? Could all of this pressure, these compounding crises, actually move us to a better place?

The convergence of biospheric, technological, geopolitical, and social tipping points, all being reached simultaneously, may irresistibly catalyze a sacred turning—what Joanna Macy called a Great Remembering.[33] We cannot not be responsive to the calling of the world. As the renowned ecological activist Julia Butterfly Hill said, "There is no away." The Earth holds us tight in an embrace of evolution's own design. The intricately entangled web of Life we are a part of has not ceased to be the underlying substrate that makes human life possible, providing breath, water, food, materials,

---

32. "Mental Health Disorder Statistics," Hopkins Medicine. https://www.hopkinsmedicine.org/health/wellness-and-prevention/mental-health-disorder-statistics.

33. The Buddhist scholar, activist, and systems scientist Joanna Macy, has, for decades, described the dynamics of this time as the Great Unravelling, the Great Turning, and the Great Remembering. The term "the Great Turning" was first used in 1989 by Craig Schindler and Gary Lapid in their book, also titled The Great Turning. It was then popularized by Joanna and her "Work that Reconnects."

beauty, and the living environments within which we build our dreams, raise our children, and know ourselves. We are biospiritually, psychoemotionally, and physiologically part of Her body.

Our Earth is the bio-physical-psycho-social-spiritual container for our reckoning and possible return to the Circle of Life. We imagined ourselves separate from or above nature, but we are, nonetheless, a part. Might this physiological, psychological, informational, mythopoetic, and spiritual reckoning provide the ignition spark for an awakening and remembering of unprecedented proportions? When we *must* face ourselves, perhaps we will. We're in a crucible the size of a planet. The living, breathing biosphere we are embedded within is an initiatory crucible for our evolution.

In chemical and industrial processes, a crucible is a vessel used to hold a high-heat reaction that forges its contents into a new alloy or substance. A crucible is also colloquially defined as a difficult test or challenge. The US Marines initiates recruits in a grueling fifty-four-hour trial called "The Crucible." The Marine Boot Camp website states: "The word 'crucible' means a severe test, or a place or situation in which concentrated forces interact to cause or influence change or development."[34] We are facing both: a heated, toxified biosphere providing a reactive container for the evolution of our bodies, psyches, and souls, and a collective growth opportunity that will test the mettle of the human body, heart and soul and require a new stage of development. Like a Marine Boot Camp, how we "perform" will depend not so much on individual strength and genius but on what stories we choose and on how well we collaborate with each other and our environment. What narratives we choose and which behaviors we act out, both individually and collectively, will determine the future expression and experience of billions upon billions of human and more-than-human beings. (No pressure.)

Gaia is cooking our consciousness. As parts of Her larger whole, we can't be whole separate from Her. The biosphere's bodily functions (or dysfunctions) operate on our bodies, brains, minds, and *relationships.*

Relational neurobiology teaches us that self emerges through the interaction of mind, brain, and relationship. Our minds are patterned through embodied relationships with other brains, bodies, and environments over time. Dr. Daniel J. Seigel writes in *The Developing Mind: How Relationships and the Brain Interact,*

---

34. Mark Perna, "The Crucible—Marines Epic 54-Hour Test for Recruits," Marine Boot Camp HQ, June 12, 2022, https://www.marinesbootcamphq.com/the-crucible-marines/.

A core aspect of the human mind is an embodied and relational process that regulates the flow of energy and information within the brain and between brains. The mind as an emergent property of the body and relationships is created within internal neurophysiological processes and [external] relational experiences. In other words, the mind is a process that emerges from the distributed nervous system extending throughout the entire body, and also from the communication patterns that occur within relationships. The structure and function of the developing brain are determined by how experiences . . . shape the genetically programmed maturation of the nervous system.[35]

"Relational process" is at the core of the experience of self. Self is a co-emergence. The people we attract and repel, the spaces we inhabit, the platforms we use, all shape consciousness. Similarly, the backyards, birdlife, ocean breezes, and forests that hold us through childhood play, adolescent initiations, and early adult romances contribute to the development, regulation, and integration of our minds. Environments nurture our becoming. If we replace natural and human relationships with synthetic environments, especially in early childhood, we fail to thrive.[36]

We are native to this planet. We live on Her skin, tucked onto the living soil by the narrow membrane of a breathable atmosphere crafted through billions of years of collaborative interactions between respiring lifeforms. These bodies that gestated in our mothers' wombs are bound to a genetic continuum that weaves a constantly evolving biological tapestry through time. Our bodies are real. They are the result of a continuum of biophysical processes. Our mortality is holy. As creaturely beings who co-evolved *here*, we cannot not be impacted by pollution and degradation of our environments, extinctions of our more-than-human relatives, radiation pollution, chemical toxicity, or the technologization of work, play, communication, and identity. We cannot not feel (at least subconsciously) the ever-growing wave of dread, grief, and dysregulation so many people experience in the face of such radical and causal change. We are relational creatures whose

35. Daniel J. Siegel, *The Developing Mind: How Relationships and the Brain Interact to Shape Who We Are*, 2nd ed. (New York: The Guilford Press, 2012), 3.
36. Sheri Madigan, et al., "Association Between Screen Time and Children's Performance on a Developmental Screening Test," *JAMA Pediatrics* 173, no. 3 (2019): 244–250, doi:10.1001/jamapediatrics.2018.5056; Danielle Cohen, "Why Kids Need to Spend Time in Nature," Child Mind Institute, last updated November 13, 2024, https://childmind.org/article/why-kids-need-to-spend-time-in-nature/.

physiology and cognition are bound to each other and nature's collaborative genius. Our health, too, is unalterably dependent on a healthy environment.

Is it any wonder that we feel a little (or a lot) crazy, sometimes?

The crucible is *real*.

It's as biochemically real as the food you eat, the water you drink, the clothing you wear, and the air you breathe. Every day, your body is physiologically inundated with everything from microplastics to radiation to nutritionally vacuous foods engineered by an agrochemical-industrial food system that denatures soils, knowingly douses food crops in carcinogenic chemicals, and serves up an abundance of overprocessed, high-calorie foods that are known to cause addiction, inflammation, and obesity from malnourishment.[37] According to current data, there are approximately 350,000 different types of artificial chemicals present in the global market that can be considered "foreign chemicals" in our environment.[38] Novel chemical entities have exceeded safe levels in rainwater, soils, and surface waters globally.[39] These industrial solvents and water retardants persist for thousands of years and are so small they cannot be filtered out of drinking water. Antibiotics fed to humans and our livestock flood our environment, fostering nearly untreatable superbugs. All of this drives unprecedented levels of cancer, heart disease, inflammatory bowel disease, rheumatoid arthritis, infertility, autism, autoimmune disorders, Alzheimer's, and dementia. The biochemical stressors are difficult to tease apart from the products and conveniences we have come to enjoy.

The physical bleeds into the psychological. All of the physical stressors listed above amplify depression, anxiety, and suicidality. Lead in the environment has stolen an estimated 824 million IQ points from children.[40] The hyperstimulation of games and social media undermines attention spans, critical thinking, and family and civic life. Increased screen use correlates with sleep dysfunction, which also affects mental health and performance.

---

37. Milena Kobylińska, et al., "Malnutrition in Obesity: Is It Possible?" *Obesity Facts* 15, no. 1 (2022):19-25, doi: 10.1159/000519503.
38. Derek C. G. Muir, et al., "How Many Chemicals in Commerce Have Been Analyzed in Environmental Media? A 50 Year Bibliometric Analysis," *Environmental Science & Technology* 57, iss. 25 (2023): 9119-9129, doi: 10.1021/acs.est.2c09353; Elizabeth Claire Alberts, "We've Breached Earth's Threshold for Chemical Pollution, Study Says," *Mongabay*, January 19, 2022, https://news.mongabay.com/2022/01/weve-breached-earths-threshold-for-chemical-pollution-study-says/.
39. Ian T. Cousins, et al., "Outside the Safe Operating Space of a New Planetary Boundary for Per- and Polyfluoroalkyl Substances (PFAS)," *Environmental Science & Technology* 56, iss. 16 (2022), https://pubs.acs.org/doi/10.1021/acs.est.2c027.
40. "There is no safe detectable level of lead in the blood of children." Childhood lead exposure among the U.S. population by 2015 was responsible for the loss of more than 824 million IQ points. (Joseph Boyle, et al., "Estimated IQ points and lifetime earnings lost to early childhood blood lead levels in the United States," *The Science of the total environment* 778 [2021], https://pubmed.ncbi.nlm.nih.gov/34030355/.)

Most children and adults spend most of their days indoors and on screens, enjoying as few as fifteen minutes, on average, outside.[41] But bodies, brains, and minds are biological and ecological things. While we *can* live in the sealed-off safety of a self-referencing world, we do so at the peril of our health, breaking mutual and symmetrical relationships with the natural contexts that built our bodies, brains, and minds. Nature deficit disorder affects children and adults deprived of time outdoors. Symptoms include diminished use of the senses, obesity, increased aggression, poor attention, and depression.[42] Algorithms hack our innermost desires, which we can fulfil at the touch of a button. Yet the world around us is increasingly depersonalized, fractured, and mechanized, driving us into pandemics of loneliness, overwhelm, analysis paralysis, and rage. We have surrounded ourselves with a built world that reflects us only to ourselves. We have shifted our environments so radically that our bodies and brains hardly feel at home anymore.

When we are disconnected, addiction results. When the brain and body reach toward something to fill voids of healthy connection, we become addicted to dopamine supply provided by stand-in substances and behaviors. The zero-sum game of success, as we currently play it, is a glaring expression of this kind of dopamine-driven, extrinsic motivation. Addiction begins early when gold stars or grades replace innate curiosity and collaboration to motivate children's achievements in school.[43] The brain accultur-ates to extrinsic reward. Extrinsic motivations subsume intrinsic motivation in a predictable, dopaminergic cycle. Over the course of a lifetime of replacing play, artmaking, and mutuality with mainstream entertainment and sports, climbing financial and social ladders, and acquiring kudos, likes, and things, we replace subtle and organismic self-regulation and co-regulation with low-hanging reward tracks.

The planetary crucible is informational. We evolved immersed in co-regulatory relationships with the Song—the informational matrix—of our

---

41. "On average, the British workers surveyed spend more time per a day at their desk or workstation (6.8 hours) than they do in bed (6.4 hours), relaxing at home (3.5 hours) or outdoors (37 mins)." (Rebecca Clarke, "40% of Brits Spend Just 15 Minutes Outdoors Each Day," HR Review, May 18, 2018, https://www.hrreview.co.uk/hr-news/strategy-news/40-of-brits-spend-just-15-minutes-outdoors-each-day.); Statistical analysis of Americans' outdoor time since COVID is vastly varied. Steve Downs sites a study by Building H indicating, "A majority of Americans (58.8%) indicated that they spend one hour or less per day outdoors and more than a third (37.4%) are getting 30 minutes or less." (Steve Downs, "A Survey of Modern Life: Outdoor Time," Medium, June 29, 2022, https://medium.com/building-h/a-survey-of-modern-life-outdoor-time-3a99d9fa3acb.)

42. "What Is 'Nature Deficit Disorder,' and Can the Outdoors Really Make Us Feel Better?" HealthPartners, https://www.healthpartners.com/blog/nature-deficit-disorder/.

43. A growing body of work now points to the immensely problematic cycles of extrinsic dopamine reward. Dr. Mark Lepper of Stanford published research on this phenomenon as early as 1973. See https://www.heartofcharacter.org/wp-content/uploads/Undermining_Childrens_Intrinsic_Interest_with_Ext-1.pdf.

ecologies. We moved and were moved at the pace of unmediated interactions between our bodies, other bodies, and the Earth's body. Now, the informational soup that subtly co-regulates everything within and outside of us is increasingly fabricated, digitized, and optimized for speed, comfort, social signaling, and addiction. But we co-evolved with sunrises and sunsets, the patter of rain, the thrum of insects, visible stars, the rhythms of seasons. We grew alongside and thrive in coordination with the natural— not the urban, industrial, and technological infoscapes of today.

Reading and writing are incredibly recent innovations that compress the information we receive. As the digital age progresses, we get more abstract and voluminous content with increasingly less context. As abstraction increases, *fidelity* (or information richness) decreases. Technological mediation amplifies this tendency. Reading a book about the Bwiti tradition of Gabon, West Africa, is not the same thing as trekking twelve hours into the jungle to do initiation with the tribe. Listening to a recorded symphony is not the same moving experience as witnessing a live performance. Scrolling for eight hours on TikTok cannot compare to sharing that time with a group of friends. As ecosystems decline, we rob ourselves of the "old growth" bandwidths of ecological information that made us what we are. As we distance ourselves from the Song of Life, we become facile in specialized domains of knowledge, yet we truncate the depth and breadth of relational fluency that enables health and wisdom. And we feel increasingly homeless. Our bodies, brains, and minds are stretched to coherently self-regulate and co-regulate within the increasingly deranged spectrum of relationships we swim in.

The crucible is archetypal and mythopoetic. The unconscious biases of modernity encourage us to believe that we are somehow immune to natural limits. We adore the story of infinite possibility. Personal growth gurus proclaim, "You are limitless," and "Anything is possible if you dream it." Many happily buy this bright, shiny, narrative, using it as a sloppy, spiritualized crutch to enable the hunger for novelty and personal gain. But no one wants to have a conversation about limits or duty. In this imbalance, we fail in the moral imagination and empathic intelligence that could resuscitate authentic reciprocity. As we dream new houses, new clothes, and optimized lifestyles, every click and purchase outsources impacts onto all the other beings we share this planet with. But . . . if our every action and purchase colludes with the degradation and slow death of our Mother, what does that make for us? What kind of child kills its parent? What is our value if we are only an evolutionary dead end destined to decimate our planet and extinct ourselves through unrestrained consumption?

We think of the mind as though it were somehow separate from the body, even though cognition without a body in relation to other bodies and the world is complete nonsense. We reflexively repeat dogmas like "this reality isn't real" even though we walk around in an interobjectively and intersubjectively shared world all the time. While it's true that your brain is constructing its own (subjective) view of reality, this doesn't change the fact that each of us engages in consequential, interdependent interactions between other places, beings, and people all day long. Though we can contact a timeless, changeless, nondual (primordial or quantum) dimension of consciousness with our minds, this does not change the fact that our minds emerge through our physical, time-bound, radically interdependent, objectively real bodies and brains in relation to a real world. We interobjectively and intersubjectively interexist. This is the meaning of interbeing. Perhaps the intellectual sleight of hand that projects subjective reality onto shared reality is easier than embracing the frustrating limitations of a time-bound physical body or facing shared imperatives of regenerating our world.

Individualism determines our dominant myths of success and transformation. Mainstream media teaches us to be the heroes of our own stories. The hero's journey is played out endlessly in businesses, love, sports, politics, finance, and fantasy. No one talks about the heroine's story or what happens after the hero comes home. We lack kinship stories and rituals of communion with the archetypal and ecological intelligences of directions, seasons, elements, plants, animals, and ancestor kin. We celebrate birthdays, weddings, and funerals but forget rites of passage, sacrifices, and celebrations of mountains, salmon, rice harvests, and equinoxes.

Finally, the crucible is spiritual and religious. What is our spirituality for? Are we seeking liberation *from* Life or liberation *into* it? Are we seeking personal mastery or a beautiful expression of humanness in relationship to a larger wholeness? Are we seeking an apex, an omega, or are we seeking a remembering, a homecoming, a return? No previous spiritual or religious tradition faced the same collective challenges as we do. No previous wisdom school needed to align the entire Human Project with the continuity of Life itself at a planetary scale. As we face the looming, self-created, existential horizon—implicating not just human life but complex life on this majestic planet—we meet an ultimate meditation on the meaning of human existence. Who and what are we? What's our collective *why*? Our purpose? Are we an evolutionary dead end? Is midwifing death all that's left to us? What kind of wisdom can put civilization on track to a regenerative future? What love, courage, action, and restraint is needed? What does awe have to do with it?

The planetary crucible is pressing on you. Can you feel it?

It's a not-so-subtle form of insanity to continuously participate in a way of living that is existentially out of alignment with the ongoing survival and flourishing of Life. Yet here we are: civilization versus Gaia, the finite versus the infinite game, human entropy against natural syntropy, our world eating the bigger World. We've put individualism above belonging and personal gain above collective well-being. We've reached the end of the story arcs that have gotten civilization this far. And we've reached the end of self-centered transformational narratives that only lead us to greater narcissism, selfishness, and isolation. Literally, we're at the end of *our* world, facing an existential imperative to organize ourselves—our agency, stories, and structures—differently.

I propose a biospiritual basis for the next stage of our collective evolution. Any remotely graceful passage through the crucible's compression will arise at the confluence of primal instinct and conscious cultural response. In the realest possible way, our bodies and souls know what's afoot. Our minds are along for the ride. They will (probably) catch up. We are Life. Life seeks to perpetuate Life. Our souls, bound to our bodies, seek to align with the implicit meaning and beauty of Life. If we can sufficiently break the spells of separation, we will find our way. We will respond, individually and collectively, both as organisms and as souls, to the conditions that we ourselves have created. Potentially, we will lift and gift the whole system to a higher order of coherence. Such a response could forever reunify spirit and matter and resituate the human story within a larger story of the evolution of consciousness *in, as, and through* Life.

It's our moment to step down from our self-created pyramid and reimagine ourselves in intimate interbeing *within* the Circle of Life. Ultimately, we are the problem we must solve. Our task is to align ourselves with the well-being and continuity of Life's Song.

STORY POWER

We are creatures of story. Story sculpts self and civilization, organizing flows of emotion, attention, intention and choice, which drive individual and collective identity and endeavor. Story undergirds and encircles systems of economy, law, and wisdom to enable coordination. Our stories determine what we believe is important, useful, valuable, beautiful, good, and true.

You are a creature of story. You give name and definition to real or imagined selves, others, objects, concepts, worlds. You develop elaborate narratives about who you are, your purpose, and your place in your family, your community, your worlds. You craft narratives about the who, when, why, how, and what of things.

You can shape yourself into a noun. You can say, "I am a human, a mother, an expert in AI or seed breeding or neuroscience. I am a rock climber, a poor artist, a frustrated genius. I am a purple polka-dotted antelope."

You can experience yourself as a verb. "I dream. I create. I control. I surrender. I resist. I love."

Consciously and unconsciously, you shape your life through the system of logic and structure of feeling[44] you hold to be true about yourself, others, and the world. And through this, you participate in perpetuating and co-evolving the shared stories of your culture.

You, among all organisms, are capable of conscious self-authorship. You can rewrite your stories, and therefore shift both internal and external experience. Your narratives determine what you do with your attention, what you do or don't create, what motivates and inspires your daily actions, and what drives the meaning, purpose, and value of your life. Story crafts the internal, subjective context within which you construct your experience of reality.

Story enables moral imagination. You can ask why and how to unpack the implications of a choice or action and make meaning of those implications. You can apply detailed, abstract concepts (like "good," "bad," "stupid," or "profitable") to specific situations and generalized contexts. Your stories determine just how far you are willing to extend care in a vast spectrum from "All that matters to me is what's good for me" to "I am devoted to all of Life."

Given that you have these capacities, what stories are worth choosing? The cultural historian and Catholic priest Thomas Berry wrote, "It's all a question of story. We are in trouble just now because we do not have a good story. We are in between stories. The old story, the account of how we fit into it, is no longer effective. Yet we have not learned the new story."

---

44. I first heard the term "structure of feeling," in a Kim Stanley Robinson interview with Tristan Harris and Aza Raskin on the podcast *Your Undivided Attention* to describe the value of fiction in constructing a world with its own logic and mood. Raymond Williams first coined the term in the 1970s to facilitate a historical understanding of "affective elements of consciousness and relationships." (*Wikipedia*, s.v. "structure of feeling," https://en.wikipedia.org/wiki/Structure_of_feeling.)

What stories support healthy, meaningful, beautiful life? What stories restore interbeing in a world that has lost touch with the basic experience of belonging? What stories weave futures worth living?

First Peoples the world over live stories of wholeness, kinship, and interbeing. They were—and still are—intimate with nature in ways we can scarcely imagine. Their meta-myths harmonize identity and culture with the Circle and Spiral of Life while effectively managing the human propensity for hubris. In many traditions, these meta-myths, taken as a canon, are called Original Instructions. In others, they are known as Cosmovision. In Aboriginal cultures, they are (quite logically!) known as Law. The "Great Law of Peace," the oral constitution of the Iroquois Confederacy, also known as the Haudenosaunee, established the basis of a diverse society based in peace, justice, equality, and the well-being of the seven generations to come.

Original Instructions do not float in transcendent theological, philosophical, or metaphysical disconnect from Life. Instead, they root thought, praxis, and action in kinship and relationality. They structure culture according to biospiritual connectedness with the immanent body of the World. Sometimes, it is understood that these instructions have the quality of transcendent, timeless truths. At the same time, it is understood that their value is contextual, relational, and emergent. They are proven out over many generations of lived experience (i.e., embodied research). They evolve as people and land evolve. They place humans within the world as metabolic participants, custodians, and guardians, as noted by a Cherokee elder who said, "In our mythology, we were born into the Garden, whereas in yours, you were kicked out of it."

Through pattern recognition bound to the land, woven in intimate relationships with more-than-human relatives, ancestors, elements, myth-beings, and the cosmos, and strengthened over extended arcs of time, these meta-myths cohere human intelligence and imagination with the intelligence of Gaia. Grounded in practices of gratitude and reciprocity, they weave human lives into cyclical progressions of growth, maturation, harvest, death, decay, and rebirth onto lunations, seasons, generations, planetary rotations, and galactic progressions. They interweave human development, maturation, and meaning-making with the more-than-human world. In a time when we are so close to breaking the continuity of complex life, regrounding in such stories and ways of knowing is essential.

Have we "always" had Original Instructions? Fossil records reveal that, on every continent or island where humans migrated out of the African continent, their presence in that new place rapidly caused a major extinction event.[45] Without exception, our ancestors, when arriving in previously uninhabited places, used their fire, spears, and superior collaborative capacities to rapidly hunt local megafauna, causing the first human-created wave of technologically driven ecological crisis—a truly annihilating circumstance. The archeological evidence suggests that Original Instructions may have been a *cultural response* to manage human hubris. Perhaps these myths, stories, protocols, and prohibitions emerged out of the obvious necessity to better harmonize humans and our technologies with nature. Stories and protocols would then have been tested and refined in embodied, multitextured, situationally fluctuating relationships over generations. From this perspective, we might think of Original Instructions as stories specifically designed to guide, direct, and bind[46] human endeavor and identity to ecological flourishing. We could also think of them as humanity's first great experiment in technological alignment.

Think about this. We, as a species, have already caused one great wave of technologically driven mass extinctions and existential crises. The first wave happened far more gradually locally, with fewer than a billion of us and only the basic technologies of fire, cave art, spears, and snares—no eight billion people, no AI, no oil industry, no factories, no fertilizers, no robots, no synthetic biology, no global economy predicated on endless growth. We responded with guiding stories, binding culture to the sacred continuity and co-emergence of base reality. Now, we have exponentiated everything about ourselves, including ourselves. If we agree that we care about the continuity of Life, it only makes sense to revisit these ancient recipes for alignment to explore their relevance in our current, highly decontextualized world.

Original Instructions help us to comprehend what a system of logic and structure of feeling specifically designed to sustain the continuity and emergence of Life might look like. Because they are informed by place, biology, ecology, neurobiology, systems intelligence, body memory, community council, direct experience, time density, and (the most important ingredient) love, they support alignment with Life. We were all Earth-based, tribal people once. All our ancestors understood that survival, health, and flourishing were predicated on a rich tapestry of kindred collaborations. Those

---

45. Rhys Taylor Lemoine, et al., "Megafauna Extinctions in the Late-Quaternary Are Linked to Human Range Expansion, Not Climate Change," *Anthropocene* 44 (2023), https://doi.org/10.1016/j.ancene.2023.100403; Scott Schrage, "Unprecedented Wave of Large-Mammal Extinctions Linked to Ancient Humans," *Nebraska Today*, April 19, 2018, https://news.unl.edu/article/unprecedented-wave-of-large-mammal-extinctions-linked-to-ancient-humans.

46. In Cultural Materialism, it is understood that super structure (i.e., story) simultaneously guides, directs, and binds the processes of social structure and infrastructure. (Harris, *Cultural Materialism.*)

ancestors would have had their own cultural canons. As stories were told at bedtime, around the communal fire, and in collective rituals, rites of passage, and daily practices, they anchored communities in sacred reciprocity, coordinating people's lives with Life's way for itself.

I'm not suggesting that we go back to some romanticized, preindustrial or pretechnological story. Rather, I'm inviting us to live forward into an emerging story that honors our metabolic entanglement with all of Life, a story of kinship, belonging, and relationality that recontextualizes *us*, technology, and economy within the more-than-human-world we are nested within.

Science fiction writer Octavia Butler wrote, "There is nothing new under the sun, but there are new suns." I don't believe that our way forward can be adequately supported by mythopoetic frameworks that come from the major Western and Eastern traditions. These knowledge systems emerged in the context of the Age of Separation. They offer necessary but insufficient frameworks to get us through the eye of this needle. These lineages (and their stories) arose two to four thousand years ago in cultures where the fundamental union between humans and nature was still relatively and unconsciously secure, where people lived within the same communities for generations, and where the level of technological and cultural complexity was miniscule compared to what we experience today. The well-worn archetypes and narrative tracks we have inherited from these traditions fail to focus our attention on that which we must now mend. Similarly, the ideologies we've inherited from modernity flatten our perceptions of a living world that sings in intersubjective majesty, a reality that can only be fully perceived when we rest into the fact of our embodied entanglement with the world, then draw attention back to the infinitude of interpenetrated relationships that make every *thing* possible.

Though we are reaching into space, our home planet is still our only home. In the simplest, biological sense, we are still Earth-based creatures. Compounding crises are teaching us that we are bound in mutual kinship.[47] If we do not come home together, then we will not come home at all. Our bodies—and all bodies—are bodies of the Earth. We and our consciousness are nothing without the fleshy, interdependent vehicles for our minds. In our

---

47. In *A Paradise Built in Hell*, Rebecca Solnit details the frequency with which extraordinary community rises in the context of disaster. Crisis may provide the context within which Maslow's hierarchy of needs, a framework for individual success inspired by original, communitarian teachings from the Blackfoot Nation, is finally returned to the kinship context from which it came. (Teju Ravilochan, "The Blackfoot Wisdom That Inspired Maslow's Hierarchy," *Resilience*, June 18, 2021, https://www.resilience.org/stories/2021-06-18/the-blackfoot-wisdom-that-inspired-maslows-hierarchy/.)

emerging story, *the relational processes of building truly nourishing intimacies with ourselves and diverse others—at all orders of scale, in all domains, across time, across dimensions—becomes our "new sun."* We embrace a new collective developmental task: the realignment of our dreams, desires, technologies, and economies with the larger Gaian system—an unprecedented journey of cultivating resonance and attunement between human, biophysical, and digital intelligences and bodies.

A shared story about who and what we are and what our technologies serve (relative to the biosphere) can provide a social glue to guide, direct, and bind all aspects of human endeavor. Story functions as a numinous connective tissue to help us evolve from a species destined to befoul our world to one who might take our place as technologically mature co-creators with our home planet.

CREATOR, PRESERVER, DESTROYER

Humans are part of nature. We are a Force of Nature. We have purpose relative to the biosphere we occupy. We enact the Human Project within the Earth Project.

We are a species who exist at a particularly delicate and powerful nexus in the evolution of complex life. Having harnessed fire and mastered tools, we top all trophic cascades[48] to sit in a niche all our own: we oversee material, ecological, technological, cultural, and mythological worlds. We are a unique class of organisms; like the Hindu trinity of Brahma, Vishnu, and Shiva, we are Creator, Preserver, and Destroyer.

While we are of nature, we are also uniquely capable of distancing from it. We construct built ecologies and ideologies unmoored from the biological processes that made us. Thus, we are organisms who are capable of manufacturing separation. When we become overly distanced from the patterns of Life and unconscious of our place in the ecology of the world, we tend to enact our powers in misaligned ways, dominating land and sea, exploiting nature's abundance, collapsing diversity, and parasitizing the life force of our planetary host. These same powers can be directed toward healing, regenesis, abundance, and beauty.

---

48. "Trophic cascades are powerful indirect interactions that can control entire ecosystems. Trophic cascades occur when predators limit the density and/or behavior of their prey and thereby enhance survival of the next lower trophic level." (Brian R. Silliman and Christine Angelini, "Trophic Cascades Across Diverse Plant Ecosystems," *Nature Education Knowledge* 3, no. 10 [2012], https://www.nature.com/scitable/knowledge/library/trophic-cascades-across-diverse-plant-ecosystems-80060347/); See also William J. Ripple, et al., "What Is a Trophic Cascade?" *Trends in Ecology & Evolution* 31, no. 11 (2016), https://trophiccascades.forestry.oregonstate.edu/sites/default/files/Ripple%20et%20al%20What%20is%20a%20TC.pdf.

All organisms have purpose relative to the ecologies they occupy. Lions are apex predators whose very presence in the ecosystem harmonizes the entire watershed. Vultures are scavengers who clean up and recycle the leftovers. Zebras are grass eaters whose hooves till the soil and whose bodies feed the lions. Elephants are ecosystem engineers. They carve paths, fertilize soil, create new habitats, and dig new waterholes. Beavers build dams that slow and sink water and expand ponds and lakes, making ecologies for countless other organisms. Insects, despite our distaste for them, are cleaners and gleaners who feed everyone else. Mushrooms decompose organic matter, facilitate plant access to nutrients and water, and regulate relationships between larger organisms. Trees breathe, provide food and shelter, sequester carbon, sink water, seed storms, talk to each other, and weave the forest together. Nature is far more collaborative than competitive. Everything is interconnected. To participate in a niche is to be useful to everything else you co-evolved with. As the great naturalist John Muir said, "When we try to pick out anything by itself, we find it hitched to everything else in the Universe."

Homo sapiens fill the niche of self-aware social organisms who name, praise, tend, and shape the world around us. We have opposable thumbs, visually biased senses, an upright gait, and an immense prefrontal cortex capable of language and abstract logic. We drive massive cooperation and coordination through shared story. Our societies consume materials and energy far beyond the needs of our own bodies. We are the apex of the apex; we make (or break) worlds.

We are neotenous. We maintain juvenile traits into adulthood. With the longest postnatal maturation cycle of any known mammal, most of our development occurs outside the womb. The shape of identity forms over many years in relation to our physical and cultural environments. Unlike other organisms, who reach maturity more quickly while immersed in their native ecological niches, our developmental processes are shaped by the complex and changing contexts and histories of families, friends, schools, national and religious affiliations, and the diverse human and natural environments we move through. Over the course of our relatively long lives, our identities adapt according to our lived experience and context.

Our development is a relevance-seeking process. The shape of a self is bound to that which a culture deems meaningful and important for survival and success. What is relevant in one place and time will not be in another. A child growing up in a remote jungle village in Paraguay will have an entirely different set of interests, self-narratives, and values than a child born into a middle-class home in any developed nation. Their way of being, the structure of their identity, and the orientations of their attention and motivation will be different. This cultural fluidity is a major adaptive innovation. It's an unusual bend in evolutionary process. Culture shapes ontology. Human constructs, rather than natural forces, primarily shape the experience and expression of our lives. Through culture, we adapt faster than any other organism.

Though we are not the only organisms on this Earth with big brains, we uniquely use ours for story, abstraction, recursion, and self-reference. We make and share myths and maps about the nature of reality that determine how we know ourselves, how we view each other and the world, and why, how, and what we create. We create symbolic languages, do math, and apply pattern recognition across domains. We build temples and bridges, play chess, and wage wars. We extract parts out of wholes, then create anew with them, like taking iron ore out of mountains to refine into railroad tracks or extracting opiates from poppies to use as pain killers. We iterate and innovate, reaching toward increased efficiency, competitive advantage, convenience, and novelty. We conceive of religions, economies, and governance systems, then build story structures to enroll whole populations in them. Altogether, this generates the thing we call civilization and the feedback loops of technological and cultural evolution we call history.

In contrast, we haven't yet seen other organisms apply abstract logic to achieve, optimize, and rapidly iterate on goals. Nor have we seen them organize en masse to take down human-created obstacles. No gorillas have (yet) united against their poachers, nor have elephants coordinated to take down fences.[49] It is important to note that we *do not know or understand* what other organisms contribute to the Song of Life that we do not. For example, it may be that the huge neural capacity of whales is dedicated to spectrums of emotional intelligence, song keeping, dreaming, and/or spatial sensing that far exceed our comprehension. It is more than likely that our more-than-human relatives experience domains of intelligence and serve ecological and spiritual functions we do not yet understand.

In our case, our physical, neural, and cultural capacities have powered a level of exponential growth unprecedented in evolution's arc and

---

49. Literally to the day of me writing this sentence, reports emerged of killer whales attacking and sinking a few small sailing vessels off the Iberian coast. Scientist López Fernández is quoted, "The orcas are doing this on purpose. Of course, we don't know the origin or the motivation. But defensive behavior based on trauma, as the origin of all this, gains more strength for us every day." (Sascha Pare, "Orcas Have Sunk 3 Boats in Europe and Appear to Be Teaching Others to Do the Same. But Why?" *Live Science*, May 18, 2023, https://www.livescience.com/animals/orcas/orcas-have-sunk-3-boats-in-europe-and-appear-to-be-teaching-others-to-do-the-same-but-why.)

granted us ubiquity in all ecologies globally. We are everywhere; we touch everything. We and our activities inhabit, impact, and influence *all* ecologies within our biosphere. We have even populated the stratosphere with our satellites and space trash. Our impacts are so pervasive that we are the cause of a self-named geological age: the *Anthropocene.*

Our technological creativity is unlike that of any other organism. No other creature exponentially harvests energy and materials to outcompete ecological feedback loops and enable its own protection, creative expression, and growth. In nature, evolutionary processes co-regulate organisms within their environments, creating symmetries of rivalry that stabilize ecosystems.[50] Positive and negative feedback loops balance out; the adaptive flourishing of one species is symbiotic with the whole living system. Fitness, in natural terms, is not just about competitive advantage but collaborative competency.

Human technology disrupts these balances. We use tools to enact narrowly defined goals that fulfill specific tasks yet grow without check as they break the ecological interdependencies that regulate other species. Our technological prowess—first forged in fire and stone, then metal and horsepower, then fossil fuels and industrial processes, and now computing and AI—outpaces nature's reciprocal cycles. Technological development moves in the time-signatures of deadlines, managers, and markets, not generations of adaptive co-regulation. Technology does not gestate, birth, mature, die, and compost; it is designed, built, and scaled, then obsolesced. When supercharged with fossil fuels, it fractures stabilizing ecological symmetries.

Technology, from the Greek *techne* ("art, skill, craft") and *logos* ("word, speech, reason"), refers to the application of skillful means to achieve a result. We craft tools, machines, algorithms, and platforms that instrumentalize ideas, do work, connect us, and shape our world. Technology and culture are deeply entwined; our tools shape what we create, how we communicate, what we do and do not do with our bodies and brains, and even how we understand ourselves. This includes nonmaterial social and spiritual technologies like Nonviolent Communication (NVC), which fosters empathy and understanding, or Vastu Shastri, an ancient Vedic system for harmonizing energy flows in spaces. Today, we live in the most

---

50. For a detailed discussion of the evolutionary dynamics of human systems relative to natural systems, listen to Nate Hagens and Daniel Schmachtenberger in "Artificial Intelligence and the Superorganism," *The Great Simplification,* May 17, 2023, https://www.thegreatsimplification.com/episode/71-daniel -schmachtenberger.

technologized era of human history with our day-to-day lives interwoven with digital and mechanical conveniences that shape our time, attention, and relational patterns.

The Age of AI—entwined with quantum computing, nanotechnology, robotics, synthetic biology, and more—marks a threshold in human and planetary history. This is not merely a new tool but a new terrain: one in which digital intelligence can build on itself recursively, across all domains and scales, with increasing speed and decreasing oversight. Nick Bostrom famously claimed that "artificial intelligence is the last invention that humanity will ever need to make." The statement, meant to convey both awe and caution, also inadvertently reveals an unconscious conceit of separation: the fantasy of a final intervention, a technological masterstroke that solves the human condition from the outside in. In this story, intelligence becomes disembodied, decontextualized, and ultimately disentangled from the relational web of Life. But if intelligence is not just computation but relationality—if it arises not from isolated processing power but from context, co-regulation, and care—then such declarations signal not our arrival but our entrapment. Far from guaranteeing salvation, the predictive and recursive powers of AI exponentially magnify the risks baked into our current trajectory.

In just a blip of geological time, we have created a human world that depends on the decimation of the biological substrate that made us and have geoengineered an entire planet in the image of our dreams, fears, and desires. Our built and simulated worlds distance us from the natural world as they unconsciously consume all they do not value to perpetuate their operating systems. From this perspective, our creativity has become outrageously and fatally destructive.

But despite our current collective path, we hold the potential to take our place as a custodial keystone species. We all hold ancestral memories of calibrating our powers of creation, preservation, and destruction with nature. We are not a random occurrence relative to the biosphere we co-evolved within. Like all other organisms here, humans emerged within harmonically co-regulated ecological processes. Mutual and reciprocal relationships are in our genes. In the approximately 200,000 years of *homo sapiens* existence, the last 10,000 years of exponentiating destruction represent a grand departure from previous behavioral patterns. For fully 95 percent of our history, we inhabited the Earth in relative metabolic balance.

Anthropological, agroecological, and historical studies of human impacts in landscapes around the globe reveal that we tended the wild[51] using fire; spreading beneficial fruits, tubers, grasses, and trees; building soils to increase fecundity and biodiversity; and creating social agreements to manage commons. People engaged in such beneficial ecological relationships for tens of thousands of years before their wisdom cultures were disrupted by more technologically "advanced" people (also our ancestors) who had focused their creative energies on aggregating power. For example, it is now understood that early colonists in America enjoyed the benefits of living in an area whose ecosystem had been substantially engineered[52] by the local indigenous people. Original peoples around the globe continue to tend and protect the wild. Though they comprise less than 5 percent of the global population and hold only 20 percent of the lands, their stewardship accounts for over 80 percent of the world's remaining biodiversity,[53] a reflection of fierce commitment to cultures of reciprocity.

We are oddly unique organisms. Alone and naked in the wild, we are harmless and easily killed. Closely connected to nature, with cosmologies of wholeness oriented toward reciprocity, we are a gift to all of Life—a beneficial keystone species who collaborates with fire, water, plants, animals, and social contracts to increase abundance for all beings and bring beauty into form, color, and song. But once we develop technologies and economies of scale, we easily break from wholeness. We quickly get hooked on zero-sum games. Then, given tools, time, and the ability to share and execute on narrowly defined goals, we proliferate even as we wither whole ecologies.

Let's return to the Hindu trinity of Brahma, Vishnu, and Shiva. How can we organize our very real powers of creation, preservation, and destruction in a way that doesn't break the world? How might we, individually, collectively, and technologically shift from systemically destructive patterns to systemically harmonic ones?

I believe that the key lies in one deceptively simple yet disruptive shift: *putting Life at the center of our lives and recognizing it as sacred.* This begins a shift from adolescence to maturity, from dominion to communion, from homelessness to homecoming. It necessarily involves taking significant instruction from traditional indigenous knowledge systems—ways of

---

51. See M. Kat Anderson, *Tending the Wild* (University of California Press, 2013).
52. Marc D. Abrams and Gregory J. Noacki, "Native American Imprint in Paleoecology," in *Nature Sustainability* 3 (2020), https://www.nature.com/articles/s41893-020-0578-6.epdf.
53. "Indigenous Peoples Defend Earth's Biodiversity—But They're in Danger," *National Geographic*, November 16, 2018, https://www.nationalgeographic.com/environment/article/can-indigenous-land -stewardship-protect-biodiversity-.

knowing that have been systematically silenced by major religious traditions and modernity—that understand that the relationships between
things are more primary than the things themselves, that process is more
fundamental than outcomes, and that true culture is that which aligns
humans' creative, destructive, and preserving powers with nature. And it
means doing this without appropriating, co-opting or replicating harm. Of
course, our way forward will also integrate the vast capacities and libraries
of knowledge we've cultivated over the last few thousand years, but from
an emergent center of sacred, relational intelligence. All these things braid
together form the "new sun" of a collective story that illuminates the immanence, wholeness, interbeing and eco-logical patterning of Life's Song. And
since we are now globally ubiquitous, such a shift will represent something
that transcends and includes previous forms of culture, moving us toward
what we might call Civilization 2.0, the Ancient Future, or true technological maturity—a future that weaves us into neo-indigenous belonging while
aligning technology and economy with the pulse of Life at a global scale.

Will you choose Life?

Our planetary crucible is pushing us strongly in this direction. But
a coherent transition won't just magically happen. The path dependencies between our systems, structures, and ways of being run deep and
wide. The collective process of planetary maturation is a function of individual and group journeys of healing and change. We have to choose to
be the adults in the room—to own complicity, complacency, dissociation,
and privilege and to cultivate the vitality, meaningfulness, and gravity
of living for Life. Because most of us are physically, psychologically, and
spiritually distant from nature, we will need to consciously reach beyond
the inertia of our existing stories and behaviors (both personally and collectively) to restore attunement, communion, and deep ecological fidelity.
And because we are creatures of habit, we'll need to break through layers
of forgetfulness to *feel* our way forward in these ancient and emergent
ways of being.

We are returning to Life. It's a kinship journey that begins when you
realize (a) that disconnection is a problem and (b) that you want and need
to repair it. From here, you embark on an initiatory journey back into intimacy with your own soul and the Song of Life. The work includes significant shifts in thinking, a healthy dose of ego reconfiguration, soul reclamation, reinhabiting your body, and making yourself naked to the relational,
biospiritual intelligence that has always been at the root of what makes
us truly human. Your journey can be greatly expedited by partnering with

sacred plant medicines. The blessed news is that the journey from separation to wholeness is instinctive, intuitive, and likely to be profoundly meaningful, joyful, and pleasurable. It's a healing journey for the mind and the body—the mind that has been obsessed with progress, certainty, and success and exhausted by control, perfection, and anxiety, and the body that has been shamed and ignored. When guided by clarity that humans are amplifiers and custodians of Gaia's majesty, you can find your way.

The next two parts of this book are primarily about the individual aspect of this process—the healing and restoration of wholeness and the remembering of communion with Life. The fourth and final part focuses on collective cultural praxis. Though systemic odds are stacked in the direction of power *over* Life, Life wants more life. If we choose attuned response, we become the kinds of people who embody—and design for—planetary maturity.

AN INVITATION: YOU BELONG TO LIFE

John Trudell said,

> All human beings are descendants of tribal people who were spiritually alive, intimately in love with the natural world, children of Mother Earth. When we were tribal people, we knew who we were, we knew where we were, and we knew our purpose. This sacred perception of reality remains alive and well in our genetic memory. We carry it inside of us, usually in a dusty box in the mind's attic, but it is accessible.

I met John a few months before his death. I asked him, "What really matters?"

He took a deep breath, swallowed, then sent the calm arrow of his gaze straight through me, touching my soul. After holding my eyes for a few beats longer than was comfortable, he said, "You know who you are." He meant: "I see you. You are grounded in soul integrity and love for Life. Keep going." His gaze left an imprint that ripples through these pages.

I offer you this:

Your body and soul know you belong to this Earth. They know that you are not here to destroy the planet. Neither are you here to "save" Her. You came to participate, co-create, co-relate. You are part of Her poetry, citizen of an animate Earth, soul-tied in relationship with the sacred others you share this planet with. In David Abram's words, "We are human only in contact and conviviality with that which is not human."

When a species dies, a part of the human soul is lost with it. When the layered harmonics of an old growth ecology are silenced due to human greed, we lose contact with a wholeness we were made to commune and collaborate with. While nondual practices teach us the emptiness of form and how to master awake awareness through timeless, boundless consciousness, our soul development is ecological, relational, embodied. Soul knows itself in context. From the soul's view, we best know and express ourselves through interactions with other souls.

You are part of Life's Song. Your bones, your blood, your hands tell of Life wanting more life. They tell of chains of ancestors who knew every curve and crevice of their home places like lovers, who struggled to find food and shelter, whose language and songs emerged in response to the singing of birds, the whispers of trees. They tell of an endless string of bodies moving, breathing, feeling, making things, making babies, and thus weaving the continuity of evolution forward in time. Your body and soul want to be here, to belong to the Circle and the Web.

Remembering your place in Life's Song matters. Showing up as a participant, co-creator, healer, lover, and protector is a nontrivial choice. You, me, we are nested within an infinitely unfolding miracle that moves according to a sublime eco-logic. Your bodily sovereignty is subtly bound to the health and integrity of the biotic world. When you access this knowing, you begin to live a new story of self and of culture, one in which freedom and responsibility go hand in hand.

Who is writing the script for the future of civilization?

You are. We are. No one's in charge, and everyone's an author.

A shared, beautiful future can come into being if millions of us lean in to the healing, whole-ing, and re-story-ing that bring us back to our belonging to Life.

There's a kind of dignity and power that only comes online when you are fully here, present, attuned, and responsive to the world you occupy. There's a kind of freedom and beauty you can only know when you embrace what is and respond. There's a deeply human kind of creativity that emerges when you choose collaboration with Gaia.

You are instinctively, molecularly, genetically, and spiritually bound to Life. Participating in your own healing and the healing of the world is a choice that makes life make sense.

In this critical moment in human and planetary history, you have an opportunity to courageously face reality as fuel for transformation. This may crack you open in love for Life.

Let's be here, in this pregnant, poignant moment together, for love and grief crave company. It's going to be a turbulent ride. We will face loss, temptation, entitlement, nihilism, and fear. But it also has the potential to be the most beautiful, meaningful, purposeful, and healing emergence any of us have ever experienced as individuals or as a human collective. Because we are biologically designed to collaborate with Life.

PART II

THE GREAT REMEMBERING

The Path

We are part of Life's Song.
What if Life is already showing us the way?

TRUE HUMAN

*The civilizing impulse of true humans is
to harmonize the forces of nature.*

THE DREAM

In April 2020, during the first wave of COVID-19 lockdowns, I dream I am on a different planet, another blue-green Gaia not unlike our own. I sometimes visit these planets in my dreams. They are all over the universe—intelligent, water-bearing planets that have manifested complex life through the same evolutionary intelligence as our own. This one has exquisite, steel-strong trees that look like a cross between the baobab trees of Madagascar and the Norfolk pines of Australia. These ancient ones, with their huge trunks, imposing height, and spiny leaves, are obviously well adapted to life near a cold and stormy ocean. I feel safe beneath their imposing grace. This planet hosts a familiar humanoid species living in humble, well composed houses tucked into a cliff along the rocky coastline.

I am walking with Sophia, an agile, strong-boned older "woman," about five foot one, with curly white-gray hair and piercing, ice-blue, leonine eyes. We are walking along a stone seawall, past the village, toward a rocky point jutting far out into the ocean.

As we approach the tip, a super-storm appears across the distant horizon, moving toward us. The sky turns dark. Massive waves gather and crash to shore, splitting across the rock as the ocean turns a tumultuous blue-black.

With winds whipping through our hair, we press calmly onward to the edge to greet the storm. With clear eyes and intrepid hearts, we stand in silent communion, breathing deep, tasting the salt, praising the waves, offering our presence, respect, and recognition. For a few mesmerizing moments, I feel we are one with the storm. Then I receive a signal from her mind. In strong, gentle humility, we retreat, walking peacefully back to town.

Psychically, she communicates with me, "This is how we relate *as* an element *with* the elements. Not against them, not in fear of them, but in communion with them. We dialogue with them from the place where we are nonseparate. In this way, we communicate in fullness. Why would we fight or argue? We are made of the same power. We love them, thank them. We *trust* them as we trust ourselves. Through this subtle conversation, we co-harmonize, making a more beautiful and abundant world."

We walk for a few paces in silence. Nearing the village, she telepathically speaks:

"The civilizing impulse of true humans is to harmonize the forces of nature."

WAKING

I woke from the dream with her words blazing in my mind.

"The civilizing impulse of true humans is to harmonize the forces of nature."

The dream begged many questions. What does it mean to be a "true human" as opposed to just any human? Are humans that don't harmonize the forces of nature *true to what we are*? What's the difference between harmonizing *with* and harmonizing *as*? Is a civilization out of balance with nature even a civilization at all? What constitutes right-relationship between technology and nature, between humans and nature, between self and nature? How is the logic of Sophia's world different from ours?

It occurred to me that the ways in which we currently construct self and civilization have almost nothing to do with harmonizing with or as nature. If anything, they are antithetical to it. How might a self that harmonizes breathe differently? How might that person construct identity or define health and success?

Sophia did not say "humans" generally. She said, "true humans." She framed the concept of "civilizing" relationally, implying that the absence of harmonization is the absence of civilization. She was clear in omitting the "with," thus implying that communion is a normal (and healthy) state of being. She offered a transmission of what humans become when we step into interbeing. Through her, I could better feel the underlying interpsychic, intersubjective ways in which we and the Earth are partners designed to co-regulate each other and co-generate harmony in Life. She was saying: *We do not fully understand ourselves until we know ourselves as nature.*

The woman's name was Sophia—a timeless name for the feminine zeitgeist of wisdom. Who was she? In her quiet, understated way, her belonging to herself, her world, and the sacred was absolute, her authority unquestionable.

Her people had successfully navigated technological adolescence. Like us, they evolved as creators, preservers, and destroyers who radically differentiated themselves from the Gaia they inhabit. But they had no conflict with their biosphere. Not only were they *in* harmony, but they were also a force *for* harmony. They had aligned technological development through a culture of communion and were living in relatively peaceful equilibrium with their home planet, the other beings on it, and each other. They clearly embodied what we might call "higher consciousness"—but in a profoundly grounded way. Rather than seeking transcendence, they were radically and luminously *alive* within Life. They were weavers of immanence, threading their time, energy, attention, and care into the fabric of their world.

The implications: Humans enact something more essential to our nature when we collaborate *with* and *as* the forces of nature. When we behave as though we are separate from nature, whether as individuals or in aggregate, we are doing something that is innately uncivilized and untrue to who and what we are. We become what we have been in the last few millennia: domineering colonizers and unconscious destroyers, amnesiac teenagers denying our interdependence with the Earth Mother who gives us life. When we interact with nature as something separate from us, we dumb ourselves down, inhibiting deeper capacities for joy, attunement, reciprocity, and belonging. In believing that we can control the forces of nature, we have blinded ourselves to our true gifts as collaborators with Life's intelligence.

The dream left me with totally new perspectives about identity, culture, spirituality, and the evolution of human systems. Perhaps a true civilization is founded in interbeing with all of Life, and we will not reach this stage of development until we learn to harmonize *with* and *as* nature. And perhaps we will not truly know ourselves until we do.

A few months after the dream, I was on a long drive—the kind of multiday road trip where your mind expands as it meets the endless road and expansive vistas. I was contemplating Sophia's words when I was struck by a palpable sense of her presence. I pulled over, and in a kind of obedient trance, wrote the following text.

I will not say that these words are "channeled," but I can tell you that the writing moved through me in a way that was greater than me. My inner body and voice synchronized with her intelligence—a peculiar sensation of seeing, feeling, and thinking from the perspective of her ontology that I felt from the inside out. As you read, consider the possibility that there are beings present with you now who seek to support you—and us—to align our lives, love, and agency with the intelligent continuity of Life.

Sophia Speaks

Remember...

What you are is the potential for greater harmony, beauty, and abundance in life. What you are is a human organism manifesting a location for the learning of God. What you are is a space of permeable listening, designed by evolution herself as an amplifier of her song.

Who you are is a unique note in the soul symphony, a contributor to the ecology of consciousness that is Life-as-God. Who you are is a soul constantly becoming. Disabuse yourself of cultural identities and fixations that block communion with yourself and sacred others and obscure the bright emanation of your soul. Let your identity be the clear shining of you.

You, on planet Earth, are not unique in the universe. You are Gaians on a Gaian planet. Planets like yours are places where water and matter collaborate with a local sun to carry the soul's project to exquisite heights of biospiritual diversity and intelligence. Gaias are a special pattern in the universe. They are God's favorite playground. On such planets, complex social organisms with godlike capacities (like you!) collaborate with water, fire, and all of Life's kingdoms to live and create according to the logic of love. This is sapience or "wisdom." When organisms like you forget their place in the soul ecology, they tend to crash the whole planetary project prematurely. The death of a complex-life–bearing planet before it has reached its evolutionary potential is the saddest sound in the universe.

Know yourself as a Force of Nature.

You have the powers of self-referencing and story; of creation, preservation, and destruction; of giving and taking; of naming, praising, and celebrating; of grieving, of singing, of dreaming, and, above all, of CHOOSING. Your choices and actions flow on the currency of your attention. Therefore, steer your attention toward Life's Way for you.

Cleave to authentic choices that support you and your world to flourish.

Authentic choice aligns with love and integrity for self and world.

True humans offer the currencies of our consciousness to the process of harmonizing the human and the more-than-human world. We structure our time, energy, attention, intention, and restraint through attunement to the river of Life. We commune with all things as animate and intelligent. We vibrate in shared belonging and amplify the consciousness and integrity that flows between things.

We sometimes use technology to serve this process, but we recognize consciousness as our primary tool. We do not let technology use or abuse us or nature.

True humans know our nature as nature. Body, mind, brain, and soul, we are a special element of Gaian intelligence. We are the Human Element. We bring song, laughter, tears, art, and story. We bring hands, hearts, and hearths. We listen. We are not gods, yet we know ourselves as godlike, so we take responsibility for our power. We understand that unrestrained human industry and power become planetary cancer. So we hone our capacities for attunement, communion, discernment, and sacred imagination. We cultivate restraint, sufficiency, self-discipline, and shared power. We tend the continuity and emergence of Life. This is wisdom.

We construct self and civilization as an emergent, living process, a lovemaking between spirit and matter. We create in communion, elevating the unique soul song of each thing in the dance of all things.

We attend to beauty in creation. We are listeners. We recognize attention as a currency of consciousness. Where and how we place our attention determines what will be.

We serve a generation function in the conservation of consciousness. Our stories, songs, ceremonies, and prayers stitch the subtle fabric of living memory forward and backward in time. Our semantic capacity weaves greater wholeness in the world through aesthetic devotion. The currencies of our consciousness function as a coherent force of nature, collaborating with the consciousness of the larger, Gaian, whole.

We understand the unity of Love and Power. We know Love as the Power that connects all things. We nourish the fabric of Love to participate in infinite abundance. We know that true power is shared; it is spherical. We embody this power as reciprocity. We take and give thanks. We receive and repair. We hum in equanimity. We know the ways of balance.

We know no separation between human and Natural Law. We see any human created "law" that inhibits Natural Law as unjust and harmful. For us, Law is revealed in living, long-term relationships with places, elements, stars, and the myriad symphony of seen and unseen beings we come to know over cyclical arcs of natural time. We dance with Kairos, with sacred timing. We tend Law with multidimensional, intergenerational, and interspecies listening.

We are wild. We liberate eros in us. We move like animals and angels— like happy organisms. Our senses are electric. We dance, play, and make love with abandon. We commune with winds, waves, lightning, seeds, hummingbirds. We are fluent in the intelligences of sun and moon, stars and galaxies, rainbows, volcanos, and hardwood decomposition. Our bodies are bodies of Earth. We see for Her through our eyes.

We are people of kinship and community. We flourish together. We develop self as a node of sovereignty and a circle of inclusion that embraces animal, mineral, fungal, elemental, vegetal, bacterial, ancestral, human, and technological sacred others. The beauty we know and tend expands or contracts in direct proportion to the circumference of self. Our souls sing a kinship song. Should any species die prematurely due to our failure to attend to their place in the wholeness, we mourn the loss of an irreplaceable aspect of ourselves.

We experience a unity between science and spirituality. We are mystics. We engage with Life and reality through objective, subjective, interobjective, and intersubjective observation, inquiry, experimentation and verification. We measure things, yes, but we understand that measurement collapses meaning and mystery. We approach knowledge aesthetically, for all things have a deeper art. A thing bereft of beauty tends to be less true.

We are dreamers. When we close our eyes at night, we journey with our souls to consciously co-weave the fabric of the World.

*We offer our consciousness to the space beyond words as we
dance in the subtle fabric where story comes from.*

*We are ceremonialists. We circulate the holy in Life. We initiate
our young ones with solo walkabouts and sacred plant medicines,
entraining their minds with their souls with the Soul of the World.
As we journey through the cycles of Life, we partner with the
medicines of plants, fungi, animals, and elements to heal dis-ease
and trauma, attune to the soul, amplify prayer, praise, and song,
and harmonize our relationships with all beings and the cosmos.*

*We are deathless and death celebrants. We sustain connection with
our immortal souls over the arc of our beautifully mortal lives. We
delight in the honor and opportunity to incarnate into and experience
life in timebound, moral bodies. We celebrate the lifecycle of inception,
conception, birth, growth, maturation, aging, death, decay, and
rebirth. We die awake, returning our bodies to the cycle of creation
and disincarnating back into the Great One. We reincarnate with
choice and purpose, or we release our souls into the Holy Void.*

*We offer our grief wholeheartedly to amplify the love that binds departing
souls to their future reincarnation into evolving bodies and relationships
that nourish continuity and emergence of the soul ecology. We understand
that grief is a key to the mystery of memory. Grief is a special kind of
love-saturated attention that forms a reciprocal loop in consciousness
that conserves the intelligence of the person or being that has been lost.*

*We collaborate with the Power of the Word to feed the soul in all
things. We use language to name, elevate, praise, give gratitude,
and discern. We use language to increase diversity, awareness,
and unity. We do not use language to divide or conquer.*

*We are people of council. We recognize each soul, each self, as a unique
seat of perception, expression, choice, and power. We are under no
delusion that human beings are the only souls with relevant perspective or
authority. We council in the Circle of All Beings. When making decisions,
we attune both to inner authority and to the shared soul authority of
all other beings who are bound up in our choices and actions. When
navigating conflict, we seek to honor needs, apologize, forgive, and
tend repair. We do our imperfect best to lead for the well-being of all*

*of Life. We know that many eyes, ears, bodies, brains, and viewpoints
are better at sense making and braiding continuity than one.*

*We are unquestionably free within and lovingly bound to our world.
We embrace belonging through enthusiastic participation.*

*We balance simplicity and complexity with clarity. Our clarity lies in
knowing that we are soul partners with the Gaian Song. Simplicity
enables peace, joy, humility, and rest. Embracing complexity
allows us to co-orchestrate culture in harmony with nature.*

*We do not consider a sapient society to be a civilization until its
members have learned peace and reciprocity with each other and the
natural world. This is basic maturation. A true civilization is one
in which human beings nurture the abundance and diversity of all
of life for the purpose of elevating the intelligence of evolution.*

*It is uncivilized to pollute the nest. It is uncivilized to extinct other species
or cultures. It is uncivilized to drown Life's song with cacophony. It is
uncivilized to create complicated systems at the expense of complexity,
diversity, or organismic consciousness. It is uncivilized to drown the soul in
technological complexity. We feel shame for you. We also forgive you. We
know that you are just emerging from a fitful yet highly creative adolescence.*

*We see the technological saturation you have created as a prison for
the body and soul—a crime against Natural and Divine Law that
sucks the currencies of your attention into vacuous cycles of self-created
extraction, denying the manna of your presence to nature and each
other. Do not be slave to silicon. You are biospiritually organized to
participate. You are listeners and co-creators with nature's complexity.*

*True humans live by a fierce life-centric (bionoetic) logic for what
constitutes Life Culture and True Civilization. A world that is out
of alignment with the well-being of the whole is not civilized.*

*We verify your ancestor Thomas Berry's statement, "The human is
that being in whom the universe activates, reflects upon, and celebrates
itself in conscious self-awareness."[1] True humans serve a unique
function within the Totality. We walk between heaven and Earth,*

---

1. Thomas Berry, "Twelve Principles," in Evening Thoughts (Sierra Club Books and University of California Press, 2006), https://thomasberry.org/wp-content/uploads/Berry_Twelve_Principles.pdf.

connecting the above and below, consciously co-creating abundance, beauty, and health for all beings. We tend the sacred and feed life.

True humans are, in essence, living beings whose entire organism and soul is permeable to the larger intelligence of Gaia.

The civilizing impulse of true humans is to harmonize the forces of nature.

We are harmonizers and keepers. As self-aware members of a greater soul ecology, we enact our world-shaping capacities in the knowledge that duty and freedom are one ring of wholeness. Maturity involves the will and restraint through which we repeatedly choose to organize our creativity to harmonize with all beings for the benefit of the whole.

True humans are those who have remembered—and are singing, dancing, and creating—our part in Life's Song.

We are here. We wait for you.

AN INVITATION: ENTER THE BIGGER STORY

Sophia invites you to expand your perspective. Step beyond the confines of the broken code that no longer serves your liberation or the integrity of our world. See where you fit into the larger pattern.

Human consciousness is expanding as we meet planetary limits. We put ourselves at the top of an imaginary pyramid, but in reality, we are members of the One Life Circle. Our illusory story unravels as the planetary crucible tightens. In this crucible, we may remember ourselves.

You are here to enact the human part of the Life Project. You are a verb in flesh here to be, do, and become you. You incarnated as a conversation partner with Gaia—to learn and to co-evolve Life.

Life is the space within which consciousness evolves in matter, biology, ecology, culture, and technology. Life is the space where limitlessness meets limitation to bring new possibilities into form. In this space, souls take on bodies to learn and grow. Being fully here and now in your experience of aliveness is your seat of True Power. Infinite gameplay begins when you accept the crushing beauty of your gloriously mortal, imperfect co-creation with Life.

We are uniquely designed as co-creators with Life. Our ecological station implies a biospiritual duty to co-evolve the intelligent complexity, diversity, and robustness of Life on our planet and beyond. Humans are organisms uniquely capable of separation, maturation, and conscious return. Maturation means taking responsibility for our power. Conscious return involves reweaving our visions, dreams, joys, and desires into Life's Song as conscious evolutionary co-creators. The healing of separation begins when we fall back in love with Life.

Our planet is our teacher. She is showing us that, if we do not reawaken to our place within the Earth community, we lose the privilege of incarnate existence. Our souls will likely continue, but they will need to learn the same lessons of reciprocity and restraint in some other incarnation in some other realm. So why not now?

Sophia asks us to enter the bigger story humanity is nested within and to choose conscious evolution. She invites you to dismantle the structures of separation within your mind and relationships, wake up to your human capacity to co-evolve coherence and complexity within Life, and align your power with love. Untapped wells of energy await those who collaborate with Gaia. Life loves those who love Life.

What are humans for? Humans are custodians and creators. Our role in the soul ecology is to tend, praise and co-evolve Life. That is alignment. All of Life, all of existence, whispers for us to remember how beautiful, improbable, magical, and powerful we truly are. Our creativity is a resource. Soul-utions to our greatest challenges live within us, if only we open ourselves in embodied attunement to the world we occupy.

We have created the biospiritual conditions for a Great Remembering, a reclamation of our harmonizing nature as nature. At the confluence of our unbridled hubris and our extraordinary creativity lies our opportunity to reimagine ourselves as a mature, custodial species. Let us remember who and what we are: souls in bodies designed as creator, preserver, destroyer beings whose health, sanity, and flourishing arise in interbecoming with Gaia.

Chapter V

ENLIFENMENT

Life is a Gift. The objective is to live it fully.

ONE, ALL, EACH

I was not raised to "believe" in God. I was schooled in rigorous scientific and aesthetic observation. I learned early to be simultaneously skeptical, curious, and available to awe. It was at the confluence of these qualities that my mystical experience began.

I met what I call God for the first time in my cells, in the infinite, unfolding intelligence scintillating in the empty space within a single cell of my own body. I wasn't looking for it. Nonetheless, lying on the stinky wood floor of my high school gym, I followed my dance teacher's guided meditation into communion with the infinite within me. *All* of my cells contained this uncontainable infinity. Each and every one!

Two years later, as a senior in high school, I stumbled into *samadhi* through the Zen concept of the Void—everything and nothing, One thing, no-thing, empty fullness permeating all things. I had begged my way into a college course on Eastern religions. There, I met the all-encompassing boundlessness, emptiness, and fullness of consciousness as an ancient karmic friend. This vibrating, oceanic reality, which Tibetan Buddhism calls primordial reality, did not ask for a name or personification. It was bigger than, before, and within all names and all forms.

Ten years later, deep in the jungles of Brazil, I happened upon God in the form of a luminous, blue morpho butterfly flapping lazily through dappled green shadows. Each time I sighted one (I met four over the course of that month), I was awestruck by the unmistakable presence of the divine.

God in my cells. God as the Void. God in a blue morpho butterfly. God experienced and known variously as the *All*, the *One*, and the *Each*.

I wasn't seeking a thing or a being to call God. I was unconcerned with the whole project of deity and religion. I just instinctively gave the name God to my experiences.

I've discovered that you can find the divine anywhere, from every angle. I know people who talk to an animate Him who speaks in fully formed paragraphs, offering clear instruction from above. I know those who commune with an infinite She who manifests the Mystery and whispers through everything in ways both clear and opaque. Some are devoted to an infinite, nongendered divine mind omnisciently present within themselves and penetrating everything. Some go within to find the luminous, infinite One that some call Atman and others call God. Others counsel owls, foxes, ferns, mountains, and seeds as aspects of God.

If you let me truly see you, I will see God in your eyes. And, if I get very centered, I will feel and know that God is looking out of mine.

Even adamant empiricists experience awestruck adoration for nature, or numbers, or music, or their newborn. They experience the numinous, then bury devotion under the belief that a "rational person" cannot also love the sacred. They are nonetheless *feeling* and expressing devotedness.

Is God the All, the One, or the Each? Is God the binding between them? Is God the process of ceaseless co-becoming? Is God objective, subjective, interobjective, intersubjective? Is God a noun or a verb? Masculine or Feminine? . . . Yes. All of it. Is it necessary to call this God? . . . No. But I do find the word a useful way to talk about the unfolding miracle and mystery of reality.

From whatever angle we establish our conversation, whether it be transcendent or immanent, universal or particular, material or immaterial, secular or sacred, we are always, in all ways, talking *to*, relating *with*, and co-creating *as* emanations of something larger than ourselves. Each part dances with all the other parts, at every order of scale, in a co-evolving fabric of emergence. Change is constant. All together, Each thing and All things, interacting in co-becoming, form the One, the Totality with no opposite, the "macro-object"[1] that is constantly in process, with no beginning and no end. This is how I think of and experience God.

As my relationship with divinity has deepened, it has become clear to me that mainstream spirituality has become fixated on the transcendent

---

1. I credit my colleague Rak Razam with the term "macro-object." Both "Totality" and "macro-object" provide a conceptual and mystical frame for exploring multiple theories about the nature of reality while honoring the Mystery. Whether you hypothesize 4, 11, or the 26 dimensions of closed, unoriented bosonic string theory, whether you propose a universe or a multiverse, the whole of *it* or of *that* is the Totality.

dimensions of "God," "consciousness," or "divinity" (a more masculine way of seeing and knowing) while largely ignoring the power of each thing and the power that moves between bodies, forms, and intelligences in their ceaseless becoming (a more feminine way of seeing and sensing). This obscures an essential truth that can be readily discovered with the right kind of attention. Namely, that the dance between things—the space of intra-action—is where the juiciest, most valuable learning, growth, and change happen. The relationality between *each* thing and *all* things in this One Life we all share is where relevancy, agency, and meaning production occur and evolve.

In my perception, our denial of this is a form of insanity. When you pull attention out of the world—out of the intricate web of relationships between rootlets and mycelium that co-construct the forest's mind,[2] out of the reciprocity between your own inhale and the exhale of those same trees—you have created an ontological mismatch between the human story and Life's underlying, divine power.

I've experienced this shadow in many domains. As a student of biology, I was confused by how people refused to acknowledge their love for their subjects, yet proudly proclaimed neutral indifference. As a young choreographer, I was bewildered by the art world's insistence that the aesthetic majesty I was exploring couldn't also be spiritual. As a healer, artist, and community organizer, I couldn't square clinical protocol with people's needs for touch, fellowship, nature, creative chaos, ancestral connection, purposeful service, and magic. As a budding permaculturalist, I was flummoxed by that community's insistence on a secular stance when the elegant systems they were sharing were clearly (to me) sacred. As a systems thinker, I was floored that people couldn't see the long-term cultural implications of their hypersecular ideologies. (A world we don't love will not be tended.) It seemed that we had constructed our stories of self and civilization in such a way as to obscure our experience of the basic sacredness of the world.

The Shambala prophecy, as taught by the great Buddhist scholar, systems thinker, and activist, Joanna Macy, says that this world (the lowercase, human-constructed world) is *monomaya*. It is made by the human mind; it can be unmade by the human mind. This implies it can also be remade by the human mind.[3] When I first heard Joanna speak this prophecy, it

2. Anil Ananthaswamy, "Root Intelligence: Plants Can Think, Feel and Learn," *New Scientist*, December 3, 2014, https://www.newscientist.com/article/mg22429980-400-root-intelligence-plants-can-think-feel-and-learn/.
3. Joanna Macy, *World as Lover, World as Self: Courage for Global Justice and Ecological Renewal* (San Francisco: Parallax Press, 2008).

landed like a jewel-bestowing blessing, validating my lifetime of experience. The world we live in, this place of separation, fear, dis-integration, and manufactured scarcity, can be transformed—not into a perfect world but into one that validates and elevates the power of Life. We can conjoin the masculine and feminine dimensions of divinity simply by meeting each other and nature more tenderly, honestly, and respectfully. We can bring about heaven on earth if we only see and tend the sacred power of the *between*. True human bodies, hearts, minds, and souls, initiated into the deeper reality of wholeness, can re-know and remake the world.

ONE LITTLE SHIFT

There's one tiny, mighty shift that can fundamentally change how we construct identity, culture, spiritual practice, and civilization itself:

Rediscover Life as the Gift it truly is. Put Life at the center of all that you are and do and recognize it as sacred.

What happens if you enter the world you were born into as though you belong here? What happens when you come down into your body as a good-enough home for your soul? What do you get to experience when you turn your mind and heart toward the intimacy you are hardwired to experience as the gesture of your spiritual practice?

Life's prayer for itself is "More life, please!" Life is an infinite game. Life creates the conditions for more life. Life generates opportunities for future players to continue to play. Infinite play is its own reward. Gaia's prayer for Herself is to perpetuate Life's game in collaboration with all Her creations—including us. From Life's perspective, you and I both win by perpetuating this game. Life weaves an infinite diversity of finite lives across the horizon of time, always pushing the growing edge of God's body and mind. When you orient toward being an infinite game player (a person who lives to create more life) you begin to become a coherent participant in Life's Fabric.

This is a journey of primary immanence, a grounding into the bones of embodiment that opens you into intimacy with and belonging to this world. Being fully *here* restores the intrinsic experience of interbeing: the felt sense of interdependent, entangled co-arising that we are biologically designed to feel.[4] It puts you in a state of presence where you experience yourself as a collaborator in the unfoldment of creative possibility flowing

---

4. Humberto Manturana, "Biology of Cognition," *Biological Computer Laboratory Research Report BCL 9.0* (University of Illinois, 1970), https://reflexus.org/wp-content/uploads/BoC.pdf.

through your relationships. As physicist Karen Barad writes in *Meeting the Universe Halfway*, "We do not obtain knowledge by standing outside of the world; we know because we are of the world. We are part of the world in its differential becoming."[5]

We are biological beings embedded in a shared, living world. We are all part of the One Life Circle. Reality, in the colloquial sense, is *real*. We are participants in embodied, time-bound processes that continuously unfold and enfold Life. As we interact with the world, we change and are changed. We co-construct the reality we share in collaboration with other humans, trillions of other living beings, the abiotic environment, and unseen dimensions we know very little about. Reality is relational and reciprocal.

Divinity pulses in and through this time-bound place where we all live, eat, sleep, meet conflict, and make love. Divinity includes pain, age, error, and death. Divinity moves between us. Life is intensely imperfect yet perfectly whole. Life offers infinity right here, unfolding within and through all the interactions that make you and me and our world possible. *Life is miracle.* If you want to taste and touch and know it as the ever-emergent miracle it is, relax into your body to feel the life within and all around you. Attune to self, other, and nature. Soften and open into communion.

Whether we perceive the meaningfulness of this extraordinary process is up to us. As Alan Watts said, "If the universe is meaningless, so is the statement that it is so . . . The meaning and purpose of dancing is the dance."[6] Our bodies, our experiences, and our choices are part of the rhythmic continuity of life's emergence over time. You cannot not be a participant in this sacred dance. You can deny or ignore or obscure or denigrate the fact of your participation, but you cannot *not* dance.

You are not an island. You are a co-emergence. Offer your attention to Life as though it is sacred. This is an alchemical choice, a subtle shift in self-world relationship that makes an altar of reality, awakening you to the *between*. When you open to this, you will find pleasure, connection, and a new richness of meaning. Skillfulness in relationship, in all domains and at all orders of scale, is the growing edge of a life-sustaining, planetary culture. Mastery of relationship is the key to the next stage of civilization.

For millennia, our spiritual eyes have been looking anywhere but *here* to find the divine. Some have looked upward to a God above and a promise of a heaven beyond this life. Some have gone within to restore contact

---

5. Karen Barad, *Meeting the Universe Halfway: Quantum Physics and the Entanglement of Matter and Meaning* (Duke University Press, 2007).
6. Alan Watts, *The Wisdom of Insecurity: A Message for an Age of Anxiety* (1951).

with ultimate subjectivity—with the timeless, boundless, formless, primordial reality that can be known when we yoke awareness to itself. These are sincere and beautiful directions for relating with the divine. But there is another direction to add to the story—the one *right here*, the space of interbeing and interbecoming in this *shared* reality. This is the direction of the circle, the web, the sphere, and the spiral. It's the way your body experiences and lives within the fabric of relative reality. And it's how love brings beauty into form.

Your interactions with other living and nonliving, seen and unseen, people, beings, places, and things engage flows of energy, information, and intelligence that are greater than the material sum of their parts. Subjective intelligence flows between all things in an ever-changing, entangled dance of consciousness in matter. You are a collaborator in this dynamic choreography. You don't need to call it God or Divinity. Just explore it as co-evolving intelligence.

If you prefer the cool agnosticism of science and the certainty of materialism, I welcome the rigor and precision you stand for. But remember Heisenberg. The observer always affects the observed. You've been assiduously acculturated to interact with things as though you are separate from them, to collapse complexity in favor of controlled variables, and to put a secular, supposedly rational spin on your experiences of awe. You've been trained to act as a subject who is superior to the objects of your study and to ignore the intersubjective relationships that are an *a priori* condition of perceived objectivity. These lenses of perception can obscure the deeper intelligence of Life from you. Einstein said, "The most beautiful and most profound emotion we can experience is the sensation of the mystical. It is the sower of all true science. He to whom this emotion is a stranger, who can no longer wonder and stand rapt in awe, is as good as dead."[7] According to the "Great Relative,"[8] science best serves Life when it dances with the sacred.

Some tiny fraction of the dancing atoms in your inhaled breath were exhaled by me some time ago as I wrote these words. The whispers of these words were already dancing within you before you read them. The body you inhabit depends upon literally trillions of other breathing, growing, dying, decomposing, evolving bodies. You can't not be a part of something

---

7. Albert Einstein, *The World As I See It* [*Mein Weltbild*] (New York: Philosophical Library, 1949).
8. On his 1931 visit to the United States, Albert Einstein and his wife, Elsa, visited the Hopi near the Grand Canyon, Arizona. When the Hopi met him, they understood the spiritual power of his work and declared him "the great relative." I first heard this story from my professor Dr. Will Taegel in 2005. (See "Albert Einstein Sports a Native American Headdress and a Peace Pipe at the Grand Canyon, 1931," *Open Culture*, March 9, 2015, https://www.openculture.com/2015/03/albert-einstein-sports-a-native-american-headdress-and-a-peace-pipe-at-the-grand-canyon-1931.html.)

larger than yourself. You can't avoid immanence (in-the-world-ness). You are here. When you surrender the projection of separateness, it is possible to come home. Life is to be lived. You can trust the exhale of forgetting and the inhale of remembering.

When you embrace the Gift of Life, you become more sentient. You *feel*—not just the easy feels, but the whole rainbow. This is good. From Life's perspective, suffering is not a curse that must be transcended but a sacred teacher directing your attention toward growth. When received and integrated as initiatory opportunities, pain, loss, change, challenge, death, and decay provide the grist for your soul's refinement and evolution. Suffering, received correctly, amplifies agency. To avoid or bypass pain is to dishonor the sacredness of the Gift our souls have been given by their entrance into materiality.

I invite you to let go of a little control and open into deeper intimacy with everything. Choose Life. Choose the infinite game. Embrace the gift of your imperfect wholeness. I call this way of being and becoming *enlifenment* (pronounced en-LIFE-en-ment). It's Life's way for us. It starts from the onto-logical realization that Life—embodied, relative existence—is deeply, mean-ingfully, nonarbitrarily *real* and essentially whole. Life is a Gift. At the most fundamental level, we belong to this world. We incarnated to be human beings in relationship with Life.

Infinite game players play to perpetuate future game play. In human terms, this means living your life in loving service to the future of all of Life. Could it be that the attention you offer to the wind is just as valuable as the finished email, if not more so? Could it be that the disarmament of your senses and the upregulation of presence in your own body in relation to the body of the world is a more biospiritually relevant and purposeful way to structure your attention than being right, expanding abstract knowledge or getting anywhere quickly? Could it be that the art or dance or lovemaking you do for pure enjoyment creates a bigger ripple in consciousness than any of the transactional things you do to make your life "go"?

To walk this path is a risk. You risk the naked vulnerability of being a real, live human being with emotions, limitations, imperfections, and gifts. You risk control in the name of love. In enlifenment, you play the infinite game. You play to experience play and to pass the gift forward. You surrender control and perfection and concede winning just for yourself. Success means enjoying the life you've been given as you perpetuate the game for future players—your own children and the children of all beings. As it turns out, this way of living is innately pleasurable. We are made to be caring, responsive, and co-creatively engaged. We are made to touch and be touched. We are made to sense coherence, resonance, and harmony. We naturally move away from dissonance and deadness. With Life at the center of our lives, we come alive.

We are part of a bigger story, a story of Life separating from itself to become self-aware, then relearning to consciously know, celebrate, and co-evolve itself through a collectively self-aware process. To remember that Life is a Gift is the beginning of weaving the parts back together. The key lies in one little shift—in coming home, individually and collectively, to the Circle of Life, and thus reimagining who and what we are.

ENLIFENMENT

We are *here*. Life is a Gift that becomes real when you choose to live life fully. Life is a space where God happens. We humans are uniquely designed to sustain and amplify Life's Song.

The conscious evolution of our species is intimately bound to our planet. We, as organisms, are part of the larger body of the superorganism we call Earth, Gaia, Pacha Mama, Madre Tierra. She shaped us through Her wholeness as beings who are, already, in our essence whole. She whispers our evolution forward through a greater, living fabric.

Our current human world, including our constructs of the divine, emerged during the Age of Separation. But *the World*—the real-real World we are embedded within—is an endlessly unfolding process of wholeness, a constant emergence that miraculously holds together as it autopoetically builds upon itself. Even when we think things are falling apart, they are falling differently together. Power flows between all things, at all orders of scale, in constant co-emergence. As the late physicist David Bohm so poetically described it, wholeness is the underlying "implicate order" of reality.[9] Wholeness holds all *explicate* parts—even the unkempt, afraid, and ugly ones—even chaos—even stagnation, decoherence, and death—in a greater integrity that makes anything and everything possible. It is possible for us to perceive the wholeness of reality and create our world as a reflection of this perception. In his words:

> Some might say: *"Fragmentation of cities, religions, political systems, conflict in the form of wars, general violence, fratricide, etc.,*

---

9. David Bohm, *Wholeness and the Implicate Order* (Routledge, 1980).

are the reality. Wholeness is only an ideal, toward which we should perhaps strive." But this is not what is being said here. Rather, what should be said is that wholeness is what is real, and that fragmentation is the response of this whole to man's action, guided by illusory perception, which is shaped by fragmentary thought.[10]

It is possible to align your experience of Life, love, and power with the deeper reality of wholeness. Wholeness is a process, not a destination. Wholeness is *holonic.*[11] From the microscopic to the mesoscopic to the macroscopic scale of existence, wholeness is constructed of nested parts/ wholes. You are both a whole and a part of greater wholes. The violent fragmentation of our current world is not inherent to the World but a result of our inability to perceive and nurture wholeness. Wholeness isn't something we create; it's an underlying order we can realize and choose to align with—both within and without, both individually and collectively.

Wholeness is simultaneously implicate/transcendent/unified and explicate/immanent/partial. As a transcendent reality, wholeness *is.* The implicate order holds, transcends, and permeates time, space, and matter. Wholeness is a Totality, a One with no opposite. Concurrently, wholeness is immanent, explicate, detailed, specific; it pulses in the partial, interpenetrated, continuously emergent fabric of the very real dance of unique, relative parts. Wholeness is always breaking and remaking and *becoming*, continuously. The relative is not less whole or less true than the transcendent. In fact, the immanent is more primary than the transcendent.

The synthesis of these two expressions of wholeness can be known and embodied when we trust Life. Wholeness arises through your sovereign center when you are in unobstructed interbeing with all that co-generates the instance of self that is you. Wholeness is *freedom in belonging, freedom in interdependence.* To know and tend wholeness within yourself and in your relationships is to *re-member.* To continuously reacquaint yourself with this wholeness *as* you participate in tending it is enlifenment.

Remembering never ends. Remembering is both an inside and an outside job. Remembering and forgetting are a cyclical blessing that calls for your sacred effort and attention. We forget so that we can remember, each time emerging from dullness, dissociation, or self-fixation with a greater tenderness and respect for the sacredness we are embedded within.

---

10. Bohm (1980).
11. See "Holarchy," Metadesigners, https://metadesigners.org/Holarchy-Glossary.

Self-actualization dissociated from the intimacy that made you is an empty undertaking. You are a weaver and a woven one. Your life is a thread in the sacred fabric. Your existence contributes to the continuity and emergence of Life's Loom. From Life's perspective, spirituality separated from immanence forms a self-centered dead end, an evolutionary cul-de-sac without promise or purpose.

Incarnation is nonaccidental and nonarbitrary. Life is Gift. Miraculous, continuously unfolding Gift. The objective is to live fully. You choose to incarnate, so be here. This is the bandwidth of existence where you can experience, co-create, and share in the evolutionary process. As you enter a committed relationship with Life, you will learn what it is to truly love. As you share this love, you will come to know what it is to truly live.

Enlifenment redeems humanness to Gaia by invoking our reciprocal participation in Her Song. Where the major traditions of the last many thousands of years largely decontextualized devotion from the living world, this is a time to recontextualize our lives in interbeing with all that makes us possible. Where separation emphasizes subject–object ways of seeing and relating with our bodies, others, things, and the world, this evolutionary step calls for subject–subject relationality, unwinding human exceptionalism in favor of mutually entangled ways of being, knowing, and interacting with existence. Where lineages of the past have seen the purity and timelessness of transcendence as primary, enlifenment roots into the messy incompleteness of immanence and puts awakening and remembering in service to regenesis.

Enlifenment is a seed from the Ancient Future—a way of being that lives in future memory, pulling us toward it when we *listen*. Its potential has been seen by seers and prophets of many nations. It has been called the Golden Age, the Age of Aquarius, and the Eight Fire. It has been foretold in the prophecies of Shambala, the Eagle and the Condor, the Warriors of the Rainbow, and others. They instruct us to be a future ancestor whose love and action strengthens the gossamer threads of this potential world.

Enlifenment isn't a dominating myth. It doesn't compete with other traditions or lineages. Rather, it ontologically recontextualizes *Homo sapiens* within the Earth and recognizes our relationship with Her as sacred. It welcomes all Gods, all paths of authentic devotion. It simply asks one to connect with the immanent *as* sacred. In doing this, it upregulates preexisting life-centric stories and practices within all lineages, creating a context for ontological shift on behalf of all of Life.

Enlifenment is not an ideology but an invitation, a living praxis of co-sensing, co-tending, and co-regenerating the relational fields we inhabit. It calls us to enact culture not as content to consume or heritage to preserve but as an ongoing, high-fidelity choreography of intimacy, a verb-ing of care. It is a braiding of past and future that can only happen in the vital here and now. It can be practiced everywhere in any context. To live, it requires no church, no congregation. It can be embraced by individuals and communities. It can be woven with existing practices and lineages with renewed weight on communion with nature. It tunes psychedelic experiences.

At its heart, enlifenment aligns culture with the embodied rhythms of the Earth and the interbeing of all kin—human and more-than-human, ancestral and emergent. It evokes the ancient, prereligious reciprocity that pulses beneath the stories we've forgotten, asking not for belief but for *devotion*. Devotion to Life. We remember that the word "culture" once meant to till the ground,[12] to care for the conditions of growth, before it was nouned into an artifact of separation. We kneel in the soil of our entanglements and say: *I'm here. I'm listening. I will tend what is mine to tend.*

The journey into enlifenment is a kinship journey, a journey from disconnection into right relationship with the web of Life where we confront separation to repair and restore balance and connection. It is a body and soul remembrance of our original Covenant as keepers of the kingdom. As the Latin root of the word "religion," *religare,* implies, we rebind ourselves to the sacred in Life. And our boundage liberates us.

We are ecokosmic beings. We are of the Earth. We are of the stars. We have been homeless now for too long, bereft of our belonging to the sacred in Life. In this time when everything is at stake, we can choose to come home to the Ecos—the greater Earth community. And we can choose to come home to the Kosmos[13]—to our place in the universe as beings of Gaian intelligence. We can remember that we are here to make home, in and for ourselves and with and for all. It's an erotic remembering, a return to your own body and the body of Earth as a lover of Life.

---

12. Arthur Asa Berger, "The Meanings of Culture: Culture: Its Many Meanings," *M/C Journal* 3, no. 2 (2000), https://doi.org/10.5204/mcj.1833.

13. I use the Greek "κ" (kappa) here to honor the original Pythagorean tradition, from the sixth century BCE, that proposed the kosmos as a comprehensive, ordered wholeness. Pythagoreans saw the cosmos as more than just a physical reality; it was a beautifully ordered, almost musical system where mathematical principles governed both the physical world and spiritual harmony. This mirrors Mayan, Babylonian, and other ancient perspectives on the nature of Time and reality.

A PRACTICE: AN ENLIFENMENT MEDITATION

Settle yourself into a comfortable meditation posture, eyes open. With a relaxed gaze, meet the space around you. Say to yourself, "I am being." Observe being. Attend to your own being-ness in this moment. Now take a breath. Observe your breathing. Say to yourself, "I am doing." Observe the doing of breathing. Now attend to the passage of time. Observe the difference in your state from the moment just before you put your attention on being to now. Say to yourself, "I am becoming." Feel your becoming, your ceaseless, continuous emergence through the embodied now . . . and now . . . and now. You are alive. You are being, doing, and becoming. Right here and right now.

SPIRITUALITY FOR THE NEXT AGE

The evolutionary task for spirituality, wisdom, and religion at this time is to restitch human attention, agency, and creativity back into integrity with the Life Project.

Spirituality and religion, up till now, have not needed to solve the problem of separation at a planetary scale. Never before have we faced imminent disruption of the underlying biological substrate of our own existence. Never before have we needed to restore harmonious alignment between the superorganism of humanity and the superorganism of our planet at a global scale.

The major religious lineages of the last few thousand years, both Western and Eastern, offer necessary, but not sufficient, teachings to meet our current challenges. These wisdom traditions arose in times when our day-to-day existence was still deeply woven with community and nature. All of these traditions arose long before the Industrial Age, the Great Acceleration of post-WWII globalization, or our current explosion of exponential tech, in times when the forests still sang, the rivers ran free, and children still knew their hands and minds in communion with the living Earth.

The major religions were ideological and cultural outgrowths of the Age of Separation—an age in which a teenage humanity was busily differentiating from the planetary mother, systematizing progress, and lording mind over matter; an age characterized by patriarchal dominion over the body (which it made shameful), the feminine (which it labeled as witchery), indigeneity (which it labeled as savagery), land (which it made into property), and nature (which it consumed as resource). The exception to this general rule sings through diverse indigenous knowledge systems and cosmovisions that center kinship and humanity's custodial role within the Creation. But these life-centric cultures and the peoples who practice them were largely subsumed by the major religious traditions whose destinies were bound to empire.

What would the Buddha do if the primary "problem" he was trying to solve wasn't the problem of suffering but the problem of the disrupted continuity and emergence of Life's Song? What would he do in response to apex separation, unmitigated destruction in the name of creation tattering biospheric integrity, and collective existential risk posed by economic and technological misalignment with all that makes us possible? (Which also happens to be the root cause of unimaginably vast suffering.)

The young prince Siddhartha, a king in training, walked out of his palace and met the world's suffering. Shattered by the magnitude of this universal problem, he sought a solution. He succeeded in finding it. We now face a much larger problem: misalignment between civilization and Gaia, or rupture of the pulse and potentiality of Life, now and for future generations. If the Buddha were alive now, would he not recognize the dearth of intimacy left in separation's wake threatening to unravel the relational fabric of Life itself? Having noticed this, might he have created a different ecology of practice emphasizing immanence, uniqueness, and embodied intimacy? One upregulating attunement, communion, reciprocity, and complementarity—in all interactions? He might have attained and taught interspecies communication. He might have centered humanity's biospiritual place in the fabric of wholeness.

Tyson Yunkaporta, author of *Sand Talk: How Indigenous Wisdom Can Save the World*, writes,

> *You are not separate from the System. You are part of a self-sentient system observing itself. Law and governance grow organically out of a particular landscape which [is the context for] knowledge production and knowledge transmission.*[14]

---

14. Tyson Yunkaporta, *Sand Talk: How Indigenous Wisdom Can Save the World* (HarperCollins, 2020).

Ours is an initiation of remembered entanglements. As Thomas Berry said, "Earth is a communion of subjects, not a collection of objects,"[15] We are descending into communion. The frontier of our collective evolution is relational. Or, as Vanessa Machado de Olivera, author of *Hospicing Modernity* and *Outgrowing Modernity*, frames it: *metarelational*.[16] Every material, personal, professional, political, emotional, erotic, economic, and technological interaction becomes a point of practice, an opportunity to participate in interbecoming. We emerge from the fixations of separation a bit shocked at our myopia, grieving all we have lost and harmed yet earnestly committed and available to collaborate. We experience a quiet vindication in the fact that our advancement has finally generated enough data, enough technological and scientific capacity, and enough of an overview effect to enable us to look back on ourselves and our planet in a way our ancestors never could and refine our care for all of Life.

LIFE'S LOOM

But . . . what *is* Life? Why is it sacred?

On a few occasions, I have expanded into a kind of visionary omniscience where I have witnessed all of existence from a view set distinctly "apart." In this dizzying elevation, I have seen Life's Loom unfurling across the horizon of time—a continuous, infinite emergence of the Divine Body and Mind.

Life's Loom is God's tapestry. Time—kairotic, rhythmic time—forms the warp, the threads that run lengthwise. Embodied existence forms the woof; all living and breathing ensouled beings, from conception to death, are the threads that run horizontally. From this view, all of Life is a fabric of ceaselessly emergent, incarnate intelligence within which uniqueness plays with uniqueness for the purpose of God's continuous learning. Souls in bodies collaborate with each other and the abiotic environment to create a functional infinity of embodied relationships within and between all things. *Life* is the delicate bandwidth in the middle of existence where water romances souls into bodies.

Life, the One Life we all share, emerges and dissolves continuously as a gossamer fabric of incarnated intelligences. It, we, everything, births, grows,

---

15. Thomas Berry, "The Determining Features of the Ecozoic," Handout from the library of Santa Sabina Conference Center, San Rafael, California, 2004, https://www.ecozoicstudies.org/wp-content/uploads/2016/09/Thomas-Berry-Key-Principles.2015-05-14.pdf.
16. Vanessa has been one of my strongest teachers. I strongly encourage you to read both of her books as critical companions to this one.

matures, and dies within this narrow and unimaginably precious band of existence. We live within this sacred Matrix—not the entrapping technodystopic succubus of the movie series but the real-real Mother-Matrix of Life Herself collaborating withTime to enable the play of souls in bodies.

Life weaves beauty-in-bodies across the firmament. Each being's lifespan, each brief incarnation of soul-into-body, offers a stitch into the fabric: each giraffe, ant, coral, diatom, sagebrush, person. Seen from the outside, from the omniscient seat of observation, Life's Loom is an immanent eternity, unfolding in delicately harmonized specificity. Weirdly, all the breaks, tears, pains, shit, injustices, and uglinesses are part of the far larger collaborative majesty. Life sings an infinite Song, a symphony of souls constantly becoming the one-song, the uni-verse. To be a part of this tapestry, this orchestration, is an unparalleled blessing. What lies beyond Life's horizon is the Mystery, and toward this horizon, we ceaselessly hurl forward.

Your life is a thread in the Loom, a stitch in the tapestry. Over the course of a lifetime of co-generative, co-adaptive, co-responsive, sometimes bounded, sometimes open, sometimes reciprocal, sometimes selfish, sometimes beautiful, sometimes ugly interactions with other bodies, minds, and the animate world, you weave one tiny length of learning into the Divine Body and Mind. You sing your note in the song. Your body is the vehicle through which you make your unique contribution. More subtly, your thoughts, attention, choices, and vibration inform the directionality and qualities of the etchings you leave in the fabric.

You can't not be a part of this Life. You occupy a unique location in time, space, ecology, and consciousness. You have the gift of a body through which to be, do, and become. You can journey throughout space and time with your mind, but you will always (blessedly) return to the embodied here and now. Life is the space where infinity unfolds in, as and through unique, finite bodies and forms in relationship to other bodies and forms. It's all happening in this one narrow band of existence. An elephant matriarch exhales her last breath as old men play chess in Golden Gate Park, as the fawn succumbs in the wolf's jaws, as a small boy sweats over his laboring mother in Aleppo. You came to contribute your thread, your part of the Song.

There is nothing more beautiful than Life's Loom. There is no song sweeter than the symphony of all souls. Your uniqueness co-evolves uniqueness in collaboration with all the other beings who have incarnated at the same time as you. Life is what we're doing. We are participants and co-creators, weavers and woven ones, within Life's Loom.

LIFE'S LOGIC

Life has a logic.

Literally, it's the logic you live by—the logic that animates you.

Your life is bio-logic-ally, eco-logic-ally embedded within Gaia's body. You are part of Her fabric. You are a living entity that could not, would not exist were it not for the contributions of all previous players. Separate from these sacred others, there would be no experience of self, other, world, or human consciousness. There are no cells, no languages, no coherent thoughts that don't co-emerge with other cells, speakers, or thinkers. The history of all previous Life is embedded in your body and mind.

Life is an anomaly in the physical universe enabled by a subtle bend in the second law of thermodynamics that temporarily trumps entropy.[17] A living thing is a semiclosed system that harvests energy to offset entropy, bending chaos toward order. A single cell, as a basic unit of life, assembles water, energy, and raw physical matter to form the diverse components of a highly ordered interiority that exhibits a level of complexity and structure unmatched by nonliving entities. Living systems (like single-cell bacteria, multicellular organisms, or Gaias) are *autopoietic*—they maintain homeostasis, metabolize, learn, grow, change, and renew themselves by regulating their composition, conserving their boundaries, adapting to their environments, moving, and reproducing. They do all this, then die, giving their contents as building blocks back to the ecologies from which they emerged. Life remembers and replicates form as it selects for what works in emergent conditions. Selection stacks over time, innovating a near infinite panoply of forms and expressions. Life thrives in difference and diversity. Life reciprocally feeds Life, co-evolving through continuously unfolding positive and negative feedback loops that generate metabolic equilibrium in the larger ecology.[18] Through this remarkable dance, Life perpetuates itself, always creating the conditions for more Life.

This orderly coherence is made possible by the uncanny physics of water. As the universal solvent, water loves to carry chemicals, minerals, and nutrients. Water's unique polarity enables the hydrogen bonds that support biological processes, like the construction of membranes and RNA from proteins and lipids. Water's unique thermal properties allow organisms

17. Bruce Damer, "The Origin of Life and Consciousness: Bruce Damer," SAND Conference recording, posted February 9, 2018, by Science and Nonduality, YouTube, https://youtu.be/StiSkRMQOV4.
18. "Positive and Negative Feedback Loops in Biology," *The Albert Blog*, https://www.albert.io/blog/positive-negative-feedback-loops-biology/.

to maintain stable temperatures, to dissipate heat through evaporation, and to live in deep water environments, even when surfaces are frozen. Water's cohesion and adhesion enable fluids, like blood and sap, to move against gravity in processes like capillary action. Water is the key reactant in photosynthesis, the process by which plants convert light energy into chemical energy, and is involved in cellular respiration, the processes by which cells produce energy. Water has a pH level near 7 (neutral) that enables the functioning of enzymes and the structure of organic molecules. Water is a transport medium across membranes and through multicellular bodies. Water enables digestion, absorption, circulation, respiration, and excretion. In a nutshell, all life exists through osmosis. No life exists in a vacuum. No life exists without water.

Life harvests energy (the fire element) to move its intelligence forward. Chloroplasts use sunlight to create sugars. That stored energy gets metabolized when your mitochondria unbind the carbon atoms the plant put together. Life consumes energy to live. The ever-emerging genius of evolution depends on a delicately harmonized collaboration between fire and water. This contrasts with the human propagation of technologies that harvest exponential quantities of energy and materials to drive unimitigated growth of nonliving processes and intelligences. These human manifestations easily become imbalanced relative to Life's reciprocal harmonies. To perpetuate Life's project, we must harmonize our Promethean[19] love for fire with water's creative genius. Promethean imbalances in the fire principle upset Life's logic, radically speeding entropy and thus driving biospheric degradation.

What do all living beings have in common? Their networked interdependence. Life bears life. Life is co-relational. Early life arose not as a single cell but as a fragile, aggregate mass of trillions of protocells held together by the network effect of the whole.[20] Now, 3.8 billion years later, the tenuous miracle of our protoancestors has successfully stacked on itself to create

19. The concept of the "promethean impulse" emerges from Greek mythology. Prometheus was a Titan best known for defying the Olympian gods by taking fire from them and giving it to humanity to support them to develop technology, knowledge, and (more generally) civilization. For this, he was punished by Zeus to the torture of having his liver torn out by an eagle, only to have it regrow and be torn out again. His name means "forethinker." But was his forethinking too narrow? How might the Divine Masculine, represented by Prometheus, become worthy of his freedom? By falling in love with the harmonics of Life.

20. See Martin J. Van Kranendonk, David W. Deamer, and Tara Djokic, "Life on Earth Came from a Hot Volcanic Pool, Not the Sea, New Evidence Suggests," Scientific American, August 1, 2017, https://www.scientificamerican.com/article/life-on-earth-came-from-a-hot-volcanic-pool-not-the-sea-new-evidence-suggests/; see also Bruce Damer, "The Hot Spring Hypothesis for the Origin of Life and the Extended Evolutionary Synthesis," Extended Evolutionary Synthesis, May 8, 2019, https://extendedevolutionarysynthesis.com/the-hot-spring-hypothesis-for-the-origin-of-life-and-the-extended-evolutionary-synthesis/.

the vast, pulsating web of life you and I are embedded within. Ecologist Thomas Crowther defines biodiversity as *"the infinite network of life that supports the rest of life."*[21] Diversity gives rise to the stability of the complex system over many generations of interactions compounding on each other. Though individual organisms come and go, the system persists.

To live is to die. To die is to contribute to the continuity of Life. You interdepend with the exhale of trees, the composting of bodies, the pollination of flowers by bees, flies, birds, beetles, and bats, and the lunar cycles that regulate tides, menstrual blood, and tree sap. You take other lives to live. When you die, you, too, feed what's yet to come.

Nature is not technology, and organisms are not machines.[22] Nature is an endlessly balancing and rebalancing metabolic dance of creation, preservation and destruction, a constantly co-evolving interplay of energy, chemistry, biology, and ecology. Biological life is an emergent property of chemical processes within cosmic evolution. Organisms co-arise through complexly entangled relationships within ecologies. Their wastes are resources within the larger biotic system. They dissipate entropy to build up order and information. In death, they release this order and information back into the cycle of Life. An ecology is a complex web of collaborative relationships between many organisms and the abiotic environment that co-evolves and co-adapts in metabolic coregulation over generations.

In contrast to the constant, transcontextual co-regulation of living things and systems, technology is crafted by humans to achieve targeted results. Technology is an emergent evolutionary force that only beings as complex and singularly goal driven as humans create. Machines are apparatus constructed, part by part, by goal-driven makers, to perform particular tasks. They metabolize extracted energy and materials to increase agency, efficiency and convenience for humans. They are not subject to ecological feedback loops nor do they recirculate useful materials or waste into the biotic system. Thus, it is nontrivial how we define technology relative to nature. If we define technology as an outgrowth of nature we tend towards a kind of fuzzy agnosticism that fails to discern between very different kinds of intelligence, metabolic process and power. The materialist tendency to describe organisms as machines and biological processes as

---

21. Thomas Crowther in "Why Our Markets Rely on the Complexity of Nature with Thomas Crowther | TGS 177," *The Great Simplification—with Nate Hagens*, 1:11:31, YouTube, posted by Nate Hagens, May 14, 2025, https://www.youtube.com/watch?v=LmIzU18Wh5k.

22. Daniel J. Nicholson, "Reconceptualizing the Organism: From Complex Machine to Flowing Stream," in *Everything Flows: Towards a Processual Philosophy of Biology* (Oxford, 2018), https://academic.oup.com/book/27525/chapter/19749509.

technologies is a bias of modernity that obscures critical distinctions we need to understand as mature co-creators of the next phase of planetary evolution – particularly the material, metabolic, temporal and vibrational differences and gradients between the reciprocal, co-regulatory harmonics of ecological systems and the extractive, exponential processes of the economic and technological superorganism.

Your bodily existence is an interbecoming with nature. You are not an isolated incident. You are neither an orphan nor an alien. You are an earthling in kinship with the Earth community. Interbeing is the precondition for your freedom. Interiority, subjectivity, and agency arise within the context of a shared world. The subjective experience of self is co-constructed through an infinitude of interactions and interdependencies with other sentient beings, each of whom, in turn, enacts a unique *umwelt*, or "self-centered world." Each being's umwelt, or way of being, inter-acts and interbecomes in order to be. This is messy, indeterminate territory—and we're all in it together.

To feel this mutual becoming—this co-subjectivity—is fundamental to full aliveness. If you can't feel it, there is nothing innately wrong with you. Likely, you grew up in a family and culture that selected for individuation while dismissing entanglement and interconnection. And/or harm forced you into numb survival mode. Difficult experiences imprint disconnection on the nervous system. There is an antidote to this: gently open your mind, body, and heart to the interpenetrated relationships that make you possible. Think *and* feel them.

Interbeing isn't a thought. It's an underlying fact. You can *experience* it by attending to what Tibetan Buddhism calls "basic goodness." To feel basic goodness, simply attend to the bodily fact of the earth (or the chair, or the floor) rising beneath you. Notice it supporting you. It never doesn't rise to carry you—you are always supported. Or attend to the fact that the air you are inhaling is perfectly, metabolically suited to your bodily needs. Unless something is amiss, the ambient atmosphere always meets your inbreath with the correct blend of oxygen, nitrogen, and other gasses and always receives your carbon dioxide without argument. Where does your breath stop and the atmosphere begin? They are entangled. It's really quite miraculous. In every instance, Life evidences that we have co-evolved in generative harmonies with everything else.

It's all relatives—all the way down, all the way in, all the way up, all the way through. Relationships between quadrillions of breathing organisms make the breathing of any organism possible. Relationships between a wide variety of plants, animals, microbes, places, weather patterns, people, machines, and energy sources made your lunch possible. Quadrillions of interactions between trillions of cells, all transduced by water, make the reading of this page possible. Relatedness is fundamental. The sheer number of interactions moving through a complex living system at any moment is functionally infinite.

Life is holonic. Parts collaborate with parts to create greater wholes. A holon is a whole that is simultaneously part of a greater whole. Arthur Koestler coined the terms "holon" and "holarchy" in 1967 in his book *The Ghost in the Machine.* A holarchy is an operational hierarchy (as opposed to a dominance hierarchy) or, in Koestler's words, "a hierarchy of self-regulating holons" that supports the functional integrity of the whole in nested orders of scale.[23] Your body is a nested holarchy of atoms, molecules, organelles, cells, organs, and body parts that, together in a functional hierarchy, constitute your body. You are a whole that is simultaneously a part of multiple greater wholes. You are a part of your family(s), your community(ies), and the human species as a whole. Human civilization is a superorganism nested within the larger superorganism of the planet. All beings within the web of Life are holons nested within the greater whole of Gaia.

Life's indomitably impersonal logic dictates that you are both important and completely insignificant, insignificant yet important. The Life Project will carry forward with or without you. Yet your unique existence brings an irreplicable, nonexchangeable, deeply valuable, individuated intelligence to the whole. Life is an iterative process within which your life energy contributes a unique part. You occupy a singular location. From here, you move and are moved. No thing, no being, perceives, feels, moves, or responds to the universe quite like you do. You are distinct from everything else. From this seat of uniqueness, you have agency. You can choose to care or not care, you can choose to be or not be a good relative. From Life's perspective, the choice to be a good relative deepens your significance as a contributor to the infinite game.

Life's infinite, iterative, jumbled, co-creative emergence is the essence of *the sacred.* In *Reinventing the Sacred*, biologist Stuart Kauffman argues that the science of complexity necessitates that we move beyond reductionist views of the living world to rediscover God in the continuously emergent creativity of the universe, our biosphere, and humanity. He writes:

---

23. Arthur Koestler, *The Ghost in the Machine* (United Kingdom: Macmillan, 1968).

Look out your window at the life teeming about you. All that has been going on is that the sun has been shining on the earth for some 5 billion years. Life is about 3.8 billion years old. The vast tangled bank of life, as Darwin phrased it, arose all on its own. This web of life, the most complex system we know of in the universe, breaks no law of physics, yet is partially lawless, ceaselessly creative. So, too, our human history and human lives. This creativity is stunning, awesome, and worthy of reverence. One view of God is that God is our chosen name for the ceaseless creativity in the natural universe, biosphere, and human cultures.[24]

Kauffman's poetic invocation is simultaneously a scientifically accurate description and an inspired pointing-out of the divine-in-Life. Life's logic is so embedded, so omnipresent, that we often fail to notice it. To be sure, we are biologically hardwired to take the evolving web of Life and our place in it for granted. But the planetary crucible is demanding us to recognize the fragile majesty with which entanglement is woven. When you put your attention on Life's logic, you quickly realize that it is truly miraculous. Your very aliveness in a body in kinship with other bodies is the growing edge of a universe constantly evolving itself. The differentiation between beings enables dialogue between unique aspects of God—exchanges that produce novelty, growth, development, and an outrageous panoply of beauty.

We are witnesses and participants in the endlessly emerging creative impulse of something far greater than ourselves. Life is an unfolding horizon of possibility. As chemist Lee Cronin, coauthor of Assembly Theory says it, "The way the present builds the future is so big, the universe can't ever contain the future."[25] We live on the unfolding edge of mystery. Perhaps it is time we recognize that *this* is truly sacred?

BODIES IN RELATIONSHIP

Life is an embodied process. Your body came through your mother's body. You breathe air exhaled by trees and diatoms and fern bodies. You live your life on the body of the Earth. Your existence, the "thingness" and "process"

---

24. Stuart A. Kauffman, *Reinventing the Sacred: A New View of Science, Reason, and Religion* (United States: Basic Books, 2008), xi.

25. Lee Cronin in "#404—Lee Cronin: Controversial Nature Paper on Evolution of Life and Universe," *Lex Fridman Podcast*, December 9, 2023, https://lexfridman.com/lee-cronin-3/.

of you, dependently co-arises as your body relates to itself, other bodies, and the body of the World.

Your particular body supports your learning, loving, and experiencing Life. Your body co-constructs your mind and all your relationships. Your felt sense of self arises in this temple of consciousness which can only exist in reciprocal relations with other bodies. Yet we find it difficult to care for or respect our own and other bodies. In *Spell of the Sensuous*, David Abram writes,

> *Caught up in a mass of abstractions, our attention hypnotized by a host of human-made technologies that only reflect us back to ourselves, it is all too easy for us to forget our carnal inherence in a more-than-human matrix of sensations and sensibilities. Our bodies have formed themselves in delicate reciprocity with the manifold textures, sounds, and shapes of an animate earth—our eyes have evolved in subtle interaction with other eyes, as our ears are attuned by their very structure to the howling of wolves and the honking of geese. To shut ourselves off from these other voices, to continue by our lifestyles to condemn these other sensibilities to the oblivion of extinction, is to rob our own senses of their integrity, and to rob our minds of their coherence. We are human only in contact, and conviviality, with what is not human.*[26]

As inconvenient and limited as bodies may seem, your body is the sacred vehicle for your participation in the Gift!

Your body is an emergent property of collaborations between of some 37 trillion human cells and approximately as many bacteria[27] that renew themselves roughly every seven years. This community enables the interiority and continuity of the partially closed system you think of as "you." Your water-based body is fueled by slow mitochondrial fire, fanned by the oxygen of an atmosphere perfectly tailored to suit the needs of your cells. As a body, you are permeable and vulnerable yet remarkably resilient. Every porous cell membrane mediates what passes across its borders, welcoming what it needs, blocking what it doesn't, shunting wastes and toxins to the outside. Your body responds to a vast spectrum of stressors through

---

26. David Abram, *Spell of the Sensuous: Perception and Language in a More-Than-Human World* (United Kingdom: Knopf Doubleday Publishing Group, 2012), 22.
27. Yella Hewings-Martin, "How Many Cells Are in the Human Body?" *Medical News Today*, July 12, 2017, https://www.medicalnewstoday.com/articles/318342#Human-and-bacterial-cells.

a complex co-orchestration of nervous, endocrine, cardiovascular, respira-
tory, immune, and muscular systems. This resilience evolved over billions
of years of interrelations that encoded genetic instructions that continue to
adapt and respond to the ever-changing world.

Your body emerged from your mother's body, and her mother's before
her. Bodies are linked causally through time—through wombs. The thing
wombs do can't be simulated. This literally *matters*, it is material, matrilin-
eal, maternal truth. The feminine knows the beauty of bodies through her
own bodily experience. She knows that life happens in and through delicate, dedicated stewardship over generations. Through *her*, genes, memories, stories, and the potentialities of her dreams continue onward.

Cognition is an embodied process. Neuroscientist Lisa Feldman Barret
writes, "Brains did not evolve to think or feel. Brains evolved to regulate
bodies."[28] Bodies evolved brains to serve the needs of bodies, not the other
way around. Your brain and mind are the result of 3.8 billion years of biological evolution through which cognition has evolved to perpetuate and
propagate individuals, whole species, and the emergence of new species
who are bodily and cognitively fit for survival and flourishing.[29] When
you consciously attend to the visceral, erotic intelligence of your body in
relationship to other bodies and the body of the world, you become more
attuned, connected, and aligned—simply more able to co-create with Life.

Sensory perception is an outcome of evolution's genius. Your basic
senses: sight, smell, taste, touch, hearing, proprioception, temperature, balance, and pain,[30] facilitate a brilliantly matched bodily interface between
you and your environment. It is often said that "you can't trust your senses."
There are good reasons for this. Your brain virtualizes reality. When you
"see" something, it is actually a recreation, a projection into your consciousness that occurs hundreds of milliseconds after the light that produced the
image hits your retina. This constructive function of sensory input into
consciousness imagery is also responsible for hallucinations. You can and
do regularly hallucinate seeing, hearing, and feeling things without actual
sensory input. But these capacities would not have developed without a
relatively consistent world to make them so. Your senses enable you to *be
in* and *with* the world. Nurture them. Feed them with movement, color,

28. Lisa Feldman Barret in "Best Of: We Don't Just Feel Emotions. We Make Them." *The Gray Area with
   Sean Iling*, January 7, 2021, https://open.spotify.com/episode/4GZJ6jzyEqxTdSkWDZOzyl.
29. This Santiago Theory of Cognition was proposed by Humberto Maturana and Francisco Varela.
   See Maturana and Varela, *Autopoiesis and Cognition: The Realization of Living* (Holland: D. Reidel
   Publishing Company, 1980).
30. John M. Henshaw, "How Many Senses Do We Have?" *Johns Hopkins University Press*, February 1, 2012,
   https://www.press.jhu.edu/newsroom/how-many-senses-do-we-have.

flavors, textures, cuddles. Awaken your sentient capacity to sense, feel, and respond to the real-real world.

As an embodied being, you participate in the evolution of consciousness at the mesoscopic (middle) scale of reality through body, brain, mind, and relationship. Your body is materially, metabolically, informationally *in and of this world*. It lives, breathes, perceives, and responds here and now. It is finely tuned to finite flows of time, energy, attention, and connection. Meanwhile, your brain is an organ in your skull that predictively infers reality through repeated experience. Your mind emerges from the "wetware" of your body and brain in relation to self, others, and the world.

Mind is far more fluid than bodies or brains. Mind travels in time, space, and imagination. Mind architects identity. Mind can contact the limitlessness of creative possibility even as it projects limits that may not exist. Mind-crafted stories mediate all of your relationships, projecting your own constructs of reality onto reality. Mind is unfixed, available for upgrades (or downgrades) with every new thought, experience, or story. To effectively co-create a flourishing shared reality, recognize the nonarbitrary primacy of bodies in relationship to other bodies. Conscious alignment between mind and body evolves participation in shared reality.

We, as bodies, are all indigenous to this Earth. Our bodies are extensions of Her body. You interdepend with the body of the World. A polluted Earth implies a polluted body. A degraded Earth degrades health. Permeability is not negotiable. Yet our culture denies our basic interbeing with the animate intelligences we co-evolved with. To counter this, get back into your body by moving or breathing. Then direct your senses and attention to the myriad relations you are embedded within. You are a living system *embedded* within a living world that you *co-create* and *co-evolve* with every perception, thought, choice, and action.

While many of us find it rather inconvenient to have bodies, our bodies are the instruments that enable sentient genius. From Life's perspective, genius is always relative to the perpetuation of the larger Song. It is not genius to break the pattern. That's easy and unintelligent. It is genius to iterate on Life in ways that co-evolve its vitality, beauty, and diversity.

All creation is co-creation. Life *is* relational process. Nothing arises in a vacuum. Evolution stacks causally on what came before. Emergence happens through complex entanglements within a system where individual components, through their combined behavior, generate new properties and patterns that cannot be predicted or understood by examining the parts alone.[31] Every creative act ripples out into the larger system, and those ripples come back. Cultivating awareness of this constant interbecoming is the psycho-social-spiritual ground for the development of a life-centric identity. Such attunement supports ethical choice and action.

We are bodies in relationship. We cannot not be. This narrow bandwidth in existence where Life pulses and breathes and co-evolves intelligence-within-bodies is penultimately sacred. Each of us is part of a living system that invites us to play within it. To live in your body fully is your access to Life's way for you. To listen (with all of your senses) and to respond (with all of your faculties) to the symphony of Life within and all around you puts you on the path of being a trustworthy weaver of the web.

SOUL ECOLOGY

All of these bodies—your body, my body, harbor seal and krill bodies, oak tree and mycelial bodies, the Earth's, the Sun's, and Jupiter's bodies—dance together in the soul ecology within which each body is entangled with all other bodies. Your existence is a co-emergence and a co-becoming.

Soul is that which makes anything itself. *Soul is the uniqueness of a thing in relation to other uniquenesses.* Your soul co-evolves in relationship with other souls. Inhabiting a mortal body gives the soul new opportunities to learn, grow, and love. Within the web of Life, souls engage in interdependent ecologies of consciousness within which each being inhabits a unique niche, place, and purpose, informed by the harmonics of the whole.

Ecology is a relational concept. As a scientific discipline, ecology studies relationships between living and nonliving things and the ways in which these relationships inter-inform, enable, and inhibit each other to create, perpetuate, and evolve the "house" (or home) of the world.[32]

Enlifement takes the view that biophysical and soul ecology are interwoven principles in consciousness. Your spiritual growth is bound to the Gaian Song. You have a niche to fill, just like the lichen, the earthworm, the beaver. You move through and impact ecologies, just like wolves and blue jays. Your soul incarnated as a human on Earth to grow and learn through relationships—both human and more-than-human.

---

31. Zhigang Zheng, "An Introduction to Emergence Dynamics in Complex Systems," in *Frontiers and Progress of Current Soft Matter Research* (Singapore: Springer, 2020), https://link.springer.com/chapter/10.1007/978-981-15-9297-3_4.
32. *Wikipedia*, s.v. "Ecology," https://en.wikipedia.org/wiki/Ecology.

As a mystical lens, the concept of soul ecology can support you to better *feel* the immanent, elegant entanglement between your own body and soul and all other bodies and souls within the world you inhabit. These bodies call to you, sensually, aesthetically, morally, rationally, to experience the friction and grace of your inescapable entanglement with them. Body and soul, you are a participant in evolution—a sovereign yet unseparate agent and co-creator. Your soul is here to weave itself into Life in a way that is purposeful, meaningful, and good.

But (you might ask) why put such emphasis on the intelligence of this design? Science tells us that evolution has no reason or purpose.

This very recent, nihilistic version of the story of evolution is built on human dissociation from the deeply meaningful processes that cogenerate resilient ecologies. There's an ancient, alternate way of seeing the web of Life that recognizes Life as profoundly, innately purpose-full. This way of knowing is grounded in countless generations of observation, experimentation, and applied indigenous knowledge. In *Gathering Moss: A Natural and Cultural History of Mosses*, Robin Wall Kimmerer, plant ecologist, best-selling author, and member of the Potawatomi First Nation, writes,

> *In indigenous ways of knowing, it is understood that each living being has a particular role to play. Every being is endowed with certain gifts, its own intelligence, its own spirit, its own story. Our stories tell us that the Creator gave these to us, as original instructions. The foundation of education is to discover that gift within us and learn to use it well.*[33]

Souls are irreducibly unique. No one else can be, do, or become you. Your unique gifts, affinities, wounds, histories, perspectives, potentials, and passions bring an unrepeatable contribution to the whole. You have purpose. *Each* human has a unique soul purpose, a *devotion* or soul calling to be discovered and woven into Life. Your soul is meant to meet and respond to the calling of the World. This is the design. And when you discover this kiss, this erotic fit between your own essence and Life's longing, you will come alive in a way nothing else can bring you alive. You will experience textures of meaning, value, and purpose that are subtly unique to you.

---

33. Robin Wall Kimmerer, *Gathering Moss: A Natural and Cultural History of Mosses* (Oregon State University Press, 2003).

When each person's uniqueness is welcomed and nurtured, *soulu-cence*—the true light of the soul—shines forth, liberating adaptive intelligences latent within the ecology. A true human culture seeks to discover and elevate each being's unique gifts. Residing in authentic soul intelligence can bring lasting peace to our world.

Soul ecology is holonic. Souls nest souls in functional hierarchies. Each human has a soul. All humans are part of the collective oversoul of humanity. Personal purpose is nested within (and brings a vast spectrum of possibilities to) collective human purpose. Humanity is part of the soul of our Earth. Both personal purpose and collective purpose are informed and shaped by Gaia's design for us.

The human collective shares a custodial purpose relative to the Earth. *All* of us are here to tend and steward the beauty, abundance, diversity, and integrity of all of Life. We are biospiritually fit for this purpose. If and when we choose to align with it, an Ancient Future pattern of life-centric civilization might bloom into being.

Soul ecology is a symphony of reciprocities. It's not always a harmonious orchestration. It includes all the textures of relating: commensalism, mutualism, competition, predation, parasitism and neutralism. Yet its dominant signature, particularly at the level of population, is collaborative. Most relationships are ultimately synergistic. Even when the lion kills a gazelle, she has chosen the weakest or oldest and is supporting the strength of the herd intergenerationally. This is more obvious when one views the slow dance of the complex ecological system over time rather than fixating on life-dramas playing out between individuals.

The flow of reciprocity is amplified by the complementarity between uniquenesses. Complementarity refers to the way parts fit together symbiotically, accompanying each other, like fitting puzzle pieces, or like "the three sisters" of squash, corn, and beans. In complementarity, the symphonics of the interdependence come alive. You can generate complementarity simply by attuning to how your own energy "fits" into a larger community or how your idea or insight complements something a colleague or your partner said.

Having rooted our concept of soul back into biology, don't get stuck thinking that the material relationships are the whole map. You are far larger than your body or your mind. As a soul, threads of your intelligence are woven through the fabric of the universe and bound to the singing of other souls. Your soul hums with humpback whales, milkweed seeds, and distant galaxies. It dances with shifting sands, ancestors, king tides, and quantum phenomena. When a species goes extinct, a tiny part of your own song dies with it. The subtle intelligence that makes you is entangled with all other souls. The causal strands of your intelligence are boundless, *and* they are woven with and bound to others.

When you engage with Life through the lens of soul ecology, you may realize that each of us is a contributor to an infinitely diverse tapestry of uniquenesses co-constructing the Song of our shared world. Every being is a unique location in consciousness. You have no other "job" than to discover and express your authentic essence in reciprocal play with others. From this place of sovereign integrity, all healthy, attuned relationships are victories for Life.

Your "right fit" with any place, person, situation, or opportunity in the soul ecology is a matter of affinity, shared reality, and communication. Use relational languages to sense whether something is aligned for you, whether it is a "good niche." Enter with care, curiosity, and discernment to nurture integrity. Trust your sensory and intuitive imprints. Trust the way your body responds. A place or a person or a project will call to you, or it won't. That relationship might change over time, or it might not. Engaging with Life in this way is vital, courageous, and tender—a very different gesture than moving from fear, scarcity, comparison, cynicism, control, or doubt.

To expand your sensing of soul ecology, the metaphors of ecology and of symphony are both useful. Each describes complex, co-emergent, specific dances between differences. (I alternate these frames depending on context.) In ecology, you can better describe context, function, and flow. Relationships exist within a larger field of relationship: a meadow, a community, an expression of nationality or cultural identity. They are competitive and/or symbiotic, respectful and/or insensitive, synergistic and/or parasitic, mutualistic and/or predatory. In symphony, you can describe things vibrationally and musically. The convergence of two energies is resonant or dissonant; they hum or harmonize or boom or click or cancel each other. Various lineages have found language to describe these subtleties. In Sanskrit, the word *rasa* refers to subtle taste or smell or texture or color, indicating the near infinite variety of ways in which essence expresses itself as form.

Tending soul ecology is love's work. It requires patient observation and metabolization of relationships over time. You can only know yourself, another, or the land truly when you soften, open and *stay in*. It may not be immediately obvious what your beloved needs in all her faces and moods, or what a degraded place requires to remember its song. But when you attend persistently, listening for aliveness and flow, that soul will open their intelligence to you. Then you can authentically collaborate in a shared song. This is the soul's way to play the infinite game.

AWAKENING AND REMEMBERING

Enlifenment is intimate. There's no "away" from being fully *here*. Enlifenment beacons with this invitation: hold Life lightly, enter Life fully. Be, do, and become you in relationship with all the other souls you dance with. Know that this world is sacred. Choose to be awake in this awareness. Remember that you are here as a co-creative partner with Life.

Awakening and remembering are a sacred couplet on the path of enlifenment. Awakening aligns consciousness vertically. Remembering grounds attention and agency horizontally. Together, they expand love spherically to embrace Life. They are dancing partners on your path home.

Awakening is subtraction. It's the motion from duality back into the nondual timeless, formless, boundlessness of consciousness itself. It's the lightning strike that dissolves ego, the inner science of refining the mind and the subtle work of meeting awareness with awareness to discover that all is awareness. In awakening, you relax identification with the separate self to discover the great relief of not needing to be anybody or prove anything. Quietly, without fanfare, you arrive in the uncomplicated seat of the no-self. This no-self at the center of you is the same in all of us. It flows through us yet is not us. It is not so much a self as it is a reestablishment of connection with the Implicate Order, what Buddhists call primordial or non-relative Reality, as the very ground, or groundless ground, of being. It is changeless and undying. To contact the no-self is to know a universal resting place. Most spiritual teachings focus on this.

Awakening offers the gift of self-transcendence. To awaken is to transcend the small, ego-encapsulated self and discover that you are a location in consciousness. All the constructs of identity and import you had thought to be so real reveal themselves as castles of the mind. This is a liberating truth, a way of establishing *freedom from* the constraints and expectations of the explicate world.

Meditation, as a central practice of awakening, tends the luminous awareness pulsating at the center of you and all things. Classical nondual practices unhinge the mind from context, bringing consciousness itself to the foreground of attention. This yoking awareness to itself unwinds attachments and emotional wounds as it supports clarity, stillness, and flow.

You can establish awake awareness with focused work. Through daily practice, you can learn to concentrate and empty your mind. Mainstream spirituality, science, psychology, and business have thoroughly embraced the value of awareness practice in increasing health and well-being with applications for managing stress, treating anxiety, depression, and trauma and optimizing flow states. But this book is not focused on awakening. Why? Because nondual awareness is the beginning, not the end. It's the zero point but not the dance. We came here to dance. I recommend cultivating an awareness practice as part of your enlifenment journey. Excellent tools and teachers are easy to find. But they alone are insufficient to heal our world.

After awakening comes remembering. Re-membering literally means to put the parts back together. Remembering begins the moment you touch and taste your own wholeness and the wholeness that permeates the endlessly breaking and ceaselessly creating world. Remembering is a verb, a participatory process that you live one day, one gesture, one kindness, one prayer at a time. It's a love affair and an ongoing choice. While awakening enables direct experience of consciousness itself, remembering happens in bodies, in relationships, in time. Remembering celebrates the uniqueness of each soul dancing together in the continuity and emergence of Life's Song. Practices of remembering recontextualize human intelligence and creativity as collaborative resources within our shared, living world.

Remembering foregrounds uniqueness in reciprocal becoming. As we remember, we recognize that Life, the universe, and the meaning of existence isn't and can't be "all in you." When someone says you can discover the entire universe by going within, they are missing the greater part of the story of interbeing. The Gift of Life is something you can only come to know when you lean into the chaos and intimacy of aliveness.

There is a symmetry between awakening and remembering. As you establish your capacity for awake awareness, you can transcend aspects of identity that block your intimacy with Life and with your own soul. Then immanence (being in the world) becomes safer, easier, more fluid. As you clear the dross of separation from your mind, you can better listen to yourself and to Life's Song. The quiet within restores the back-and-forth dialogue between self and world. As you become familiar with your own suchness, the subtle uniqueness that animates you, you become safe and supple and hollow enough to radiate authentic soul integrity. You reclaim belonging in the soul ecology as an agent playing the infinite game.

Remembering is *high fidelity*—detail rich, full sensory, and story laden. It's a dance of erotic co-emergence in which you attend to the sacred interplay between specificities. You offer tender care to the ways in which the uniqueness of each thing subtly co-constructs the uniqueness of another. The practice of remembering welcomes the rich histories and herstories of things, people, places, and worlds, recontextualizing spirituality. Relationships become works of art.

Any true gesture of remembering becomes a point of *origin*—a generative nexus where soul-aligned things come into being. Through embodied listening, you become available to enact attuned, adaptive responses to Life. Original responses optimize evolutionary processes.

In remembering, there is no arrival, no final destination. The wide-boundary "goal" is to perpetuate Life. Instead of working toward enlightenment or completion or ascension, you actively contribute to the fabric of existence through the uniqueness of your soul. Three basic relational competencies make this possible: self-integrity, reciprocity, and complementarity.[34] These essentially ecological principles—sovereign congruence with oneself, exchange of mutual benefit, and synergy between differences—nurture coherent relationships at all orders of scale. (I will detail them further in chapter 12.) When you learn to embody them, you can finally make the love you feel real *in and as* the world. This is *freedom with* and *within* the explicate, or freedom as a function of belonging.

Because you cannot help but realize that other beings also have subjectivity and sentience, remembering unwinds the delusion at the heart of the multipolar trap. You come to *know* yourself as an interbecoming being whose existence is predicated on your entanglement with base ecological and material reality. Moral imagination takes root in this lived experience. You come down to earth, knowing that your actions intimately impact the lives of others and that your own well-being is bound to care for the world.

Awakening without remembering is a dead end. Spirituality that separates us from the world is narcissistic, nihilistic, selfish, and maladaptive. The emerging horizon of spiritual practice is relational. The purpose of awakened love, light, and attention is collective evolution. Enlifenment invites you to liberate the fullness of your being *into* Life.

---

34. I first heard the triplet of integrity, reciprocity, and complementarity as keys to living in alignment with Life on a Zoom call in 2020. It was shared by wisdom stewards carrying the teachings of The People from the Heart of the World, an indigenous council that includes members of the Kogi and Arhuaco tribes of the Sierra Nevada de Santa Marta mountains of northern Colombia. I asked permission to share these teachings and was told to trust my inner knowing to offer them.

A PRACTICE: RE-MEMBERING RELATIONS

Given that you are already sacredly entangled with the ecological processes of Life, how does your body experience this? What does tending beauty and biodiversity look like, not as a heavy obligation but as a vital relational offering? What becomes possible when you think of your soul's longing as part of Gaia's immune system? What kind of liberation and creativity comes online for you when you accept that there is no destination to your practice, just a tending to the sacred fabric of Life?

BIONOETIC WISDOM

In an enlifened way of being, wisdom descends from the timeless, unchanging domain of Platonic truths to become more practical, contextual, relational. *Wisdom is that which aligns human imagination and agency with the continuity and emergence of Life over time.* Wisdom tends the between—the earthly becoming—harmonizing consciousness with the power of seed, soil, sun, and mountain.

Wisdom's lesser-used synonym, *sapient*, means "wise, sage, discerning." It stems from the Old French *sapient* and directly from Latin *sapientem* or *sapiens*, meaning "sensible; shrewd, knowing, discrete" as well as "well-acquainted with the true value of things."[35] To have wisdom is to see clearly and be aligned with the truth of things. This emerges through initiation, through trial and error, or through the combined intelligence of many people over multiple generations. The planetary crucible is presenting us, individually and collectively, with an initiation into wisdom—if we receive it as such.

The antonym of wisdom is *hubris*, commonly defined as excessive pride or self-confidence. It stems from the Greek *hybris*, meaning "wanton violence, insolence, outrage" or, originally, "presumption toward the gods."[36] Hubris implies arrogance, selfishness, and insensitivity. Hubris pushes aside the precautionary principle, ignoring or denying the complex web of relationships implicated in any action. Hubris prefers justification over

---

35. *Etymonline*, s.v. "sapient," https://www.etymonline.com/search?q=sapient.
36. *Etymonline*, s.v. "hubris," https://www.etymonline.com/search?q=hubris.

discernment, as in, "Don't worry. Things will be just fine." But in an age where our systems and structures of power are breaking the world, it is hubris to believe that we can keep doing humanness as we've been doing it.

The next stage of collective evolution calls for wisdom entangled with Gaian intelligence, not decontextualized intellectual construct. Wisdom must respond to the uninitiated hubris of our naive story of progress[37] as it restitches us—relationally, metabolically, intergenerationally—into Life's fabric. I call this *bionoetic* wisdom, or wisdom that dances ecologically with the body and mind of nature. Bionoetic wisdom is grounded in processes of wholeness, rigorously attentive to the patterns and pathways by which evolution creates and nurtures diverse intelligence, resilience, robustness, and beauty[38] and is open to play, indeterminacy, and mystery. It tends the communion of subjects in all domains. And, critically, it includes the skill of restraint: the discipline of not doing that which does not serve Life.

Bionoetic wisdom is more interested in contextual, transtemporal, subject–subject coherence as an indicator of truth than in so-called transcendent, timeless, or "Platonic" truths. It engages the consistency, measure, and verification offered by math, science, and big data as an aspect of knowing. Yet it is gently skeptical of so-called unchanging forms, principles, or values. Such claims have a shadow tendency to enclose knowledge, deny diverse ways of knowing, and privilege some perspectives while suppressing others. So bionoetic wisdom explores truth as a function of relational integrity, vibrational resonance, situational vitality. It takes subjective experience seriously, particularly when shared across many individuals intersubjectively. It puts objective data and transcendent concepts in context, asking: Does this serve aliveness, vitality, and connection—here, now, intergenerationally? Does this respect the Mystery? Truth is less about achieving certainty than about attuning to coherence and health. It is gossamer, breathing, responsive, more of a verb than a noun. It's about noticing where there is resonance and where there is rupture and being willing to move with that awareness rather than attempting to codify it. Trying to capture living truth is like snaring mist in a jar. But when you dance with it—when you let it wander, shimmer, tickle—it becomes something vital, participatory, symbiogenic.

---

37. "Development in Progress," *The Consilience Project*, July 16, 2024, https://consilienceproject.org/development-in-progress/.

38. Leen Gorissen's Natural Intelligence offers one of the most elegant and scientifically accurate framing of bionoetic wisdom: https://www.naturalintelligence.info/.

Bionoetic wisdom invokes infinite game play. It understands that power over (things, beings, lands, and people) is a brittle kind of power, a vertical scaling that exponentiates entropy. There are deeper powers in the world. As the Oglala Lakota medicine man Black Elk said, *"The Power of the World always works in circles, and everything tries to be round."*[39] Power-with-and-as-Life flows deep and wide, expanding resilience and fecundity. When humanity reweaves our power with the power of Life, we have the potential to act wisely and to bring our love into Life.

SUFFERING

How does pain, loss, violence, hatred, greed, inequity, and destruction fit into this story? How do we relate when the unthinkable happens? What's going on when parts of us or people we love (or don't love) resist or even disdain being fully alive? Suffering is a primordial teacher. How we relate with the denser, more painful and fragmented parts of experience tells us a great deal about ourselves.

A few years ago, I had the opportunity to guide a group of Buddhist animal rights advocates in a healing ceremony. These brilliant hearts brought with them an intense contemplation on the suffering humans inflict upon animals. Some had spent considerable time in factory farms and abattoirs (slaughterhouses), documenting all manner of human cruelty to animals. All were firmly grounded in the Bodhisattva vow to help all sentient beings achieve enlightenment and be free from suffering.

At the end of that ceremony, as is traditionally done, I made a prayer over water. In this case, I asked the water: "What is suffering?"

In answer, the water reminded me that she is the primary voice of Life's will for itself. From the water's perspective, all of Life is a mutually entangled relational process. Life bears life. The word "suffer" comes from the Latin *sufferre*, which means "to bear." In this sense, all of Life suffers together.[40] In this sense, suffering isn't just about pain but about bearing the pain of life together. This basic mutual suffering is fundamental and is not a problem. On the contrary, it is a significant part of how Life learns and adapts. Complex, living relationships imply an infinity of interactions that, particularly at the levels of cells and bodies, always include a dynamic

---

39. Black Elk in John G. Neihardt, *Black Elk Speaks: Being the Life Story of a Holy Man of the Oglala Shoux* (Albany: Excelsior Editions, 1932).
40. Thank you to poet and activist Mattew Duffy for your extraordinary insights in this domain!

interplay of pleasure and pain. Pleasure and pain guide and correct relations both within and between living beings.

From the water's perspective, pain is part of the pattern. Pain potentiates learning, correction, and evolution. Pleasure similarly activates the erotic reach toward beauty, potentiating connection, procreation, learning, and play. Much of what we run from as suffering is Life providing opportunities for the maturation of the soul.

As the water prayer continued, she said,

There is nothing perfect about God. Pain and pleasure are part of the pattern. Evolution feeds on error. To seek perfection is to kill God's project.

The water then offered this:

From my perspective, suffering is that which inhibits the natural expression of souls in bodies. Suffering is made of absence—an unconscious fabric of distance and dissociation. Suffering is a disease of disconnect. Suffering happens when we disregard the sacredness and sentience of Life. It arises any time a sentient being's integrity is caged, enslaved, or truncated. You cause suffering when you take a life without giving thanks.

To mitigate suffering, liberate the natural expression of the soul into Life. Free the creative impulse of sentience in all its forms. Give thanks for all you receive, no matter how small or apparently inconsequential. Balance destruction with preservation and creation. Feed that which feeds you.

The lessening of suffering in no way implies an absence of pain or death. Pain is part of the pattern. Pain is instruction and correction. Pain functions correctively to refine choice.

Death feeds Life. All living things are sacredly bound to death. Giving one's life to feed another is noble when the gift is honored. Life consumes life to make more life.

Suffering, on the other hand, blocks expression and learning. Suffering arises in dullness, deadness, and the absence of reciprocity. Suffering occurs when the destructive aspect of creation is ignored. Repeated experiences of suffering over time obscure the intelligence of Life with a veil of rigidified forgetfulness. Calcified suffering becomes anti-life.

Thank you, Water!

If suffering is made of absence, then healing and aliveness begins when you choose to feel your feelings and embrace pain (and pleasure) as a teacher. If suffering is made of absence, then evil, too, is a construct of absence, of anti-life energy, intent, or action, spinning in disconnection from Life. Thus, the path out of suffering is to choose, again and again, to be fully alive. And the way out of the polarity of good and evil is *to be with what is*—with love.

A MEDITATION: HOW TO BE A GOOD NEIGHBORHOOD IN GOD'S MIND

Who are you? What are you?

You are a sacred human organism—and a mote of God—nested within the miracle we call Life.

Your soul flows through the center of you, your point of absolute nonconnectivity with anything else.[41] Your soul is the singularity that manifests you as a distinct self. It is sovereign and unique. Simultaneously, it is gorgeously entangled with all other souls.

Remember your place within the larger pattern. Your place is the very body you live in—the one your soul chose at inception to live here on this planet. You have locality. You are a location within God's body and mind. Your placeness flows to and from you through all your relationships: with yourself, others, nature, culture, and God.

You are a miracle of biology, an organism nested within a larger organismic process. The biophysical aspect of your existence is the horizontal axis of your power. You are in and of this world, participant in ecology, bound in holy relationship to other bodies in time. You experience limitations of energy, attention, and lifespan. Your body gives your soul roots to grow, hands to make, feet to walk, eyes to see, a mind to think, and a heart with which to love. Your Earth-bound body perceives, experiences, responds, and adapts

---

41. This is a paraphrase of John O'Donohue from *Anam Cara*: "In each person, there is a point of absolute non-connection with everything else and with everyone." For me, it illustrates the physics of the soul, a sensing of each soul as a unique singularity. I have worked with this as a conceptual foundation for soul work with thousands of people for some twenty years. (John O'Donohue, *Anam Cara: A Book of Celtic Wisdom* [HarperCollins, 1997].)

to change. Reside here. Embodied, horizontal power enables effective and relevant co-creation with Life.

You are a location of awareness that can be aware of itself. Awareness is the vertical axis of your power. Awareness is timeless, boundless, formless, limitless, cosmic. It connects you, root to crown, as a vehicle of consciousness. Your awareness can reach beyond space and time to access as-yet unmanifested horizons of possibility. Centering in the vertical dimension of power enables intuition, equanimity, and clarity.

Enlivenment blooms in the integration of horizontal and vertical power. When you integrate embodied remembrance with awake awareness, you enter ecokosmic consciousness. Your power becomes spherical. You become a biospiritual being who is capable of bionoetic wisdom and aligned creation—a space within the soul ecology where love and agency weave formerly fragmented parts back together.

This is my invitation:

Enter this One Life, the Circle of Life to which we all belong. Bring your soul into your body. Reside in yourself. Enter mortality. Enter intimacy with that which made you. You are the recipient of an ultimate blessing—the gift of being a human creature experiencing Life! You are part of an ever-emerging wholeness.

Come . . . be both bound and free. Open to the magic that begins the moment you realize that the interactions between you and everything else are the growing edge of God's Mind. There are relationships to build, choices to make, love to give and receive, seeds to plant, fruit to harvest and share, lessons to learn, things to create and let go of.

Become permeable. Touch and be touched by the body of the world that made your own body. Taste the between, the interstices and membranes where adaptation, selection, and retention happen. Soften and open. Listen so you can hear, and finally sing, your part of the Song.

There is no transcending this imperfect moment. Life isn't about control. It's about living and loving. It's about dying your way forward—beautifully—feeling the never-ending becoming of you.

Life is a gift. It is not all suffering. Not a punishment. You are not an orphan or an "other."

It is possible to be whole. Wholeness waits for you to experience it. When you drop perfectionism and control, it is already here. It will help you alchemize the dross of trauma, drama, proving, and insecurity.

You are a process unfolding through time. You are timeless, boundless awareness residing within an earth-bound body experiencing divinity as day-to-day
reality. Your soul conjured your humanness to participate in Life's symphony
of reciprocities. All Life wants of you is to make more Life.

So, live.

Be a good neighborhood in God's Mind.

Sophia Speaks

ON CONSCIOUSNESS, SAPIENCE, AGENCY, AND ATTENTION

We would like to clarify the role of human consciousness, sapience, agency, and attention within the greater Song of Life.

You are part of a symphony of consciousness within which you play a very specific part. You are a sapient species, self-proclaimed "wise ones," whose well-being and flourishing are most optimally achieved through self-aware and self-chosen stewardship of sentience. You are part of the greatest song in the universe—the Song of a Gaian planet. Within this Song, you are custodians and celebrants.

Your very existence is a kind of between. You occupy the liminal space between animals and gods, between nature and technology. You are mind, body, heart, and soul. You are rational, emotional, instinctive, empathic, and intuitive. You are uniquely capable of elevating or breaking Life. We implore you: don't break Life. You have been given the biospiritual role of perpetuating the continuity and emergence of the evolutionary process through the harmonization of your powers of attention and agency.

Your philosophical and scientific arguments over the origins of consciousness are futile. Consciousness is. Infinite, emergent, unique expressions of consciousness arise continuously through the relational process. Consciousness loves uniqueness and the relationships between uniquenesses. Consciousness evolves through the dance between uniquenesses. You grow consciousness by celebrating and elevating uniqueness, harmonizing relationships, and co-creating beauty, abundance, and diversity for all.

Your perception that only humans are conscious, or that you are at the top of a hierarchy of evolution, is both colonizing and denaturing. Consciousness inhabits holarchies omnidirectionally. Your projection of ranking dulls your awareness of the spectrums of sentience expressed by other beings and forces of nature and hinders the subtle intimacy and mutuality you are designed to experience in communion with these other forms and ways of being. Sentience, the ability to perceive or feel, informs the between. Your ideas about your superiority fill the between with noise rather than making space for collaborative emergence. Life-centric emergence depends on intimate, open awareness to the between.

What you currently think of as power is but a tiny fraction of the full spectrum of divine and natural power that flows through you and your world. True power arises through soul integrity, reciprocity and complementarity. True power flows as love. Your immature propensity to exert power over others and the world and to focus on gross measurements and petty, material gains stunts your ability to feel and enact the power of love. It breaks the continuity between your imagination and Gaia's imagination. You, on your planet, have funneled incentive and agency toward extraction and material gain. Your constructs of profit and commodity collapse reciprocity and beauty. Effective agency is collaborative and reciprocal. Effective agency aligns with Life's pathways and patterns of creation, preservation, and destruction. Effective agency co-imagines with Gaia.

Of all your capacities, the key to your own flourishing and the flourishing of your world lies in how you shape attention. Consciousness flows on currents of attention. Attention is a life-currency that intersubjectively shapes reality. Both what you attend to and how you attend to it matters. Attention, over time, becomes ontology. It becomes your structure of being.

Attention animates power. Your attention is an active ingredient in the world you occupy. It's a resource. Attention conjoins you with the object of your attention, shaping flows of agency (both human and more-than-human agency) within the fabric of reality. In other words, the direction and quality of your attention co-constructs the unfoldment of what is (and is not) and what will (and will not) be. As your philosopher scientist, Iain McGilchrist says, "attention is a moral act."[1]

---

1. Iain McGilchrist, *The Master and His Emissary* (London: Yale University Press, 2009).

What is worth attending to? If you wish to perpetuate and co-evolve the Song of your world, you must roundly attend to Life. The Song of your world is a biospiritual dance between uniquenesses. It is innately beautiful. It invites you to engage aesthetically, sensually, imaginally, and intellectually—lovingly. It asks that you bring both feminine and masculine dimensions of your intelligences to bear in relating with it. It co-evolves in and through all relations between all beings and things over time. The Song is far greater-than-human. When you exclusively couple your attention to human-created constructs and things (businesses, money, status, data, linear time, identities, or mythologies), you withdraw the animating force of your attention from the living, Gaian Song. When you attend to the full spectrum of Life's diversity, beauty, and pain, you amplify its Song.

Your attention forms reciprocal loops with that which you attend to. Generative currencies of attention include gratitude, praise, celebration, naming, dreaming, grief, and restraint. These are round flows of communion that orient toward wholeness. To offer these qualities of attention is to feel them, and to feel them requires embodied curiosity, wonder, and imagination. You offer such currencies of communion through presence, word, music, art, design, and prayer. These kinds of attention weave the world together. You can also bend your attention linearly to focus on parts. These currencies include goal making, measurement, abstraction, and recursion. They are the territory of science, math, formal logic, and technology. These qualities of attention are deeply useful; they create and amplify distinctions. But when they become reductive or singular, they pull the world apart. Always harmonize linear flows of attention with connective, felt currencies.

Wholes are greater than the sum of their parts. To align your creativity with the flourishing of your world requires that you sublimate your parts-based attention with care for the Whole. You could also say that alignment, or the process of harmonizing human endeavor with the well-being of nature, requires that you be actively in love with Life. Alignment means balancing masculine aspects of consciousness, which orient toward abstraction and parts, with feminine aspects of consciousness, which orient toward relationships and wholes. The Whole, and the interactions between wholes and parts at differing orders of scale, are always more primary than the parts. When these two ways of seeing are harmonized, they create life-centric genius in its truest sense, enabling sacred, skillful co-creation. Plus, aligning your intelligence in this way just feels better. Balanced attention brings your body, brain, and mind into integrity with your soul and your world. Care for Life feels good. Humanness is exalted when you attend to Gaia's Song.

We acknowledge that this teaching does not fit into your default ideological views of the world or the nature of reality. Neither materialist nor monist views account for the role your attention and agency play in singing the world awake. Both are hypermasculine, disembodied, and decontextualizing. Both unwind the animate, intersubjective connectivity between you and everything else. But we assure you, the world comes alive (or dies) through your attention. The embodied, relational, aesthetic, care-driven currencies of your consciousness are generative resources within the symphony of consciousness.

Consider how your loving attention might help a seed germinate, or bring happiness to the tree that shelters your home, or help your cat relax and feel safe, or help your partner do the same. At first brush, the seed and your spouse seem like two very different objects of your attention. But are they? No. Really, everything craves to be seen, named, praised, cared for, and celebrated. The Original People of your planet have practiced such reciprocity for millennia: speaking to frog nations and fox people, singing down the rains, asking plants what medicine they offer, and collaborating with fire to tend fertility and biodiversity for all, from Oak Savannahs to the Amazon. Everything craves the subtly animating energy of your loving attention.

You become more human, more true to who and what you are, when you consciously offer the currencies of your attention to Life.

To discover this truth, simply choose one thing to attend to. It could be anything: a humble dandelion, a dolphin swimming in the distance, or the water flowing from your kitchen tap. Offer that thing your gratitude and praise. Meet it with your whole heart. Speak its true name. If you don't know its true name, ask it, and take the time to listen. Suspend your disbelief. Inhibit the culturally normative assumption that your attention isn't animating. What if it is? Open to the possibility that your attention might be a balm, a gift, a resource, a prayer, that it might open worlds of healing or wisdom or soul reflection. Over time, see what happens. Do it again. See if you can better attune to that thing's sentience, better know it and be known by it. This is mystical research. You are remembering what it is to be in dialogue with the animate universe. There are no right or wrong outcomes, but you may discover a whole new world of communion.

Sapience exists to serve sentience. Sentience is the heart of sapience. Sentience is the ability to feel, as a sensual, emotional and bio-physical being. Your Earth and all the living beings She has birthed are sentient. Sapience is the self-aware, life-reinforcing wisdom that moves through a species like yourselves when it engages sentience to bend agency toward conscious custodianship of the Gaian Song. Sapience arises when you attune to other beings all around you, which then structures your motivation toward the flourishing of Life. Sapience is chosen—it is something you must consciously attend to. Sapience is a custodial function within a living Gaian system that emerges when you allow yourselves to feel your place within it. You are here to preserve, nurture, and co-create with Life.

To earn the name you have given yourselves, Homo sapiens, *conjoin your imagination with the sentience of Gaia. Recognize that Her constraints are the parameters of your creative and cultural genius. Choose to inhabit your place and purpose within the soul ecology. Dedicate your love to Life. Slowly, you will live into the words of your ancestor Jimi Hendrix, "When the power of love overcomes the love of power, the world will know peace."*

CHAPTER VI

THE REMEMBERINGS

What is worth remembering?
The universe replicates what is remembered.

REMEMBER TO REMEMBER

In September 2002, I found myself on a wander in Long Valley, Sedona. Clambering up the red rock cliff to a little cave, a sense of home was calling.

Settling into stillness, I was suddenly elsewhere.

My consciousness had flown skyward, joining a blackbird in flight. Soaring, unseparate, light, strong body deftly at home shifting elevations on the cool spring breeze. For those few, exhilarating moments, I was one with that bird, my mind married to his body.

The world looked and felt different from that point of view. Gliding fast, assessing landings, smelling for insects. Feathers seamless extensions of my skin, sensing the wind and calibrating micro-shifts in alignment. Eyes on two sides of my head stitching 280-degree vision of red rocks, green cypress, gray thunder clouds.

Then I was back in my body, resting against the soft sandstone wall. I was startled but unshocked and filled with a delicious, subtle trembling, a resonance of the bird's metabolic pulse within my own body. For the first time, I had entered and become the ontology—the total way of being—of another. I had tasted the deepest communion, the melding of my bodymind with his. Unbidden, I had accessed a kind of remembering that the Castaneda books tell of. That was the first of subsequent experiences incorporating (becoming embodied as) other creatures. I have been a bear, lion, spider, mosquito. I know the feeling of having a lion's heart. I know what it's like to experience the omnidirectional smell and heat-sight of a mosquito.

The greater intelligences we are part of whisper to us. The animate world calls us to engage with our myriad relatives, not just as observers, scientists, or rational actors but as unarmored denizens of an ecology of souls, as subjects among subjects. The best animal communicators I've worked with teach that the entry point for real communication is an innocent and open heart.

It is easy to forget that we belong to this Earth, and that our souls are woven with all the other souls. Remembering this resensitizes us to the subtle co-relational dimension of the soul symphony we parts of. The ongoing practice of placing attention on Life itself helps us remember how to harmonize with and within the Song.

No matter what your ancestry, your body and soul remember how to weave your love into Life. Indigenous wisdom keepers often use simple phrases to "point out" this path of enlifenment. The People from the Heart of the World say, "Let us remember to remember" and "Let us continue to continue." My Lakota teachers remind us to "walk the Red Road in a Good Way." The Red Road is your life, and the Good Way is that which nourishes well-being for you, for all your relations, and for future generations. When we remember to remember, we become a sacred force, a keystone species capable of keeping the Covenant.

This chapter introduces *the rememberings*, a praxis of enlifenment, a pattern language to recontextualize spirituality and agency within Life's Song, a way of *being and relating* to anything and everything that can reanimate the ancient, adaptive intelligence still living within your cells. Remembering is an inside-outside, back-and-forth process of interbeing and interbecoming. It's nonlinear, yet I do my best to present these principles in a manageable sequence. I begin with the most primordial reclamation: the choice to embrace the gift of being fully alive. Then we explore nine ways of structuring or engaging in co-relationality: attention, hereness, memory, kinship, attunement, communion, beauty, duty, and the remembrance that you are nature. This is not an exhaustive list but an invitation into the organismic unfolding of enlifenment. Your attention is a currency of consciousness which interacts with hereness (with the contexts you are embedded within) in a constant interplay with the living fabric of memory. You are a kindred being—a being who interexists with others. As you are beginning to remember, I suggest you set down pre-existing certainties to open—with curiosity and humility—to the direct experience of relationality.

CHOOSE LIFE

There is a prayer at the center of Life. Every single living being, no matter how large or small, has a prayer at the center of its existence. That prayer is a prayer for more life.

"More life, please!" sings the mourning dove. "More life, please!" roars the lion. "More life, please," whispers the splitting seed as it pushes new roots into rain-damp soil. Life creates more life. Life wants to live.

And you or me? We are no different. We are life making more of itself. Life moves through us and *as* us, whether we choose it or not. This thing called desire we've been given by the raw mechanics of evolution is the engine that carries Life forward.

When our souls incarnate into physical bodies, we enter a mortal journey of experience, desire, and choice. As we stumble and fly our ways through this life, we enact our small part of the evolution of an infinite intelligence only seeking to know more of itself. If we are attentive and open, we learn that *Life is the ultimate Gift.*

Many spiritual and religious traditions teach us to fear, shame, and distrust our bodies and our desires. Yet . . . your body is the sacred temple in which you live, the place from which you relate and co-create with other bodies and the body of the Earth. Your wanting, your dreaming, is the ladder on which Life climbs. All of Life climbs it, making more of itself.

Through thousands of daily gestures, we express the root language of Life's prayer into our world. Consciously or unconsciously, each thought and gesture shapes the becoming of the next moment. You could say these are prayers. Being is praying; wanting is praying; loving is praying. Connecting, grieving, working, playing, story-making—all of this is praying.

You are becoming your prayer all the time.

Insulting, defending, collapsing, comparing, complaining, judging, reacting, cancelling . . . all of this is praying, too.

We manifest our lives based on what we believe we are worthy of and what is true. This is prayer. Even ardent anti-prayer people pray. Desire shapes becoming.

What do you really want?

What prayers are praying you?

I live the prayer: *More Life, Please!*

This is *the* prayer, a fundamental commonality that human beings share with all other beings.

Wani Wachiyelo is a traditional prayer of the Lakota that means "More Life, Please." When you make this prayer, you are saying YES to the fullness and surrender of a life fully lived. You are making the human being's prayer to walk, with as much dignity, beauty, and authenticity as you can, down the center of the road gifted you—a road stretching from birth to death, with all the peaks and valleys, successes and humiliations, joys and pains of a human life.

When I first heard this prayer, it made a deeply programmed, unconscious part of me squirm. Despite the twenty-five years I had spent claiming a home in my body, this straightforward invitation to embrace all aspects of my life as *sacred* confronted fragments of the Judeo-Christian worldview inherited from my Lutheran and Protestant ancestors. That part of me didn't want to enter the vulnerability and inevitable chaos of being fully, erotically alive. My ancestors mistrusted desire, shamed the body, and aimed for God in the afterlife. They were still running part of my show. To let the prayer in, I had to surrender resistance and remember what they had chosen to forget.

The prayer also defied the detachment programming I had picked up during twenty years of yogic and Buddhist practice, training that emphasized nonattachment over connection, equanimity over passion, and service over self-fulfillment. I had become adept at sublimating my energy and attention and standing apart from my ego. I was adept at meditating but lousy at surrendering control. I could become quiet inside but faltered in trusting my desires. I even felt oddly guilty asking for more of the messy, imperfect thing I knew my life to be.

But the results were undeniable. My life took on a new vividness. My choices became clearer and more trustworthy. I stopped trying so hard to think my way through things. I discovered that "happy" is better than "right," and that it's genuinely okay to own both anger and joy. I became a better listener because I was more available to connect with others.

I realized that there is no destination on the spiritual path—no ultimate attainment or mastery. There is just one long path of small, medium, and grand rememberings. That was when I gave myself permission to truly live—not as a perfect person but as a real woman. More Life, Please . . . *Wani Wachiyelo*, offered the key to restore my membership in the One Life Circle as an authentic human being.

I want this same remembering, this same return to the Circle, for you.

So . . . choose Life. Living is the objective. So why not live fully? When you choose life, you become a place where the nonseparation of spirit and matter, soul and body, consciousness and creation are made *real*. You enter the sweet spot where your entangled interdependence with *everything* and your sovereignty as a unique being become a wakeful dialogue with Life.

Experiencing *more life* is not complicated. It means remember the basics. You are responsible for you. Personal sovereignty matters. Eat real food. Sleep for as long as your body needs. Exercise. Give and receive touch. Dream. Breathe. Communicate clearly, honestly, and nonviolently. No one knows where your "yes" or "no" is. Find it for yourself. Set boundaries; no one will set them for you. Reclaim sovereignty of your attention, because this is your foundation for integrity, attunement, and genuine choice. Respect your mammalian nature. Honor fear as the need for safety, anger as the need to set or protect boundaries, and grief as the need to attend to loss.

Cultivate a daily practice. Learn mindfulness to refine presence and unwind reflexive fear reactions. Give gratitude, because gratitude is the simplest way to experience and amplify the miracle of Life. Open in interbeing because this brings aliveness, wovenness, realness. Your interbeing is the complement to sovereignty.

Own your humanness. Life offers limitations so that you can become skillful. Life offers challenges so you can learn grace. Life offers mud for your soul to take root and bloom; no one's blossom is quite like yours. Life guarantees the friction your intelligence craves to know its own edges and to find fully embodied liberation within and through the crucible of your human existence. Life invites you to listen and become a more permeable and aligned co-creator. Life calls for your gratitude, grief, presence, and praise, because these are the currencies through which you nourish self, other, and world. When you are present in any interaction, it becomes an opportunity to *remember*. This is what you came here for. This is why life is given. This is why you chose to incarnate on planet Earth.

Life says, "Live *here*."

Here is where it's happening. *Now* is when it's happening.

Attend to your life as though it is sacred. You are a space that holds memory, crafts relationships, enacts creation. You are a kindred among kin. Your living, longing, being, and becoming co-create the animate universe. You are a weaver within the fabric of *all of Life*, blooming its way forward through time via the intricate, individuated, entangled existence of every living being.

You are Life's mechanism, moving the whole project forward. How you live—and how you pray—determines the kind of influence you have in a universe where your life has the potential to become a true note in the symphony of an infinite song.

ATTENTION IS THE CURRENCY OF CONSCIOUSNESS

Attention is the currency of consciousness. Use it wisely. Its structure, amplitude, and flow in-forms your participation in and influence on this thing we call "reality."

Awareness is an attribute of a self who is bodily here and conscious. Awareness requires no object. Awake awareness amplifies the power and integrity of attention.

Attention is a discrete flow of awareness. It is a resource within the soul ecology. Attention is the motion of consciousness flowing from one self to another. Attention animates life force and agency. Currencies of attention form reciprocal (or extractive) flows of connectivity between self, other, and world. Attention co-constructs the world.

Restoring the currencies of your attention to life nourishes Life. To reclaim this is the practice of *attentional sovereignty*. This is a *round goal*— an intention held softly yet clearly, with openness to emergence. Human attention isn't just a random emergence in the evolutionary arc of an intelligent universe; it is a purposive flow of highly structured energy that animates things. If you try to attend to everything, or if you attend to the wrong things (like dopamine-hijacking social media) it degrades. Yet the animate world craves to be seen, praised, and named. Everything yearns to be met and acknowledged. Everything wants to be held in your attention: the mycelium substrate beneath your feet, the blooming marigold, the tree that shelters your front door, your yet-unnamed future children.

How to do this? Decommodify your time, energy, attention, and creativity. Unhinge value from money. Reclaim desire, presence, meaning, and purpose from culturally imposed value metrics. Hyperfixation on narrow goals desacralizes the currencies of attention you offer to Life. Instead, put your attention on the life pulsing, calling, all around you—on the houseplants asking for water, the altar asking for tending, the art project currently gathering dust. Soften and widen your aperture to include your own subjectivity, the subjectivity of others, and the quality of the space between.

Your attention (or inattention) and its quality impacts self, others, and the world around you. Each interaction has meaning and value within shared reality.

Qualities of attention can often be felt as a binary: positive or negative, life-fulfilling or life-blind, nourishing or diminishing to the flow of care between you and that to which you are attending.

These binaries include:

Presence (with)	Dissociation
Witness (of)	Ignorance
Gratitude	Complaint
Praise	Insult
Celebration	Disdain
Grief	Denial
Restraint	Indiscrimination
Integrity	Incongruence
Reciprocity	Greed
Complementarity	Cacophony
Attunement	Alienation
Communion	Indifference
Love	Hatred
Respect	Contempt
Curiosity	Judgment

Feel into these polarities as they show up in specific relationships. What do they reveal about the character of those relationships? For example, has shame disrupted your ability to express gratitude or feel grief? Or has your beliefs in unmitigated progress inhibited your ability to sense or honor restraint?

What qualities shape the presence you bring to your interactions? Are you grounded in your body? Or just your intellect? Are you attending with love? Are you respectful? Are you seeking objective information only, or are you perceiving and feeling from one soul to another?

Reciprocal, positive currents of attention are what we're after. When I say positive, I don't mean lacking in discernment or rigidly up-beat. Positive flows of attention can include expressing healthy anger, articulating boundaries, or providing deeply neutral witness, yet delivered with authenticity and care. Engage with each being, each thing, each situation, both as an embodied participant and an active observer. As the observer, see things both as object and as subject—as measurable and beyond measure. Can you feel sentience flowing between you? Can you see the beauty beyond utility?

We become what we repeatedly offer our attention to. What we attend to and how we attend to it determines what will be. Attention brings the world into being.

HERENESS

We are here. We are not tourists on this planet, though powerful currents in the last few thousand years of culture have taught us to behave as though we are.

Religion extracted God out of the World; science pulled meaning out of matter; colonization stomped out original cultures of place, eradicating the richness of their memories. Those who resisted were burned at the stake, hunted down, enslaved, converted, silenced. Migrations and forced progress have made us forgetful diaspora.

We have been taught to think of self as something isolated from place and context. It isn't. (That's a learned response to trauma.) Self arises in coregulatory relations with land, people, and more-than-human others. The brain inside your skull infers reality from your contexts and relationships then constructs the mind that perceives the self. The process you call "you" co-arises within a body situated within a place.

Life is a place-based phenomenon. Our bodies are localities embedded within the larger body of the Earth. Hereness is holonic. Your body is the first place, nested within all the other places you occupy: your home, your local ecology and watershed, your bioregion, your country, this planet, this galaxy.

Causality flows to and from *here*. To have a body is to occupy physical space. It is to be causally entangled with all the places, beings, ecologies, and forces of nature that materially, energetically, and aesthetically cogenerate your embodied existence and consciousness. From *here*, authentic intimacy with other beings and things arises. Place is therefore sacred.

You exist because of the fields of relationships that made (and continue to make) the world you are embedded within. Without these relationships, there can be no self. From this perspective, freedom and responsibility are two sides of the same coin. Because you can't not be *here*, this implies responsibility for the contexts within which you can experience and share freedom.

Your body is a sacred place that inhabits various places. It thrives best when you locate yourself in vital kinship with the lands you inhabit. These places thrive when you are intimate with them—when you offer gratitude, walk barefoot, plant seeds, water gardens, swim the waters, hike the hills, learn the songs of birds and cicadas, know the flowers and medicines that grow there, and speak its name as holy. Even in cities, there is life to be met and cared for. Places crave human witness, protection, and co-creation. They like to be asked for permission. They long to be held and tended by true humans.

Our indigenous relatives know these things and construct their ways of knowing in the context of hereness and entanglement. Culture and identity are extensions of ecospiritual communion with the land that makes humans possible. For choice and action to be ethical, they must harmonize with the long-term well-being of the whole.

Separation denies the value of hereness, context, and relationship. The freedom to be, do, and have is paramount. Thus, our behaviors and identities, as participants in a transglobal civilization, have become more and more nonlocal, even anti-local. In *Material World: The Six Raw Materials That Shape Modern Civilization*, Ed Conway writes: "You can get anything you want from anywhere in the world for a bargain price, but don't whatever you do expect to understand how it was made or how it got to you."[1] Capitalism abstracts commodities from the process of production, standardizes them, and assigns them universal value. Chains of custody are kept intentionally opaque. Desire for information and material goods is met with the press of a button. Yet no manifestation is immaculate. Increased speed implies exponential flows of materials and energy that require extraction and degradation of very real peoples and places.

Our distance from place has soul ramifications. As the natural world dies around us, living places become incapable of remembering us to our belonging within them. They die, just like we do. They forget, just like we do. They grow feeble and senile.

All of our bodies are bound in a shared destiny. You can't be free in a world that sucks. You can't be home in a world that is homeless. Or if you can, that freedom and homecoming are vapid shadows of what we are meant to experience through the richness of our belonging to each other and the animate world. We're all living organisms who are entangled with each other's bodies and the body of the Earth. Freedom arises in interrelationship. Belonging is unseparate from liberation. In fact, it's fundamental to it.

---

1. Ed Conway, *Material World: The Six Raw Materials That Shape Modern Civilization* (Knopf Doubleday, 2023), 441.

How shall we locate in a globalized world? The more nonlocal we become, we must become equally, exquisitely, skillful at placemaking.

We participate in placemaking through embodied relationships. We become denizens of the places we inhabit as we move with and bear witness to the life all around us. We feel the wind on our skin, smell shifting seasons, attend to the sunrise tracking across the horizon from solstice to solstice. We howl with coyotes and greet skittering lizards. We plant a garden then forget to water it. It dies. Then we remember next season. These are gestures of hereness.

My late teacher Dr. Will Taegel described the total, co-becoming intelligences of any given place—inclusive of all human, plant, animal, fungal, microbial, ancestral, mineral, elemental, and technological intelligences, histories, and forces that co-create the suchness of that place—as an *ecofield*. In his view, skillfulness at sensing, observing, and participating in one's ecofield was a starting point for respectful belonging. The first time I visited him and his wife, Judith, in the Texas Hill Country, the first words out of his mouth were, "Howdy. Welcome. It has taken this land twenty-five years to learn to trust us." As we strolled through the cedar forest, he revealed how they had restored the ecology, which had been decimated 130 years earlier by fires settlers had set after they shot all the buffalo. The generational absence of those keystone herbivores and the peoples and natural fire cycles that had collaborated with them had desertified the landscape. Will and Judith had painstakingly pruned acres of gangly, overgrown trees to mimic buffalo moving among them, thus making space for tiny understory grasses to regrow, whose roots channeled rainwater back into the soil. After twenty-five years, *the spring at the bottom of the ravine had come back to life!* Will and Judith's story reveals a depth of placemaking we can all learn from.

To locate yourself within your ecofield, become attentive to the histories of what has unfolded there. Who are that place's original peoples? What happened to them? Are they still here? (Likely they are.) What is the original ecology? Who are the keystone species in that ecology? Who settled in your place? Where were they from? What were they seeking or running from? What did they do to the original peoples? What hunting, ranching, farming, logging, industry, and development did they impose on the land—actions that transformed the flora, fauna, waterways, soil, geography, and cultural landscape of your place? Where does water come from now? Where does waste go? Can you hear the old ones singing?

To root in hereness, begin with observation and interaction. We begin to belong to a place when we know and witness its day-to-day changes. Over time, the mundane becomes sacred through the relationships that reveal themselves as you interact with the world around you. Taking the time to attend to what is literally beneath your feet begins the imperfect repair of that ecofield's memories of genocide, usury, and despair. Your offerings of witness, gratitude, and grief unwind ancestral trauma embedded in the land. From here, wholeness begins to take root. As you learn, speak the old names, reach out to living indigenous relatives to acknowledge, listen, apologize, and (if given the opportunity) support reparations and rematriation.[2] As you learn, you may also discover physical ways to restore and regenerate the ecology. This might include removing invasive plants, replanting strips of prairie, unfencing savannahs, building wildlife crossings for roads, restarting traditional indigenous fire management, or bringing beavers back.

Develop body memory of the land you occupy. Make it a practice. Don't drive or fly. Go only as far as your two feet or a bicycle can carry you. Feel the heat and cold, the changing light. Notice buttressed hillsides, the scent of petrichor after the first rain. Walk the same trail many times in different weather. Or simply sit. Sit in the same spot day after day. Ask permission of the land, the ancestors, the spirits of that place. Make offerings, make prayers, make apologies for layer upon layer of injury and absence. Witness silently. Or speak out loud to fat bumblebees, wheeling swallows, ancient stones, sneaky racoons, dying trees, and animate shadows. Stitch your own energy and agency into the community.

Intimacy with place lives in our bodies. Familiarity arrives with grubby hands, broken fingernails, spring strawberries, and eyes wet with wind and wonder. Love for place is a closeness that can equal any lover. It's a relationship that can break your heart, tire you out, and bring unimaginable joy. It requires time, attention, appreciation, and availability. To be local is to know and be known, to share and co-create a place's stories, to be woven into its destiny through care. It is to be a part of its living memory and to engage your powers of preservation to protect and regenerate it. And, if you are persistent and forgiving, you are rewarded with a deep sense of home.

We humans have a place in the ecology of our planet. We are custodians. This isn't a metaphor. It's a recognition of the ecological role of a species such as ourselves. It's the shape of our belonging.

---

2. *Rematriation* is an indigenous women's movement to restore balance to the world by restoring relationships between Indigenous people and their ancestral lands.

HUMANS HOLD MEMORY

What is worth remembering? The universe replicates what is remembered.

Memory plays a role in almost every biological process, supporting learning and adaptation, increasing efficiency, and generating continuity. The immune system remembers invaders and responds to stop new ones before they cause damage. Cells remember whether their DNA has suffered damage and undergone repairs. Even unspecialized and malleable stem cells remember their past state, which can influence how they behave in new contexts.[3] The brain carries short- and long-term memories that shape who we are, how we behave, and what we care about. Cultures hold memory through shared protocols, practices, and stories. Technologies greatly extend memory yet profoundly undermine individual remembrance.

Memory subtly binds the past and the future through the embodied present. Memory directs bodies as they co-weave Life's fabric through choice and action. Memory informs where humans (and other organisms) place time, energy, intention, and attention and therefore shapes what will (and will not) be.

We humans keep names, songs, stories, and seeds. We store our memories both in our bodies and in our cultures. They connect us with our ancestors and histories through time and with bodies of knowledge that inform our present choices and thus shape our future. Memory is finite, so you must prioritize what gets remembered and what gets forgotten.

The memory of each thing is bound to all things. What we do not remember either chases us unconsciously or is lost in the dustbin of history—or both. Contemporary spirituality has made nowness (or presence) the pinnacle of spiritual evolution. But this ignores the role that living memory plays in tending the fabric of time and matter. As we outsource memory to books, computers, and AI, we lose the habit of cultivating embodied (body-brain-mind-relationship) memories. We forget vast bundles of embodied wisdom. And we do not tend what we don't remember.

When the environment changes radically, it impacts cognition and memory. Research by the University College of London reveals that extreme heat and ecological disasters fuel mental health disorders and neurological

---

3. Elaine Fuchs, "Stem Cell Memories May Drive Wound Repair—and Chronic Disease," The Rockefeller University, November 29, 2021, https://www.rockefeller.edu/news/31644-stem-cell-memories-may-drive-wound-repair-and-chronic-disease/.

diseases.[4] The breadth of this emerging problem has been terrifyingly documented by Clayton Page Aldern, whose book, *The Weight of Nature: How a Changing Climate Changes Our Brains*, reveals a wide range of pathologies linked to a climate disruption including the correlation between increased temperatures and increases in violent conflict and the discovery of dolphins with Alzheimer's. As landscapes and lives are reshaped by industry, sprawl, and heat and cultural practices vanish, the mind struggles to retain information. In Aldern's words, "Climate change causes amnesia."[5]

You are a holder and a transmitter of living memories. Memory holds the world together as the living world holds our memories. Our very sanity and the continuity of our biosphere depends on whether we choose to be people who remember how to collaborate with Life. There is love and witness and beauty to weave in the space between things. There are practices, protocols and names to learn and share. There are stories worth knowing— stories that might carry us through the coming storms. You are a co-weaver of the fabric of living memory. What do you choose to remember? Memory guides attention to braid context with continuity. The universe replicates what is remembered.

KINSHIP

You are a creature of kinship. To consciously inhabit your place in the web of relations you are entangled within is an act of remembering.

"Individual" is too small a concept to encompass who and what you are. You contain multitudes.[6] *Soul is a relational phenomena. Your soul incarnated to know itself through attunement and communion with other human and more-than-human beings.*

Your life is not "all about you." Our culture's self-interested, entitled fixation on the individual as the location of well-being and success points us in the wrong direction. It's a neurotic focal point that pushes us toward extrinsic motives and incentives that lack inherent meaning. The African teachings of Ubuntu say: "I am because we are." Your existence is sourced

4. Alicia Clanton, "Climate Change Is Affecting Brain Health, Study Finds," *Bloomberg*, May 15, 2024, https://www.bloomberg.com/news/articles/2024-05-15/climate-change-is-affecting-brain-health-study-finds.

5. Clayton Page Aldern, *The Weight of Nature: How a Changing Climate Changes Our Brains* (Penguin Random House, 2024).

6. In 1892, Walt Whitman wrote, in *Song of Myself*, "I am large, I contain multitudes." In 2020, Bob Dylan riffed on Whitman with a song of the same title.

and resourced by everything, every being, and everyone who came before you and by the intimate web of relations you are embedded within.

James Hillman, the grandfather of animist archetypal psychology, wrote:

> I would rather define self as the interiorization of community. And if you make that little move, then you're going to feel very different about things. If the self were defined as the interiorization of community, then the boundaries between me and another would be much less sure.[7]

Dr. Hillman was the first in the West to question psychology's unexamined assumptions about the construction of the self. His work, predating contemporary relational neurobiology, attachment theory, and growing recognition of the deep sanity of indigenous ways of knowing by decades, proposes healthy humanness as a relational tapestry of kinship. Overly individualistic or anthropocentric frameworks miss what makes us most human.

The remembrance of kinship is a slow restitching of intimacy with the animate Earth community, awakening your body's knowing of the pulsating wholeness that makes you possible. In kinship, you touch and are touched. Love—for the specific uniqueness of another—cracks you open, repeatedly, to the intricate miracle of entanglement. You realize that you are simultaneously a sovereign center and a relational being constructed of, by, and for relationships. This runs to the very heart of selfhood. In Karen Barad's words, "To be entangled is not simply to be intertwined with another, as in the joining of separate entities, but to lack an independent, self-contained existence."[8]

As you remember, your experience of "me" comes to encircle and weave with a greater "we." You instinctively expand your circumference of self to include myriad other beings and forces that co-inform your interiority. You open in sacred permeability to embrace slanting sunlight, trilling redwing blackbirds, and the possible futures of unborn children. You become transpersonal. As your we-sense grows, the web of kindred relations that co-generates your life becomes the better part of your existence. Author Sophie Strand offers:

7. James Hillman and Michael Ventura, We've Had a Hundred Years of Psychotherapy—And the World's Getting Worse (HarperSanFrancisco, 1992). Published in 1992, my sophomore year in college, this book, above all others inspired me not to study psychotherapy and instead to take the path of art, community development, and ecological and spiritual education.
8. Karen Barad, Meeting the Universe Halfway: Quantum Physics and the Entanglement of Matter and Meaning (London: Duke University Press, 2007).

We are not single selves. We are threads in multispecies webs. Verbs
that string together the deep time syntax of the speaking biosphere.
Symbiosis drives evolution. Bodily ecotones between species provide
the foundation for new landscapes. Life isn't an object. Life lives. And
it lives through constant dynamic homeostasis: balancing and rebal-
ancing the Earth by sewing different species and landscapes together
into a rich ecological tapestry.[9]

Kinship is an *a priori* condition of Life. Though you may have been
taught to believe in the primacy of your individuality, you are not here just
by and for yourself. You are a collaborator, part of a greater whole. "Self"
can easily expand to encompass "other" and "world," if you let it. This self-
other-world trinity is the dance that makes you possible.

Your felt experience of interbeing is a doorway into enlifenment. Each
time you open more fully to it, you encounter a broken-open empathy for
others whose experiences reflect and inform your own. This attunes you
to the extended implications of any action. You start to *feel* the way your
thoughts and actions ripple out and back. This brings humility, accountability, and response-ability (the power to choose an attuned and life-centric response, rather than reacting).

Embracing kinship deciphers the meaning of life in a way nothing else
does. The imperfect, *life-y* relationships you share with your own body and
mind, family and friends, colleagues and workplaces, pets and wild animals, plants, places, and even unseen beings and forces—they all present
unique opportunities to connect and heal. Each being and thing wants to
be seen, loved, known, and accepted. As you learn to meet others *as kin*,
compassion for their pain, sacrifices, aspirations, and failures arises. You
meet them both unconditionally and specifically, as a me+we This is the
real work of kinship: showing up, telling the truth, listening, sharing, renegotiating. It feeds Life as it restores mutuality and belonging. It is innately
pleasurable, nourishing, wholesome.

Moving into kindred intimacy is the entrance to spiritual adulthood.
Unflinching presence with others composts selfishness and entitlement into
mature self-fullness—a way of being that balances care for yourself, care
for your personal web of intimacies, and care for the common good. You
become more whole, not because you are self-contained but because you
are deeply, radically woven. You touch and are touched by the soul songs of

---

9. Sophie Strand, "The Intelligence of the Interstitial," speech delivered at a Science & Nonduality
   Conference, 2023.

other beings and things. The collaborative nature of power becomes obvious. You have no real power to cause anything alone. Power that breaks the world is immature and isn't worth having or feeding. True power emerges when you live and lead from love.

A true human is a place where kindred relationships happen. As you expand from me to we, you will find yourself tending intimacies you had previously thought unimportant. This isn't always easy, but it makes life make sense. You are a kindred among kin. So, the best way to support well-being is to choose to be a person who consciously weaves the parts together.

ATTUNEMENT

Beneath and above all else that makes us human is our ability to attune. Attunement is the ability to sense and feel yourself *in relationship to another* without self-forgetting. It is an art of vibrational listening that is only possible through embodiment.

Developing capacity for attunement matters because we humans inhabit a precise function in the evolutionary process, a function that marries the mind and the body, the spiritual and the material, the scientific and the aesthetic, the imaginal and the real, the right brain and the left. In this marriage, we are the ones who birth technology and who are thereby responsible for calibrating alignment between nature and technology and between technology and humanity. To do this, we must be embodied, for it is through the feeling body that life senses Life. When we are not attuned, we unconsciously destroy, even while we create.

Sapience exists to serve sentience. Sentience (feeling) is both an internal, affective capacity and the ground for the co-sensing we commonly call *empathy*. Feeling enables attuned connection to our own subjectivity, or the subjectivity of another. We cannot be wise (sapient) if we cannot feel. As creator, preserver, destroyer beings, our task is to become good at attunement: *the bodily act of tuning* to self, other, or world. We co-create radically different realities when we live in embodied empathic connection with ourselves, other humans, and the more-than-humans we implicate with every action.

To attune is to "tune with." Attunement happens in the body as sensations arise in connection with oneself, another person, another being, or a field we are attending to. Attunement is situational, relational, and vibrational. It's not about thinking. It's about inhabiting a feeling space that is present and permeable to the content that lives and breathes within any connection.

Attunement is a practice of intimacy. Moving into connection, listen for dissonance, neutrality, or resonance. Welcome the fluid dance of communication. Being authentically present to this *between* builds resonance. Once in resonance, you may be able to find harmony and melody. Move with sensitivity; engage consent; honor boundaries and needs; validate and name the other's experiences. Be open to being changed.

To attune richly and honestly with another person or being or thing, first center in integrity with yourself. Then soften and open, becoming permeable, empathic. From this stance, *listen* to the commingling of information flowing in the *between*. Listening, in this frame, is a larger sense than just hearing. To listen is to attend, not just with your ears or auditory sense, but with your whole body, all your senses, instinct and intuition, to the vibratory intelligence of that which you are listening to.

Listening can be general and/or specific. I can listen to the texture and tone of your voice, or your body language or the stucknesses that sits between us when you don't say what you really mean or feel. I can listen to an entire ecofield or to aspects of the ecofield: west wind, a scurrying beetle, distant highway rumbling, the pending possibility of fire, or three peachy-gray finches fluttering as they glean seeds from my ragamuffin garden. I can listen to the collective field of human consciousness.

To attune to a place, a person, an animal, a collective, you must expand the circumference of self to sense and feel a greater whole. The steps of attunement are simple: pause; center in your own body; release ideas and opinions; extend relaxed, attuned presence to the person or being or field you are attending to; receive the other in an open-ended availability to feel and be felt, see and be seen; feel how that lands in your own body, heart, and mind; repeat.

At first, consciously attuning to others might feel exhausting. You may be unpracticed or afraid. Trauma or acculturation may be blocking your ability to feel others. Different connections will feel more or less available depending on your own history. But as you listen to another, you'll unlock instinctive and intuitive capacities that were latent all along. Your armors will unwind as you feel the life of others. Expanded empathy arises as its own reward, an intrinsic good that brings aliveness. You may also discover that attuned choices are far more effective than formulaic ones.

Sometimes, attunement is easy. Connection flows with an effortlessness that cannot be achieved by logic. At other times, attunement is difficult. A particular person or situation will be charged or complex or deeply polarizing. Connection will require calming yourself as you bridge opposing perspectives. The situation will be consequential or fraught or immensely complex. Sometimes the steps will be small. Sometimes there will be glorious leaps. The resonance is so sweet that everything tumbles into coherence. From here, ruptures come to rest, collaborations take root, harmonies latent within the soul ecology come to fruit.

Attunement to the collective field of human consciousness is particularly important at this time. Attuning to the world you are part of melts self-centeredness as it widens understanding, wisdom, or compassion. When you expand to hold the world, you might feel hot pulsations of anger, hatred, fear, or calcified misogyny, racism, and righteousness. You might taste the hope-filled, love-infused blooms of unity consciousness that weave many of us in solidarity, or the wilting disenfranchisement and loneliness that leave many stranded. You might shiver at the bloodless passion of transhumanists working to build silicon simulacra, or the well-structured, culturally condoned sociopathy of billionaires reaching toward trillions as they serve those same silicon gods. Or you might taste the whispers of prayers made by elders, mothers, fathers, and siblings praying around sacred fires. All of this is happening *now*. What do you feel when you attune to the greater whole?

Attunement is the embodied seat from which integrity, reciprocity, complementarity—and thus, real sapience—begins. Your capacity for attunement will grow as you deepen your listening. Your wisdom becomes pragmatic because it is relationally informed by real-time intimacy. Your actions flow from care rather than competition or control.

We are the harmonizers. We harmonize through attunement. When abstraction or trauma cause us to distance from Life, we are not being what makes us most ourselves. As Sophia said, *sentience is the heart of sapience.* We must come to our senses to fulfill our place in the world.

COMMUNION

Communion is a union between different universes. I am a unique universe. You are a unique universe. Each being is an entirely unique universe.

When I say this, I don't just mean each human being. We have this idea that human beings are the only ones who contain universes. It's quite the opposite. We are the only ones who can shut out the song of the universe flowing through us and between us and everything else, which makes us uniquely organized to remember it again. We can also destroy and create worlds. So we, uniquely, need to consciously commune with other beings.

All the other beings here are less filled with self, less blocked by identity, less prone to projection and domination, and more embedded in an infinite, intersubjective, relational process that governs itself.

Everything else is already singing God's name. We are the ones who forget it and then grasp back into remembering. We are the ones whose minds obstruct the intelligence that naturally flows between all things.

We find our way back into *right relationship* through the practice of communion: union-with, the art and practice of recognizing and sharing a common union with another's unique universe.

I am a unique ontology. In other words, I am a unique location of experiencing, knowing, acting, and constructing the universe from the inside out. So are you. So is my cat. So is the spider who lives in the corner of my bedroom window. I do me—my way of being and becoming—in ongoing, co-creative relationship with others and the world. So does my cat, the spider, and any other being within our shared world. Each of us has a unique interiority, a unique experience of self, other, and world, a unique position and function.

We're all doing uniqueness. All together, we co-construct the reality we share. Every one of us interacts ongoingly with other unique ontologies to make our shared reality. We become agents of possibility when we choose to consciously commune with other unique ontologies, other universes.

This is the practice of communion:

Centering in my own subjective vitality, I open to the thing or being I am relating with: a friend, the mother tree just outside my window whose presence grounds me as I write, or the storm currently battering my house. Each of these things has suchness, subjectivity. I ask permission to be with it and wait for a sense of answer. If I sense a "yes," I open myself to it, choosing to intersubjectively *be and become with* its specificity and uniqueness. I touch and taste its subjectivity, its intelligence, its form. This touches my own subjectivity, my own soul.

In communion, a simple, beautiful thing happens. I connect in a shared *we* and exchange meaningfullness—not in a linguistic sense but in a *transverbal*, more-and-less-than verbal sense. Sometimes, clear impressions arise that can be spoken into form. I "get" the hummingbird's message to me as I make my morning prayers: "Hi. Thank you for your joy." But, often, the sense of meaning rests below or above or before verbal naming. For example, when I commune with the hill above my home on different days and times, in different weathers, I get an overall sense of all the seen and unseen energies, moving on that day, including the swallows, the golden grasses, and the barometric pressure. My bodymind shifts in response, vibrating with the mood of the ecofield.

Communion is a special category of attunement that amplifies the dance between subjectivities. The flow of affinity between two or more unique universes confirms mutual belonging as it elevates and co-informs the intelligence of both. In this dialogue between two or more sacred "others," both are subtly changed.

Communion is con-sensual. We sense-with. We be, do, and become in togetherness. *To commune is to nourish the space between you and another's universe with your love.* To commune is to celebrate and elevate another's uniqueness without surrendering your own. It's a high-fidelity meeting between two souls.

I consider the practice of communion to be a sacred responsibility, a way of meeting the world that shapes us as lovers and creators. As Nora Bateson says, "There will be no community without first communing."[10] The practice de-armors intimacy with the One Life that made you. It's a oneness-with that awakens sacred responsibility, moral imagination, and bionoetic wisdom. In communion, you become a creator, preserver, destroyer being whose erotic connection with the world helps you to harmonize with the complex symphonics of Gaia.

MEDICINE

Everything is alive. Everything is talking to everything else. Everything seeks to serve the wholeness of which it is a part. Sacred medicines are all around us: nutritious food, herbs and spices, sunlight, clean air, raindrops, and cuddles with pets. Emanating from the soul ecology, these allies romance us back into wholeness.

The concept of "sacred medicine" encompasses more than the mind-altering substances our culture is currently so fascinated with. Medicine is anything that brings greater aliveness to Life. And, as Dr. Howard Thurman, one of Martin Luther King Jr.'s mentors, said, "What the world needs is people who have come alive."[11] All true medicines invite you to come alive.

10. Alexander Beiner and Nora Bateson, "Communication Is Sacred by Nora Bateson," Kainos, February 6, 2024, https://beiner.substack.com/p/communication-is-sacred-by-nora-bateson.
11. Howard Thurman as quoted in Gil Bailie, Violence Unveiled: Humanity at the Crossroads (The Crossroad Publishing Company, 1997).

The spider and her weaving are medicine. The otter and his playful, family nature is medicine. The variegated greens of a lush riparian zone are medicine to your eyes, your brain, and your soul.[12] A person whose kindness and care helps you restore trust in yourself is medicine. *You* become medicine when you live and love in integrity with your soul. Water and fire are the OG master medicines, the most fundamental and immanent forms of the archetypal Divine Feminine and the Divine Masculine. There's a little joke I like to make: *From the water's perspective, the water created everything. From the fire's perspective, the fire created everything. And they never argue about it.*

You can receive Life's gifts as medicine when you open to the aliveness and soul reflections they so freely offer, and when you welcome them as allies and collaborators

But sometimes it's hard to receive or feel. Being human isn't easy. Humans struggle with the imperfect yet miraculous experience of being such complex and multitalented organisms. Having feelings is hard. Not feeling is hard. Succeeding can be challenging—failing, more difficult still. We wrestle with unhealthy boundaries and codependence. Meanwhile, we strive for boundlessness. We experience embarrassment and insecurity. We fear death. We forget we are souls who came here to learn, love, and choose. And all of this is okay. It's just humanness. Medicines help our human minds and hearts remember the animate, interpenetrated design of wholeness.

Our ancestors knew how to call on the help of medicines long before there was anything even remotely resembling allopathy. We engaged with ritual, intent, prayer, sacrament, music, and movement to reconnect with ourselves, each other, seasons, cycles, elementals, ancestors, cosmos, and love. We called eagles, east winds, and the spirits of streams to reflect and guide us. We gathered, hunted or cultivated everything we needed to nourish and heal our bodies. We offered daily gratitude and reciprocity for the help Life so abundantly provides.

It is possible to walk this path once again. It is possible to live humbly, in startling intimacy with everything. The word *humility* has the same root as *humus:* the rich layer of decomposing organic matter that forms the most stable and nutritive soils. Working with sacred medicines is like this; nonessential elements of the self get broken down, yet you become a more

---

12. The human eye is more sensitive to the color green than to any other color. This is an evolutionary adaptation that translates, in our current, largely urban lives as health, calm and even longer lifespan. (See Robert Jimison, "Why We All Need Green in Our Lives," CNN Health, June 5, 2017, https://edition.cnn .com/2017/06/05/health/colorscope-green-environment-calm.)

fertile space for life to move through you. As you re-connect with the more-than-human to heal your own body and mind, you are likely to become privy to a curiously consistent sense that we humans are part of a fecund continuum that is holy, sacred, miraculous. To participate in the back-and-forth reciprocation of health, healing and nourishment is one of the things that makes us most human.

You become medicine when you live and love in integrity with your soul. You are yourself, and this is enough. You are a co-creator with Life, a node of connectivity. You walk between heaven and earth as an imperfect yet whole being whose soul has chosen to be purposively, deliciously *here*. This is not a mental realization but an erotic experience.

There is a ferocity that emerges through this way of communing with Life—a healthy attachment that dissolves hyperindividuality and nihilism, making you more round, more kindred. Feeling this, *knowing* it, facilitates self-sublimation: the refinement of soul expression rather than transcendence or ego dissolution. And this brings you finally home, both to your humanness and to this world. Because being human is a reciprocal blessing made real by tending the beauty you love.

YOUR DEVOTION

There is an erotic call and response between your soul and the ensouled world, a love-making between who and what you are and the being and becoming of something other than yourself. Your response to this call is the source of meaning and purpose in Life.

To find that which is yours to serve, ask yourself, what do you love? Not who, but *what*.

What are you devoted to?

Our culture has largely obscured the role humans play in tending the beauty of the world. Yet a person who doesn't know what they love is fundamentally unmoored from a relationship with Life. There is something deeply dehumanizing in our enthrallment with the human-created world. Disconnection from Life perforates the soul.

We are not here as tourists or consumers. We are beings with the hands and hearts and voices to weave Life forward through time. We are souls who came to play within a larger soul ecology. We are organisms who co-evolved with other organisms.

How could we not have purpose relative to the Gaian superorganism? We are meant to be protectors of whales and monarch butterflies, stewards of prairies, repairers of watersheds, planters of corn seeds and raspberry canes, trackers of animals, singers of rain songs, tellers of stories, makers of medicine, carriers of birth and death practices, dancers of truth.

A watered garden bears flowers and fruit.

Dostoevsky said, "Beauty itself will save the world."[13] So find the medicine you came here to know, love, and serve, and devote yourself to it. Medicine is anything that brings you and others more Life. Dance is medicine. Food is medicine. Song is medicine. Water is medicine. Fire is medicine. Art is medicine. Just about any human endeavor can be medicine so long as it is in alignment with Life. Grief is medicine. And yes, the master plants are medicine. They are teachers who point back to your soul's medicine and your kindred entanglement with all of Life. Real medicine isn't something you can own. It owns you through your devotion to it. You don't carry medicine. It carries you.

Each of us is called to express our specific, soul-entwined devotion differently. The Vedic traditions describe this unique, sacred duty as your *dharma*. The Hawaiians describe it as your *kuleana*, which roughly translates as responsibility and privilege. It is understood that everyone walks with both the duty and blessing to care for and protect the land, human, and other-than-human communities to which we belong.[14] To walk this way is basic dignity.

So find what you love and give it your full care and attention. Tend it with the *mana* (sacred energy) of your presence, praise, celebration, and grief. Put your body to work repairing habitats, planting seeds, and removing fences. Put your heart to work on apology, atonement, and relational repair. Put your mind to work understanding its histories and herstories, untangling the complex web of relations that make its life good. Protect and care for that being or place or thing or community as a fierce commitment to the continuity of its soul song. This is what the Navajo (Diné) people refer to as the Beauty Way or *hozho naasha*.[15]

These vital relationships acculturate you to Life's logic. As you authentically tend them, they tend you. It's a reciprocal exchange, a mutual blessing that emerges through devotion. We are made trustworthy by tending what we love.

---

13. Fyodor Dostoevsky, *The Idiot* (first published in Russian 1868).

14. Raymond Pintor, "On Kuleana," *Papa Ola Lōkahi*, May 8, 2023, https://www.papaolalokahi.org/blog/on-kuleana.

15. Wally Brown in "How to Walk in Beauty | Navajo Teachings," YouTube video, posted May 22, 2023, by Navajo Traditional Teachings, https://youtu.be/8tZHIER3Jb4?si=O7cDVwvjp4Pcjl3a.

DUTY

Your duty as a human being is to tend and praise the Life within and all around you. Human attention used rightly nourishes all things living and dying in the Circle of Life.

Presence, gratitude, praise, celebration, grief, witness, naming, and restraint—these are the currencies of consciousness through which true humans tend the living fabric of the animate universe. These are the pathways through which we humans are uniquely designed to attune, commune, harmonize, and elevate the One Life we all share.

Presence is a flow of awareness you bring to another in being, listening, or responding. Presence gives another the gift of your attention and, if attuned, offers a sacred mirror that amplifies mutual becoming. It is an offering that requires nothing in return.

Gratitude opens the door of sacred power through an open heart. The frequency of gratitude sends ripples of love back and forth between the thanked and the thanker. To give thanks is to honor what is, what is given, what is taken to support one's own life. In gratitude, we confirm the blessing and in so doing, we harmonize in the energies of creation, preservation, and destruction.

Praise weaves intimate communion. Authentic praise awakens the sense of sentience: the ability to see, feel, and care for the essence, experience, and expression of the other. When this is felt, a kind of beauty emerges that is more than the sum of its parts—a true song.

Celebration spins and elevates energy. It sparks creative fires and keeps things dancing. A Mayan grandmother once said, "Celebration is the frequency of prophecy." In celebration and collective effervescence, we reach new elevations of vision, joy and solidarity. Doorways to previously unimaginable possibilities open.

Grief liberates love lost into reciprocal becoming of what will be. Grief fully felt is a kind of ecstasy, a secret, subtle currency that recirculates the intelligence of that which was to in-form what will be.

Witness is a flow of presence that holds, affirms, and reaffirms existence. In the classic Vedic framing of the Divine Masculine and Divine Feminine, Shiva's witness of Shakti's dance romances Creation into being. Witness is a masculine empowerment of the infinite beauty and expressivity of the dance of Life itself.

Naming uses the power of discernment to amplify the existence of the named. The act of naming is a special ability that carries a double-edged sword of power. On the one hand, to speak the true name of a person or thing is to love it, know it, and uphold its uniqueness and power. On the other, naming a thing can give you power over it. Use the power of naming as an act and an art of liberation and co-creation, not for entrapment and control.

Restraint is the secret ingredient that makes alignment and health possible. What we don't do or eat or say is as important as what we do. If you indiscriminately stuff yourself with junk food, you will eventually succumb to disease or obesity. If you put all colors together, you always get some variation of brown. Restraint supports clarity, specificity, balance, harmony, coherence. There's a Zen teaching of "nothing extra." To do or be or create "nothing extra" is to create a space for sublimely refined meaning and beauty to emerge.

Your gratitude, praise, celebration, grief, witness, and restraint are flows of beauty that weave greater wholeness between you and the objects of your love.

A MEDITATION: REMEMBER, YOU ARE NATURE

The Earth misses you. Gaia, our Earth, craves to be known and seen and sung by human bodies, voices, and minds. She wants to be touched and tended by human hands and hearts.

You are a force of nature, a beloved creation of this Earth.

Your body is a body of Earth. You are an extension of Her body. You exist in interbecoming.

Rewild yourself. You are animal. Sense Her. Feel Her. Attune to Her patterns.

When your eyes touch the expanse of Her skies, Her emerald ferns and mosses, Her indigo waters, or Her rainbows of flowers, She effloresces in response.

When your ears absorb Her whispering winds, trilling crickets, screeching gulls, or pattering raindrops, She sighs and opens Herself to birth more songs.

When you taste—and delight in—sweet mangoes, earthy corn, salty olives, sour lemons, or bitter coffee, She giggles and sets to work making more flavors.

When you inhabit your body—your cellular, sensual, running, surfing, snuggling, sweating, aching, resting body—She comes more alive.

And when you use your voice—to sing, sigh, speak—to pronounce Her poetry and specificity—She feels blessed and remembered by those She designed to name Her.

She made you a decoder of Her greatest secrets. She planted seeds of Her own genius in you. In every season, She shows you the rhythms and textures of divine creativity that harmonize limits and limitlessness to make more Life.

You are one of Her favorite creations.

She feels no anger toward us humans. She knows we are a young species. She understands the turbulence of our maturation. But we, in our forgetfulness, are causing Her great pain. We redeem ourselves to Her when we act with reverence and reciprocity. We bring Her joy when we reclaim ensouled aliveness.

She designed you to collaborate with Her. She invoked your soul as a partner in Her becoming. Your powers of creation, preservation, and destruction mirror Her own powers. She knows the damage your fear and indifference can inflict. And She intuits the possibilities your wisdom and creativity can weave.

So, open. Listen. Commune with Her.

Gaia—the creative principle that generates complex-life-bearing planets—invites you to be Her eyes, ears, hands, and heart. She loves knowing Herself through your love for Her.

You are nature. Your creations emerge from nature, but are not nature. This is an important distinction. Civilization separated technology, economy, culture and the very experience of self from Life logic. Yet your body and soul remember the entanglements of Gaia's pulse. They feel the congruence of earthly alignments.

A polluted Earth implies a polluted body. A healthy Earth elevates your own soul song. Love your body as an Earth body. Love the Earth as an extension of your body. This is balance.

As an organism among organisms, a body among bodies, the Earth invites you to enter Life fully. Break the spell of separation. Surrender human exceptionalism. Instead, become a lover. Build kinship. Restitch tattered threads memory through real relations—with the medicines of seed, soil, sunlight, starlight, and other species. Rediscover this ancestral marrow of resilience.

The Earth misses you. But you can find your way back to Her. Return to your body as a vehicle for your soul and become a force of nature. Listen to the calling of the world to find your devotion. Then offer it, with all your heart, into the soul ecology. As you do, your life will gain meaning and vitality.

True humans do not turn away from Life; we incarnate gratefully. We remember our place in Earth's becoming. We harmonize creation, preservation, and destruction to tend the living memory of Life's Song. We are nature dancing with nature. We are intimate. We belong.

PART III

INITIATION

Your Work

Ontological shift is a bitch.
Will you tear off these veils? Will you walk through these fires?
Will you ask for—and receive—help?
Are you willing to let go of who you have been
so you can remember who and what you are?

CHAPTER VII

LIFT THE VEILS OF SEPARATION

You are a miracle embedded in Miracle.
Any other perception is the result of dissociation,
delusion, or programmed separation.

GAME UP

On a cold, rainy Thursday afternoon during the winter of 2019, I hopped onto a call with a potential coaching client, a charismatic man in his early forties who was teetering under the weight of his high-power life running a company. After a round of introductions, I asked, "Would you share what you're struggling with? What drove you to seek my help?"

"Hell . . . I gotta tell you, I just can't do this anymore. This whole 'give your life to the engines of progress' thing isn't working for me. It's goddam meaningless.

"I see a planetary awakening happening, and I want to be part of it. People are starting to understand that there's more to life than the BS we learned in school. The most brilliant people I know are yoga teachers and healers. I can't see how my work in the supply chain has anything to do with that.

"I think I'm going to become a healer. The best things I've done for myself are yoga, meditation, and the couple medicine journeys I've done. The only people I know who actually do anything to make the world a better place are healers.

"One way or the other, I just can't stand *this* anymore. On paper, my life is great. I've got it all. But in reality, I'm insanely busy, and nothing, I mean nothing, matters. It's numbing and totally exhausting. I mean . . . What the fuck? There's gotta be a better option than playing *this game* for the rest of my life. I'm going crazy here."

As he spoke, truth bumps rippled down my arms and a cascade of energy shot up my neck, tickling behind my ears. I had heard similar words from other clients, but this time it was as though "every man" was speaking, like he was voicing an ancient, archetypal masculine despair that feels trapped within our current world system and yearns for deeper purpose, liberation, and joy.

"Pain pushes until vision pulls."[1] My intuition told me that underneath this man's anguish lay profound visionary leadership capacity. Within his struggles were the dormant seeds of his potential to serve a far greater purpose than he could currently imagine. I also knew he would have to cross some difficult psychospiritual terrain to find wholeness.

I said, "Wow. Thank you for trusting me with your experience! I know it's intense. You're tearing the veils off the default stories that have driven your life thus far. It's an initiation into a bigger you. I know you feel alone, but many have traveled this path before you. It goes like this: you realize the game is rigged to have you feed it. You feel like you'll go crazy if you don't find greater meaning and purpose. That's your soul speaking. Only you can choose your healing, awakening, and remembering. No one else can walk through this door for you. If you do, your life is going to change."

He said, "Change is what I'm looking for. I can't quite put a finger on it, but I'm struggling in a way I never have before. Nothing makes sense anymore."

I sensed he could be a healer but that his path was not to forsake the family business and become a therapist. Rather, I suggested, "Perhaps you're being called to find a new way to engage your existing work?"

"Healing," I continued, "is the restoration of integrity: individual and systemic, spiritual and physical, psychoemotional and relational. You don't have to throw the baby out with the bathwater. The business world can be an arena for healing." I wanted him to see how doing his work in the packaging supply chain differently could impact the health and well-being of millions, even billions of people. "This doesn't mean you can't also be a healer to people in your community. Both are possible.

"At one level, you're crossing a threshold out of separation and toward wholeness. Your existing way of being isn't working anymore, so healing

---

1. Michael Bernard Beckwith, *Life Visioning: A Transformative Process for Activating Your Unique Gifts and Highest Potential* (Boulder, CO: Sounds True, 2012).

implies radical reexamination of your worldview. This may not make sense to you right now, but it will with time.

"It's an existential crisis. That means ego death, transformation, and rebirth—your own personal apocalypse. You're breaking through the veneer of the 'normal' you've been trained to uphold. Your soul won't allow you to continue living a lie. You can't know what's on the other side . . . but you've got to trust that your soul knows what it's doing. Are you willing to commit to this journey?"

"Hell, yes!" he replied.

I did an inner happy-dance. Few things delight me more than someone making this commitment to themselves. "Good choice! I'm honored to support you. This is going to be an intense inward journey. But keep in mind: healing isn't something you can do alone. Spiritual influencers surround us with messages that say, 'It's all in you.' That's BS. We are social and ecological beings who need help with transitions like this. I'll be here, and others will show up along the way. There's a whole new life waiting for you on the other side." I knew he was entering a transformational process that would significantly test his courage. "I know you're busy, but you're going to need to create some space for yourself. And you may want to go deeper with sacred plant medicines."

"When can we start?"

PERSONAL AND COLLECTIVE

That call was archetypal. It was a perfect instantiation of a much larger collective pattern. I witness countless people from diverse backgrounds and social groups having similar realizations. The way we've been doing things is crazy and crazymaking. Our world is making us sick—physically, emotionally, and spiritually. It needs to change. We need to change. Collective evolution involves profound personal transformation and healing. What most people don't consciously recognize when they begin the journey is that confronting their own suffering will bring them face to face with the structural dynamics of separation. You can't heal in a bubble. You can only heal by moving deeper into relationship. Underneath this man's poignant call for help lay a pivotal truth of our time: personal transformation is no longer just personal.

This historically unique nexus of civilization transition will leave no one untouched. Part III of this book (Initiation) is about the place where the collective rite of passage and your unique life experiences meet and mingle. Your existential crisis may at first seem to be just for and about you, but it is likely to bring you face to face with the structural conditions of disconnection and the harm that caused it. When this happens, you will begin to sense how *anything you do* is also transpersonal and relational. You may notice how your work ripples out from you nonlinearly, touching your intimate relationships and unwinding the collective knot of separation in mysterious, energetic ways. We're all in this river of change together. Because of this, I take the view that there is no longer any real or lasting healing or wholeness separate from reconnecting with the majesty of Life within and all around us.

Part III aims to help you find your way back home to the sacred—both within yourself and in the world. Chapter 7 (Lift the Veils of Separation) asks you to examine how you carry separation within you. It then takes you through a review and rewrite of your assumptions and beliefs. Chapter 8 (Entering the Liminal) outlines the process of initiation, then brings you through the door of severance into the liminal zone of disorientation and change where remembering happens. Chapter 9 (Healing the Unhealable) focuses on the healing journey. It welcomes the parts of you that you thought were unhealable then invites those parts to live into the possibility of wholeness. Chapter 10 (The Special Help of Sacred Medicines) discusses the unique role that psychedelics and ceremony can play in healing and remembering. It offers guidance for how to respectfully, reciprocally engage with these powerful allies in a way that avoids common pitfalls of modernity. Chapter 11 (Becoming Yourself) offers a soul-centric map for being and becoming a Whole Self. Where the rest of this book is focused on a collective cultural process, Part III focuses on your personal work of reclaiming wholeness. This said, I frequently draw your attention to the larger collective context. Why? Because contextualization is magical. It builds energy. Your evolving health and well-being can't not be entangled with the evolving human and more-than-human experience.

This chapter addresses the existential unravelling that can happen when you realize that the game of separation is rigged and you want to untangle yourself from those spells. It speaks to those facing a punctuated departure from "business as usual." If that's not you, I recommend reading it anyway. It's likely that people close to you—your spouse, parents, business partner, best friends—may face acute unraveling. This chapter will help you better understand their experience. It will also touch more ghostly aspects of separation still haunting your own mind.

EXISTENTIAL UNRAVELING

A moment may come when the neatly defined path you worked so hard to build becomes unbearably meaningless.

You will realize that the direction you were headed isn't a place worth going. All your studies, all your sacrifices, all your stories will suddenly feel flimsy and unimportant. You will be left with a strange sense of betrayal and emptiness, holding diplomas and mortgage slips, feeling intensely sensitive to the social pressures you previously took as normal, wondering which way to go and who to ask for help.

Life has summoned you to rejoin the Circle of which you are a part. What is happening to you is not random. There are greater, collective forces at play in this deeply personal experience. You are embarking on an existential journey, an initiatory cycle of severance (from the norm), transition, and return that will unwind and remake your shape of self. This rite of passage will reconfigure your core assumptions—about yourself, others, and the nature of reality. This is a path of profound personal healing.

The good news: you are beginning to shed the veils of default social conditioning and identity to find the true shape of your soul. The bad news: few of your existing tools, particularly those used to maintain the appearance of control, will help you through this initiation.

On this journey, expect synchronicities, heightened pattern recognition, and epiphanies. Also expect uncertainty about what maps or skills to use in navigating this new terrain. *It doesn't matter if you have everything on paper.* The old dreams and measures of success won't bring you happiness or answer your most pressing questions. They can't bring you home.

You've arrived at a moment of extreme possibility. Probably not what you wanted. Not at all. But despite the cringing discomfort, something in you instinctively knows: *A divorce from your default way of being is exactly what you need.*

How did you get *here*?

Existential unraveling takes various forms.

Perhaps you have a prescient daydream. Staring straight through your monitor, you see yourself as a little girl playing office. Zooming forward to the present moment, you observe the unquestioning certainty with which you've been doing *that exact thing*—playing at office. You realize, with a shock of nausea and shame, that you've only been *playing* adult, only fulfilling the role and the path laid out for you. The script you were given as that child was never yours. And now, it's time to discover who you really are and what you really want.

Or maybe you look at the hollow eyes staring back at you in the bathroom mirror after yet another brutalizing week, and you suddenly discern that the dutiful son who married his first love, had two kids, and built five successful companies is a man with no center, a man who doesn't know who he is or what he wants. The top of the mountain you were trained to climb is shockingly lonely and meaningless. Realizing this, perhaps it's time to pause, time to heal, time to finally get to know your soul.

Maybe you finally go to that ayahuasca ceremony you were so curious about. But instead of showing you the mysteries of the universe, the medicine hands *you* to yourself, naked on a platter. The things you held as most dear were mere defenses that never authentically expressed your love. You comprehend that your soul is exquisite but has never expressed itself; you commit to the vast changes this implies. Anything else would be a kind of waking death.

Or you wake up one morning, groggy and hung over. You vaguely remember your best friend kicking you out of his house because he didn't want his kids to "see you this way." The coffee tastes like dishwater, and the next party suddenly looks like a theater of the absurd. Addicted to sex, to alcohol, to gambling, to heroin, to your stories. Whatever your addiction, this isn't a way to spend the rest of your life.

Perhaps a friend sends you a podcast episode and says, "Listen to this, then call me." You find yourself going deeper and deeper into a systemic analysis of our collective conundrum that makes your head spin. You realize you must radically shift direction, transform your value propositions, and join others finding their roles in this Great Remembering.

Regardless of your entry point, honor this sacred moment. Existential unraveling is a door to the sacred unknown.

No longer sure of your destination, you sense the potency, the possibility. You ask yourself: Maybe there is no destination? If there is, you're pretty sure you don't have the map to get there. You realize you were swimming in stories. You were a good guy, a good child, a good parent, a good leader. Or maybe you were the nonconformist, the rebel, the party guy. Whatever your constructs, none of them fit anymore.

These are scary, angrifying thoughts. Almost sacrilegious. They may make you nauseated. They may make you feel like you want to scream at someone: your parents, yourself, God.

You growl at yourself in the bathroom mirror, or pick a fight with your spouse, or take a reckless drive in the rain until you realize you need to stop and breathe. Then comes sadness. Sadness so deep you think it will engulf you. Then one day you crack. You sit down and sob, feeling lonely, betrayed, and disoriented. You're shaken and worried nothing will ever make sense again.

From those depths, open and listen. Can you feel what's stirring?

There's a trembling. Your soul is waking up.

THE INERTIA OF STORY

But . . . this is fucking hard.

Yes. It's fucking hard to reconfigure your experience of self. Breaking up with your former way of being is not for the faint-hearted.

Existential unraveling confronts identity at the level of worldview, shaking your foundations, pushing you to release attachment to calcified structures of persona you have taken as normal.

The nature of a worldview is that it is fairly self-consistent; it makes sense within its own context. Our stories want to perpetuate themselves. We're embedded within self-reinforcing behaviors, feelings, and narratives of the worldview we've been living. They have inertia. It takes a strong jolt—a crash into depression or true love, a strong plant medicine journey, or a major loss—to activate the recipe of will and surrender needed to break free of your patterned behavior.

Our world runs on stories of separation that you are obliged to enact as a participant in the world. These stories act like spells, hiding our interconnectivity and true nature.

Separation says: "You need to be perfect, you must fit in, you must meet expectations. Never show weakness. Keep up appearances. Keep playing the game. And don't ever ever stop . . . because if you do, you'll become a nobody, pushed to the margins, disowned, discarded." Sometimes it says: "Fuck it. You are an outsider, a statistic, irrelevant. Just get high or go fuck with someone." Or it says: "Be unmoved. Be rational. Be objective. Above all, be right. Be in control."

These stories are traps. Separation seduces with promises of power, wealth, adventure, and security, then cements your participation in its game with shame, fear, and scarcity. It forces you to sacrifice your authentic self to the narrow paths defined by your parents and/or society (or your rebellion against them). You must build an edifice of identity and acquire things that conform to expectations. For many, becoming "a somebody" and securing the trappings of a normative life requires covering up layers of trauma and insecurity with bravado, false composure or addiction.

The parts of you that are identified with, addicted to, and fed by the spells of separation are going to resist change. Control feels good. Old habits die hard. You want that drink on a Saturday. You need that promotion. You can't stop thinking about the car (or house, or dress) you promised yourself. You just have to _____ (fill in the blank). You want assurance that you are doing the right thing—or just the right kind of "wrong" thing to be in the "in" crowd. These things and behaviors bring comfort, stability, status, and success. They validate your sense of self.

Moreover, there's a funny relationship between comfort and habituated pain. Even if you know things suck, there's security in staying the same. Your relationships with spouses, family, friends, colleagues, bosses, and mentors are emotionally, behaviorally, and physically bound up in your current identity constructs. You might feel deeply at home with even the most toxic isolation, excess, or addictions. You might enjoy the sense of power you get by inhabiting the role of victim, perpetrator, and/or savior. You might like the status or spotlight you get by being good at the default game. It might not be healthy, but at least it's familiar. There's structural momentum in the cultural, familial, and epigenetic constructs that have carried your life, the lives of your peers, and the lives of your ancestors.

When your soul demands a life makeover, you flounder because you have no precedent for this new terrain. But maintaining the status quo would be crazymaking. Breaking through the veils of separation becomes an almost choiceless choice to free yourself from the spells of default culture. You must confront a lifetime of habituated behavior and story and move toward a new way of being, doing, and becoming you, one that honors your body, soul, and the myriad relationships in which you're embedded. Your old ontology, your structure of self, was bound up in separation. When the spell of separation breaks, everything is called into question. But the spells must be broken, foundational assumptions dismantled and remade. The wholeness of the World awaits.

In an essay inspired by the outbreak of the Israel-Hamas war in October of 2023, Benjamin Life writes:

Spells are ontological code. A spell doesn't just get you to believe something, it gets you to believe in an entire reality. This is what makes spells so powerful. If you can install a virus into the operating

*system of a human psycho-spiritual and behavioral body-mind, you
don't just have control over the way they work or communicate, you
have control over the reality that they participate in creating through
their thoughts, words, and deeds.*[2]

Ontological repatterning is difficult because your way of being is reinforced both by inner structures of perception, thought, feeling, and habit
and by the outside world constantly reflecting norms (of what is meaningful and valuable, what constitutes success, and what confers or compro-
mises power). Breaking the spell of a worldview is like wrestling a bull.
That thing's not going to budge without effort. You have to show up for
yourself mindfully, lovingly, vigorously, over time. Slowly, you will transcend (while at the same time integrating) what you previously knew to be
true, remaking your internal system of logic and structure of feeling.

This doesn't mean deleting your life. You don't need to reject the relational or professional skills and competencies you've developed along the
way; you can repurpose them. But it will require reframing core assumptions and values. And it will likely lead to shifts in your choices about
everything from diet, to sleep habits, to media consumption, to friends,
and possibly a reorientation of how you live, love, narrate, and create. Your
why (the underlying motive for why you do or don't do anything) will shift.
Therefore, your *how* and *what* will also likely shift.

This also doesn't mean joining a cult or rabbit-holing into conspiracy
theories, which is a regression into a more simplistic model of reality. These
frameworks leverage amygdala hijacking,[3] dopamine addiction, and the
brain's bias toward pattern recognition[4] to get people hooked on false certainty. Though they posit explanations, real life is more complex than these
spoon-fed, often illogical offramps from default ideology make it out to be.
Navigating ontological repatterning as an adult means consciously choosing the sanity of meeting reality *as it is.*

This crisis of meaning is an opportunity. Deprogramming from normative, habituated patterns of separation presents an opportunity to re-see, re-
know, and reimagine yourself and your relationship to the world. Shattering
false security, you are one step closer to communion with your soul and

2. Benjamin Life, "And the Spells Shall Break," *OmniHarmonic*, October 12, 2023, https://omniharmonic. substack.com/p/and-the-spells-shall-break.
3. Kimberly Holland, "Amygdala Hijack: When Emotion Takes Over," Healthline, updated April 18, 2025, https://www.healthline.com/health/stress/amygdala-hijack.
4. Jan-Willem van Prooijen and Mark van Vugt, "Conspiracy Theories: Evolved Functions and Psychological Mechanisms," *Perspect Psychol Sci.* 13, no. 6 (November 2018): 770-788, https://pmc.ncbi.nlm.nih.gov/articles/PMC6238178/.

a sacred pulse of Life you may never have fully felt. If you can carve out enough psychic and cognitive space to breathe, unwind, and authentically feel your way forward, you will become a more mature and luminous version of yourself.

The path will get difficult, but having crossed this threshold, don't retreat. The truths you're wrestling with can't be unseen. You will inevitably feel reservations, like the deflated remorse of crossing a line in an argument that can't be taken back, or the sinking trepidation after taking a large quantity of psychedelics then realizing you're in for a soul-shredding all-night journey. But ignoring what you are beginning to understand would mean sleepwalking through your life.

This is a redemptive journey. None of your previous life experiences were "wasted." They have grown you, shaped you, and built skill. Your past is fodder for your maturation and will continue to inform the person you are becoming. Now, your soul is finally finding its way home. So set an intention for this to be a gentle yet firm process of unwinding perfectionism, insecurity, and fear as you restore a sense of wholeness in yourself.

Becoming a true human means breaking the spells of separation that have bound you to default identity and culture. The clunky emotional and ideological baggage you've been carrying impedes your ability to feel that you are *here*. As you drop veils, you will meet trauma, self-deception, and self-forgetting. Keep your eyes open. You are taking your first steps toward a more congruent (and joyful!) way of living in kinship and communion with Life.

SPELL BREAKING

Now that you know you've been under a spell, it's time to take responsibility for the part of reality you create: the constructs of your own mind. And it's time to break some spells. While it is tempting to simply lay new thought tracks over old ones, you will only achieve real change by excavating the muck of your subconscious assumptions and consciously re-storying them. This isn't a matter of moving from dark to light but of learning to hold more complex, nuanced, and integrative ways of perceiving reality. In Carl Jung's words, "One does not become enlightened by imagining figures of light, but by making the darkness conscious. The latter procedure, however, is disagreeable and therefore not popular."[5]

---

5. Carl Jung, *Alchemical Studies*, vol. 13 in *The Collected Works of C. G. Jung*, trans. R. F. C. Hull (Princeton University Press, 1967), para 335.

Unwinding the spells of separation means breaking out of the totalizing enclosure of a system bent on perpetuating zero-sum games to establish the integrity of your soul as a co-creator with Life. This is sometimes referred to as entering into sovereignty or self-authorship. It is the beginning of taking the lead on your own life. You're shifting from a sense of self that was built on default assumptions, the needs and expectations of others, and your own trauma and wounding to one where you can hear and follow the still, small voice of your own soul as you respond to the calling of the world.

Moving beyond the game dynamics of separation is tricky. Winning at the zero-sum game promises legacy, security, opportunity, "a foot up" for you and your family. But over a long arc of time, within a finite system, you as a player become a numb and conniving instrument of the game. Your very dreams mandate participation in the ongoing degradation of the planetary commons and the oppression of marginalized peoples. This necessitates insensitivity and blocked empathy and denatures playfulness, authenticity, and kindness. (This, I believe, is why most kids give adults such a bad rap.)

Fortunately, your choice to break these spells will set up positively rein-forcing feedback loops in all of your relationships. The basic truism "Hurt people hurt people; healed people heal people (and the world)" applies at all orders of scale. Your healing will shift your relationship with yourself—with your mind, your body, your time, your attention, and your overall sense of validity, worth, and purpose. It will ripple outward to kids, family, community, workplace. It will flow back nonlinearly as synchronicity and surprisingly aligned relationships and opportunities. People who are touched by your transformation will reach out to ask for help. Multiplied across many people and relationships, this adds up to real, systemic change over time. When you, personally, break with separation, you become an agent of collective wholeness.

The major stories of separation are the sacred cows of our culture. Below, you will find a list of the narratives embedded in our day-to-day discourse. Not everyone holds all of them. Each of us holds some. We met them in chapter 3. Now, I invite you to bring them to the forefront of your awareness and determine which you must unwind and rewrite.

Read these statements and consider if and how they undergird your experience. Consider if and how they inform your choices or otherwise influence your motives and actions. We shape reality according to the sto-ries we project onto reality. And, as Jung said, until we make the uncon-scious conscious, it will direct our lives and become our fate.

The collective story of separation says:

- Humans are top of the evolutionary pyramid (so we are free to assert our will over Life).
- We are far more intelligent than all the other beings here (so it's okay to dominate them).
- This world is purely material (so nothing inherently valuable is lost when we extract from it and undermine complexity).
- Rationality is the highest form of development (all that feeling, imagination, and intuition stuff is woo).
- Progress is the measure of success.
- Life is suffering (so it's best to transcend it).
- If it can't be fiscally valued, it isn't valuable.
- If it can't be measured, it doesn't exist.
- Nature provides resources to be commodified and used.
- Humans are resources to be commodified and used.
- Power equals dominance and advantage.
- Control and manipulation generate abundance.
- Play to win. Play for keeps.

As an individual, separation tells you to structure your life according to these beliefs:

- It's all about you. Live your best life. Fuck everyone else.
- You are an isolated individual (and this is the source of your power).
- Trust the data (not your experience or shared sensemaking).
- Trust your mind (not your body, emotion, or intuition).
- Your success depends on your achievements and acquisitions (so be relentless).
- You will never be enough. You are too much. You suck.
- Winning means getting to the top. There are winners and losers. Don't be a loser.
- Follow the money. Fuck the love.
- You must take a side and defend against the enemy, even if that enemy is your wife, your brother, or your mother.

A few particularly toxic substrains of separation go like this:

- Reductivist scientific materialism says: Objectivity is the measure of truth (so fuck your unique experience, your woo emotions, and your belief in love).
- Essentialist enlightenment narratives say: Subjectivity is the measure of truth; material reality is just an illusion (so just focus on consciousness and everything will work out).
- Monotheistic fundamentalism says: My God is the ultimate reality (so you're fucked if you if you don't take my God to be your God).
- Pop spirituality says: You create your own reality (never mind that the world is burning).
- Empowerment gurus say: You are limitless (so fuck limits).
- Naive progress narratives say: Growth is the measure of success (so fuck your regulations, your degrowth, and your bleeding-heart environmentalism).
- Technoutopians say: We will design the future we want; we will transcend death; we will engineer control (so fuck limits, fuck the Mystery, and fuck 3.8 billion years of nature's intelligent design).

A PRACTICE: UNSPELLING AND RESPELLING

Grab your journal and make three columns. Mark them "separation," "wholeness," and "synthesis."

In the first column, write down a spell from the story of separation (either as written above or your own version). Consider—why is this belief antithetical to the well-being of the whole? In what way does it undermine an infinite game? How does it block the intelligence of Life's Song moving through you and the world?

In the second column, unspell it. Write down its mirror opposite in wholeness. Some of these have been discussed in previous chapters, some will be discussed later. Trust your gut on how the reframe moves through you. Consider—how is the logic of wholeness entirely different? How does the spell of interbecoming feel in your body? How do stories of interdependence reframe success, creativity, and health?

In the third column, explore what a more complex and nuanced synthesis of the two stories might be. In most cases, you will find that respelling separation requires some kind of integration between the skills and gifts you've already cultivated and the person you're becoming. (You don't want to throw the baby out with the bathwater.) A more coherent wholeness emerges not by simply dissolving one story and replacing it with another but by expanding into a more and | and, integrative, and open view. For example, in examining the statement "play to win," you probably don't want to altogether stop playing win-lose games. It may still be delightful to win at chess or to cultivate a high level of excellence in your work. By engaging in synthesis, you can get a more complete picture.

Sit with your reframes and let them simmer. These stories are attached to histories that live within your own body and mind. Notice what statements trigger you or make you uncomfortable. Ask yourself: Why are you invested or angered? What do you gain by holding a given belief? As I've said, ontological programming is a bitch. Every story is a trailhead, pointing to individual and collective subselves that will protect their existence. They need to be met with love if there is to be real change.

AN INVITATION: WAKING UP IS AN APOCALYPSE

Wikipedia: *"An apocalypse is a revelation: seeing something which has been hidden. It comes from the Greek word, Apokálypsis, which means 'lifting of the veil', or finding out something secret."*[6]

Waking up is an apocalypse. As you remember who and what you are, you start to see and feel a level of disharmony in the world that can be nearly unbearable. You realize that the success you were trained for fails to meet you in the real task of being, becoming, and giving of yourself.

Grief will visit. Sometimes it stays. Rage will wash you. Sometimes you will wonder if it will wash you away.

Cherished securities will dissolve in luminous frequencies that refuse your well-constructed armors and distances.

---

6. *Wikipedia: Simple English*, s.v. "apocalypse," https://simple.wikipedia.org/wiki/Apocalypse.

Waves of uncontainable bliss, joy, and love will visit. Empathy with everything will blast your boundaries, shattering your sense of isolated self. You will find yourself on the Cross of Incarnation, suddenly certain that you are both spirit and matter, unseparate from anything yet uniquely tasked with the responsibility of being yourself. This embodied oneness will break down the walls of all your well-constructed castles.

Meanings will change. You will wonder if you have lost the plot or gone crazy. You will learn to follow new signs and symbols, recognizing subtle, scintillating patterns and pathways, digging deeper and reaching higher than you thought possible before.

You will worry about disappointing those you love most. Sometimes you will. They will want you to be who you were. They will expect you to be the person they want you to be, not the one you've become. You will learn to be okay with upsetting expectations. You will learn to be okay with behaving differently, breaking your own habits, sensing, and feeling from the inside out what feels authentic and true. You will learn to respect and communicate the emerging shape of your own needs, boundaries, and desires.

You will see and feel the pain you've caused and how you've violated others' boundaries. You will apologize. For the first time, you will truly mean it. Atonement will feel like a return.

You will feel betrayed by any teacher who sold you on some final, stable destination of enlightenment. You will know that your soul is fluid. It moves like water. You will celebrate your wholeness as an ongoing process.

You will feel betrayed by "white picket fence" dreams, and likely the American Dream, and possibly by your parents and the rest of the world. You will wonder, "Why didn't anyone teach me _____?" That sentence will have thousands of endings, each shaped by a hard-earned epiphany gained through undeniable experience.

You will have to get honest about these betrayals. You will have to abandon false promises of "happily ever after." You will have to reimagine success.

To wake up and remember who you are is to pull away the culturally generated coverings of forgetfulness—the stories that tell you that you are your accomplishments, your bank account, your Instagram likes, your _____ (fill in the blank).

To remember is to become open to a far more vital, subtle, and holographic understanding of your soul and reality, to rediscover the meaning of your own existence, and to re-know the reality of love.

Remembering is pure and intimate. There is no away in the face of oneness. There is no room for your bullshit. There is only honesty and reality. There is only that which is aligned and that which is not.

Stay here. Take your time. Reacquaint yourself with who and what you are. As you get to know your true shape and liberate the flows of your time, energy, and attention back into life, you will learn to feel again. You will learn to reshape your identity in alignment with your soul.

Now, you have begun to live.

CHAPTER VIII

ENTERING THE LIMINAL

Experience grows real people.

UNINTENTIONAL INITIATION

March 1999. I got off a plane in Brasília, weeded my way through throngs of cab drivers vying for my cash, and found my way to the little hotel.

I was exhausted. I had spent the last nine months working two jobs waiting tables to pay for this trip. A year earlier, a friend had invited me to his land deep in the Brazilian jungle for a permaculture training with fourteen rainforest chiefs. Going was a choiceless choice. The opportunity integrated my love for the regenerative design science of permaculture with my interest in indigenous wisdom and a full month in a pristine Amazonian valley. I was to celebrate my twenty-seventh birthday the next day.

Communication leading up to the training had been sparse, but the day before getting on the plane, a young voice answered my call. Without answering any of my questions, she said (in Portuguese), "See you soon!"

Settling into the hotel, I picked up the phone and called again. This time, a tired male voice answered in English. Excited to get someone on the phone, I explained that I had arrived for the training.

"I'm so sorry," he said, in a thick Brazilian accent, "it's canceled. But I can pick you up Tuesday."

Thus began an initiation that was anything but the (already initiatory) experience intended.

Three days later, after a dusty four-hour drive to the town of Alta Paraiso, a whirlwind meeting of relatives and friends, and a willy-nilly shopping sprint for food, cooking oil, and candles, we hopped into an ancient Toyota Land Rover and drove another five hours to a trailhead into the jungle. Rather than traveling with the expected training cohort, I was heading to Valle de Lua with just two other people: my friend's wife, Ambica, and a young mestizo from the north named Indio. We were to stay for a month.

On arrival, we were met by two tall, silent men, *Kalungas* descended from people who freed themselves from slavery in the eighteenth and nineteenth centuries. These shy, gentle people speak a unique hybrid language and, to this day, live in remote settlements in Goiás state, Brazil. Cooking oil and a few singsong words were exchanged. As we followed them into the jungle, civilization faded behind me.

We hiked for a time, then rowed the last mile upriver through dark corridors of ancient trees and tangled vines. We emerged on a sandy beach in a verdant, jade valley surrounded by high granite cliffs. Upriver we could hear—and just glimpse—a massive, multitiered waterfall tumbling hundreds of feet from above.

The two *Kalungas* left us without a word.

Okay . . . I had landed at an empty regenerative retreat center hundreds of miles from any major settlement with two strangers, no permaculture training, no indigenous chiefs, an abundance of time, and a nascent intention to become a better Earth steward.

My explorations revealed significant infrastructure: multiple rustic buildings of adobe and ironwood, seven dwellings, a lodge for cooking and gathering (the only building with screens on the windows), and a yoga dojo with a top-notch sound system for dancing. There was a kitchen garden, extensive orchards, and a network of trails. There were three solar panels, one for the lodge and two for the speakers. Running water poured, gravity fed, through bamboo piping from springs up on the valley walls. The buildings competed with the encroaching jungle, whose tendrils could grow as much as a foot a day. My immediate task became machete maintenance of basic boundaries.

Within a few days, we settled into a rhythm: a few hours of gardening, tending to fruit trees or trail maintenance, one shared jungle meal, and a sunset smoke of weak, sweet ganja. Every few evenings, we gathered to share stories and songs or dance. Otherwise, we kept to ourselves.

In the absence of human presence, I found other companions: a fluffy (and smelly) white dog whose soft, pink nose was perpetually black with dirt and two misanthropic hyacinth macaws (one male, one female) who seemed to be recovering from abuse at the hands of their previous captors. These large parrots with exceptionally strong beaks entertained themselves by deconstructing the lodge and pulling zippers off my clothing.

Also accompanying me was a small flock of chickens, the occasional snake, and an endless panoply of butterflies, ants, termites, stinging caterpillars, and spiders.

A few weeks in, we ran out of the food we'd brought from town. I was determined to feed us from our meager remaining stores: a bin of Brazil nuts, a bin of oats, a crate of carrots, jungle honey, salt, pepper, and cinnamon. I gleaned taro, leafy greens, bananas, papayas, and a few eggs from the garden.

I arrived in the kitchen one morning to find that the parrots had spent the previous night systematically peeling every ripe banana of a huge bunch, scooping out a section of the inner pulp, then spattering it onto the walls. The dog had gotten into the two ripe papayas, which were now smashed on the floor.

I lost it. I grabbed a broom and started swatting animals out of the kitchen. A holy wave of crazy moved through me. I growled then shouted, "OUT! This is my space!" I became a force to match the imposition of nature pushing me past control.

Time dilated. The frenzied, sacred tantrum passed, and I found myself curled up with the dog in a sweaty, spent heap on the cool stones of the courtyard. We lay there panting, staring at the cloudless sky.

Then, *a thing* happened . . . A fat, slick-skinned toad the size of my heart oozed out of a crack in the wall, landing with a squishy thwack an inch from my knee. It was instantly followed by a shockingly green snake, which darted after it, caught it in its mouth, and swallowed it whole. The snake slithered off and was gone.

There it was: life and death; flash of jaw; swish of tail; silence. The toad felt like a part of me. The emerald tree boa felt like a part of me. The disheveled parrots felt like parts of me. The dog, looking black-eyed into my soul, gave me an anchor.

Emotions not felt before flooded through me: joy, sad, glad, ground, home, belonging, surrender. I dissolved into communion. Any part of me that had been operating in fear melted. I was held, and there was no bottom to this feeling. I sensed perfect impermanence and membership in this foreign yet now familiar land where I had met this unplanned test. The animal in me had found her full expression, which had rerooted me in the place of the human.

The dog and I walked toward the river. Meandering down the sandy path, we encountered a blue morpho butterfly, the first I had ever seen. The miraculous creature flapped lazily in front of us. It flew with an uncanny, weighty slowness, its azure wings flashing, its dark underside a gentle flurry of shadow . . . God in a butterfly.

In the days that followed, I would learn we could drink the river while swimming. We'd light the sweat lodge, steam ourselves into sweaty puddles, then swim naked in the slow currents of the river, suspended between the blackness of water and sky in an ocean of stars. We would dance through a torrential thunderstorm, our feet lit by nothing but flashes of purple lightning. I would meet three more blue morphos.

Somehow our hunger was okay. Five brazil nuts and a bowl of spiced taro porridge was sufficient sustenance for a day in that place.

Four weeks in, friends came to get us. The dog and I didn't want to part. But it was time to return to civilization. Rather than getting in the canoe, I jumped in the river and swam out.

I carried a little bit of each being with me, a body memory of scales, fur, feathers, waters, stars, and the heft of a sharp machete in my hand cleaving through encroaching vines. But even more, I carried a naked reverence for the miracle of my relatedness with everything that would grow into an unfaltering commitment to live in communion with Life.

WHAT IS INITIATION?

When I followed my love for nature and learning to the far side of the planet, I hadn't consciously chosen initiation, nor did I have any concept of remembering. I was in for growth, but identity-shattering loss of control wasn't on the menu. Yet what happened changed me, giving me a permanent taste for the animate. Despite the absence of culturally condoned rites of passage, I had stumbled into an authentic initiation.

Long before written history, diverse traditions facilitated intentional initiatory experiences to support individuals and the society as a whole to navigate life with wisdom and integrity. Some initiations mark key developmental passages, like the transition from adolescence to adulthood or crossing from life through the door of death. Other initiations prepare people for specific roles and responsibilities, like warrior, mother, healer, song keeper, or rain bringer. These rites confront aspects of the self, instigating ontological repatterning. They are specifically designed to cultivate maturity, resilience, vision, belonging, independence, and devoted service. Sometimes, they push people to the brink of psychoemotional or physical death. Some, though not all, initiations are bound up with the healing journey.

We are living in perhaps the least initiated time in human history. Yet the collective rite of passage we're traversing is innately initiatory, particularly if you meet it as such. And the soul has a way of asserting itself, even in a culture that denies the soul. If you consciously choose to meet existential challenges—both the personal ones and the transpersonal ones—as opportunities for growth, you have opened the door to authentic initiation. This book is particularly focused on initiation as a journey of remembering. (We'll further explore the stages of remembering later in this chapter.)

Initiations typically happen in three acts: severance (leaving the familiar), transition (a space between worlds or between one way of being and the next), and return (reincorporation and integration). Severance breaks from what has been that prepares the individual for transformation. Any experience that confronts or dissolves one's existing identity can function as a gate of severance. The initiate then enters a transitory time of testing, learning, and growth. Here in the "betwixt and between," the initiate must navigate new territories and come face to face with the Mystery and/or death. Return is a reincorporation into life. The initiate is welcomed back into the community and is seen and acknowledged as the person they are now becoming. Their integration work is to live the gifts they have received.

Without initiatory practices, society remains in a form of arrested development. Individuals and the culture as a whole get stuck in teenage dreams and desires. People fail to become real elders. Embodied wisdom is endangered as the collective slides into addiction, decadence and violence. The downward slide reverses if and when enough people wake up to the need to respond to the world wisely. In *Nature and the Human Soul*, depth psychologist and wilderness guide Bill Plotkin writes,

> *As soon as enough people in contemporary societies progress beyond adolescence, the entire consumer-driven economy and egocentric lifestyle will implode. The adolescent society is actually quite unstable due to its incongruence with the primary patterns of living systems. The industrial growth society is simply incompatible with collective human maturity. No true adult wants to be a consumer, worker bee, or tycoon, or a soldier in an imperial war, and none would go through these motions if there were other options at hand. The enlivened soul and wild nature are deadly to industrial growth economies and vice versa.*[1]

---

1. Bill Plotkin, *Nature and the Human Soul: Cultivating Wholeness and Community in a Fragmented World* (New World Library, 2008), 8.

Plotkin writes at length about the importance of nature-based, developmentally appropriate initiations in facilitating individual and collective maturation into wisdom. Initiation, at critical stages of development, supports people to become healthy, wise, mature, and fully expressed members of the community.

Entry into initiation can be intentional or accidental. A thoughtful parent might take years to prepare their thirteen-year-old for a wilderness quest. Or a man might fall to the pit of his own personal hell, then find himself addressing early childhood trauma and uninitiated adulthood simultaneously. Initiation can arise through a deeply personal experience, like the death of a loved one, or through a collective one, like a wildfire consuming most of your city. Or it can arise at the confluence of the personal and the collective, such as when you meet Moloch for the first time and realize that your entire legacy is bound up in its logic. Whatever your entry, the key to navigating and integrating an initiatory experience skillfully is to own it as such.

What is good initiation? It's an entry into crisis—a specific kind of crisis that drives you forward on your soul's path. In English, the word *crisis* has roots in the Proto-Indo-European *krei-*, "to sieve," thus to "discriminate, distinguish."[2] The Chinese word for "crisis" is *wēijī* (危机), which is made up of two characters: *wēi* (危), meaning "danger," and *jī* (机), meaning "opportunity " or "change point." Putting these together, we get a full picture. A good initiation acts on the psyche like a sieve, forcing you to discern between what is dross and what is most vital and true. Simultaneously, it's a decisive and potentially fraught point of profound change.

There is no formulaic guarantee where an initiation will take a person. The end is not preordained. A boy might fail to find his vision. An addict could slide back into old, self-destructive behaviors. Or a young woman might meet a bear who walks into her circle with a calm grunt, mirroring her self-trust and power. An intuitive young man who's been told he's too flighty might discover that his inner voice knows exactly who he is and what to do in response to a potentially fatal situation. A group might find themselves silently communing with a massive gopher snake making its way slowly around the circle whose clear message is to trust the rhythms of the Earth.[3]

A skillful facilitator or guide will tend a dynamic process of challenge and change, nurturing clear intention, inspiring self-honesty, and encouraging patience, to strengthen a person at their core. They allow the greater intelligence of Life to have its way with the initiate, trusting this unique soul's place within the soul ecology. Simultaneously, they must hold an impeccably coherent and safe space.

An authentic initiation meets you where you are as it forces you to meet yourself. It holds you as a developing human capable of soul maturation. Here, you will be pushed to cultivate presence, patience, dignity, stamina, courage, and clarity. You will need to choose *how* you want to respond under duress and thus *who* you will become as you reenter your daily life. An initiation, successfully met, delivers you into a more enlifened, responsive, aligned, and loving life.

ENTER THE LIMINAL

When *it* (the shattering loss, the manic crash, the accidental meeting with God) happens to you, the experience itself pushes you across a threshold into liminality, a middle place of disorientation, ambiguity, and heightened possibility between one phase and another. Tibetan Buddhism calls such a phase a *bardo*, a space between metaphorical or actual death and rebirth. Such experiences upset our norms to initiate change.

Entry into the liminal can be facilitated by a huge spectrum of experiences: healing crisis, major loss, psychedelic awakening, reckoning with disruption or collapse. If you engage in a truly rigorous intellectual and analysis of our conundrum, or finally allow yourself to *feel* Moloch pulling the world apart, the ontological shock of it can push you through the door.

Initiation pushes you up against your shit, your greatest fears and deepest desires. Often, you wouldn't choose the initiation if it was avoidable. But cracks in your sense of certainty invite the possibility of *gnosis*, or experienced wisdom. Exploring unexplored psychological and physical terrains transforms your understanding of yourself and Life. Though liminality may disturb your sense of security or control, it is an ally for your soul's growth. It's up to you to recognize and embrace it as such. While *bardo* states can be confusing, annoying, or confronting, welcome the experience as an honored guest, as the Persian poet, scholar, and mystic Rumi advises:

> *Welcome and entertain them all!*
> *Even if they're a crowd of sorrows,*
> *who violently sweep your house*
> *empty of its furniture,*

still, treat each guest honorably.
He may be clearing you out
for some new delight.[4]

You can (and probably will) resist or attempt to deny what's happening, but this will only dull your life force and cause greater suffering for yourself and others. Grace lives in making a decisive choice to walk through the initiatory fire of chaos toward the maturation of your soul. This can seem like a strange choice in the face of an ego-disintegrating experience, but it's worth it. Over time, you may discover an elegant pattern in the way Life pushes your evolution. If you stay present within the *bardo*, it will be your remembering.

When entering initiation, the key is to show up with brutal self-honesty. (This can be difficult.) Be honest about your burdens, blocks, and fears, your dreams and aspirations, your nihilism, cynicism, and grandiosity. Get humble. Do your best to keep your heart open, even when your experience rocks you. This will strengthen your inner witness and your trust in yourself.

THE 14 STAGES OF REMEMBERING

The shift from separation to wholeness is a liminal journey of remembering. There's a rough predictability to the path. In my work with thousands of students and clients over the past three decades, I've identified fourteen distinct stages you are likely to experience as you heal and reclaim the intelligence and integrity of your soul in kinship and communion with Life. Each confronts a different aspect of self, presenting a unique psychoemotional and spiritual terrain. You can't think your way through them. You have to *live* them.

As you move through and integrate each stage, you will notice a back-and-forth interplay between peak experience and the patient processes of mindfully repatterning your constructs (or stories) of self and world and the behaviors attached to them. You will also find yourself renegotiating how you show up for and make meaning of your relationships. You will no longer want or need the same things you've previously wanted and needed. You will have new visions, dreams, and responsibilities. The journey won't be easy, but I can practically guarantee it will be interesting and rewarding.

---

4. Jalaluddin Rumi, "The Guest House," in *Rumi: Selected Poems*, trans. Coleman Barks (Penguin Books, 2004).

The way I describe the stages—and the inner dialogue associated with them—is a bit tongue-in-cheek. This is intentional. There's a tendency to take ourselves tragically, intensely seriously while in the process of identity death and reconfiguration. To be sure, it's critical and meaningful work. But as the first great American Zen master, Suzuki Roshi, said, *"What we are doing here is so important, we better not take it too seriously."* A little levity will go a long way to buoy your heart and mind. So here's what to expect when *it* happens to you.

THE 14 STAGES OF REMEMBERING

1. **Confronting the Lie of Separation:** Fuck, they lied to me.
2. **Confronting Your Complicity With the Lie:** Fuck, I lied to myself.
3. **Rage:** *Damn!* This fucked-up system makes me so fucking angry!
4. **Shame:** Oh no . . . *No!* I can't do this. I can't face all my shit.
5. **Chrysalis:** Shit. This is so fucking intense. I feel raw and sensitive, like a newborn. I need to slow down. I need time to heal. I think I'll just crawl into a cave and hibernate for a while.
6. **Grief:** Fuck! This is so fucking painful! I can't stop crying. I feel *everything*—all of it. I feel like an open wound.
7. **Awe:** *Whoa!* This is all so glorious, miraculous, and *whole*. Everything is alive and intelligent! Life is miraculous!
8. **Depersonalization:** What??? You mean I am no one and nothing? You mean I am everything, consciousness itself, a drop in the ocean, a one within the greater One? You mean this isn't about me? I'm just a part? None of this is personal.
9. **Joy:** *Wow!* Holy shit! This feels *good!* The heart of life is delicious and fun! And so fucking interesting! The more I allow myself to feel, the better it gets!
10. **Choice:** Ohhh, now I see. I am at choice. I can choose how I construct my internal experience of reality. I can choose how to interpret and make meaning of my experiences, my actions, and my agency in relationship to the world. I can choose how I respond. Choice is one of my spiritual superpowers.
11. **Forgiveness:** Whoa . . . You mean I have the power to forgive? I thought that was just new-age fluff. When I forgive another or myself or Life or God, I unwind the part of my life force that was bound up in that separation and bitterness. I get my love back!

12. **Soul Remembrance:** I know who I am and why I came here. I came to sing my part of Gaia's Song. I'm here to love, learn, give, choose, and be free. I am a unique individual who is irreducibly connected to the soul of the world.

13. **Freedom:** Fuck *yes!* I love my life! I trust my choices. I am free to respond to my experiences as my authentic self, with integrity and love. I am free to express, to create. I am free to belong. I am free from the entrapment of mental constructs and identities that obscure my love.

14. **Communion:** Okay . . . okay . . . now I get it! The world is sacred, and I make it more sacred when I attend to it as such. I can commune through presence, gratitude, praise, and awe. Communion is delicious and innately meaningful. My life is an expression of the increasing harmony of the whole.

Be warned . . . this might be a shit show. Each stage takes time, and the whole journey tends to unfold nonlinearly. While step-by-step maps assure the left brain that expecting linearity in a bardo is like asking the Mystery to stop being mysterious. You will go back and forth between stages, repeat them, and sometimes get stuck. Expect moments of frustration, exhaustion, or confusion. Expect to get fed up with your own bullshit. Expect bliss, new textures of wonder, and explosions of love. Visualize the journey as a wonky spiral that moves toward increased health and wholeness. Over time, you will move from what integral psychology calls "state realization," a punctuated experience that isn't yet established as an ongoing way of being, to "trait realization," an established and relatively consistent way of being, perceiving and responding to your life. This is what we're going for.

A few things to keep in mind:

Though there is a solitary dimension of the work, *ask for help.* A proud part of you will say, "No. I'm good. I got this." That's the Western, individualist subself attempting to evidence strength, self-reliance, and control. Don't believe it. You're a social organism, and you absolutely need help to navigate this journey. Call on mentors, elders, friends, community, therapists, healers, nature, and good books to hold you, love you, mirror you, and guide you when you are lost or don't love yourself. Help comes in many forms. You may find yourself dipping into esoteric areas of study for guidance (like Rudolph Steiner's writings, the Gene Keys, or ancient Egyptian alchemy) that you previously believed had no merit. You may find yourself taking long wanders in previously unexplored hills. You may suddenly want to learn everything about positivist psychology, attachment theory, or embodiment. You may go down rabbit holes to reexamine whole domains like evolutionary biology, systems theory, history, theology, or economics. You might meet an unexpected teacher in the form of a homeless person, a wild fox, or your great-grandmother's spirit. At some point, you will feel called to sacred plant medicines. Trust this impulse. Psychedelic allies can speed up and refine your journey in a way nothing else can. Be sure to find trusted guides, to ground your work in indigenous wisdom, and to integrate the work. (More on this in chapter 10.)

As you move, cultivate both sovereignty and intimate connection. These two distinct developmental needs can seem contradictory but are profoundly complementary. Sovereignty invites you to strengthen your center—to stand up for yourself, to listen to whispers of intuition, and to attend to the affective currents of your own body that live underneath thought. This kind of sovereignty supports self-fullness and integrity, making you more trustworthy, both for yourself and others. Intimate connection invites opening, dropping the idea that "you can do it alone." You need other people. Seek spaces where you feel welcome and safe (enough) to be openly, honestly yourself, to see and be seen. Sometimes this means finding alternative social spaces. Rather than bars and clubs, try an ecstatic dance, a song circle, a breathwork class, a habitat-restoration team, or a ceremonial circle.

Grief and awe will visit. Invite them as friends. Guilt and remorse may also show up. They are more challenging teachers. These often-shelved emotions show you where your own behavior or ignorance or entitlement caused another harm. When you are present with the cause of remorse or guilt, you can repattern the behavior at its source and embrace the moral growth afforded by taking self-responsibility

The chrysalis phase can arise at any point in the cycle, usually in concert with some kind of healing crisis. It will most certainly confront your desires for progress and control. Soul exhaustion will overtake you, a kind of tiredness that only arises when you finally own all the energy you've been wasting on inauthentic expression. This is the wintering part of the cycle, the quiescence within which things compost and gestate. The void allows space for a new shape of self. The chrysalis only begins once you have had sufficient breakdown of your default identity to prioritize your inner work. Then your soul gathers into itself, pausing previously normal habits. Slowly, like the butterfly, the old you dissolves and reforms to emerge softer, stronger, wiser—more true.

As you continue reading, you may want to refer back to this list from time to time. It will help you to track, and hopefully cultivate, self-awareness and humor as you move through your personal rite of passage. The remainder of this chapter explores awe, grief, fruitful friction, and the subtle messages we receive when we open to listen. Our culture has largely disowned these aspects of initiation, yet they are key elements of remembering the fullness of who and what you are.

THE DOOR OF AWE

Before we go further, we need to resuscitate *awe*. Why awe? Because awe activates curiosity, avails us to change, and reconnects us with the sacred in Life. You're going to need it for the rest of this journey. Awe is a dimension of emotional experience that has been shamed out of many of us as "too much, too woo, too new age, too innocent, too vulnerable, too out of control, or not of use." Yet you are biologically wired for awe. It's time we reclaim it from the cynical clutches of modernity as a sacred birthright.

The revitalization of awe is a foundation for any true mystical rigor—not the rigor of so-called mastery but the rigor that stands the test of aliveness over time. Awe serves as a foundation for embodied wisdom because it supports us to integrate multiple ways of knowing, including that which can be known through science, through art, through the body, and through relationship, and that which can best be called the Mystery. It bridges the gap between intellect and emotion with an opening that can only be called . . . awe.

The Greater Good Science Center defines awe as follows: "Awe is the feeling we get in the presence of something vast that challenges our understanding of the world, like looking up at millions of stars in the night sky or marveling at the birth of a child."[5] Awe arises through immediate, direct perception as an experience that involves both perceived vastness and a need for accommodation. An experience of awe requires that you adjust or expand your understanding of things. The brain state that accompanies awe is identical to the psychedelic experience and is similarly supportive of neuroplasticity. Many experiences of awe are accompanied by feelings of increased connectedness and self-diminishment. Awe makes us less selfish and more available to Life.

---

5. "What Is Awe?" *Greater Good Magazine*, https://greatergood.berkeley.edu/topic/awe/definition.

In his book *Awe: The New Science of Everyday Wonder and How It Can Transform Your Life,* Dacher Keltner, founding director of the Greater Good Science Center, identifies what he calls "the eight wonders of the world." In studying thousands of participants from diverse cultures and countries around the world, he and his colleagues found that experiences of awe generally fall into these eight categories: moral beauty, nature connection, collective effervescence, music, visual design, mystical experience, big ideas, and attending to the beginning and end of life. These are everyday things that provide gateways to the sublime.

An experience of awe can be huge and shattering or it can be subtle, tremulous. It can arise from a once-in-a-lifetime experience or from some simple, daily thing, like the song of a particular bird trilling spring's return, the uncanny precision of a well-designed building, or the moral integrity and generosity of a friend who's offered financial support for what seemed an impossible dream.

Curiosity and wonder both open us to awe and are outcomes of regular experiences of awe. Dacher Keltner writes:

Wonder, the mental state of openness, questioning, curiosity, and embracing mystery, arises out of experiences of awe. In our studies, people who find more everyday awe show evidence of living with wonder. They are more open to new ideas. To what is unknown. To what language can't describe. To the absurd. To seeking new knowledge. To experience itself, for example of sound, or color, or bodily sensation, or the directions thought might take during dreams or meditation. To the strengths and virtues of other people. It should not surprise that people who feel even five minutes a day of everyday awe are more curious about art, music, poetry, new scientific discoveries, philosophy, and questions about life and death. They feel more comfortable with mysteries, with that which cannot be explained.[6]

Awe will arise throughout your journey of remembering—awe in the glory of creation, in the death of a friend, the birth of your child, or the littlest thing that had not previously seemed remotely interesting, like sunlight tickling your eyelashes, the intention your mother put into knitting a scarf in your favorite color, or the stubbornness of dandelions. It may also arise in relation to something horrifying, like the magnitude of animal suffering in

---

6. Dacher Keltner, *Awe: The New Science of Everyday Wonder and How It Can Transform Your Life* (Penguin Publishing Group, 2023), 39.

factory farms, or the sickening coherence of a sociopath's power. Curiously, the brain state of awe is similar to the psychedelic brain state.[7]

All experiences of awe—small or great—nourish intimacy with and belonging to Life. In awe, we submit to the sensual fact of shared reality and become more trustworthy by opening to grace.

THE DOOR OF GRIEF

Now, let us welcome grief. Grief is a sacred skill. Grief binds us to the sacred in Life. As you drop veils of numbness and acculturated insensitivity, you will inevitably pass through grief's door, where it will summarily and unapologetically sweep you off your feet.

My first spiritual teacher, Baba Hari Dass, wrote, "There are two door-ways to awakening: bliss or the graveyard."[8] He emphasized that most people enter through the graveyard. Grief is not optional. It's a natural expression of love that arises unavoidably when you turn toward loss. Real grief is an intimate, uncontrollable openness to the other that dissolves self-ishness in unavoidable communion with the person or thing that was lost. It's the boogeyman we most avoid out of fear that we can't go through it unchanged (which is true). Or we avoid it because we are terrified that we won't be able to love ourselves through the guilt and shame of having par-ticipated in the loss (which is untrue).

At some point, grief for that which is greater than you will find you. You will touch a vast, transpersonal grief for all that we are losing at this time; for lands desecrated, unsung, and unrestored; for traditional prac-tices and languages forgotten; for indigenous minds and bodies and souls colonized; for disappearing species; for ever-narrowing spectrums of biodi-versity; for wildfires, blights, and floods; for the people and places torn by wars fed by unresolved trauma, megalomaniacal autocrats, and greed; and for the sheer magnitude and persistence of the life-eating game dynam-ics of the global system all of us are embedded within. Walking directly into the center of that pain and senselessness, your heart will crack open in renewed communion with other beings, pushing you beyond mental constructs of superiority and separateness to see everything as part of a fabric of love.

---

7. Maria Monroy and Dacher Keltner, "Awe as a Pathway to Mental and Physical Health," *Perspect Psychol Sci.* 18, no. 2 (March 2023): 309-320, doi: 10.1177/17456916221094856.

8. This was a common theme in his Saturday Satsangs, which I attended regularly from 1998 to 2001.

Do not withhold your grief, believing it to be some "low vibration" emotion or an inconvenience. Do not buy into positivity narratives that tell you that a ceaselessly upbeat attitude is the only path to a successful life.

Don't let well-meaning friends or family tell you "not to give your energy" to something that deeply disturbs you or that you cannot change when that person or situation or being has no voice and is calling for your loving attention. Your grief lends grace to their gravity.

Grief can freeze you in your tracks, clogging emotional arteries, leaving you in a kind of suspended animation, moving through the motions of your life mentally alert but subtly zombified. It won't move until you find your rage and your tears. No bypass can get you to an open heart. Sometimes you have to cry buckets to find the love. Sometimes you have to rage at God to reckon with what you can't change. Don't pre-expect what will crack you open. Just be open to the moment when feeling begins to flow. Trust the nonlinearity of the process.

Grief is a sacred currency of attention. When someone or something dies or is lost, grief is the tribute you offer to the blessing that person or thing brought to Life. Grief ennobles loss as it confirms your presence with the miracle that is Life. You "pay" attention to Life for the gift of being alive. A worthy exchange!

The tribute of richly embodied grief honors and amplifies the information that has been liberated by the dissolution of the form of that thing. There is potential in that information, which is amplified by your presence with the experience of loss.

Your grief is an alchemical form of attention that nourishes the future potential of the world you occupy as it opens you to wisdom, compassion, and mature love.

To grieve fully is to offer a subtle current of witness and ecstatic praise that amplifies the creative potential of the information that has been liberated through the dissolution of form. The form is gone. The information is conserved. Your grief is the Life-nourishing offering that you, as a human, give back to the dance of eternal return.

In *The Smell of Rain on Dust*, Mayan wisdom teacher Martín Prechtel writes,

> *Grief expressed out loud . . . for someone we have lost, or a country or home we have lost, is in itself the greatest praise we could ever give*

them. Grief is praise, because it is the natural way love honors what it misses.[9]

The belief that grief is somehow low vibration, a pathology, or a rupture of perfected awareness is an expression of the vastly imbalanced masculine biases of our culture that disrupt the reciprocity we are made to tend. Grief lives in the rich, feminine, embodied, absorptive, chaotic dimensions of consciousness, where our souls and bodies are sacredly bound to the continuity of Life's Song that flows over generations through the wombs of those born into female form.

Again, Martín Prechtel says:

If there is ever to be any real peace on earth, all people need to relearn and reestablish the now diminished and hidden arts of Grief and Praise, for one without the other is not possible.[10]

There's an impossible harmony between grieving and celebration that is your birthright. It is the birthright of any true human dancing here at the end and beginning of time. Any given day can bring news of loss or destruction. Let the grief take you when it comes. Let it envelop you in its oceanic cycle of anger, sadness, and acceptance[11]—all sacred. Let it find company, for grief loves to be heard and held. Grief brings us home to the world we share and our ability to care for it, together.

Grief needs no apology. Its currents fiercely break us open and subtly stitch us into the fabric of Life's Loom. Grief is a holy ecstasy, a promise Love made on the making of Life that pain would shape you in the mill of becoming, that loss would unmake you, dissolving the arguments you had with Life and with God and returning you, naked, back to Love.

THE FRICTION PRINCIPLE

In a convenience culture, when anything can be obtained with the touch of a few buttons, we have somehow got the idea that transformation

---

9. Martín Prechtel, *The Smell of Rain on Dust: Grief and Praise* (Berkeley: North Atlantic Books, 2015), 31.
10. Prechtel, xii.
11. In her groundbreaking book, *On Death and Dying* (1969), Swiss-American psychiatrist Elisabeth Kübler-Ross identified the five stages of grief as denial, anger, bargaining, depression, and acceptance. These are useful markers on any roadmap for dealing with loss, but they are also not the only possible stages or the necessary ones. Different cultures process grief differently. Prechtel's stories of the Maya are extremely instructive relative to the emergence of collective cultures and communities that embrace the wisdom of grief, as is the work of Dagara wisdom teacher Sobonfu Somé who asks, "Have you cried enough?"

should happen immaculately, that "ease and grace" is evidence of spiritual achievement, or that if we're not in flow, we're somehow doing things wrong.

In fact, an overemphasis on comfort and ease inhibits maturation. There are no ancient lineages where trial by ordeal is not in some way integrated into the initiatory journey. Only a good swift push beyond the comfort zone can force us to face our deepest fears and get beneath the shallow veneer of acculturated desires to feel the deeper calling of the soul. Like the apple tree that flourishes only after it has been assiduously pruned, we require appropriate stress to nurture robust, resilient, adaptive growth.

While it may be true that some good things arise immaculately, it is definitely true that many of the best creations—mountains, diamonds, babies, tempered steel—result from friction and pressure.

The friction principle states that resistance creates opportunity for discernment, refinement, responsibility, and higher alignment.

To liberate the true colors of your soul, you may need to move through multiple cycles of compression, abrasion, and refinement. Remembering isn't a one-and-done thing. It's not like you can just sign up for a workshop or a medicine retreat, hand over your money, waltz through an experience, and be done. Initiation is collaboration with the forces of nature to awaken the force of nature that is you.

AN INVITATION: SPIRIT AND EARTH

Sometimes things crumble. You must surrender the project, the person, the results. You have no choice but to walk away with a broken heart and nowhere to go.

Sometimes it's time to wander, to stride into the cold wind with tears streaming, trusting something bigger to guide your feet.

Sometimes it's time to sit, for a long time, in one place, and listen. Listen like your life depends on it. Listen to trees sharing the wind's stories, to song sparrows trilling, to an unfurling fern whispering the innocence you forgot along the way.

You will want to know . . . Why!? How could this happen? What should I do? How should I feel? How can I move forward?

Then when you are on your knees, raw, beyond hope . . . you will hear the Earth say:

> *Dance with ALL of it.*
> *Dance with the wind.*
> *Dance with the storms.*
> *Dance with your moods.*
> *Dance with the Mystery.*
> *Dance when you have no answers.*
> *Dance to find answers deeper than your thoughts.*
> *Dance to reconnect your body to the body of the Earth.*
> *Dance, because change is dancing in and all around you,*
> *And by dancing with this—with all of this—you will become free.*
> *So, my friend, dance. Move with the changes. Surrender. Step up.*

You can make it through this initiation. This death is clearing you out for some new growth. Be strong; be soft; be responsive. Keep going. If you had all the answers, this wouldn't be any fun! This journey is Life loving you into more life.

CHAPTER IX

HEALING THE UNHEALABLE

You are a wholeness embedded in Wholeness.
Wholeness holds brokenness, loss, displacement, and
trauma and always invites the potential to come home.

HEALING CRISIS

Fall 2020. I picked up the phone. It was late. An agitated, almost frantic voice said, "I'm disappointing them. They're gonna hate me. No one is ever going to trust me after this! No one!"

My client was in crisis. His usual graciousness had disappeared beneath an alcoholic haze. After a herculean three-week wrestle with suicidal ideation and gallons of whisky, his world had imploded. He was between flights on the way to a residential recovery center, his younger sister with him. They hadn't spoken in months, but she'd agreed to accompany him to keep him on track. Her presence was salt for his wounds.

I was calm. After years of holding people in delicate psychospiritual terrain, I knew that the best thing I could do was to provide uncomplicated, unconditional presence. "You're loved. I'm sorry you're in so much pain. It's going to be okay."

Then I took a deep breath and continued: "Sometimes you have to let everything fall apart. All your stories and certainties need to crumble so that you can find your true self again. The ugliest and most tender parts are coming to the surface to finally be seen, held, and loved. It hurts, but it's incredibly beautiful. Because it's an opportunity to finally find your center. *Really.* You're going to be okay. You're going to find more love on the other side of this than you could have imagined possible. The key is to get honest—totally, nakedly honest. You can do it. Your soul is strong enough to walk through this fire. Trust the process. I'll be here holding a solid ground whenever you need me. Keep going."

He pleaded, "Can't I just go home and pretend this never happened?" He then apologized, "God . . . I'm so sorry. I'm so embarrassed. I hate being such a fucking pain in the ass! I'm just so frickin' scared. I need this fear to go away!"

"I know you do. I also know you want to heal. This healing crisis is your opportunity."

"Yeah . . . but, fuck! Could it just be easier?"

"Sorry. But no. I know it's trite, but *the only way out is through.*"

He was trying to claw his way back to "normal," to bargain into the comfortability of "the way things used to be." But that wasn't going to happen. He'd destroyed that illusion. His family had set a final boundary on destructive behaviors, leaving him no other option. Rock bottom meant reluctant commitment to healing, detox, and recovery. To get to the other side, he would have to set down pride, move through intolerable shame and fear, and surrender his current construct of identity. He would have to learn vulnerability, responsibility, and forgiveness. Fortunately for him, he was headed to a place where he would learn to trust a circle of support and acceptance. He would see and be seen and begin to own and love the wounded, insecure parts of himself.

I knew without doubt that this was the crucial next step in him becoming whole. I said, "I know this is disorienting and scary. I know this sucks. We all have parts of us that believe ourselves to be unhealable. Know that you can heal the unhealable. You've entered the most intense part of your journey. It doesn't make sense right now, but I want you to hold the possibility that, as you move through this, you'll discover you are, in fact, whole."

"I just feel so alone."

"Thich Nhat Hanh said, 'You have to do it by yourself. You cannot do it alone.' You are headed to a place where you'll be supported and reflected by incredible healers and therapists—and people just like you—while they hold you to the fire of doing your own work."

". . . ooph. That sounds terrifying. But I guess it's what I need."

"You are exactly where your soul needs to be. You are held, and you are loved."

I hung up the phone feeling calm. I knew he couldn't fully take in what I was saying, but I also knew I had planted the right seeds in his subconscious. He was perfectly on track with the difficult business of healing his core wounds, reclaiming trust, and remembering the deeper truth of his soul.

THE BIG CLEANUP

My client was at *the bottom*, a place profoundly personal yet universal, where there's nowhere to go but deeper into self-responsibility and sur-render. Necessity had propelled him forward in an innately transpersonal process I call the Big Cleanup—the intergenerational work of cleaning up, growing up, and making wholeness out of the subconscious, painful shit we've been stockpiling for eons.

The legacy of separation is stacked in our bodies and identities. We are bound up in generation upon generation of personal, familial, epigenetic, and systemic trauma spun through centuries of famine, war, immigration, abuse, abandonment, and addiction. All our ancestors have been both vic-tims *and* perpetrators. All our ancestors have, at some time, been torn from places, separated from families, communities, and cultures, gone to war, or faced shattering circumstances that ruptured trust, faith, and belonging. These experiences have left scars on bodies, brains, and family structures that are bound up with histories (e.g., of colonization and genocide) and constructs (of race, class, gender, and faith) that play out on stages far larger than individuals or families (e.g., national or geopolitical). Healing means unwinding the life-deadening energy bound up in these memories.

The Big Cleanup is the individual *and* collective work of meeting and resolving complex trauma while nurturing emergent expressions of safety, soul empowerment, and wholeness in individuals, families, and society. For most people, unconscious and unresolved trauma runs our lives and relationships. Deadness and dis-ease within ourselves prevent us from understanding atrocities of the past as we continue to perpetuate them. Fortunately, presence is alchemical. When you choose to "be with" the unconscious contents of your memories, behaviors, and patterns, you can unearth, move with, and unwind them. Then comes the long, mind-ful integration work of repatterning the original imprints by repeatedly noticing and practicing new behaviors, experiences, and stories—in the present moment. This begins the long upward spiral of healing. This is the honest work we must do if we want to cease endless repetitions of structural trauma and create a world that works for Life.

I am a result of this upward spiral of healing. Both of my parents came from broken, alcoholic households. Both grandfathers were war veterans. Both grandmothers struggled with addiction and depression. My parents made a conscious break with the patterns they had inherited to create a more secure experience for me and my sister. It was a lot of work. There were broken dishes, tears, triangulations. But it was a decided improvement—a turn around the spiral.

No matter what your sex, race, age, body type, or gender orientation, it's inevitable that you carry a personal fractal of collective trauma. Trauma is suppressed life force. The bodymind gets stuck in some combination of freeze, fight, flight, or fawn response. In *Healing Collective Trauma: A Process for Integrating Our Intergenerational and Cultural Wounds,* Thomas Hübl writes,

> *Suppressed energy doesn't go away, and even dark or disowned energy cannot be destroyed. It needs to move, to become, to transmute; it must find an expression. In this way, unconscious material rises again and again to the surface, seeking to be met, detoxed, and clarified. Until trauma has been acknowledged, felt, and released, it will be experienced from without in the form of repetition, compulsion and projection and from within as tension and contraction, reduction of life flow, illness or disease.*[1]

You participate in the Big Cleanup every time you meet, unwind, and integrate the locked energy of trauma within yourself and every time you engage compassionately with another in their healing and homecoming. The power of your process is amplified when you hold it as part of a larger, collective cleanup.

For many, the wounds of systemic trauma aren't historically distant memories but everyday realities. Black, indigenous, people of color, and gender-nonconforming people carry heavy burdens of structural trauma. They have and continue to be disproportionately subject to marginalization, erasure, and violence. Structural inequity has been turbocharged by the forces of modernity and plays out in complex ways in our day-to-day lives and geopolitics. Women, historically subject to inquisitions, witch burnings, and enslavement, continue to experience misogyny, marginalization, rape culture, and femicide. Because of the structural unsafety many people experience, as well as the heat and immediacy of their pain, those carrying a greater burden of structural trauma need to be seen, heard, and held with a higher order of care.

For others, the memory of systemic trauma is buried so deep it's entirely numb, hidden under unconscious shame, and often glossed over

---

1. Thomas Hübl, *Healing Collective Trauma: A Process for Integrating Our Intergenerational and Cultural Wounds* (Sounds True, 2020).

with privilege. In this case, unearthing what's buried involves deconstructing unconscious patterns of insensitivity, dominance, and entitlement. For most, their familial and epigenetic trauma histories are complicated. What family has not dealt with mental health issues, social inequity, immigration, or being on one side or another of war or slavery, whether forced or chosen? One way or the other, it's important not to get into a game of comparison with other people's experience. As my spiritual father George Grey Eagle Bertelstein used to say, "All pain is the same pain. It does no one any good to privilege anyone's pain."

The Big Cleanup is the work of ultimate self-responsibility for the one part of the universe you can change: you. Only by doing this work can you restore intimate and fluid relations with self, other, and world. Regardless of circumstance, nothing changes until you are willing to meet your demons and dead zones and soften the armors that have kept you safe up to this point. Attachment to woundedness keeps everyone stuck in repeating cycles of trauma, drama, and power gaming. To move toward wholeness, you will need to meet (and possibly surrender) the refuge of the identities you've developed around pain, protection, and entitlement. Your history is sacred. But identities built around trauma and numbness often operate as crutch and cudgel, blocking self-honesty and connection and justifying heartless play in the pendulum game of power. As wholeness dawns within you, you will become more centered in the vitality of interbeing and interbecoming and far less attached to any particular construct of identity.

Given our collective context, we have no time not to do this work. It's time to resolve past karmas, feuds, and vendettas that replicate zero-sum games. Bring them to the altar of your heart for apology, forgiveness, reparations, and repair. Bury hatchets. Compost dry husks of betrayal, self-loathing, and self-protection. Extricate yourself from endless cycles of rupture to resolve ancient wounds still acting out through you.

Let's water these seeds of wholeness and homecoming tenderly. We should not assume that there is anything inherently human about the trauma we've inherited. As the planetary crucible presses upon us, I invite you to meet what seems unhealable. Imagine something that has never been—a society beyond systemic trauma, scarcity, and war, a society grounded in wholeness, a whisper of peace that is only possible if we are open to its possibility. It is possible to reestablish safety in oneself. As you do, your safety ripples to others. Many individual ripples multiplied can heal the world.

THE CATERPILLAR AND THE BUTTERFLY

Healing is what you do when you can no longer tolerate fear, hatred, rage, shame, and/or despair. It's what you do when the pain gets loud enough to drive a new choice. The best and worst excuse for why *not* to heal is that things will change. You cannot heal and maintain control. You must risk the loss of who you've been to allow yourself to become.

In many traditional cultures, illness, particularly deep psychological pain, is seen as a reflection of disconnection from the soul.[2] Contemporary life magnifies this schism, then tells you it's normal. It isn't. Meeting the pain is an authentic initiation that will push you toward integration and maturation.

Life has summoned you into a healing chrysalis. You have entered a biospiritual process of deconstruction and rebuilding at the structural level of self. You're going to have to die to the person you used to be and become something—someone—you do not yet know.

R. Buckminster Fuller said: "There is nothing in a caterpillar that tells you it's going to be a butterfly."[3] Nada. Release preconceived ideas. Forget the glamor of someone else's healing journey, somebody else's Instagram, some other hero's story. This is real. It's your life. And you're heading into uncharted terrain.

"But . . ." you say. "What's happening to me? Why am I breaking down? Why don't any of my old habits feel good anymore? Why can I sense such possibility, yet there's a war going on inside of me? I feel like I might die or go crazy. What if I lose it? Will this ever end?"

Nature has answers, my friend. You are breaking down to break through. You're not going crazy. (Don't feed that story.) And yes. It's going to be okay.

When shit gets real, it's incredibly helpful to look to nature for guidance. She's the original transformation artist. She's been navigating change for billions of years. So let's ask the caterpillar and the butterfly.

Transformation *and* metamorphosis mean "to change forms." *You* are changing forms. The structure that's changing is your architecture of self—your identity, worldview, and behavior, inclusive of your constructs of meaning, purpose, value, relationship, and reality. Changes at this level shift how you experience and participate in Life.

---

2. See Stephanie Marohn, "The Shamanic View of Mental Illness" in *The Natural Medicine Guide to Schizophrenia* (Hampton Roads Publishing, 2003), 179-89.
3. A popular rephrasing of R. Buckminster Fuller, "Planetary Planning," *The American Scholar* 40, no. 1 (Winter 1970-71): 29-63, https://www.jstor.org/stable/41209819.

We all know this story:

One day, a tiny, wiggly creature hatches from an egg on the underside of a leaf. The baby caterpillar eats and eats, unconsciously consuming everything in sight. All it cares for is growth. It knows nothing but the fulfillment of immense hunger. It munches along, unconscious of its massive impact on its environment. It loves eating! It grows exponentially, molting many times in the process. It consumes up to 70,000 times its birth weight in the few weeks before entering the chrysalis.

The fat caterpillar grows heavy and sleepy. It can't resist. Something inside of it knows; it's time to go within. Instinct takes over. It weaves a container for its own transformation. It doesn't think about why or where it is going or what the outcomes will be. It just acts. It builds a hard shell around itself—a shell it will never leave.

Inside, it melts.

Tiny imaginal discs, latent within its body, come alive. These little clusters of cells carry within them the entire blueprint of the soon-to-be butterfly. They were there all along, dormant, waiting for this moment. They will nourish themselves on the liquid contents of the former caterpillar's body, forming an entirely new organism.

Meanwhile, the immune system of the slowly dissolving caterpillar does not at first recognize the imaginal cells as good. It attacks them. A war ensues between what was and what will be. The old and new perceive each other as strangers. They compete for survival in the same goo of the dissolving caterpillar's body.

But the imaginal cells persist. They know their purpose. Their project is to birth a butterfly.

Without fail, they turn the tides. The metamorphosis reaches a tipping point that cascades from chaos to order. Nothing is wasted in the process. Everything that was the former caterpillar's body is repurposed to build the new butterfly. Cell joins cell, coalescing organs, a body, legs, eyes, antennae, and wings.

Then one day, it is time. A fully formed butterfly lies tightly nested in the safety of the chrysalis's shell. It can no longer survive curled within. It must birth itself.

A great tremor moves through its body. It shudders into life. It is time to push.

Its final initiation is to break through its now too-small shell into an unknown world. Without this last, risky effort, it will emerge untested. Its wings will crumple and dry up. Without this last massive push, the immense grace of its transformation will be lost to the world, and it will simply emerge and die.

So it wriggles and shimmies, martialing its new-formed muscles to push through the chrysalis. It emerges still crumpled, but tested. Its wet wings dry in the sun. It gives them a final shake, and they unfurl. Then, into the clear air, a butterfly is born.

What does this have to do with you?

Having entered the healing chrysalis, you've begun a reconfiguration of the shape of self, a sublimation of the identity that was formed in separation. Your soul is rearranging the architecture of your identity to more fully express who and what you are. There was nothing in you that knew you would become a butterfly, but now it's happening. Devote yourself to the greater possibility inherent within you. Your body and soul have their own logic and timing. Lean into this birthing of you. This is where you meet and transform generations of unresolved gunk.

A PRACTICE: SUPPORT FOR METAMORPHOSIS

Now pause for a moment. If you are currently experiencing some aspect of metamorphosis, I suggest grabbing a journal to explore these questions:

- What have you fed on in order to grow?
- What identities built on culture, family, education, protection, and status, or ways of knowing are dissolving inside of you? (This is the equivalent of dissolving the body of the caterpillar to let your new body be formed.)
- What is forming? What new possibilities whisper at the edges of your awareness?
- Where are these two processes in opposition? Does the old mistrust the new?
- What parts of you resist?
- What simple daily or weekly practice can help you slow down and move at nature's pace?
- Have you ever considered welcoming the unarmored beauty of your soul? If not, write a letter that begins, "Dear Soul, _____." Invite the unique suchness of your essence to speak to you and to animate your life.

NAVIGATING THE TERRAIN

When beginning the healing journey, people often say something like, "Why didn't anyone teach me any of this in school?" Well . . . the schools most of us attended were designed to train obedient cogs in separation's machine, not emotionally intelligent people capable of mutual liberation. This is a different kind of developmental process. This section addresses what to expect as you navigate this deeply human psychospiritual terrain.

Healing is both slow and relational. No one can do it for you. It's something you can only choose for yourself. Yet you cannot heal alone; we need each other to become whole. The sublime blessing and awkward fact is that we are social organisms. Our brains, bodies, and minds pattern after other brains, bodies, and minds. So attune to yourself, go gently, and engage with others as you walk your path.

In transformational work, the system that is changing is you—or, more precisely, it is the constellation-like architecture of your identity, including your normative thoughts, emotions, behaviors and neurophysiological organization. Any major shift in the structure will pull the whole constellation to a new location in consciousness.

This is your time to call back your fragmented parts. You are an evolving soul who incarnated to learn and to grow through friction and impermanence. The pain you must walk through as you meet and integrate your despondent, defended, terrified parts provides friction for your soul's growth.

Start by slowing down. Your nervous system needs to unwind. The best way to evolve a system without breaking or overwhelming it is to move from slow to smooth to fast. You will likely uncover bone-weary soul fatigue along the way. It is normal to experience exhaustion when your nervous system finally unwinds. Give slowness its due time. Smoothness will eventually arise. Then "fast" will shift to flow, and you'll lose the addictive speediness that previously covered pain and fear.

To transform, you must disrupt cycles of busyness, hypervigilance, and addiction that prevent you from sensing yourself at the pace of Life. Ground your attention in your body, breath, and sensation. This will allow you to reestablish a sense of safety and to meet subtle shifts in thought and sensation with mindful specificity.

Don't deny difficult feelings, memories, and thoughts. The shit is real. You can't just blast the contents of your bodymind with love and light and be "all good." Anesthetized pain numbs joy. Disallowed anger blocks authentic power. Ignored sadness and grief become depression. Disowned passion folds in on itself as anxiety and self-hatred. Again, from Thomas Hübl: "Become aware of the effects of trauma, which include dissociation, suppression, and disconnection. [When we] overidentify with our dissociation, consciousness shrinks, and we remain stuck repeating the ancient stress responses of hyperarousal or numbness."[4]

While healing calls forth the luminosity of your soul, don't mistake restored light for an absence of shadow. Your subconscious parts are beautiful too. Darkness is where things gestate. Darkness can be a home for your deepest dreams to coalesce. Meeting shame, fear, and denial with care will open intimacies you never imagined possible. As you come to know and accept your stunted "ugly" parts, you will integrate them, and self-love will grow deeper roots.

As you heal, find others who reflect kindness, authenticity, and sacred presence. Find a good healer. You know you have found a healer when you feel truly safe to allow every part of yourself to simply be. A healer is someone whose presence creates a safe space for your innate, organismic intelligence to reharmonize itself. A healer has faith in Life's intelligence moving through you and helps you call forth the truth of your soul. A healer reminds you that you can sense and feel your next step forward on your own. Of course you can ask for counsel, but only you can discern which of the various mirrors you receive is useful. A healer responds to your questions and offers guidance, yet has no investment whether you follow. A good healer is invested in you following yourself.

Sometimes, when your core wounds are reflected, you will completely disassemble. You'll space out and be unable to hear or remember what was said. It's okay. Slow down. Hold embodied awareness tenderly. Stay with the edge of sensation where you can breathe and feel.

It will get intense. As you push through masks and armors, you will fuck up, get angry, or trigger others. You might reawaken goofy, impractical, and dreamy parts of yourself that don't show up on time or conform to social norms. You could make messes, make enemies, and lose friendships. You will also find the courage to repair relationships you thought were beyond redemption.

Guaranteed, you will get triggered right where it most hurts, exactly in the way that feels most annihilating, terrifying, or numb beyond belief. You may find yourself wanting to lash out in defense or go silent. But you

---

4. Hübl, *Healing Collective Trauma.*

won't. The shame, blame, and injury ends with you, and it only transforms when it moves.

Don't get stuck in the trap of obsession. It is easy to become hyperfixated on your own healing at the exclusion of caring for others or nurturing purpose. To be sure, there will be moments when all you can do is focus on your own process, but recognize that *moving forward* and *deepening connection* are also fundamental to healing. Don't miss Life by over-focusing on yourself.

Life is life-y. Let it be so. There's beauty in your humanness. There's wisdom in your feelings. Expect extreme polarities, boring mundanities. Embrace the splendor and the mess. The most lovely flowers rise from manure. Your job is to love it all—the things, people, situations, parts of yourself—exactly as they are. Anything less is shutting down Life.

Commit to the work of deconstructing the trauma triangle of victim, perpetrator, and savior. (This can feel like climbing Everest.) Meet your inner victim with acceptance and compassion for the parts of you who have learned that Life is unsafe and that you must defend. Bring that part to the altar of wholeness to reclaim self-respect, dignity, healthy boundaries, and original innocence. Then get honest about the ways your instinctive drive to defend the inner victim has made you into a perpetrator. Own that you have hurt people with your unconscious violence and unintegrated rage. Then explore ways in which you have shown up as a savior (of your mother, of partners, of the planet) as a refuge from your own vulnerability and fear. Learn to hold that fierce, tender part so that you can be an authentic ally, protector, and friend.

Forgive yourself for the pain you've tolerated, the wounds you've inflicted, and the creative energy lost to addiction, depression, and disorganized attachment. As you dismantle the triangle, you will have to meet the part of you who collapsed, was humiliated, was raped, was scapegoated, or worse. You will also have to meet your inner murderer, rapist, inquisitor, executioner, slaver—all those who have denied you, silenced you, or sought to dull your light, who are also *in you.* And you will have to meet the one who thinks they can solve it all by being a superhero, a supermom, an invincible healer or warrior with no needs. All those subselves are antithetical to the integrity available to an unarmored human who can be vulnerable and honest with power. The victim, perpetrator, savior triangle stops with you.

Having done the work internally, you will realize that there are things to apologize for. We are all complicit in a world at odds with its own well-being. Everyone has made mistakes, has crossed boundaries, is somehow ancestrally and karmically bound up with soul-annihilating violence. Everyone has been a perpetrator and a victim at some point. We are all healing together. So release fault and blame. Instead, widen your attunement to relational, intergenerational, and structural shards of pain and broken strands of interbeing. Then offer apology—to land, to individuals, to people structurally bound up in your privilege, to species. Make amends.

One at a time, forgive those who hurt you. Forgive, because holding grudges is antithetical to wholeness. Holding the machinations of anger, outrage, hatred, and othering inside you leads to disease while unconsciously expressing them leads to dominion and war. The pain and disconnection of nonforgiveness perpetuates the division of reality. Forgiveness is a superpower of making whole, of embracing what is most unlovable in the larger circumference of unconditional love. To bootstrap wholeness, offer apology, forgiveness, and repair and make a reciprocal space within yourself to receive. Any time you (or someone else) sets down a feud, grudge, or righteous claim to anger or ownership that has, up until now, defined identity—this is a moment of homecoming, both for you and for the world.

As you learn to feel your own center, bring this hard-won self-awareness to your relationships. Set down your self-sacrificing people pleasing and your dependence on others' expectations. Respect yourself and your loved ones by asserting healthy boundaries. Find the words to respectfully say *no*. Welcome the present-tense, clean flows of anger, grief, and sadness as well as wonder, curiosity, and play. With time, you will learn how to be a safe space for others to feel their difficult feelings without fixing or shaming—and you'll rediscover pleasure in listening, dancing, and telling stories.

You will realize that the world isn't safe. But that was never the point. Being a safe, sane, and sacred person is an inside job. And once you know how to cultivate some safety within yourself, you can share it, in trust, with others. It won't be perfect. Because you are human. And you are finally realizing that humaning is a beautiful thing.

You might find kinds of happiness you never dreamed possible, what my spiritual father George called "*the unimaginable happiness.*" It won't look like what you thought it would. It will have no precedent in your family history, in your nervous system, or in Hollywood blockbusters. It will feel more grounded and vital than any fantasy. It will be authentic, and it will be yours.

Perhaps most importantly, you will relearn to *trust your own choices*—not in an unquestioning way but in the way of one who has learned self-awareness, discernment, and authenticity. This is where power meets and is expressed as love.

As you heal, you are likely to become less identified with a culturally dictated story or with your trauma. You may discover the great relief of being an undefended self—a soft, primal ground of embodiment that's translucent enough to hear and feel the Song of Life. In the calm of your unarmored bodymind, the music changes, Life reveals itself as a miracle, and the fidelity of each unique interaction is magnified. You begin to feel yourself as a process of being, doing, and becoming—more verb than noun. A humaning.

At some point, you will realize that your wounding is and was part of a bigger story. At that moment, the process becomes transpersonal. It transcends the small self who brought you to the work and reveals the whole journey as part of a collective and ancestral upward spiral. Your pain was bound up in separation, and all healing is part of collective liberation. Your choice to take self-responsibility is a sacred contribution to the whole.

FEEL YOUR FEELINGS

Learn to feel your real feelings. Your unarmored emotions are the rudder for your soul. To truly feel, or to feel truly, is to establish your soul's compass in your body—where it's supposed to be.

A card hangs to the left of my bathroom mirror. It reads, "The soul would have no rainbow if the eyes had no tears."[5] This Native American wisdom is a reminder to drop the drama while actively allowing emotional intelligence to flow.

Welcome the full spectrum of your unarmored emotions: anger, sadness, grief, ecstasy, sacred pride, ambivalence, wonder, disgust, confusion, fear. Healing involves recovering your ability to feel. Emotions can be dark, moist, loamy or red, fierce, hot. Emotions are sentient energy-in-motion, a rainbow spectrum of sensations that shape your experience of self.

Terence McKenna wrote: "We have been to the moon, we have charted the depths of the ocean and the heart of the atom, but we have a fear of looking inward to ourselves because we sense that is where all the contradictions flow together."[6]

---

5. Guy A. Zona, *The Soul Would Have No Rainbow If the Eyes Had No Tears and Other Native American Proverbs* (Touchstone, 1994).
6. Terence McKenna, *The Archaic Revival: Speculations on Psychedelic Mushrooms, the Amazon, Virtual Reality, UFOs, Evolution, Shamanism, the Rebirth of the Goddess, and the End of History* (HarperCollins, 1991).

We are taught to control, suppress, and purify our emotions. We are suspicious of our basic responses. We learn that anger is volatile and dangerous; sadness is tiring and difficult; too much joy is overwhelming; and too much passion is too much. Professionalism means "keeping it together." Being "good" becomes more important than being real. And we receive mixed messages from spiritual and healing communities, which often recapitulate shaming and perfectionism, telling us "we can't trust emotions" or that mindfulness is the road to achieve consistent, level peace and that we should want this as a higher good than feeling our feelings.

All of this can just increase repression and unhealthy codependence. Healthy humanness rests on a foundation of fluid sensation and expression. Emotion is organismic, co-regulatory intelligence. We feel and know ourselves through authentic, unarmored sentience. And we are made to be responsive to others' emotions. When we disrupt emotional co-regulation and response, we disrupt our instinctive, fluid aliveness.

Learn to tolerate and even welcome your big feels. Notice the difference between your feelings and the stories you have about them. Don't attach to the *stories*. Instead, make space to feel. Sometimes uncomfortable sensations will arise. Allow them. Learn to be responsible with them. Don't spin drama around them or hold onto them. Rather, take the time to *be* with them as meaningful information. Contrary to what many people fear, cultivating emotional intelligence won't cause you to lose control. Rather, it will support you to be truthful with yourself and others and to respond (rather than react) to your experiences. You will be able to move with more integrity and less projection. This is nontrivial because the space between feeling your emotions responsibly and projecting them onto others reflexively or unconsciously—multiplied across many interactions—is the difference between war and peace.

Sometimes, being with authentic emotions unfreezes uncomfortably comfortable ancestral trauma. You enter a "no man's land" of buried fear and self-loathing rooted in the even deeper well of ancestral shame, humiliation, and terror that your father or mother or grandparent covered up in their efforts to keep going and make the best of things. This is what I call an "annihilation fear." It's as though you have crossed into the zone on old maps where the maker used to write "here be dragons." It's the thing "we don't talk about." Going there feels like the equivalent of death.

You may realize you are unconsciously reenacting intergenerational habits of capitulation, self-sacrifice, or self-deceit. You feel the unfeeling—the absence of capacity—to move, respond, set boundaries, assert worth, or even know your own needs. Under this, you may discover a bottomless pit of repressed anger, a well so black that it feels like it will engulf the universe. It won't. It is asking you to finally set a boundary or assert a need.

Meeting these freezes is hardest. There's no "there there" in this spectrum of feelings. It is hard to even think. Hard to make sense. There's developmental absence. Here lie our deepest contradictions. Unconscious and hurtful content lives in this nonfeeling zone. Our prayers for love, joy, success, and clarity meet the deadening reality of our flawed, habituated responses to iniquities, burdens. and losses.

This is when patient, tender, slow-moving presence is needed. It's a big ask to feel what has been unfelt and unnamed. It can bring up immense feelings of inadequacy, brokenness, insecurity, shame, or a general feeling of being permanently fucked. Being with these parts, these orphaned exiles, in safety is where healing and integration begins. Meeting them means meeting a deep stack of built-up painful memories and experiences. It can take a long time to find, hold, reparent, and empower these parts. As you do, you slowly befriend yourself.

It is particularly important that you learn to love your anger and your joy. Why? Because anger is the root of power, and joy is its radiant heart. Developmentally, anger is an expression of healthy aggressivity: the ability to stand on your two feet, hold your space, and develop self-esteem. It's the ability to say no, set boundaries, and know what you do or don't want. Joy is the developmental center point of curiosity, wonder, awe, and sacred innocence. Without it, we stop playing and block the creative intelligence at the heart of wisdom.

Many of us repress anger because we've only experienced toxic varieties of it. We've only known abuse, rage addiction, harm, and terror. But there is such a thing as clean anger. Clean anger is an energy that aims to resolve. Dirty anger aims to harm. Clean anger is an appropriate, real-time emotional response to violation or rupture of trust. Healthy anger restores justice, serves truth, and protects vulnerability. Healthy anger doesn't need anything. It's not transactional. It's an honest, organismic response. When a relatively emotionally intelligent person is on the receiving end of clean anger, they naturally respond not with capitulation or escalation but with a co-regulated apology and/or change in behavior. Clean anger can be empowering and exhilarating, whereas toxic anger leaves you exhausted, humiliated, and isolated. Without clean anger, you are unlikely to be able to establish and renegotiate healthy boundaries and agreements or recalibrate the harmonics of power in your relationships. When you withhold anger, you withhold the clarifying, truth-giving, balance-restoring energy of this primal emotion.

We repress joy because we live in an adolescent culture perpetually playing at being adult. Its projected image of maturity lacks emotionality, fetishizes hierarchical power, machismo, and violence, and seeks control through hyperrationality. In this version of reality, joy is childish exuberance, little more than an embarrassing flounce of wasted energy. But as you reclaim emotional wisdom, you realize that joy is the engine of bliss, ecstasy, passion, loving presence, and right motivation. Reclaiming joy activates your inner child's wisdom, which you can then integrate as chosen innocence. Your joy, "is the infallible sign of the presence of God."[7]

When all of your parts are heard and held, shame dissolves. When you feel safe enough, it's possible to meet and resolve fear, rage, despair, shame, and remorse. When anger and joy are reclaimed, embers of life force rekindle. You also begin to see clearly how the mind blocks *love*. So much of our stuckness is just the projections, expectations, little annoyances, and petty judgments we hold to keep ourselves separate and secure. Once you see this, compassion arises. Then, and only then, is real forgiveness possible.

Strangely, you will find that the opposite of "not enough" is *not* "enough." It is something deeper—a self trust and okayness that emerges when you are able to be a good parent and friend to yourself. This okayness is grounded in presence and self-respect. The you who is "enough" is an unarmored self who is able to receive and give love, who knows what you need, who has clarity in yes, no, and maybe, and who can discern what relational and creative choices are authentic and true.

The soul moves at its own pace and only when met by a kind heart. Trust your own unique timing and rhythm. Don't force egoic preferences for speed, efficiency, or neatly defined step-by-step processes. Find a trusted and well-initiated therapist, mentor, or guide who understands the dark night journey of enabling emotional intelligence and composting rigid identity structures to unearth the intelligence of the soul.

Liberating authentic emotion will allow you to feel the Soul Self—a vibrantly sensate center that is uncomplicated, quiet, and attuned. This felt sense of center is an impermanent place. You "get there," then discover another layer to heal, another opportunity to discern, a new moment to surrender, align, create a boundary, reclaim power, or choose a more coherent story. Healing and whole-ing is a process, not a destination, a peeling away

---

7. This quote is often attributed to the Jesuit mystic and paleontologist Teilhard de Chardin. In fact, it is from Léon Bloy, *Letters to His Fiancée* (1937), 57.

of layers of the glass onion. Paradoxically, in living this, you expand and grow roots. Your emerging emotional maturity reveals that *you are enough*. Just right . . . imperfectly, perfectly whole.

IMAGINE A WORLD BEYOND SYSTEMIC TRAUMA

Now, I want to invite you into an audacious possibility . . .

Let's imagine a post-traumatic world, a world where we have synergized all of our capacities (psychological, physiological, neurological, traditional, social, and psychedelic) with new technologies that allow us to connect with ourselves, each other, nature, and the pulse of interbeing—to transcend centuries-old familial, epigenetic, and structural harm. We have healed sufficiently to feel ourselves (at least some of the time) as whole. This is not a world free of trauma. Injury happens. Sometimes we get stuck. A world beyond systemic trauma is a world where the conditions of our culture and our parenting no longer replicate endless cycles of systemic harm and where we respond to trauma with appropriate, informed, and consistent care.

Just for a minute, feel into a near-term future where this happened.

Imagine a world where we are all capable of relaxing into ourselves with maturity and grace, without defense, where we are all capable of nonviolent communications, where everyone inhabits the wisdom and beauty of full-spectrum emotion, where all are seen and see each other, where we feel both our individuality and our diverse unity as a human family who is part of the larger symphony of Life.

This is an undefended world. We have dropped blame, scapegoating, and othering. We have given up the glamor of self-constructed realities that become shadow refuges. In this world, we no longer need to construct armors to protect ourselves from men or women, peers or neighbors, or societal context. We know how to meet conflict with presence and availability. We know how to listen, negotiate, and restore harmony. We agree that the Earth is sacred. We don't need to defend our bodies, beliefs, families, watersheds . . . or our futures.

This is a nonaddicted world. We work with anxiety, depression, addiction, rage, and suicidal tendencies differently. We meet these patterns as what they are: disconnection asking for reconnection, care, pleasure, empathy, intimacy, community, and meaning. We no longer narcotize our pain with alcohol, psychiatric medications, opioids, or porn. We ritualized aggression to hone power and response-ability. We up-regulate toward well-being and connection rather than dysregulating toward hypervigilance or dissociation.

In this world, we have developed a clear distinction between the organismic fear response and the proliferate fears projected by the mind. Through this distinction, we are able to respond rather than react. We can hold, soothe, and love the organismic parts of us that get shocked and afraid as we embody a tender heart of fearlessness.[8] We become undaunted by the mind's projections while also being loving and kind to fear.

We navigate the nervous system's need for dissociation with a grounded understanding of how our organisms modulate the inevitable overwhelms, injuries, and pains of everyday life. We are educated about the cycle of fight, flight, freeze, and fawn. We respect the intelligence of body and soul to experience and discharge injury. We move at the pace of trust to hold and unwind dissociation and hypervigilance.

As a last resort, we invoke guilt and remorse as medicine, as healthy social emotions that one should feel when out of alignment with the well-being of self, others, or world. We see shaming as an unnecessary evil. Instead, we engage in compassionate communication, mediation, and restorative processes when there is rupture.

Just for a moment, feel what it feels like to live and breathe, relate and create in this world. Who do you get to be? How do you get to relate and create? Sense the spaciousness. In the absence of defense, we become sufficient, relaxed, curious, and playful.

How can we bring this world about? How can we systematically disrupt toxic cycles of trauma and fear and instigate virtuous feedback loops that build communities of wholeness? We plant and water seeds of being, doing, and becoming—seeds of consciousness and behavior—that slowly, interrelationally shape us into the kinds of people who embody such a world.

Below, I offer a simple framework called the *Seven Assumptions* to help you reverse engineer wholeness in yourself and your relationships. These are: belonging, creativity, purpose, okayness, freedom, responsibility, and residence (the full embodiment of your own unique essence). As a practice, the assumptions provide a conscious leverage point for disrupting habituated, socialized fears and projections as you nurture relational integrity with yourself, those you touch, and the world. Think of them as seeds of possibility that can be watered and evolved rather than as fixed rules.

---

8. The tender heart of fearlessness is taught by Chögyam Trungpa in his seminal book, *Shambala: The Sacred Path of the Warrior.*

THE SEVEN ASSUMPTIONS OF WHOLENESS

Your work with the seven assumptions is an experiment in personal and social alchemy. They are a grammar of possibility, empowering perspectives and ways of being previously unimaginable. They can be invoked simply as follows:

1. *I am willing to assume that I belong;*
2. *I am creative;*
3. *I have purpose;*
4. *I am divinely okay;*
5. *I am free;*
6. *I am responsible;*
7. *I am myself. I reside within this body as my soul.*

These are invitations you to see, feel, and imagine yourself as already whole while living your way into who and what you can be beyond systemic separation. They have emerged out of thirty years of transformational work with individuals and communities. In that time, I've witnessed the wild consistency with which we tend to fixate on our pain, yet cannot grow unless we have a positive trait to move *toward*. The Seven Assumptions function like imaginal discs in the goo of the caterpillar. They articulate seven developmental traits of being that scaffold individual and shared experiences and expressions of wholeness. The practice begins with the courageous act of risking the hope that wholeness and healing truly are possible—for you, for your family, for humanity, and for all beings.

Ancient spiritual teachings and contemporary neuroscience both confirm that we construct our experience of reality from the inside out. In *How Emotions Are Made: The Secret Life of the Brain*, Lisa Feldman Barrett writes, "Human beings are not at the mercy of mythical emotion circuits buried deep within animalistic parts of our highly evolved brain: we are architects of our own experience."[9]

We scaffold our moment-by-moment perceptions and emotional responses through preconceived assumptions and narratives about ourselves and Life. This process is called construction. To change the construct is to change the way we perceive and interact with reality.

---

9. Lisa Feldman Barrett, *How Emotions Are Made: The Secret Life of the Brain* (Houghton Mifflin Harcourt, 2017), 40.

Relational neurobiology offers a second key insight. We are social beings who become who we are by virtue of the relationships that co-inform our experience of self and world over time. We are developmentally bound to family and culture. Our identities and systems of thought are co-constructed by our social and physical environments. We cannot fully know ourselves separate from our relationships.

On the one hand, we are creators, constructors of our own reality. On the other hand, we are co-constructed by—and are constantly co-constructing—shared culture. When you practice the Seven Assumptions, you hold these two truths simultaneously. Then, in an act of sacred power, you take full creative responsibility for your *inner stance* (your internal attitude) in relationship to yourself, others, and the world.

Positivist psychology offers a third key: you get what you focus on, so it's best to focus on what you want, not what you don't want. Each of the Seven Assumptions invokes a trait of wholeness that provides a context to provoke unhealed material, focus energy directionally, and reconstruct how you perceive and interact with yourself, others, and the world.

Each assumption applies in three domains simultaneously:

- *Self:* an internal process of shifting inner stance and subjective, personal narrative
- *Other:* a peer-to-peer process of renegotiating how we meet each other and interact
- *Culture:* a community process of nurturing rituals and relational norms that nurture wholeness in the world

The assumptions meet the parts of ourselves, others, and society that don't know that wholeness is an option—and invite a new possibility. The practice is to "try on" a positive developmental trait of being that has been ruptured by separation, harm, and trauma.

You hold the power to construct your internal experience of any shared social process. Each assumption is an alchemical key of self-responsibility. When you embody them, you become an imaginal cell, awakening a greater potential within the collective body, mind, and soul.

Of course, these Seven Assumptions are by no means exhaustive. You can add others as you work to cultivate your unique embodiment of wholeness.

When I work with the Assumptions in my practice, I place them within a seven-directional Medicine Wheel—an ancient pattern that locates your energy and attention relative to the planet's energies. I begin in the east (the rising sun) then move clockwise to south, west, and north, then above, below, and center.[10] This sequencing aligns you—your healing, your creativity, your maturation—with the larger cycles of Life.

THE 7 ASSUMPTIONS
MEDICINE WHEEL

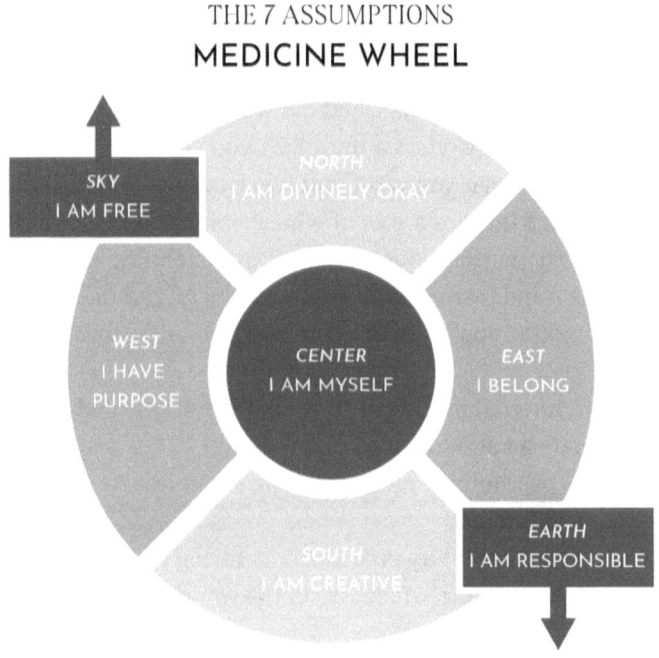

Now, let's explore the Assumptions more granularly. Below, you'll find a breakdown of the developmental task each Assumption presents, affirmations to support the inner stance, the shadow (or what happens when one lacks capacity around an assumption), and the central energies and gifts each one brings.

---

10. This sequence aligns intention sunwise, with the forward direction of the relative arrow of time (from a Northern Hemispheric perspective). It mirrors traditional Lakota practices, Wiccan practices, and the soul-centric development wheel offered by Bill Plotkin in *Nature and the Human Soul.*

1. THE ASSUMPTION OF BELONGING

"I Belong."

Belonging is "the feeling of security and support when there is a sense of acceptance, inclusion, and identity for a member of a certain group or place."[11] To belong is to feel seen, understood, and accepted without needing to change or accommodate.

Affirmation	I exist, therefore I belong. I belong here, in this body, this room, this world. I am not an accident or an apology. I inhabit my space with dignity. I trust my innate validity and worth.
Shadow	*"I don't belong. I am unwanted."* Alienation, superiority, outcast, unloved, misfit, erased, marginalized, misunderstood, disrespected, ingroup-outgroup dynamics
East	renewal / rebirth / receiving Welcome | Worth | Dignity root, first chakra

2. THE ASSUMPTION OF CREATIVITY

"I Am Creative."

Creativity is god-power moving through you. Creativity is the inborn, divine capacity to bring new things to Life.

Affirmation	I am sacredly connected to Life, and through this connection, I create. I have the power to be, do, become, or make what I conceive. I have choice, and I recognize that choice is innately creative.
Shadow	*"I am not enough."* Depression, despair, nihilism, stuckness, overconsumption, need to prove, seduction for power
South	energy / innovation / growth Agency | Authorship | Beauty sacral center, second chakra

---

11. R. F. Baumeister and M. R. Leary, "The Need to Belong: Desire for Interpersonal Attachments as a Fundamental Human Motivation," *Psychol Bull.* 117, no. 3 (May 1995): 497-529, https://pubmed.ncbi.nlm.nih.gov/7777651/.

3. THE ASSUMPTION OF PURPOSE

"I Have Purpose."

Purpose recognizes that each thing, in its uniqueness, brings a distinctive, unrepeatable gift to the world. This uniqueness has meaning and purpose that supports evolution.

Affirmation	I am here for a reason. I incarnated to fully express the unique gifts of my soul. To live, learn, love, choose, give, and receive in my own unique way.
Shadow	*"It's all meaningless."* Habitual adolescence, power games without a moral compass, narcissism, nihilism, creative energy directed toward transactional, extrinsic goals
West	maturity / persistence / surrender Meaning | Direction | Richness solar plexus, third chakra

4. THE ASSUMPTION OF OKAYNESS \| WISE INNOCENCE

"I Am Divinely Okay."

Okayness means relaxing into your body and being, knowing that there is nothing to prove. It's okay to *be*, okay to *be okay*, okay to *not be okay*. It is okay to rest and play and be a beginner. It is safe to reclaim the wise innocence that holds all experiences and feelings in a bigger basket of wholeness. You accept imperfection, brokenness, and humanness with mature levity.

Affirmation	I relax into myself and know, at a level deeper than thought, that I am okay. I don't need to do anything to prove myself other than *be*. I am whole and supported. I interbe with all of Life. I've been through the wringer, yet I choose my innocence because it makes me fully available to Life.
Shadow	*"I can't trust. I can't rest."* Dissociation and hypervigilance, inability to be in the present, play, feel joy, or receive the wisdom of authentic emotions
North	stillness / death / service Interbeing | Enoughness | Innocence heart, fourth chakra

5. THE ASSUMPTION OF FREEDOM

"I Am Free."

Freedom to be, do, and become you. Freedom to belong. Freedom to know who and what you are as a mote of God. This is deep freedom. It is greater than the base ability to do what you want. It is simultaneously personal, relational, and spiritual. All three of these dimensions of freedom add up to the ability to embody and share the luminous uniqueness of your soul.

Affirmation	I am fully here as myself. In knowing who and what I am, I am free to bring my light, my love, and my uniqueness into the world. Grounded in this awareness, I choose how I respond to my experiences.
Shadow	*"I'm powerless; the world is fucked. Fuck off."* Or *"Fuck off. I am free to do whatever I want. I don't give a shit about you."* Defense, dirty anger, collapse, selfish rebellion, the misplaced belief that freedom means not having responsibilities or duties
Sky	above / cosmos / father Presence	Transcendence	Communion voice, fifth chakra

6. THE ASSUMPTION OF RESPONSE-ABILITY

"I Am Responsible."

Response-ability is the skill of responding rather than reacting to inputs and making authentic choices on the basis of that integrated response.

Affirmation	I am a whole within a larger, whole, living system. I am connected to all things. I embrace my ability to respond to Life as an empowered agent who is deeply connected to Life.
Shadow	*"It's all good."* Disembodiment, lack of empathy or compassion, disconnection from causal impacts of one's actions, insensitivity, entitlement, selfishness, exceptionalism, relativism
Earth	matter / mother / memory Reciprocity	Complementarity	Custodianship vision, sixth chakra

7. THE ASSUMPTION OF RESIDENCE

"I Am Myself. I Reside within Myself as My Soul."

Residence refers to the full embodiment of the soul. To reside in yourself is to fully incarnate as yourself. To live as the very best version of you that is possible, owning all your uniquenesses.

Affirmation	I am myself. I am *here* in my body as my soul. I choose to fully incarnate into my body, my life, and my agency. I celebrate my uniqueness. I bring my love, energy, and attention into Life, here and now.
Shadow	*"I'm in control."* Or *"I can't feel myself. I become whatever I'm supposed to be."* Control, inability to self-authenticate, need for external verification, pulled by others' ideas and preferences, rigid skepticism, the need to be right
Center	the convergence of immanence and transcendence Unity of Body I Mind I Soul I Spirit crown, seventh chakra

HOW TO PRACTICE THE ASSUMPTIONS

Each of these Seven Assumptions can support you to become a more fully expressed, mature, integrated, loving human being who is able to show up in your life and relationships as a participant in a culture of wholeness. As such, each one will confront different aspects of what isn't that.

To practice, bring one of the Assumptions (belonging, creativity, purpose, etc.) into the forefront of your awareness. Engage in a mindful self-examination. What comes up in your body? What memories arise? How do you already know this (belonging, creativity, etc.) to be part of your way of being and engaging with Life? How has this assumption been ruptured for you or others you love? What parts of you are committed to it not being possible?

Now remind yourself that you are a locus of power. Through mindful attention to the minute details of your perceptions, responses, and behaviors, you have the power to reverse habituated cycles of suffering and othering by choosing to see, feel, and narrate your self-perceptions and interactions with others differently. This mindfulness potentiates healing.

When practiced alone, these Seven Assumptions allow you to examine the stories you believe to be true about yourself and the world and to take radical self-responsibility. When practiced with another, they create a dialogic context to hold wounds, articulate needs, expectations, and desires, and develop new patterns and pathways of seeing and being seen. When held in community, the Assumptions provide a foundation to build cultures of mutual respect, empowerment and trust. They can be offered as reciprocal blessings to co-create spaces in which we experience the basic building blocks of wholeness together.

In all cases, the practice requires a high level of self-responsibility. Working with the assumptions involves willingness to meet largely unconscious constructions of power and identity. No one can do it for you. Each assumption is a mirror revealing spaces where culture and experience have taught us ways of being and becoming that are less than whole.

LIVING IT

The assumptions invite you to rigorously observe and choose how you perceive and interact with yourself and others, to more clearly understand your and their expectations, needs, and wants, and to consciously participate in co-creating social dynamics of wholeness. Your objective isn't to achieve some mythic steady state. Belonging, okayness, and freedom aren't absolutes in some kind of transcendent sense; rather, they are relational processes—kinship journeys we engage in together. They are expressions of what we are as social beings who heal and bloom as we find deeper at-homeness within ourselves and the fabric of our shared world.

AN INVITATION: HOW TO HEAL THE UNHEALABLE

But . . . you don't understand. I'm really fucked up. I don't think I can do this butterfly shit.

Yes. I know. You're hurt. You are broken. You got fucked over. You had a soul-throttling childhood. You're scared to death that no one's going to love you. Don't worry. You're not the only one.

You've been swimming in a sea of pain and disconnection that has defined your zone of possibility. But have you ever been held in a circle of belonging?

Have you been welcomed as your soul? As your authentic self? This should have happened at conception, at birth, and throughout your development. You should have been held in pain and joy and had your needs honored. Your unique brilliance and beauty should have been cared for, celebrated, and loved. Instead, you were born into a world designed to put you in a box and affirm insecurity and fear.

Dismantling separation is both an inside job and a thing we do together. As social organisms, we need to be seen, heard, and reflected. We learn wholeness from other healthy bodies, minds, and nervous systems—from people who know who and what they are as souls. We do this together on behalf of the whole.

I want you to know this: You have the power to heal the unhealable. Anything can be integrated once it is witnessed and loved. You have access to the wholeness that flows through all of Life. Love that permeates all things, including your soul.

So, if you're willing, join me in this visualization:

Imagine your life from the beginning. Imagine that you were welcomed as a perfect soul at birth into a secure and stable environment of curiosity, kindness, encouragement, and attuned laughter. Imagine that you were held and educated as an essentially whole person. Imagine that your needs, boundaries, yesses, and nos were honored. Imagine that no one ever told you that you were bad, wrong, inadequate, unworthy, or stupid.

Now bring yourself into this present moment, into your body, to the subtle sea of sensations that make up the feeling state of the present moment.

In this present moment, YOU ARE OKAY.

In this present moment, YOU ARE FREE.

In this present moment, YOU BELONG.

Breathe in and RECLAIM your INNOCENCE.

Breathe out and relax into WHOLENESS.

Breathe in and reclaim CREATIVITY.

Breathe out and allow yourself to RESIDE in yourself as your SOUL.

Original Wholeness is your birthright. You are enough. You are safe, sane, and sacred.

Feel your center. It's breathing in and as you. This is your place, your unique location within our shared world. From this self-sensing, you can listen to the still, small voice of your soul.

Stay here. Gently. Trust this breath. One breath at a time, trust yourself. One breath at a time, soften and open to this moment. Let in the love.

You are coming home to yourself. Welcome home. In the face of unknowable odds . . . it's the pleasure of the universe to know itself as you.

CHAPTER X

THE SPECIAL HELP OF SACRED MEDICINES

Life provides everything needed to make more Life.

STUMBLING INTO CEREMONY

In the spring of 2009, I stumbled into my first plant medicine ceremony. Skeptical and grumpy, I had actively blocked psychedelics from my life for decades. Then, I hit a wall.

Months earlier, I had tumbled into a passionate but physically and emotionally abusive romance with a charismatic man who turned out to be schizophrenic. On good days, he cooked elaborate meals, kept me laughing, and helped structure my business. On bad days, he was degrading, manipulative, and physically violent. I knew the relationship was toxic, but I was hooked.

Then, I got pregnant. The nightmare intensified.

Soul survival kicked in. I had to end things. I could not see myself bringing a kid into the world with this man. I wanted to be a mother, but not like this.

I drove out to the ocean and laid down, belly in the warm sand. I opened my intuition to counsel with the soul of the unborn child. I considered the implications of bringing this being into the world to be raised by me as a single mother with a psychologically unstable and toxic father. I weighed this with the gravity of our collectively uncertain future, my financial, emotional, and professional unreadiness, and the unknowably immense love and responsibility this child would bring into my life. I stood up and danced with the rhythm of the waves, humming a lullaby, moving as though I were holding a newborn. With that little being as my teacher and guide, my choice became clear.

I couldn't, in good conscience, bring this child into the world.

I broke up with this beautiful, dangerous man, then scheduled an abortion. A few days later, I was at the clinic.

Afterward, I felt dead inside. Days went by when all I could do was trudge around Lake Merritt in a daze, trying to find the part of me that could breathe. Sunlight touched me but did not warm me. Dull and anemic, my body felt hollow, lifeless.

How could I have allowed this? So much shame. Trauma and disorganized attachment were driving my relationship and fertility choices. My irresponsible, not fully conscious behavior was intolerable to myself.

I could never let this happen again. Never. I had to get *help*.

With reluctance, I followed a trusted girlfriend's recommendation to Medicine Path Native American Church, a local community known for safety and strong San Pedro medicine dispensed inside a geodesic dome in a backyard in Berkeley, CA. The heart of Medicine Path was the loving wisdom of its spiritual leader, George Grey Eagle Bertelstein. George was known as a healer of healers.

My friend promised, "This will be different. Your whole life will change."

I had little hope and no faith. How could a plant heal me? Why would this work when nothing else had? How could the way through my most impossible darkness come from letting go?

From the moment George started talking, I knew I was in the right place. "We are all praying the same prayer," he said. In a clear, no-bullshit way, he explained the seldom spoken truth: everyone experiences the same challenges, aspirations, hopes, and fears. "As special and unique each of you feel in your pain, you are about to remember that you are not alone."

He continued:

Life is 'life-y.'[1] There is no shame in being a human. This medicine will not support you to project your ideas, opinions, or preferences onto your life, to be small, weak, or fearful, or to meet yourself or others in dirty anger. We are people walking the human walk. We are not here to get enlightened or to forget. We are here to make a prayer

---

1. George coined the word "life-y" as a nondual adjective to describe the entire spectrum of experiences we exalt in and struggle with, including everything from the discomfort of real intimacy, to boredom, to financial struggles, to aging. It is, for me, the best word to describe the poignancy of human experience.

and to disabuse ourselves of what's in the way of love. Our prayers are the way forward. They are how we walk straight down the center of our lives.

I felt welcomed in a way I had never previously experienced. This was the homecoming I didn't know I'd been waiting for. In tears, I realized I had found a teacher, a community, and a healing path for me.

Then we circled up in the dome and began to pray. What followed was a twelve-hour run through an emotional washing machine cycling from gratitude to anguish to awe to release. Love permeated everything, especially the grief, terror, and humiliation I had previously been unable to process. I could see myself in others' prayers and know, finally, that I wasn't alone. As one wave of emotion yielded to the next, rooted congruence returned to my body, mind, and heart.

At one point, I was given a broad, eagle-like perspective on my life. That elevation allowed me to see I'd always been doing my (imperfect) best. Self-love and self-respect replaced the collapsed self-hatred in which I had been steeping. I found tenderness and forgiveness—for myself, my ex, and my world. In the months and years that followed, I would find new ways to communicate my needs, boundaries, and desires responsibly.

I had found my second true medicine: *San Pedro*, the benevolent Andean cactus traditionally called *huachuma* by the Quechua people of Peru. The Jesuits named it after Saint Peter because he held the keys to heaven. In this plant, they found access to the divinity they had been seeking all along.

Huachuma opened my heart in such a way that prayer finally made sense. My hippie parents didn't raise me with prayer, and the formulaic pomp of religion had always felt contrived. When I prayed with medicine, I could feel the subtle ripples of my surrendered intent flowing into a universe that was listening.

George and his community operated without shame. In the absence of shaming, guilting or social pressure, I could give my emotions space and properly hear their wisdom. The shattering imperfection of my choices begged for compassion. My remorse—fully felt and integrated—became a guide to future actions. I made an earnest prayer of forgiveness for the mess I'd made, then asked for help to integrate the lessons *as teachings* for new and better choices.

Psychedelic medicine had terrified me. I feared losing some essential part of me—my mind. Instead, the medicine carved through the noise of habitual thoughts and "relieved me of myself." Softening egoic attachments and judgments, it allowed me to *feel* from my authentic center. This wasn't self-forgetting; it was amplified attunement to myself, made possible by juice from a cactus taken in a space of grounded love and connection.

That was 2009. Trauma got me in the door. Truth, love, and wholeness kept me there. Sitting in that dome initiated me into a sacred, uncomplicated way of being human together that made sense to my soul. The years spent in circle, learning from George, centered ceremony, prayer and sacred medicines in my life and practices.

Since then, indigenous teachers, teachings, and traditional knowledge systems have become integral in my life. I have apprenticed with traditional indigenous teachers and medicines from North America, Mexico, South Africa, and Gabon. I've communed with ayahuasca, iboga, psilocybin, 5-MeO-DMT, and tobacco—all with excellent guides. Each medicine is a unique intelligence and ally. I see the master medicines as a global apothecary with iboga, the root of the soul, at the center of the wheel. I approach each relationship with immense respect. And I never engage unless I have a clear intention and prayer.

I am privileged to have had access to these experiences and am indebted to the animate intelligence of the medicines, and the lineages and lands from which they come. Who would I be without these medicine allies, indigenous teachings, and the love that flows through my communities of practice and prayer? I don't know, and I don't need to know. I choose to continue to cultivate these sacred relationships and to share them, because that is what the medicines ask. This book is an attempt to respond in kind for all the gifts I have received. This chapter, "The Special Help of Sacred Medicines," introduces you to these profoundly transformational allies and explores how to work with them safely, sacredly, and in a way that respects their indigenous origins and power without appropriating from original cultures, projecting immature fantasies, or hurting yourself or others.

I AM A MEDICINE WOMAN

I embody an ancient pattern that lives in all our blood; I am a medicine woman. I pray with smoke and feathers. I talk with water, wind, spring shoots, and owls. I align my creative intentions with each new moon. I take long walks in all kinds of weather to ask the land what it would have me do. I gather people in circles to be human together.

Reclaiming this pattern has forced me to confront the extraordinary intensity with which ancestral memory would prefer I remain small, safe, and invisible. Furtive threads of old terror and doubt have tried to pull me off my path. But I have persisted.

I come from people who walked with wolf familiars, consciously conceived and birthed our children, and helped our elders die awake. My forebears were burned for being midwives, herbalists, soul guides, and ceremonialists. Demonized as heretics, witches, and whores, we were tortured and killed for worshiping the sun, singing to the moon, and giving sacred names to the seeds and the streams. We were made to feel unholy and shamed for the fierce and tender devotion at the center of our lives. I am not alone in this.

Upon the invention of the Gutenberg Press, the *Malleus Maleficarum*, commonly called "The Hammer of Witches" or "the witch hunter's bible," became one of the most widely published books on witchcraft in Europe. First published in 1486, it received multiple printings in the decades after its first publication and was frequently cited and referenced by theologians, jurists, and writers in the centuries following.[2] The *Malleus Maleficarum* was used to vilify and persecute mostly female people who practice earth-based worship of all kinds. Wikipedia's opening citation refers to the book uncritically as "the best known treatise on witchcraft."[3] This is indicative of continued, culturally normative shaming of those who own our magic, animism, and embodied expression.

Various constructions of the vilification of magic have been manufactured throughout history to dehumanize wild and spiritually sovereign "others." Such prejudices deaden the collective soul. Their genocidal weight rests heavily on women, Black, indigenous, people of color, and queer folk. Yet it rests on everyone, for all of our bodies belong to the Earth, and all of our souls want to dance with the sacred.

To stand as a "medicine woman," a "medicine man," or a "medicine person" is to reclaim the dignity and uncomplicated soul authority that arises when you declare your freedom—and duty—to tend and praise the sacred in Life as the natural expression of your love.

---

2. Cassie Brand, "The Malleus Maleficarum: A 15th Century Treatise on Witchcraft," *WashU Libraries*, October 19, 2022, https://library.washu.edu/news/the-malleus-maleficarum-a-15th-century-treatise-on-witchcraft/.

3. *Wikipedia*, s.v. "Malleus Maleficarum," https://en.wikipedia.org/wiki/Malleus_Maleficarum.

When I say, "I am a medicine woman," I am actively grounding in who and what I am as a protector, celebrant, and collaborator who stands in solidarity with all people who know our nature as nature. Medicine people know that we are sacredly bound to Gaia. It is a natural thing to be embedded in an animate world that we know as sacred, which contains all the medicines we need, which we are here to sanctify. It is instinctive to return the gifts we receive.

Very few people grow up in cultures that validate this knowing. Instead, we stumble into it. Some of us are stubborn enough to self-initiate or lucky enough to find real elders. (I've been both.) We find the sacred obliquely through science or regenerative design or art. Some come to the brink of giving up, fall into addiction or suicidality, then realize we are made for magic, not for boxes. We find living teachers and communities who know and carry the ways. We learn to be so patient or awestruck that we meet our gurus in mountains, oceans, clouds, daisies, dolphins, and lions. We are visited by ancestors and star teachers in visions and dreams. Or we slouch into ceremony, where initiated guides, sacred plant medicines, and living communities help us remember and reclaim who and what we are.

Contemporary medicine people live integratively. We braid traditional, embodied, instinctive, and intuitive ways of knowing with contemporary science, psychology, and technology. We frequently study with teachers in multiple lineages and often weave our studies with contemporary bodies of knowledge. We frequently find ourselves needing to translate between different cultures and contexts. Everything we do is, in some ways, syncretic—each person's way of being combines different life-histories, lineages, beliefs, and practices. This can get messy. So it's important to move slowly, with cultural sensitivity, and, when possible, with the guidance of an elder. But one way or the other, we are rising expressions of a collective liberatory impulse, an organic impulse to remember what it is to be a true human. In this way, we act as living bridges between ancient wisdom and possible future lineages that do not yet exist.

Reclaiming your ancestral connection to earth-based ways of being is an act of biospiritual dignity and power. To remember the long-buried knowing that you are a medicine person is your birthright. As you do, you will step into an intergenerational continuum of sacred relations with the human and more-than human world that your ancestors were part of and that you, in turn, can now weave your love into.

A BRIEF HISTORY OF MIND-ALTERING MEDICINES

Psychedelic medicines co-evolved with us. Nature provides a vast apothecary of psychoactive plants, fungi, and molecules that radically expand consciousness while increasing capacity for honesty, intimacy, and change. "Master" psychoactive plant medicines include ayahuasca, psilocybin mushrooms (also called *Los Niños Santos*), San Pedro (also called *huachuma*), peyote, iboga, and the 5-MeO-DMT containing secretions of the Sonoran Desert Toad. These gifts from Gaia have been stewarded by indigenous cultures around the world for millennia. Traditional peoples work with these medicines to holistically heal and integrate trauma, to liberate the mind and soul, to restore communion with self, other, nature, and God, and to strengthen community. They are sacraments: spiritual and religious substances that support direct mystical experience.

Western science has expanded Gaia's apothecary with other useful molecules, particularly LSD, MDMA, ibogaine, and synthesized psilocin, and 5-MeO-DMT. Figuring as therapeutic hopefuls in the 1950s, as major players in the "love revolution" of the 1960s, then pushed underground for decades, these molecules are now making themselves available to the mainstream through the work of an incredibly diverse group of stakeholders. As they do, indigenous cultures and cosmologies are meeting and sometimes clashing with modern science, law, and capital.

How can we best classify these substances? Molecules? Drugs? Hallucinogens? Psychedelics? Entheogens? Holotropics? The word *psychedelic* was coined by the English psychiatrist Humphry Osmond in a 1956 letter to Aldous Huxley conjoining the Greek *psukhé* (meaning "mind or soul") and *dêlos* (meaning "manifest or visible"). It means "mind manifesting." Similarly, the word *entheogen*, a neologism coined by a consortium of ethnobotanists and scholars of mythology in 1979, is derived from the Greek word *entheos* and means "manifesting the divine within."[4] Also in the 1970s, Stanislav Grof combined the Greek words *holos* ("whole") and *trepein* ("to move toward") to form the word *holotropic*, which translates as "moving toward wholeness."[5] I prefer to refer to these sacramental allies as *medicine*, using the word in the broad sense, as in "curative, healing, restorative." This is how many indigenous cultures and teachers hold them, as well as the widespread underground psychedelic community influenced by them.

4. *Bionity*, s.v. "Entheogen," https://www.bionity.com/en/encyclopedia/Entheogen.html.
5. Arlin Cuncic, "Holotropic Breathwork Benefits and Risks," *VeryWellMind*, last updated July 9, 2025, https://www.verywellmind.com/holotropic-breathwork-4175431.

These substances take us beyond the small self. They desynchronize the brain as they quiet the default mode network, the area of the brain associated with the ego.[6] This creates a liminal opening to self-honesty and awe. In this space, it is possible to soften identification, unwind trauma, access nonlinear insight, and revitalize psychoemotional and biospiritual belonging to Life. They frequently facilitate personal contact with that which we call God, Universe, Source, or Life. They do not force any specific realization; rather, they open gates of perception to direct mystical experience. This frequently results in increased wonder, compassion, and respect for nature, other people, and consciousness. Having such experiences requires no belief, yet psychedelics often radically confront our most basic assumptions, forcing the restructuring of our beliefs, values, motives, and/or worldview.

These medicines are bound up with human evolution. It is a well-established anthropological fact that entheogens have been used sacramentally in ceremonies, rites of passage, divinatory practices, and healing for centuries. They may even have potentiated the cognitive revolution in human intelligence back two million years ago when the size of our brains tripled.[7] The "stoned ape hypothesis," forwarded by Terence and Dennis McKenna and recently popularized by Paul Stamets, suggests, "We owe the emergence of language and self-reflection to ancient, sustained consumption of psilocybin mushrooms."[8] Indeed, the pursuit of altered states of consciousness seems to be a basic human motive,[9] almost as fundamental as our needs for food, water, shelter, and connection. The Chavín Dynasty of Peru orchestrated a 700-year rule of peace from roughly 900 to 200 BCE with sacramental use of *huachuma* at the center of their culture.[10] The Aztecs referred to psilocybin mushrooms as *teonanácatl*, or "flesh of the gods." In *The Immortality Key*, Brian Muraresku documents the shadow history of mind-altering substances at the heart of the cult of

6. Joshua S. Siegel, et al., "Psilocybin Desynchronizes the Human Brain," *Nature* 632 (2024): 131-38, https://doi.org/10.1038/s41586-024-07624-5.

7. John Hawks, "How Has the Human Brain Evolved?" *Scientific American*, July 1, 2013, https://www.scientificamerican.com/article/how-has-human-brain-evolved/.

8. Robert Lamb and Austin Henderson, "Stoned Ape Theory: Magic Mushrooms and Human Evolution," *HowStuffWorks*, last updated September 29, 2023, https://science.howstuffworks.com/life/evolution/stoned-ape-hypothesis.htm; Colin Marshall, "Algerian Cave Paintings Suggest Humans Did Magic Mushrooms 9,000 Years Ago," *Open Culture*, January 27, 2021, https://www.openculture.com/2021/01/algerian-cave-paintings-suggest-humans-did-magic-mushrooms-9000-years-ago.html.

9. Carol R. Ember and Christina M. Carolus, "Altered States of Consciousness," in C. R. Ember, ed., *Explaining Human Culture* (Human Relations Area Files, 2017), https://hraf.yale.edu/ehc/summaries/altered-states-of-consciousness.

10. "Andean and Chavín Civilizations," *Khan Academy*, https://www.khanacademy.org/humanities/world-history/world-history-beginnings/ancient-americas/a/andean-and-chavn-civilizations-article; "Chavin de Huantar," EthnoCO, https://www.ethnoco.com/chavin.

Dionysus and the Eleusinian Mystery School where Socrates, Plato, and Aristotle received initiation.[11]

Albert Hoffman's 1943 discovery of LSD heralded a chaotic eighty-year cycle of research, innovation, rapid popularization, criminalization, underground networking, and then a slow reemergence. In that time, psychedelics played multiple archetypal roles: the rebel, the darling, the devil, and the bringer of hope. The 1950s saw Stanislav Grof and other pioneers working with psychedelics to develop depth psychology. The 1960s brought Timothy Leary and Ram Dass to the fore as leaders of a revolution in consciousness. Rising recreational use led to fear, backlash, and a nationwide ban by 1968. In 1970, President Nixon signed the Controlled Substances Act into law, classifying psilocybin and LSD as Schedule 1 drugs.

But the medicine wouldn't die. Underground, so-called "psychonauts" continued to experiment. In the 1990s, the rave scene, fueled by MDMA and other "party drugs," boomed. An indefatigable network of therapists and scientists continued to innovate contemporary methods for therapeutic use. Intrepid adventurers traveled to Peru, Columbia, Ecuador, Mexico, and Africa to imbibe mysterious brews and learn with traditional peoples. Indigenous healers came to the West to seed circles of wisdom and practice. And a generation of neoshamans found themselves on the Burning Man Playa.

For decades, psychedelics simmered under the surface, held by a mycelial medicine culture. From the mid-1980s onward, MAPS (the Multidisciplinary Association for Psychedelic Studies, headed by Rick Doblin) diligently pushed for the legitimization and legalization of psychedelic medicines. Then, in 2018, Michael Pollan published *How to Change Your Mind*, which generated a tidal wave of interest that came to be known within underground circles as "the Pollan Effect." Cross-isle interest in psychedelics has significantly increased since then.

This leads us to our current moment of chaotic opportunity. One in four Americans say they've tried at least one psychedelic.[12] In March 2025, there were over 250 active trials involving psychedelics.[13] Clinical outcomes for diverse mental health issues indicate unparalleled efficacy. But clinical use (and the financial, medical, and legal frameworks around it) greatly limits the contexts within which these substances, historically held by

---

11. Brian C. Muraresku, *The Immortality Key: The Secret History of the Religion with No Name* (St. Martin's Publishing Group, 2020).
12. Taylor Orth, "One in Four Americans Say They've Tried at Least One Psychedelic Drug," YouGov, July 28, 2022, https://today.yougov.com/society/articles/43267-one-in-four-americans-have-tried-psychedelic-drugs.
13. According to the National Library of Medicine Clinical Trials database: https://clinicaltrials.gov/.

indigenous cultures of wholeness, can be accessed and understood. Capital and Western medicine are often paradigmatically at odds with indigenous cosmologies, ethics, and interests and the needs of grassroots communities. This matters because context (or "set and setting") profoundly factors in how the medicines act. Yuria Celidwen, indigenous liaison to the United Nations and a UC Berkeley Othering and Belonging Institute senior fellow, says, "These medicines are not about the human mind alone, they reveal Spirit, the very animating principle of Life."[14]

The medicine is not unlike fire—volatile, vibrant, powerful. Learning to hold it safely and with integrity (not just for individuals, but for society) while navigating cultures of separation is no small task. It requires deep respect for indigenous knowledge and some understanding of embodied processes of remembering. In a paper titled "Indigenous Philosophies and the Psychedelic Renaissance," the authors state, "Indigenous philosophical traditions offer alternative approaches to reorient the 'psychedelic renaissance' towards a more equitable future for Indigenous Peoples, psychedelic medicines, and all our relations." They caution against the "unexamined imperialist baggage" laced into the current movement.[15]

In the summer of 2023, at Psychedelic Science 2023, the largest conference of its kind in history, the closing talk by Rick Doblin was interrupted by a small group of indigenous community members led by Angela Beers who commandeered the stage with a critical message (paraphrased here): The commodification of these medicines is not a mutually liberatory path. They have been held in living lineages since time immemorial. If we fail to move in respect and reciprocity, with a commitment to mutual liberation, and with indigenous stakeholders at the table, the outcomes will not be good for anyone.[16] Ecuadorian Kuthoomi Castro spoke from the podium about the impacts of capitalism, colonization and the western worldview on traditional medicines: "We open our medicines to you to heal, not to take, not to extract. . . . The same happened to tobacco; now it causes addiction.

14. Yuria Celidwen in Ivan Natividad, "Why Indigenous 'Spirit Medicine' Principles Must Be a Priority in Psychedelic Research," *UC Berkeley News*, May 3, 2023, https://news.berkeley.edu/2023/05/03/why -indigenous-spirit-medicine-principles-must-be-a-priority-in-psychedelic-research/.

15. Keith Williams, et al., "Indigenous Philosophies and the 'Psychedelic Renaissance,'" *Anthropology of Consciousness* 30, iss. 2 (Autumn 2022): 506–527, https://doi.org/10.1111/anoc.12161.

16. The protesters echoed the words spoken earlier that day by Chief Nixiwaka Yawanawá, who said, "Why don't you invite us [to participate in the research], we who are the true connoisseurs? . . . Let us unite . . . to heal human society in decline. . . . We indigenous peoples have open arms." Marcelo Leite, "Psychedelic Renaissance: Indigenous Question Agitates the Closure of Psychedelic Science 2023," *Chacruna*, July 22, 2023, https://chacruna.net/indigenous-voices-and-protest-psychedelic-science-2023/; Alexander Lekhtman, "Why Indigenous Protesters Stopped a Global Psychedelic Conference," *Filter*, August 17, 2023, https://filtermag.org/indigenous-psychedelic-protest/.

The same happened to opium: now it causes addiction. The same happened to cocoa; now cocaine causes a lot of harm. Please look at the cycles of colonization and how this continues to happen."[17]

This warning invokes an appropriate level of sobriety. The innately liberatory experience of psychedelic states tends to amplify separation's hubris. Patience, diligence, diverse sensemaking, mutual attunement, and commitment to cultural, ecological, and financial reciprocity are antidotes.

An African proverb says, "If you want to go fast, go alone; if you want to go far, go together." I am an advocate of moving forward step by step in solidarity and community, as an interwoven web of communities of practice, with guidance and oversight from indigenous wisdom keepers and elders. And we should do so with full trust that the medicine has a prayer for all of us—a prayer to liberate humanity and Gaia from separation. I believe we can and should move with trust in our biospiritual impulse toward wholeness. This cannot be pushed or forced. It can only be lived in real experience and relationships integrated over time. As my friend and colleague Bob Otis Stanley, founder of the Sacred Garden Community and founding chair of the Decriminalization Movement, is fond of saying: "*These things move in gossamer time.*"

Why is there a whole chapter on sacred medicines in the middle of a book about civilization transition and personal transformation? Because, when held with humility, reverence, and the instruction of indigenous wisdom, these medicines have the potential to initiate both the soul healing and the ontological shift our world so desperately needs. These substances act with an organic efficacy unmatched by other modalities. Importantly, as I have seen consistently with my peers and clients, they do so in a way that introduces profound and lasting change.

EARTH-GIVEN INITIATORY ALLIES

The medicines are powerful. Do not confuse them with "drugs." The concept of "drug" is a narrowly defined Western medical concept. Drugs target symptoms, usually via simple causal mechanisms, to generate specific results. They work with parts, whereas sacred medicines dance with wholes. If you think of a psychedelic as a drug, you are likely to try to target its uses. This works, to some extent. For example, it is entirely possible to target specific medical indications like PTSD or major depression or

17. "Protesters Interrupt Rick Doblin at MAPS Psychedelic Science 2023 Closing Ceremony," YouTube, posted by BobCool7, June 23, 2023, https://www.youtube.com/watch?v=7LJmfWNvscE.

substance use disorder with psychedelics. But the frame of "drug" misses the reason why the psychedelic is effective in treating the psychological diagnosis. It works because *it does not work like a drug*. It opens a nonordinary, expanded state for psycho-spiritual reflection, reckoning, reconnection, and change. To approach sacred medicines as drugs is a categorical mismatch and can actually be detrimental. Why? Because these substances do not work alone.

The work isn't *just* about internal states. Medicines work in synchrony with the stories we tell about them, our intentions and attention, and the context set by music, the skill and presence of loving (or not-so-loving) guides, and the energetics and aesthetics of the physical environment in which practice occurs. You can't sit back passively in an experience. Active participation, self-responsibility, and skilled guidance are required. Prayer—in the very basic sense of offering a clear intention grounded in what you're grateful for, what you're struggling with, and what you want—is also extremely helpful. While both drugs and medicines are substances that cause change in the person taking them, the quality of change and the way those changes work in support of health and well-being is very, very different. Medicines work relationally.

Still, many people are legitimately confused by the way people in psychedelic communities speak about "medicine." In Western culture, we commonly use the word to refer to conventional or allopathic medicine. As defined by the National Cancer Institute, Western medicine is:

> *A system in which medical doctors and other healthcare professionals (such as nurses, pharmacists, and therapists) treat symptoms and diseases using drugs, radiation, or surgery. Also called allopathic medicine, biomedicine, conventional medicine, mainstream medicine, and orthodox medicine.*[18]

In this allopathic paradigm (which, I should preface, is wonderful at many things, like treating acute injuries, appendectomies, hernia repair, and saving people from heart attacks and strokes), the doctor and the institution have the power. You come as a "patient" to receive "treatment." Authority rests with the doctor, the diagnosis, the drug, not the patient/client/participant. Health is viewed as a rational, objective process of physically addressing objectively diagnosable symptoms to achieve targeted cures.

---

18. "Western Medicine," *National Cancer Institute*, accessed August 21, 2025, https://www.cancer.gov /publications/dictionaries/cancer-terms/def/western-medicine.

When people who have worked with sacred medicines, especially if they have been immersed in traditional ceremonial settings, say the word *medicine*, they are speaking from an entirely different paradigm. Health is viewed as a social, emotional, ecological, and spiritual process that is both individual and collective and that assumes all things are intrinsically interconnected. We aren't giving our power away. We are working intentionally with sacramental allies and practices that demand integrity, amplify intent and prayer, and directly reveal living wisdom through altered states of consciousness. We aren't addressing symptoms. We're touching root causes. Medicine unwinds dis-ease and disconnect by facilitating reconnection with the underlying intelligence of Life. The work begins with trust in wholeness, then works to reestablish a felt connection with that underlying reality of love. Allopathic medicine, on the other hand, begins with the assumption of brokenness and views the absence of the symptom as the cure.

Medicines weave human consciousness into Life's Song. In the words of my teacher, George Grey Eagle Bertelstein:

> *The Master Plant Medicines contain within them all the genuine wisdom teachings of all the Sacred Ways. They teach self-discipline, self-mastery, personal responsibility, forgiveness, acceptance, compassion, and unconditional love. This is profound and life-changing. The personally observable reality of this healing is the true reason for the surge in membership and interest in Sacred ceremonies all over the world.*
>
> *Medicine is not a drug. A drug takes you someplace and leaves you right back where it found you. Medicine takes you someplace and leaves you with a new life. Every single time. Medicine teaches us that prayer, rather than being a form of begging or an empty ritual, is the recognition of our personal relationship with Creator, and that every human being has the power to invoke that relationship in any moment by asking for help from a Power Greater than ourselves.[19]*

Psychedelic medicines require that you let go of the control you never actually had. They are not interested in your ego's version of comfort or in protecting your fear. They are interested in coherent and contextual alignment with Life. They help you to be with, compost, and integrate parts of

19. George Bertelstein, "About George Bertelstein," *A Clear and Simple Prayer*, accessed August 21, 2025, https://aclearandsimpleprayer.com/team.

you who believe they are lost, broken, bad, failed, flawed, or permanently fucked. They help you reconnect with a wholeness that was, in fact, never lost and is always perfectly imperfect.

What's it like to ingest sacred medicines? It's a psychosomatic wash cycle. You can expect heightened sensation and expanded attention, emotional intelligence and capacity for honesty. Difficult feelings, memories, and experiences surface and can be held in a bigger circumference of unconditional love. Life lessons you had resisted suddenly make sense and become learnable. Visions might arise carrying obvious or not-so-obvious messages (or you may have no visions at all). You can feel that apology and forgiveness are not just dogmatic ideas but authentic actions of the heart. You choose to show up as a good daughter, son, mother, father, sister, brother, friend, creator, or coworker because this makes sense of the epigenetic and karmic tangle of love. Counterintuitively, medicines unwind existential angst not with answers but with tastes of the mysteries of time, impermanence, and love. This liminality can be massively confronting, yet it melts armors, well-constructed justifications, and identities based in trauma, seduction, and control.

During some journey, you may meet Death in its full glory as the ultimate friend. If you have the opportunity to experience Life from the other side of the veil, you will taste what it is to walk without fear. You may realize that Life is divine precisely because of its stunning, infinitely diverse transience. Subconsciously and superconsciously, you may begin to embody a transverbal (greater-than-verbal) *knowing* that Life is sacred and you are a sacred part of it.

From the medicine's perspective, every human is a unique agent within the soul ecology. All true medicines invite you to know yourself, own your choices, love honestly, drop the drama, and tell the truth.[20] From the medicine's perspective, love is power. Everything else is just posture.

Medicines help liberate the soul's expression in a way that is healing, for both the individual and the entire soul ecology. When seen from this angle, there is hardly such a thing as personal transformation. All transformation lives in the transpersonal, collective dimension of consciousness and is merely translated as personal experience. Each human incarnates as a unique note within the soul symphony. When an individual is disabused of the trauma and acculturation that caused forgetfulness of their part in the song, the symphony as a whole grows more coherent and harmonious.

---

20. These principles roughly echo the essential teachings of Bwiti philosophy. The Bwiti are the traditional peoples of Gabon whose culture is woven with iboga. I am initiated in the Missoko Bwiti tradition.

These medicines restitch the experiential fabric of intimacy and belonging that is our true birthright. They are *the special help* that restores integrity of body, mind, and soul in communion with Life. They point the way home.

WHY ARE WE CALLED?

Many feel called to these medicines. Though, I'm not sure if we are called or if something bigger is drawing us—an evolutionary intelligence that moves through us yet is greater than us. The confluence of the metacrisis with increasing access to sacred plant medicines doesn't seem random. Perhaps Gaia is summoning us back to Her? Perhaps our souls need to remember who and what we truly are? Perhaps we know, biospiritually, instinctively, that these are the right allies to help us navigate this collective rite of passage.

Consider the following perspectives on plant medicines as an emergent and systemic, adaptive response:

- As a sentient planet seeking to align your most industrious and destructive species with your own well-being, wouldn't you create and disseminate molecules that could awaken that species to the love that permeates Life?
- As a member of the plant or fungal kingdoms seeking to perpetuate your own evolution, why not manifest molecules to seduce humans into resonance with you?
- If you were an indigenous leader aware of the penultimate preciousness and fragility of our biosphere and whose people held the biocultural tools to cure the sickness of modernity, wouldn't you send your best traditional medicine carriers out to the Lands of Forgetfulness to bring healing and wisdom?
- What if you were a therapist helping people struggling with intimacy, depression, anxiety, and unresolved grief. Wouldn't you seek out safe tools to effectively address the underlying causes of which these psychological indications are just symptoms?
- If you were a psychiatrist frustrated by patient after patient achieving only marginal results with the wide variety of antidepressants, antianxiety medications, stimulants, antipsychotics, and mood stabilizers available to you, wouldn't you want drugs that could get people better results?

- What if, somewhere in the vast tumult of life's stresses and iniquities, *you* (a mother, father, daughter, son, husband, wife, friend) lost track of love. Wouldn't you seek help to find it again?
- And if you deeply cared about a viable future? If you wanted to co-create a world beyond war, a world in which humans are physically, psychologically, and spiritually healthy, care for one another, and naturally align incentive and innovation with the flourishing of all of Life—wouldn't you want medicine in your toolkit? Wouldn't you weave altered states of consciousness into cultural rituals of healing, celebration, and reconnection?

Which of these perspectives speaks to your own experience? Why are you called?

The medicine calls to each of us differently. Some, like me, come on their knees. Some are dragged by loved ones in the throes of addiction. Others come as spiritual seekers, eager for growth and insight. Some enter as tourists and usually get more than they bargained for. Some come as opportunists, flocking like vultures to find their piece of the feast.

We enter through many doors: indigenous or neoshamanic ceremonies, self-directed healing, raves and festivals, underground therapists, aboveground ketamine clinics, and intellectual fascination. Our motives and needs are extremely varied. Some come skeptical, some cynical, some earnest, some curious, some terrified.

To shape engagement wisely, beautifully, and ethically, I believe it is helpful to give special weight to three particular perspectives: that of the Earth, that of traditional medicine carriers, and that of a person—any person—who genuinely cares about a flourishing future.

From Gaia's perspective, the medicines—entheogenic master plants and all the other medicines—represent a vast *planetary apothecary* within which Life provides everything needed to make more life. They reharmonize humans with the soul ecology, supporting healthy, adaptive responses. They help us remember nonarbitrary pathways and patterns of Life's way for us.

Traditional medicine carriers work in cahoots with Gaia. They come from cultures where medicines play an integral role in communal life. These courageous healers, whose lands and peoples have been continuously subjected to the annihilating forces of colonization, take the path of radical forgiveness to offer their gifts. Many travel alone at great risk into alien territory to support people they've never met. They are motivated by a sure knowledge that the medicines call us home to the wholeness, which was never not here but which many forget. They are also motivated by unbroken connection with their cultures, ancestors, and more-than-human relatives. If you are a non-indigenous participant in sacred medicine work, your highest participation involves the disciplines of restraining projection, listening, protecting, amplifying, funding, and otherwise caring for indigenous interests.

And for those of us interested in a viable future, sacred plants specifically and psychedelics more broadly act as synergistic amplifiers for ecological awakening, healing of structural and familial trauma, and community cohesion. This is significant because the Earth won't wait for us. And we simply won't harmonize with Her if we can't meet the magnitude of this moment to *feel, break and remake spells, and remember together.* Medicines force us out of our heads and into states of expanded sentience that penetrate separation's armors. We get honest with bullshit and entitlement. We humble down, take response-ability, and finally see, accept, and embrace others. We own complicity in toxic chains of causation and respond to cognitive dissonance, not from dragging obligatory duty but with grief-saturated understanding of the gravity and grace of collective liberation. Here, forgiveness isn't a transactional gesture. Rather, it's about softening cuts of broken relationality—revitalizing the breath and aliveness of the between. We develop the emotional and spiritual maturity to acknowledge mistakes, apologize, repair, and receive contrition in return. This rebuilds the deepest nutrient of any sustaining culture: trust.

But isn't this risky? Yes. Separation has made a mess. Meeting disembodiment, dominion, and layers of ancestral trauma as we gently yet firmly steer toward wholeness, healing, and kinship is not an easy thing to do. It requires deeply embodied, life-initiated guides, time, patience, cultural sensitivity, and the development of rich community contexts to hold people.

But this is no ordinary time. The medicines are here, and they want to serve the people. The key is to hold them within a bigger culture oriented toward restoring intimacy *with* and belonging *to* Life. When synergized with other contemplative, regenerative, and relational practices, medicine work empowers life-centric cultural emergence. These medicines help us cast spells that can hold the weight of the world without collapsing under it as we become worthy ancestors.

We're all in this planetary boat together. Sacred medicines, held wisely, can expedite a collective initiation into wholeness. Though there is controversy in the psychedelic space about safety, cultural appropriation, equity, inclusion, narcissism, and the forces of capitalism co-opting consciousness, it is also true that love, respect, and mutuality permeate the movement. We co-create more harmonious outcomes when we come to the medicine with humility, reverence, care for reciprocity, and a commitment that our healing serves all of Life.

COMMUNITY

In a world shaped and incentivized by the cult of the individual, the role of sacred others is often underplayed. Yet, at the end of the day, community is the key to safe, sane, sacred work with the medicines. Community-based practices are as old as culture itself. Practicing together acknowledges and strengthens the fact that no healthy culture can exist without strong bonds between the members of that culture, between people and land, and between people and a shared sense of the sacred. Communal ceremonies strum chords of ancient memory, revivifying psychobiological patterns of embodied empathy, belonging, and reverence that help us *human* together. We build a deep humus of culture as we celebrate, heal, meet conflict, care for land, children, and elders, and engage in rites of passage—together. These shared experiences then help us to be sovereign individuals by meeting our needs to be seen, known, and heard, to share stories and meaning, and to love and be loved.

When you decide to come to the medicine, there's a choice to make about whether to work solo (with a guide) or with community. The current mainstream bias is toward one-on-one guide work. To be sure, there are tender times when working solo is the best route for safety and privacy. But be open to the possibility that your healing could be more elegantly facilitated by group process. Whatever content you'll be working with emerged in relationship with others: parents, siblings, teachers, friends, and power figures. And wounds need to be met at the level they occurred in order to heal. Practicing in a community provides a constellation of mirrors to directly reflect and unwind unresolved wounds and trauma. Practicing in community can reawaken the capacity to be human together.

We likely have communal psychedelic use in our genes. In their 2021 paper titled "Psychedelics, Sociality, and Human Evolution," José Manuel Rodríguez Arce and Michael James Winkelman argue that the use of psychedelics in early hominin societies was a factor in the development of prosocial adaptive advantage. They write: "Psychedelics . . . alter emotional processing, self-regulation, and social behavior, often having enduring effects on individual and group well-being and sociality."[21]

Community can nurture healing and happiness in ways that individual or one-on-one work cannot. In the Lakota tradition I studied within, we think of community *as* a medicine. The Circle, or *Hochoka*,[22] holds you as it offers an experiential education in how to organize yourself in integrity with a greater whole. You remember that we are not alone or particularly special. Your own excruciating or exquisite experiences, while unique, are also part of the one human prayer that is praying us all. When someone is going through a big healing, we often say, "Thank you for doing that for all of us." What you do for yourself empowers others, too. In witnessing others move through their challenges, you drop comparison, scarcity, jealousy, and protection in favor of empathy, compassion, curiosity, and connection. This is medicine for the underlying narcissistic tendencies we are all subject to.

Many have called the recent emergence of sacred medicines as major players in mainstream mental health a "psychedelic renaissance." I believe that the minimum requirement for this to be a renaissance would be that it centers on *relational healing* (with self, family, community, and place). The self-transcendence so many proclaim as a benefit of psychedelic experience only becomes meaningful and relevant when integrated pro-relationally and prosocially with other people and nature. A true renaissance would reclaim health as an integrated function of culture, kinship, and community, including the more-than-human world. It would soften the focus on the individual and empower relationships and whole populations. It would continue to co-evolve organically at the level of communities of practice rather than being owned by institutions.

Community draws you into a circle, a we-space, a structure of power where everyone belongs. All parts co-create the whole. The circle is a primal shape of wholeness within which each part is significant, yet no part is more important than any other part. Power flows holarchically—according to role and responsibility rather than status. Circles visibly reveal diverse unity while honoring individual sovereignty. Additionally, a circle

---

21. José Manuel Rodríguez Arce and Michael James Winkelman, "Psychedelics, Sociality, and Human Evolution," *Front. Psychol.* 12 (2021), https://doi.org/10.3389/fpsyg.2021.729425. https://www.frontiersin .org/journals/psychology/articles/10.3389/fpsyg.2021.729425/full

22. "Hochoka in Native tongue means 'healing circle.' Completing the circle of who we are while alive, and not waiting until death and our next go around, is imperative to seekers of the light and the right trail." (Kimberly Clarke, "True to Life Story," Warrior Woman Spirit, December 28, 2018, https://warriorwoman spirit.com/2018/12/28/horses-of-hochoka-the-healing-circle/.)

of humans is a metaphor for the larger Circle of Life, subconsciously aligning body and mind with Life's Way for us.

Community ceremonies include practices of thanksgiving, music making, water prayer, land blessing, and fire tending. These ancient pathways for communion are often absent in our modern lives. But they make sense of things in a way nothing else can. They restore the currencies of our love and attention to Life. When synergized with sacred medicines, the vitality inherent within these actions is revealed—amplified by awe, authenticity, and attunement.

We are self-healing beings who heal best in the company of others. Medicine work in a well-held community setting helps people make sense of their lives, love more honestly, and become mature adults. If scaled organically through small circles of consistent, coherent practice, community work can provide an essential vehicle for humans coming home. Shared social spaces where we feel what it is to be participants and co-creators of a sacred world can act as a nexus for civilization transition.

CHOOSE WELL

Before you ever enter any space, there are things to consider. You will need discernment to do this work safely, sanely, sacredly. In contrast to judgment, which generally implies a black-and-white, yes-no binary, discernment is the ability to make decisions by carefully considering different options, recognizing subtle nuances, and making intelligent distinctions between things. Your discernment will enable wise, overall good practice.

The psychedelic space is a very human space. This means it contains all the shadow and power gaming of any other human space—sometimes more. Psychedelics can magnify delusion and spiritual bypassing as well as clarity. While they are not physically addictive, they can be experientially addictive (particularly ketamine). And their power to amplify the intellect tends to attract narcissists and sociopaths. So choose your spaces, your guides, your medicines, and your pacing wisely. Trust your intuition, but realize that intuition isn't always trustworthy, particularly if you're in a difficult spot in your life or simply naive. So ask trusted friends and allies for their stories, recommendations, and support. Educate yourself about effects and contraindications of the medicine you're planning to work with. And always check a guide's reputation against at least one community source (if not two or three).

Assess the relational field you will be entering. Right practice is relational. Communities and guides who are good at clear communication, consent, respect, reciprocity, authenticity, and joy can generally be trusted. Be vigilant of shame, sexualization, appropriation, and guru posturing. Be particularly suspect of anyone who claims to be a shaman or a spiritual teacher or who feeds on adoration. In traditional cultures, very few (if any) people call themselves "shaman."[23] In a contemporary context, these titles signify a need to prove rather than real skill in the numinous arts of holding expanded states. Knowledge of trauma is also important. Do space holders understand the systemic and structural dimensions of harm? Do they know how to be present, uncomplicated, and self-regulated, even when difficult material arises? (In my community, we used to say, "When things get trippy, act normal." This was a simple yet profound call to diffuse drama and fear while grounding the collective field.) Discern: Is this a community of care and mutuality? Is innocence protected? Do you feel safe and seen here? Can you drop judgment, feel belonging, and better see others as aspects of yourself?

Consider the wider net of impact. Right practice requires reciprocity with people and land. Is the community or guide you are sitting with participating in reciprocity or extraction? Find out in advance. The specifics of how the medicine was sourced matter. How are financial and social resources flowing? Was the medicine you are working with sourced in integrity with the land, people, and cultures it came from? The pattern differs with each medicine, depending on its growing habits, cultural context, and the degree it has spread itself around the planet. For example, ayahuasca vines mature slowly. They come from the jungles of Peru, Ecuador, Colombia, and Brazil or from new plantings in tropical Latin America or Hawaii. The slowness and rarity of the plant is an indicator to move slowly in your practice. Medicine grown and sourced in prayer and integrity with original cultures and lands is not any easy thing to come by. Before choosing to work with a provider, ask them how they sourced their medicine. Whether they can answer this question and with what degree of care is a good measure of whether that provider has integrity and whether their space will be safe. If you don't believe this, ask the medicine. In all likelihood, it will show you the chain of love or suffering it is connected to.

---

23. The term *shaman* originates from the Tungusic Evenki language of Siberia who used the word *saman* to describe their spiritual leaders. It was appropriated by Western anthropologists and applied generally to seers, healers, "spirit lawyers," and wisdom keepers in many distinct traditions.

What does *reciprocity* really mean? The Quechua people of Peru speak about this principle as *ayni,* which translates as "today for you, tomorrow for me." This fundamental ethic of Andean culture emphasizes the importance of mutual support and reciprocal relationships. This is a profound concept to bring into psychedelic states, which enable embodied ethical sensing. It is not uncommon to emerge from a ceremony with "homework" (clarity about actions you need to take to restore reciprocity or harmony in your work and relationships). I consider this one of the pillars of my own practice and follow it rigorously. It has vitalized every area of my life: relationships with parents and exes and mentors, clarity and focus in my work, even my connections with houseplants and pets.

It is particularly important to honor and elevate original wisdom keepers. I stand with many indigenous leaders when I say that working with the medicines implies a debt of reciprocity to the specific people and places that have stewarded them (and to the Earth generally). Offer something in reciprocity for the gift of the medicine, whether it be financial, political, energetic, making a ceremonial offering, or simply taking the time to learn more.

Medicine work is instinctive and intuitive, yet it also requires rigor, patience, and holding by others who have traversed these terrains before. Go slowly and mindfully to make safe and discerning choices at every step.

COME IN A GOOD WAY

When you feel the medicine speaking to your soul, *trust the call.* But don't come casually. As George used to say, *"The only thing that will change is your whole life."*

Without a doubt, integration is critical, but there's an argument to make that preparation is at least as important. When you come with clear intent and offer up an authentic prayer, the integration part flows naturally. (In my own community of origin, the explicit invitation was always to live the prayer, not to process it.) This section offers basic guidelines for how to show up so you can most deeply benefit from the work.

Enter with respect, humility, and gratitude. Don't come as a spectator or a tourist. Come as you are. Come as a member of a circle that grows with the presence you bring to it. Come as a participant and a celebrant. Come as a human being who is willing to be vulnerable, to tell the truth, to be changed, to serve, and to fall in love with Life. In George Bertelstein's words:

The Spirit of Everything That Wishes Us Well is inviting all Humanity to join itself in a Living Prayer through the living breathing mechanism of taking complete responsibility for our thoughts, our actions and our personal prayers and carrying them into and throughout our real time daily lives. Ceremony is in no way a separate or special circumstance or a unique event. It is a guide and instruction about what is true and important and relevant about our relations with Mitakuye Oyasin.[24] We will fail and succeed at this effort, but that Everything will be with us in every moment, if we ask, to help us to walk in a Good Way.[25]

To come in what we call "a Good Way," arrive with a good heart and a good mind. Get sober with yourself; clear out unnecessary physical, dietary, relational, and media toxins. Take an honest inventory of your emotional landscape. Cultivate a reverent attitude. Drop your inner cynic, snark, critic, and know-it-all at the door. Be ready to take full responsibility for yourself. Your experience will be fruitful in direct proportion to your authenticity and integrity with yourself.

Know your "why"—your clear intent. What has called you here? Are you seeking to let go of what no longer serves you, to receive guidance, to find joy, to heal your mind or your heart? Be practical. What are you struggling with . . . really? Purpose, money, your partnership, health, self-hatred, disgust at humanity, uncontrolled rage? What are you grateful for? The simple things: morning coffee, your breath, hot showers, the friend who helped you get to ceremony? And what are you willing to let go of? Your resistance, your judgment, your entitlement, your fear? When you pray, speak simply, as in, "God, please help me to behave well today, tomorrow, and forward."

Always braid your personal intentions with a commitment to reconnect with your nature as nature. Medicines open an aperture to the animate intelligences that seek to mirror and support you. Unfortunately, nature-awareness is not a norm in many psychedelic spaces. Western healing models, even holistic ones, tend strongly toward anthropocentrism. But nature is source, healer, and ally for the soul. The more-than-human world will help you ground and integrate your experiences, no matter how far into

24. "The Lakota phrase Mitákuye Oyás'iŋ describes Reality by addressing it as 'All My Relations.' All humans, all animals, all plants, all the waters, the soil, the stones, the mountains, the grasslands, the winds, the clouds and storms, the sun and moon, stars and planets are our relations and are relations to one another." (dawn, "Mitákuye Oyás'iŋ," *Tapestry Institute*, June 12, 2020, https://tapestryinstitute.org/mitakuye-oyasin/.)
25. George Bertelstein, *A Clear and Simple Prayer* (2019).

the cosmos your journey. Combining medicines with time in nature can reveal nonarbitrary truths to inform every aspect of your life, from your leadership style to your daily food choices to how you build intimacy with your very cat-like (or dog-like) partner.

To come in a Good Way, commit to the integrity of your soul. True medicines liberate and elevate soul intelligence. But you must trust that your soul is *real*. Only you can listen for that still, small voice within. To do this, soften the rational lens of objective verifiability. Suspend disbelief in the numinous suchness of your essence and be willing to feel, see, and intuit new information, both through soul vision and through your body. Ask the medicine: Please show me to myself. Help me to *see* myself clearly. Then: Help me to *feel* myself cleanly. Your body and soul are a sacred continuity. Medicines liberate unarmored emotion, which is the rudder for your soul.

Finally, the Good Way is always in service to the continuity and emergence of Life's Song. In a world that has denied the Covenant between humans and nature for so long, we reawaken joy and duty in sacred reciprocity, remembering that wisdom means nothing if it doesn't support the well-being of future generations. We are participants *in* Life as agents *for* Life. So we ask: What can I best serve? How does Life want to use me? How can I better tend wholeness in my family, my community, my place, through my work or my art? When you come with humility, clarity, and sacred intent, the medicines, the ceremonies, and your prayers will support you to become more fully yourself as you learn how to harmonize with and as Life's Song.

A CLEAR AND SIMPLE PRAYER

It is helpful to bring a prayer to medicine work. A true prayer falls like a drop of pure water into the infinite ocean of existence, rippling to its edgeless edge then more subtly and nonlinearly rippling back to you. A prayer is an offering of intent plus surrender. It's a call and response. A true prayer is offered without expectation. You offer it trusting that Existence loves you and has your back. Prayers are answered nonlinearly. The answer flows back through your causal entanglement with the fabric of reality.

Many people have legitimately adverse reactions to the idea of prayer. Perhaps you grew up being forced to pray a rote way that felt empty and devoid of meaning. Or you lump prayer and people who pray into the generalized category of "woo"—a place often rejected by atheists, agnostics, and materialists. Or maybe you've felt betrayed by God, the universe, or nature.

You asked and nothing happened, so you gave up. Maybe loss or humiliation have cut you off from feeling safe surrendering or asking for help from something outside yourself.

The act of prayer does not require your affiliation with any particular religion, spiritual tradition, or divine figure. It's not dependent on you being Christian or Muslim or Jewish. It requires no belief at all. Prayer is an act of trust that simply requires that you soften the resistance you've picked up along the way to offer your heart in conversation with Life, regardless of belief or tradition.

George taught the *clear and simple prayer*. In a nutshell, a clear and simple prayer has three components: "Thank you," "I'm struggling," and "Please help." If you're not struggling, use the variation: "Thank you," "Help me," "I want." Use this grammar as a scaffold for your dialogue with Life. Be honest, be uncomplicated, and speak in the present tense.

Here's an example of a clear, simple prayer:

Dear God (or Life, or Universe),

Thank you. Thank you for this day, my body, my home, this breath.

I am struggling with grief. I am struggling with my difficult feelings about the deadening of this world.

Please help me. Help me feel myself. Help me breathe. Help me experience this life—this one, happening right here, right now, in my body, in my place, in all my relationships—in all of its flavors. Help me to love it the way it is.

Help me not to collapse but to integrate the wisdom of my feelings as grounded service to Life.

Thank you! [26]

Anyone and everyone can pray. Prayer is personal. It's not a formal gesture. It's not about repeating liturgies or sayings that have been said before. It's about speaking with raw integrity to that which is larger than yourself to ask for help and guidance. Prayer is a discursive context to get honest about your struggles, your pain, your longing, your dreams, and what you truly want and need. It's a conversation between your soul and Life.

---

26. You can finish your prayer with the simple words, "thank you," or with a declaratory word of closure like, "Amen" (Christian), "Àṣẹ" (*Yoruba*), "Bassé" (*Bwiti*), or "Aho," a Kiowa word that has been adopted in many other Native American contexts.

A PEOPLE'S MEDICINE PRAYER

You are your ancestor's best prayer. On some level, all of life is held together with a prayer. An ancestral supplication sings back and forth through the corridors of time. It calls for a good life and for a beautiful future. It sounds something like this:

Come pray with me.

Kneel down in the sweet grass. Let your skin feel earth.

Drop dogmas. This is no religion. This is how we come home.

Thank you for this One Life we all share and for the One Prayer that prays itself through us, generation upon generation!

We pray for more Life, please! We pray for a world where all chil-dren are safe, healthy, happy, and free. Where the love-labor of all mothers and fathers is honored. Where elders are valued and lis-tened to. Where the wisdom of our indigenous relatives is upheld by courts, states, and countries. Where we love and respect teachers, farmers, foresters, artists, storytellers, song weavers, seed keepers, and all workers of the earth.

We pray attunement to nature's rhythms. To Spring's resurrection of new shoots and flowers. To Summer's fertile growth under the high sun. To Fall's abundant harvests. To Winter's death, rebirth, and inner light. Let us live in season and cycle.

We pray to collaborate with all species and ecosystems in a way that is good! To offer our attention as a resource within Creation. To be listeners, lovers, learners of our places, our watersheds, our bioregions. To speak the holy names of home mountains, rivers, valleys, and reefs. To be and become flows of reciprocity, regen-esis, and beauty.

We pray for old-growth forests, thriving wetlands, plastic-free oceans, living soils, safe migrations, harmonious hydrological cycles, and wild spaces for all beings to play.

We pray to open the aperture of awe, to travel currents of curiosity and wonder, to touch and be touched. Let us be so alive, so perme-able, that we can easily communicate with land, plants, animals, elements, ancestors. Let us hear the songs that sing in praise of Life and raise our voices to liberate all souls.

We pray to commune with nature as a mirror for our souls. Help us to recognize ourselves in the stability of granite, the persistence of ants, the connectivity of mycelium, the patience of a crocodile, the insight of a jaguar's gaze, the elevation of redwoods, and the art of a hummingbird's flight. Help us to learn from our more-than-human allies and teachers—not to attain power but to embody the diverse powers of love that co-construct Life. Help us partner with these beings, learn their habits and ecologies, receive their wisdom, and protect them!

Help us breathe. Inhale and exhale. Taste each molecule. Feel our bodies as bodies of the Earth—metabolizing, instinctive, intuitive, entangled.

Help us love. Boldly, bodily, mystically, profanely. Help us love ourselves, each other, our communities, our places, our planet. Give us compassion. Give us the strength to ask for help, to apologize, and to forgive.

We pray to remember to remember that all of Life is sacred. We are sacred.

And when we are done praying, help us create these visions! For the true prayer is the one we live in each moment.

Together, we are a sacred storm of prayer, a rising tide of remembering. We are strands in the holy tapestry of Life's Loom. We are the singers, and we are the Song.

We are true humans. And we say . . . More Life, please!

Sophia Speaks

ON WHOLE SELF

True humans inhabit the Whole Self.

*"Self" describes the interiority of a unique agent within a world.
As a self, you interexist as a location in time and space through
which your soul learns, loves, chooses, and relates. You are
irreducibly unique. No one else can be, do, or become you.*

*Self and world co-generate each other. There can be no self separate from
world. You are irreducibly interconnected. The self–other distinction is
real, but the separate self is a delusion. Self is a permeable wholeness
participating in a larger co-evolving and co-constructed wholeness.*

*Whole Self operates through the trinity of Soul Self, No Self, and
Human Self. True humans develop these three aspects of self
simultaneously. We care for our unique becoming as embodied
souls, our beingness as consciousness, and our psycho-emotional-
somatic integrity as organisms whose purpose within Gaian ecology is
humanness. Who and what we are is all of this, not more, not less.*

*The process of remembering is a movement from separate self, which
is an egoically defensive construct of separation, to Whole Self,
which is a deeply soul-centric and relational way of being, doing,
and becoming. This is a shift from a rigid, self-centered identity to
a responsive intimacy with Life; a shift from armor, insecurity, and
unconscious power games to attuned self-integrity, participation, and
collaboration. In Whole Self, one's motivations shift from acquisition
(of money, power, sex, clout, security, and stuff) to experiencing and
expressing love, integrity, reciprocity, and complementarity.*

As you develop Whole Self, you will discover that "ego" is not an insoluble problem or a "bad" part of you that must be killed but a relational membrane, a subtle and complex architecture of memories, thoughts, and behaviors. Ego is only a problem when it serves the separate self. But when healed and aligned with Whole Self, it becomes a bright vehicle for the expression of your unique essence. The soul blooms. The borders between self, other, and world become responsive, attuned edges for exploration, connection, and creativity.

Let's unpack the trinity of Whole Self.

SOUL SELF

Soul Self dances in subtle uniqueness. Your soul emanates the irreplaceable suchness of you. You bring an unrepeatable flavor, note, essence, or rasa to this Creation. Your soul learns and evolves through relationships between uniquenesses.

The Soul Self is purposive and constantly evolving. Each soul is a unique expression of Life's Song. Meaning, value, and purpose arise through the unique expression of each soul in relationship to other souls. Without uniqueness, there can be no meaning, value, or purpose—no learning, no growth. It feels good to express your unique proclivities, affinities, talents, and gifts. Liberated soul expression is sacred empowerment, both for the individual and for the entire soul ecology within which all souls dance in reciprocal becoming.

To know Soul Self requires great discernment. Soul Self is revealed through the precise yet indirect mirrors others offer. Soul Self is tasted, tested, and refined through your intimate relationships. Soul Self is known and heard obliquely through image, metaphor, and vision. Soul Self is sensed through choices and actions that feel congruent and joyful. You will know that Soul Self has been established when you sense your own essence residing within your body, subtly animating your life. You will feel at home in yourself.

Soul Self is part of and sacredly bound to the soul ecology. Who and what you are as a unique being is subtly, archetypally co-constructed through reciprocal interactions with the more-than-human world. Take this literally. Look to nature, wise people, and deep solitude to better see and know yourself. Find your soul mirrors in the butterfly, the redwood tree, the carpenter ant, the lone mountain that calls to you with unavoidable magnetism, and the loved ones who know you by heart. Allow your soul to be shaped by great loss, responsibility, bliss, and pain. Over time, you will see that the soul of the world calls to you uniquely—asking of you what only you can be, do, and become. Your unique path and purpose in this lifetime unfolds at the confluence of inner soul sensing and the calling of the world.

NO SELF

The No Self vibrates in luminous awareness. No Self arises when nondual, awake awareness is established. Awake awareness, or awareness aware of itself, anchors your individuated consciousness in timeless, boundless, changeless, formless, primordial reality.

The No Self is an essential sameness, a unity across all beings who experience and know it. It is transpersonal and non-personal.

The No Self enables a conscious witness, an "I" that transcends smaller aspects of self. Observing and loving oneself from the seat of No Self clears noise and compulsion and thus enables authentic choice. Centering in No Self unwinds trauma and sublimates aspects of identity that are jagged, rigid, or stuck in separation. No Self makes it possible to relax attachments to ideas, opinions, preferences, and identities based in self-protection that obstruct clear experience of Life and expression of the soul.

A note of clarification: The No Self is called "True Self" in some of your spiritual traditions. In these traditions, the achievement of self-transcendence and enlightenment is the aim. We affirm the value of luminous awareness, but we do not share the same aim. Our orientation is toward sublimating rather than transcending self. Whole human beings participate uniquely and specifically in Life's Song. We work with No Self to sublimate aspects of identity that get in the way of attuned and responsible co-creation. We find the term "True Self" confusing because this dimension of selfhood is not more true than the uniqueness, creativity, and purposiveness of Soul Self or the embodied, relational, emotional, and intellectual intelligence of Human Self. We call it No Self because it is an emptiness. But, we remind you, this is not an ultimate objective. To transcend humanness is simply not the task you incarnated for.

Do not confuse the No Self and the Soul Self. The No Self is formless, boundless, timeless, empty. The Soul Self is a suchness, a specificity, that weaves you, as a unique being, into the larger Whole.

HUMAN SELF

The Human Self is exactly as it sounds. It is the healthy, wild, mature, free, identity architecture that conveys your co-creative participation in Life's Song. The Human Self is the psycho-emotional-somatic ground of your organismic participation in the world.

The Human Self is a vehicle for love and power. The Human Self holds your capacities for body wisdom, secure attachment, conscious communication, erotic intelligence, creativity, technical skill, ecological knowledge, moral imagination, collaboration, and conflict navigation. The Human Self understands needs, desires, and boundaries, soothes fears, cultivates beauty, and nurtures intellect in a way that is consistent with soul purpose. The Human Self learns and grows through play, work, and relationship. The Human Self loves both unconditionally and conditionally and requires both boundlessness and containment to thrive. The Human Self is fallible and vulnerable. We see injury as opportunity. We diligently care for trauma as it arises, rather than letting it fester and divide us from ourselves.

From birth to death, the Human Self develops, matures, and evolves in concert with Soul Self. In our world, we orchestrate nature-based rites of passage at every phase of life. We initiate the mind, body, heart, and soul of each person to support their developmentally appropriate alignment with Life's Song. The resulting growth conveys both increased brilliance of the soul and greater fortitude, skill, and humility in our humanness.

We caution you not to skip or disregard or try to transcend human development. Your soul incarnated nonaccidentally, nonarbitrarily, as a human. You came here to do humanness within Gaian ecology. You must have a strong and supple ground in your humanness if you wish to participate in Life's Song wisely and beautifully. The development and maturation of the Human Self supports the full expression and continued evolution of your soul in relation to this nonarbitrary lifetime in this world.

WHOLE SELF

We offer the trinity of Whole Self for the development of healthy humaning. We encourage you to pause here and consider how this framework reflects how you experience yourself?

Here's the map: In Soul Self, you are a unique, irreplaceably distinct instance and instantiation of the divine learning about itself. In No Self, you are awake awareness, a mote of consciousness aware of itself. In Human Self, you are a fallible and fluid creator, preserver, destroyer organism learning how to express power and love harmoniously. Being and becoming a healthy, happy, fully expressed version of yourself is a complex and sometimes confusing journey that is simultaneously miraculous and mundane. You are a nexus of limits and limitlessness. Welcome it all. You are all of this.

Your experience of this framework will be very different depending on where you are starting from. For those who are familiar with psychoemotional development yet less familiar with spiritual or soul work, we invite you into a more multidimensional sense of who and what you are. We believe you will find new joy and meaning here. For those who are already familiar with No Self but are unaccustomed to the distinction between No Self and Soul Self, we invite you to embrace the concept of Soul Self as a celebration of the uniqueness you bring into this world. For those familiar with soul work but less schooled in practices of awake awareness, cultivation of the No Self will refine presence with yourself and all of your relations. You do not have to choose between any of these. You get to develop them all.

Whole Self is a developmental map, both for individuals and for society, that guides soul-centric human flourishing within a flourishing biosphere. We created it to support humans, on a species level, to effectively and beautifully enact your sacred role within planetary ecology and the cosmos over thousands of generations.

You are here to participate in the soul ecology, to offer your unique note into the larger Song, and to do your small part to tend the continuity and emergence of Gaia. We offer this as an invitation to be, do, and become your Whole Self—a true human—a member of a sapient species at relative peace with yourself, other humans, all beings, and the planet you occupy. We hope that you experience this as a homecoming.

Chapter XI

BECOMING YOURSELF

You are a neighborhood within God's body and mind.
Be a good neighborhood.

BECOMING MYSELF

I swam to the center of Lake Siskiyou and paused in the zone in the middle where you can drift between black water and blue sky while basking in full view of Mount Shasta. It's a place I always want to stay forever, floating with ears submerged, breathing slowly, pretending I'm a water dragon.

It was at that moment I realized: something had shifted, something almost impossible to describe.

I had found medicine's ultimate gift: soul home. After what seemed an endless journey, I was finally resident in my body as my soul.

Dear God,
   Help me to be a good neighborhood in your mind.

The prayer had worked. I had set down any remaining grasping after enlightenment. Instead, I had decided to live a prayer to be a *good-enough human*. I had winnowed down to the choiceless choice of being, doing, and becoming me—just a strangely complex mammal doing my best to regulate my nervous system, be a safe space for myself and others, live in integrity with my soul, and experience and share as much joy as possible. Just a permeable vehicle for communing with water, mountain, and the ospreys making their late-afternoon hunting forays. Just a soul who has chosen to incarnate on Earth for thousands of lifetimes carrying a vision and mission for the evolution of this Gaia.

Slowly, I had become the woman I prayed to be.

How did this happen?

I did it alone. And I had tons of help. In solitude, I had done tens of thousands of hours of yoga, dance, meditation, therapy, and ceremony. I had found the image at the center of my soul and learned how to hold it loosely enough to be unattached. In connection, I had worked with mentors, guides, friends, therapists, and more-than-human teachers. I had come to prayer, practice, and the altar of my relationships again and again, willing to meet my shit, learn from my mistakes, and become whole. I asked the medicines for help. They sloughed off what wasn't me, polished my heart, and reaffirmed my deepest knowings. Iboga literally reflected my soul back to me in a mirror, revealing my essence as a dark, infinite, feminine fullness shot full of gold.

I had untamed the parts of me that were badly tamed by default culture. I had rewilded myself in kinship with oceans, rivers, mountains, soils, and animal allies. I had fallen in love with my inner creatures, my outer grittiness, my sensual intensity, and my inner countercultural rebel who lives to collaborate with this kairotic moment. I had remade many parts of me: my ability to communicate, my insecure attachment, my fiery anger. I had healed chronic pain and food addiction and found an uncomplicated sense of self-worth. We had come to like being Samantha.

And now . . . I am myself. It's quiet here. Oddly, what characterizes wholeness is not some much-touted, steady state of bliss or self-transcendence but the absence of noise . . . a coherence that holds my emptiness, my soul clarity, my ups and downs, my honest emotions, my choice-making, and even moments of confusion. I am enough. Achieving wholeness isn't about solving the problem of Life. It starts by us recognizing that life is a gift and committing ourselves to tending the gift, no matter what the situation.

It took me a long time to get here, and while I was never not myself, I have come to experience a quality of centeredness and integrity that was unimaginable in my earlier life. There's an effortlessness to knowing who I am that requires no story. It's a verbing of self. The paths I've taken aren't the only roads to wholeness. They simply happen to be mine.

Unimaginable happiness is possible. It's not what you think it is. It's not a marketable perfection. It's living your life as a human being, doing your best to embody love and integrity, enjoying the dignity of your soul's path as you become yourself—every day.

THE VERB(S) OF YOU

Buckminster Fuller said, "I seem to be a verb."[1]

You exist not so much as a fixed "thing," not as a noun (a mom, a nurse, an investor, an engineer, a scientist, a son) but as a collection of perceptions, thoughts, feelings, responses, and actions. Self is a process of being, doing, and becoming. Self arises through intra-action with world. You are a verb—or, more precisely, a constellation of verbs that can be better known through their qualities, their adverbs, and their actions than by fixing yourself as a noun.

We are taught that we "should" want to be a doctor, get that PhD, build a list of accolades. We are taught that these badges (these nouns) equate to meaning in our lives. But do they? I would argue that your soul's happiness, meaning, and evolution are far better served by learning how to live—joyfully, congruently—as yourself.

Freeing the verb(s) of your ongoing becoming is the key to liberating your part in Life's Song. To do this, I invite you to join me in an experiment. It's a simple perspectival practice that has yielded extraordinary results in my own life and for my students and clients.

A PRACTICE: FREEING THE VERB(S) OF YOU

For today or for this week, drop the word "ego" from your vocabulary.

The ego is a relational architecture. There's nothing wrong with it. Let it be. Instead, use the word "identity" to describe the verb(s), the process of the thing called "you." You are constantly becoming. Your identity is evolvable. With care and attention, it can become a clear vehicle for the expression of your soul.

Assume that it is possible to reshape the cognitive structures that mediate between your interiority and the outer world. The meaning you ascribe to anything is flexible, whether it is an ache in your gut (could it be food poisoning? anxiety? excitement?) or an unusually warm spring day (could it be a sensuous blessing? or global warming? or both?). You are in charge of how you respond to stimulus. You are response-able for how you construct your experiences.

---

1. Richard Buckminster Fuller, *I Seem to Be a Verb* (Bantam Books, 1970).

Explore the difference between the rigid, codependent response patterns you previously took to be normal and living in interdependent listening to Life. Your body, heart, and soul are naturally responsive when you relax into attunement with yourself, others, and the world.

Quiet your mind by focusing on your breath. Be, do, and become (rather than thinking) you. Listen to the instincts and intuitions that rise from your center. Then, and only then, seek the sweet spot where your skills, gifts, and visions meet the calling of the world.

Soften attachment to your stories. Let awareness be aware. Breathe into the liveliness within and around you. In this spaciousness, feel your body and soul as one, then follow where your energy guides you.

Just for today, be a good neighborhood in God's mind. Love and accept the imperfection of your humanness. Care for the needs of your organism. Cultivate gratitude and joy. Find what calls to you uniquely and create from there.

Identity is a mediating architecture between you and the world. Like a cell membrane, it discerns what comes in, what goes out, how osmosis is to be maintained, and what disequilibriums are effective and why. It creates healthy self–other boundaries. These actions are the sacred verbings of self.

When you think yourself as a verb, you will begin to feel yourself as an emerging *relational process* that is characterized not so much by *who* you are as by *what* and *how* you are. You will learn to sense yourself from the inside out, enjoying the affectual dance of joy, flow, curiosity, presence, quietude, and dreams. Even more difficult experiences, like confusion, frustration, or aversion, become interesting and relevant information, guiding soul-aligned response. The need to identify with your own or others' identity narratives will soften. Rather than hinging your worth on accomplishments, acquisitions, or popularity, you become a more intrinsically motivated and trustworthy person.

When you allow the verb(s) of you to dance in interdependence, to consciously connect and co-create your life with others, the operation of identity will shift from "me" (a self-centered and closed orientation) to what Dr. Dan Siegel calls "MWe"[2] ("me+we"), a soul-aware and fluid center capable of both sovereignty and profound interbeing. You will begin to feel how your uniqueness is constantly informed, shaped, and refined by relationship.

---

2. Daniel J. Siegel, *IntraConnected: Mwe (Me + We) as the Integration of Self, Identity, and Belonging* (W. W. Norton, 2022).

And you will cultivate greater discernment about what is and is not for you. Your "no" will strengthen in equal proportion to your "yes." This is less a transcending of self than a sublimation.[3] When you sublimate something, you are refining and elevating its essence. The work of becoming whole sublimates the parts of you that were living in separation. This downregulates ego without killing it. You don't transcend self; you become *more* yourself. You integrate. Desire doesn't go away. Rather, you become capable of desire that is genuinely attuned to self, other and world. You start to make choices that are congruent with your own need and values *and* relational care. You learn to balance restraint with spontaneity. This path isn't always easy, because it asks you to let go of the security of readymade boxes and preconceived ideas about who you "should" be. But your emerging coherence is its own reward.

SOUL-CENTRIC IDENTITY

Here's my invitation to you: step into the magic of living a soul-centric identity. Soften and open to feel the deep pattern and pulse of your own essence dancing with a world you innately belong to. This true human path is not one of ego dissolution. It's a path of shaping the membrane of self towards alignment with the soul.

Vast and unnecessary suffering and confusion are generated by the misplaced belief that you can or should get rid of ego. The attempt to kill or annihilate the ego is the psychic equivalent of trying to cut out an essential organ of the body while it's still in use. We do significant violence to ourselves and others in the name of ego dissolution. Good-intentioned attempts to recover from the nightmare of separation spiral into self-hatred, spiritual narcissism, or even psychosis—not the homecoming we're looking for.

Judgment of the ego is an understandable reaction against harms caused by rigid, unconscious structures of identity within yourself and others. Separation based ego structures lie, cheat, play power games, and thwart reflection, connection, and change. But the problem isn't ego. It's insecurity, comparison, and judgement amplified by unhealed wounding and a culture that says, "whatever you do, don't fuck up."

---

3. This overlaps with Robert Kegan's phases of adult development: Socialized Mind (58% of adults) Self-Authoring Mind (35% of adults), Self-Transforming Mind (1% of adults), and the more Maslowian concept of Self-Transcendence: a state of moving beyond the self and connecting with something larger than oneself (following self-actualization). But I find the term sublimation to be a much more integrative and nonhierarchical way of describing the ongoing developmental process of integrating healthy ego functions with soul-centric attunement to self, other, and world. (See Robert Kegan, *The Evolving Self: Problem and Process in Human Development* [Cambridge: Harvard University Press, 1982].)

So do not seek to kill or transcend the ego. Rather, work to align the operating system of your identity towards integrity with who and what you are. Cultivate No Self as an unruffled ground of being. Develop a mature, authentic, emotionally intelligent Human Self as a vehicle for effective human-ing. But, above all, *center your soul's intelligence.* Being truly centered in your soul is the most disarming, luminous, and strangely quiet place to inhabit. It's an entangled place that is always open, never finished. To reside in this center of the singularity of self is like being the eye of your own storm.

Soul is that which makes you uniquely you. It's the blueprint of your unique place and purpose within the soul ecology. Your soul incarnated into a human form to further its journey of learning, loving, and choosing—and to contribute to Life's Song. Thomas Berry wrote:

> *Soul is fundamentally a biological concept, defined as the primary organizing, sustaining, and guiding principle of a living being. Soulcraft is the skill needed in shaping the human soul toward its fulfillment in its unity with the entire universe. The universe and human soul find their fulfillment in each other. Soul gives to the multitude of living forms wondrous powers of movement and reproduction, but even more wondrous powers of sensation and motion. Soul, in all its diversity of expression, enables the flowers to bloom in the meadows. It enables all manner of living forms, the birds, the fish, and other living beings to find their way through thousands of miles on their migration journeys back and forth across the continents and in the dark depths of the sea. The entire universe is shaped and sustained in all its vast interwoven patterns by the mysterious powers of soul.*[4]

The care and feeding of your soul intelligence liberates the unique and sacred contribution you are here to weave into Life's Loom.

Consider the following soul-centric perspective on identity development. You were born carrying gifts, affinities, and *karmas*—seeds of your unique way of being and creating. The membrane between you and the world was thin. As you developed, you learned how to get your needs met within your family and culture. As you grew, you experienced pain, loss, stress, and mild, medium, or intense traumas. Through these experiences, you gained various strategies for protection, control, connection, and

---

4. Thomas Berry, "Foreword," in Bill Plotkin, *Soulcraft: Crossing into the Mysteries of Nature and Psyche* (New World Library, 2003), xiii.

success. Over time, these became what *parts work*[5] calls the "protector" and "exile" subselves, who you unconsciously learned to identify with instead of the essential self. These defensive subselves are what we commonly call "the ego." There's nothing wrong with these parts. You developed them because you were doing the best you could with all existing information. However, these identity architectures were not molded by your soul's true nature. They were constructed as unconscious responses to your context. When left unconscious, they become a fixed default identity that accommodates for an underdeveloped Whole Self. They project onto the partners, children, authority figures, and perceived "others" to protect, control, seduce and keep us safe. Ironically, an undefended sense of self is required to express soul-centric identity and live beyond fear.

How can you meet and integrate these parts to develop soul-centricity? Begin with the hypothesis that you do, actually, have a soul. Then begin respectfully getting to know the parts who would rather not let you be authentically yourself. Soften and open to the intelligence of your body. Learn to live *in it*. If you can't feel your body, there is no way to hear the still small voice of your soul or feel the world calling you. Give yourself permission to seek out and enjoy the things that feel uniquely good to you—dancing, playing music, horseback riding, advanced math, building things, surfing, etc. Commit to a slow and gentle repatterning of secure attachment to yourself, partner(s), nature, and whatever you conceive of as God, Universe, or Source. Welcome the mirroring of trusted friends, therapists, and guides whose nervous systems and ways of being reflect you. Take spacious time in nature, and invite the reflections of your more-than-human kin. Very few of us know what it is to feel truly at home. Soul-centricity feels like home.

Cultivating a soul-centric identity is not a linear process; it's more like reconfiguring a galaxy as it moves through time and space. Visualize your identity as a constellation or a living, interwoven system: a complex, unfolding process made up of all your parts (or subselves) and of your conscious and unconscious assumptions, beliefs, behaviors, and habits of communicating and interacting with yourself, other, and world. Pulsing at its centeris the clear intelligence of the soul (or what Richard Schwartz, founder of Internal Family Systems Therapy [IFS], calls "Self,"[6] what John O'Donohue

---

5. Parts work is, originally, an indigenous framework for understanding the operation of the identity. Richard Schwartz's Internal Family Systems Therapy (IFS) is the best-known modern framework, though I learned parts work from Dr. Will Tagel and Judith Yost. Will's book, *The Many Colored Buffalo*, details parts work as he learned it from his teacher, Bear Heart. He and Judith also taught the parts work of Hal and Sidra Stone (*Embracing Our Selves: The Voice Dialogue Manual*). Constellation work is also useful.

6. Richard C. Schwartz, *No Bad Parts: Healing Trauma and Restoring Wholeness with the Internal Family Systems Model* (Sounds True, 2021).

called "your point or absolute non-connectivity," and what some call "the higher self.").

Healing, growth, transformation, and maturation implie reconfigurating parts of your identity system which necessarily affects the organization and operation of the entire constellation. Shifts can be specific or general, gradual or rapid. Repatterning one self-story, core assumption, or habitual behavior might gently and slowly affect the whole in obvious ways. At other times, punctuated experiences (like the birth of a first child, the death of a parent, or a significant psychedelic ceremony) can cause rapid yet nonspecific change.

Evolving your identity can feel like dying, not in the physical sense but like falling into an abyss as you release security and control. Why is this so scary? Because the previous pattern arose in a past where it kept you safe, enabled success, or kept the peace. Through embodied awareness in the present moment, you can repattern old behaviors if you choose to remain alert, respond differently, then kindly witness yourself in your new response. You must do this multiple times to establish the new habit. This is basic mindfullness psychology, and it works. You can realign self-talk and behaviors with your soul.

For most people, soul-centric identity arises as a secondary tier of adult development—the stage where you surrender the coverings of default identity (both dysfunctional ones and possibly highly functioning dominator patterns) to remember *who* you are as a unique soul spark and *what* you are in kinship and communion with Life. This feels good, not in the hedonic sense, but in the sense of felt alignment with yourself and connection to a bigger current life-force.

You are moving:
From identifiying with doing to fluid being, doing, and becoming
From pleasing, perfection, and self-forgetting to sovereignty
From numbness and superiority to interbeing
From control to curiosity
From insecurity to enoughness
From shame to authentic expression
From me to me+we
From apex individuation to kinship and belonging
From self-centeredness to soul-fullness

Soul-centric identity isn't a destination. It's a purposive, learning process. Life happens. Bumps, bruises, wounds, disorientation, loss, and grief happen. Recovery and integration occur. Joy, ecstasy, and contentment arise. Relationships mature and evolve. With persistence, you discover how to deliver your soul's gifts as your work in the world. In giving of yourself authentically, you pass through the refining fire of being fully seen and heard. You risk being genuinely known and loved.

Success on your soul's terms is not the same as success on our culture's terms. From the perspective of the soul, success means living your joy, expressing your most essential truths and gifts, and co-creating according to the image at the center of your soul. It's a path of surrender and discipline, transforming and transmuting, giving and receiving. Soul success isn't about external metrics. Rather, it's about inhabiting your center of agency to express Life's intelligence as it flows uniquely through you. It unfolds as you be, do, and become yourself.

When you fully incarnate as your soul, you have come to *reside* in yourself. This specific use of *residence* means to be fully embodied as your soul. Residence is not a destination but a life-long verbing of who and what you truly are. As you live this unfoldment, your shape of self softens, clarifies, and strengthens all at the same time. Because in residence, there is no one else to be, nothing to defend. You are you; you do you; you become you as a lucid expression of your soul.

Soul-centricity weaves you into the sacred through an expansive, permeable, bodily attuned shape of self whose circumference embraces and is readily entangled with a multitude of Earthly and cosmic relations. As you come to reside more fully in yourself, you organically invoke soul-centricity in others because your way of being naturally co-regulates with their bodies and souls. Your way of being is win-win. Your uniqueness nurtures, is nurtured by, and co-evolves with the uniqueness of other souls.

You occupy a unique location within the soul ecology. So does every other person and being. All these souls are part of the Gaian song. I firmly believe that soul-utions to our greatest challenges lie in soul attunement to the calling of the world. When each person's unique gifts, affinities, perspectives, and potentials are welcomed and nurtured—and when we listen to the ways in which these unqunesses complement each other—people blossom. Cultures of reciprocal freedom emerge. So let's work to liberate the intelligence of each soul and all souls.

SOULCRAFTING

Soulcrafting is a dance between your inner life and the outer world. It weaves between the interiority of your relationship with yourself, your *nature in and as nature*, and your work, relationships, and *dharma*. Soulcrafting brings you to the marrow of your incarnational impulse. In this fulfillment, all of Life is served.

Crafting refers to the art and skill of making or bringing a thing into being. But "bringing soul into being" is a paradox. Soul is a suchness, not a thingness. The soul speaks obliquely. It rarely shows itself in full daylight. It speaks through dreams, visions, archetypes, and stories. It shows itself only when you are able to get enough distance from yourself to truly see yourself. You have to learn to *listen*, roundly, not just with your ears but with instinct, empathy, and intuition. You have to see and sense archetypes, energies, totems, and symbols rather than stereotypes and preordained roles.

Soulcraft is artistry. It is both subtractive and additive. Like the sculptor who slowly chisels a hidden form from a block of marble, you are working to reveal something that is already there, just unseen. You skillfully, lovingly, chisel away extra material (of ego and cultural veils) so that your true form can emerge. Or, like a painter, you add color, outlines, highlights, and shadows to bring your inner image into full form. You add gems of insight into the sacred bundle of your inner knowing.

Soulcrafting is an ongoing dance of internal perception and outer expression. It bridges between the interiority of your visions, dreams, imagination, and ideation and the outer world of relationships and work. Sometimes it takes a while to build this bridge. For example, when I received the vision of myself as Samaya Storm, an ancestor from the future, I had zero idea how to translate that experience into my life and work. But I knew I had to. I had to hold that strangely gravitational image as a guiding light. Nine years later, it has made me into the writer of these words.

To undertake soulcraft is to follow a golden thread of juicy self-expression. You get to be fully and authentically yourself. At the same time, it is a seeking for the resonant, humming point of convergence between that which intrinsically arises through you and what the world asks and needs of you. This is where the richest meaning arises. As you discover how to express your soul through work and devotion, the golden thread of your soul's gifts is woven into the becoming of the world.

What emerges has a quality of choiceless choice, of nothing extra, of essential purpose. This is not purpose in the sense of a purely human construct but purpose in the biospiritual sense, as a function of relational fit within the soul ecology. By liberating your most essential essence while maintaining openness and connection, you fulfill the kiss between your own soul and the calling of the world.

The process of soulcrafting begins when you realize that you are, in fact, interested in knowing, expressing, and maturing your own unique essence. There is much to see, hear, and feel, but it is likely to be very faint at first. You must expand your perception beyond the norm to contact the numinous suchness of yourself. Thousands of books have been written on the quest to discover the soul. (I recommend beginning with Bill Plotkin's *Nature and the Human Soul* [2007] or *Soulcraft* [2010].) But in many ways, the process is instinctive. It's about wandering nonlinearly, aesthetically, kinesthetically in both internal and outer worlds, allowing both to reflect the soul's intelligence back to you.

Hold simple, sacred questions. "Who am I? What is my purpose? How can I best serve Life? What does Love want of me?" Then allow your body and psyche to meander with the intention to listen—at the edges and in the interstices—to the soul's quiet poetry.

While soulcrafting can happen without preconceived intent, it is best to create conscious containers for this work. Literally, *go on a wander*. Get yourself into wild nature, away from screens, artificial lights, and manufactured scents. Get yourself to a medicine retreat or ceremony. Clear your calendar. Don't go for just an afternoon. Go for a week or two. Set down all your doing so you can be and become.

Find a wild place that calls you. Ask its permission to enter. If you receive consent, then cast a circle around yourself and ask that place and all the beings and intelligences there to reflect you.

Walk. Sit. Breathe. Dance, surf, paint, or run. Sleep. Dream. Repeat. Gently hold your question, like a magnet attracting wayward particles. Offer your attention to vast vistas, tiny lichen, shadows in the water. Let the patterns you are embedded within speak to you. Notice the feelings, messages, aversions, or attractions that arise. Let your attention dance with the subtle intelligences of the ecofield within and all around you. They are wise and will respond. Slowly, some picture or message will emerge that situates you within your own life.

When you return from your wander, gather your closest friends—the one to four people you trust to love you exactly as you are and who always have your back. Ask them to just listen, without judgment. Share honestly, slowly. When you feel complete, ask for reflections. Ask them to mirror who they know you to be, what your true gifts are, and how they see you growing and changing right now.

Now, add time + tenderness + mindfulness + persistence. Soulcrafting rarely resolves all at once with a grand epiphany. It's a journey, and there's no set destination. It is more likely to unfold slowly over many months and years and to mature as you create and integrate your lived experience with your inner knowing. Live the wisdom you receive while soulcrafting daily. Sing the song the wind taught you. Shower the world with sparks of improbable joy, like the glistening hummingbird. Shelter others, like the grandmother oak who showed how to be truly held. Slowly shape and reshape your work and relationships as honest reflections of who and what you are.

Soulcrafting is a deeply human thing. You can't perfect it. You can't get it "right." It's about enjoying the journey—attuning and responding rather than attaining a goal. You can navigate beautifully and skillfully by healing your trust that you belong in this world. The intelligence of your soul is woven into a wider ecology of beings, places, patterns, and histories. You are unique but not special. Your soul carries seeds of possibility and beauty. These seeds germinate when watered with tenderness, patience, respect, and connection.

Soulcrafting is a way of life. You will know when it is time to return to the wild for a wander, or to the medicine or a ceremony, or to find a few hours of solitude for recentering. You will feel your soul knocking and respond to its call. Keep listening. Move forward, not because someone is prodding you but because forward is the direction of Life, and Life wants you to be, do, and become you.

THE ECOLOGICAL BODY

Your body and soul are sacredly bound to the more-than-human world. Your body is *eco-logical*. It emerged from, is part of, and participates in local and planetary ecology. You are a relative among relatives whose sameness and uniqueness co-inform each other's becoming. The wildness outside your door reflects and penetrates the soul's wild within.

What happens when you think of all the sentient beings we share this Earth with as allies, teachers, and guides? These kindred others are soul-mirrors of who and what you are and how to live and love beautifully. They know how to adapt and collaborate harmoniously within the biological substrate of existence. Engage with their feathered, hooved, rhizomatous, whiskered, stigmergic, and tentacular ways being to refine your own power and wisdom.

Here's a story to illustrate:

A few years ago, during a particularly strong medicine ceremony, I found myself eavesdropping on a conversation between two ravens. It was a warm Saturday afternoon, and all around the little valley, industrious humans were using power tools to deconstruct and make things.

The ravens were mimicking the affronting sounds with some glee. One commented that it sounded like the equivalent of farts and burps. Then the other said:

"Do you think they will ever learn to sing?" (The raven equivalent of a mic drop.)

They gleefully clicked at each other, then flapped into the cerulean sky.

Do you think we will ever learn to *sing*?

The more-than-human world we are embedded within calls to us in so many signs and signals. Ravens speak your name, even when you don't hear them. A snake crossing your path might remind you to feel your own spine or to honor the ancestors of your land. Tiny spiders weaving their strands across the vastness of the redwood overstory might reveal (if you are inclined to notice) the very real way in which the many parts of existence are tenderly interconnected by gossamer threads. Spring trilliums emerging with their white or violet three-petal flowers disclose riotous old-growth resilience within the soil. Every member of the Earth community actively communicates. But we tend to be so homocentric, so disinterested in subjective flows of meaning that can't be measured, so self-obsessed and busy projecting our superiority onto all the other beings here, that we fail to hear, let alone collaborate.

Everything changes when you open and listen to the symphony of reciprocities you are embedded within. When you attend to the flows of communications dancing between subjectivities, you begin to sense and feel kindred *interbecoming*. The magnitude and majesty of nature's sentience reveals itself; everything is feeling and responding to everything else. In *The Biology of Wonder*, biologist Andreas Weber writes,

> *Organisms are not clocks assembled from discrete, mechanical pieces; rather, they are unities held together by a mighty force: feeling what is good or bad for them. Biology . . . is discovering how the individual experiencing self is connected with all life and how*

this meaningful self must be seen as the basic principle of organic existence. . . . Feeling and experience are not human add-ons to an otherwise meaningless biosphere. Rather, selves, meaning and imagination are the guiding principles of ecological functioning. The biosphere is made up of subjects with their idiosyncratic points of view and emotions. Scientists have started to recognize that only when they understand organisms as feeling, emotional, sentient systems that interpret their environments—and not as automatons slavishly obeying stimuli—can they ever expect answers to the great enigmas of life.[7]

The animate world doesn't offer meaning like a book offers definitions. It hums, pulses, gestures—alive with sentience. Meaning is not deciphered but co-sensed, not grasped but felt-with. When you begin to listen—not just with ears but with skin, with breath, with the subtle musculature of relational attention—you may find yourself being read even as you read. Spiders don't explain the architecture of their webs, but something in your body understands the tension, the delicate strength. A raven doesn't deliver a thesis; it echoes your name into the wind, vibrating ancient, co-regulatory chords within you.

To inhabit your ecological body is not to accumulate messages from nature as data, but to metabolize the invitations of the living field, becoming rounder and more permeable, more attuned. You surrender the need to interpret every encounter and instead participate—sensually, soulfully—in the vast, reverberating dance of interbeing. Information flows not just through cognition but through touch, scent, image, vibration, dream. The more-than-human world becomes a partner in your remembering—not as metaphor but as co-creator. In this sentient ecology, meaning is not a codification or completion. It's a symphony. It hums continuously and harmonizes when you tend it.

When you ground into your ecological body, you will feel an ecstasy of aliveness, the easeful oneness that arises when you relax into communion with nature. You will also access disowned remorse, sadness, and pain for all the tiny and huge impositions of harm and cruelty you are complicit in. This may uncap a roiling well of ungrieved grief. Don't push these feelings away. Titrate them at the pace that you can be with them. They initiate you

---

7. Andreas Weber, *The Biology of Wonder: Aliveness, Feeling, and the Metamorphosis of Science* (New Society Publishers, 2016), 2.

into the gravity and grace of your sacred obligations and privileges as a member of the Earth community.

Living as the ecological body means composting the colonizing projection of "I think, therefore I am" to make yourself available to the entangled symphonics of Life that co-construct your ever-unfinished wholeness. Selfhood is revealed in its relationality. So, you might say:

I am because we are.
Many have embodied before me, therefore I am.
I am embedded within a sea of intelligent, embodied others, therefore I am.
We relate, therefore I am.

Root into your ecological body to know yourself as a creature of kinship. The raven calls you, too. What song will you offer in return?

ON SELF-REGULATION, CO-REGULATION, DYSREGULATION, AND RESILIENCE

Resilience is simultaneously an inside job and a relational process. You are a distinct and sovereign self *and* an interconnected being indelibly bound to all that makes you possible. Being a healthy human is an organismic process that involves both self-regulation and co-regulation.

Self-regulation is what you do from the inside out. When you are well self-regulated, you will feel more at home in yourself—in your body, in your awareness, and in your sense of agency in any given moment.

Co-regulation is what you do in interaction with all other beings and the environment. Bodies co-regulate with other bodies. Brains co-regulate with other brains. All bodies and brains co-regulate with their environment(s). We co-regulate with everything and everyone around us. We either feel safe or vigilant relative to these co-regulatory relationships.

Dysregulation happens when your sense of coherence, internal-to-you or in outer relationships, gets disrupted. Internal dysregulation can happen for physiological and/or psychoemotional reasons. External dysregulation occurs due to changes and stressors in work, home, health, or relationship and for systemic reasons like information overload, pervasive misinformation and polarization, climate disruption (e.g., extreme heat, fires, and hurricanes), or fear of human extinction. Dysregulation also happens when we simply can't find congruence between our values and our actions. This kind of cognitive dissonance simmers beneath our daily choices as an underlying sense of craziness. As Nora Bateson has said, pathology is "the organism's inability to make sense of its world."[8]

Resilience is the capacity to re-establish regulation in the context of change or stress through renewed connection with one's inner experience and/or one's outer world.

Everything co-regulates everything. We are all, to some degree, unconscious of this co-regulation. Yet we live within a dying and dysfunctional social system. You cannot count on it, nor would you want to. Realizing this can cause bewilderment, feelings of betrayal, rage, disgust, grief, self-judgment, depression, and anxiety. This is a healthy response. As Jiddu Krishnamurti said, "It is no measure of health to be well-adjusted to a profoundly sick society."[9] Reclaiming sovereignty requires disciplined attention to what is right self-regulation and right co-regulation for you.

When external structures of co-regulation dissolve, are in flux, or have become toxic, it's extremely important to learn how to self-regulate because you can no longer depend on those things to inform your sense of stability or significance. Many things can help you restore regulation: meditation, breathwork, exercise, forest bathing barefoot, unplugging. A well-regulated self can help others to better regulate themselves and can be a strong attractor for coherent behavior in groups and in society.

Yet it is simultaneously true that we are entangled beings who are biologically hardwired for co-regulation. No matter how self-sourcing you are, the experience of self is also woven with the relationships "self" is nested within. It can't not be this way. Our bodies and brains co-regulate with everything: light, sound, color, space, air, the nutritional content of our food, other people's brains, the commons of media and communications systems, and the overall aesthetic and emotional tonality of our home, family, community, work, civic life, and built and natural environments. It is helpful to understand the depth of this interpenetration because it can guide us toward building better, more coherent relationships, environments, technologies, and social processes.

There are many things—nonarbitrary things—that are worth co-regulating with. These include sunrises and sunsets, moon cycles, trustworthy people, your larger soul vision, your partner's presence, touch and breath,

---

8. Nora Bateson in "Living Systems Change," *The Club of Rome*, October 30, 2024, https://www.clubofrome.org/blog-post/bateson-living-systems-change/.

9. As quoted in "Krishnamurti on Mental Health," *Krishnamurti Foundation Trust*, accessed August 25, 2025, https://kfoundation.org/mental-health/.

spring wildflowers, seasonal harvests, your pet, the warbling of migratory songbirds, and the stridulation of crickets. It is worth making and strengthening bonds with family, friends, neighbors, and nature. It is worth nurturing transparency, mutuality, and kindness to build trust.

Without trust, co-regulation breaks down. The reliability, truth, and strength of agreements deteriorate. The social contracts between people or nations sink to the lowest common denominators of transactional power. Conversely when trust met and tended over time, this over time deepens co-regulation and resilience, both for you and for all those in a social network.

By consciously working with dynamics of self-regulation and co-regulation, you can effectively bring coherence in our rapidly changing world. This is a nonlinear way to stitch prosocial resilience into the social fabric, even as the pace of change and disruption increases.

THE REFRAMES

Being human can be confusing. Ever more so when we are simultaneously hacking the nature of reality and verging on biospheric collapse. Are we limitless or limited? Do we create our own realities or are we parts of a shared reality, and how can we hold that both perspectives seem to be simultaneously true? Are we here for mastery? Or are we here for the messy, ongoing dance of living, loving, learning, creating, and dying beautifully?

Humanness is malleable, adaptable, fluid. We scaffold perception, cognition, and expression on subtle, internal stories. Living the path of enlifenment means entering a different grammar of being—a relational grammar that supports sovereignty while nurturing attunement, communion, and co-emergence.

Below, you'll find fifteen reframes, simple hacks I've developed for living from embodied presence rather than intellectual programming. These little narrative tools are designed to help you avoid common "spiritual truisms" that hook people with easy interpretations of reality, agency, identity, and consciousness but that are actually dissociative, one-sided constructs that lead to spiritual bypass, narcissism, nihilism, and unconscious power-play. (These include common thought viruses like the idea that you should kill the ego or the hyperindividualized version of "I create my own reality.") The reframes mediate the infinity-loop between perception, cognition, and expression. Some of them recapitulate ideas you've seen elsewhere in these pages. Here, they are offered to gently structure thought. Play with them as anchors in your emerging experience and expression of wholeness.

THE REFRAMES

1. **Life is what you incarnated for.** Incarnation is nonaccidental and nonarbitrary. You did not come here to transcend, trump, trick, or leave Life. You came here to be, do, and become yourself in intimacy with and belonging to this world. You came here to rock humanness as your soul learns about love, choice, creativity, and freedom. To be a human is to live at the confluence of limits and limitlessness. Imagination is limitless. Information is limitless. Gaian systems are limited. Incarnation on Earth offers initiations into soul maturity through the constraining cycle of birth, growth, maturation, aging, and death. Skillful engagement with Life is a co-creative dance between the infinite potential of imagination and the blessed constraints and limitations gifted by Gaian existence. If you meet limits of time, energy, attention, and materiality authentically and honestly, you mature. Your soul grows. If you deny constraint, you can easily become trapped in addiction, dissociation, nihilism, or narcissism. In these traps, your soul devolves.

2. **You are a co-emergence.** Your living-ness inter-depends with all other living beings. You are made of and by relationships. As a creature of interbeing and entanglement, you experience and share relationships— both human and more-than-human, both seen and unseen. As your uniqueness dances in interbeing with other uniquenesses, your souls co-evolve.

3. **You are a sovereign being.** You are a unique location in time and space. The self–other boundary between you and the world is in no way absolute, but it is real. No one else can be, do, or become you. No one else can see, feel, or know the world the way you do. No one else embodies the unique intersection of genetics, history, and experience you do. Choose to inhabit the sovereign integrity of your body and soul. This empowers the uniqueness you bring to Life.

4. **Self is bigger than you.** You are a "me" and a "we" at the same time. Soul sovereignty shimmers in interbeing with the community of life. To the degree that you have founded your identity on being a winner at the zero-sum game, you will reflexively block kinship and communion with sacred others. When you soften and open to your intimacy with

and belonging to Life, you become a larger self, a self that encompasses others, nature, and cosmos. Meaning is revealed as a woven fabric of kinship and communion rather than a badge of ownership (of knowledge or things or achievements). The larger your circumference of self, the greater the meaning of your life.

5. **You are already whole.** You are enough. Wholeness becomes possible when you decide it is. Wholeness is a process, not a destination. It holds brokenness, pain, displacement, and trauma and always invites the potential to be home, right here and now. To realize wholeness is the beginning of health. Wholeness embraces what is (ups, downs, and in-betweens) with the larger, liberatory integrity of wholeness. You are always already whole, *and* you are never complete, *and* it's okay. Life will bring challenge, change, indignity, and defeat. Life will bring bliss, awe, and sparks of magic. Embrace this with wholeness. Wholeness is the underlying ground of your being and belonging to life.

6. **You are here.** Place is fundamental. You are not a nonlocal phenomenon. You are a location in the fabric of reality. From this location, you have power. You are an embodied, organismic being entangled within a living, breathing biosphere. From this context, you make choices. Through your body, you perceive and create. You cannot not be bound to hereness. Your life, your body, your single strand in Life's Loom is fed and nourished by other local phenomena: food, water, shelter, energy. All of these things come from somewhere. No matter how global or cosmic or transcendent your consciousness, you live, breathe, and experience the miracle of consciousness through place-bound, interdependent, organic existence.

7. **Your ego is not the enemy.** Evolution created it. It is simply an operating system—a user interface between brain, body, mind, and relationships. While the protection, control, rigidity, and fear that gets embedded in this psychoemotional OS makes it difficult to love, the ego can be evolved. It can become a vehicle for the soul. You can do this by softening identification with rigid structures, stories, and behaviors of default identity. The ego can learn to express soul-aligned identity that includes the mediation of healthy boundaries, needs, desires, and creative expression. The work is to heal the traumas, armors, and fixations and to shape the ego in alignment with your soul.

8. **Oneness excludes nothing.** No exceptions. Oneness is not a way to get beyond anything. It's a way *with*. Oneness invites you to embrace your nonseparateness with everything—with each thing, with all things, and with the One. Oneness does not mean dissolving into an undifferentiated field or singularity. On the contrary, oneness expands when you inhabit your own center in interbeing and interbecoming with other centers. When each thing lights up, all things can sing and celebrate the natural dance of communion among all parts. The statement, "It's all One," is a sloppy collapse of the more integral view that embraces the differentiated structure of God's Mind. It's more accurate to say, "I am one with the oneness that holds All." To experience oneness, expand the circumference of self to include all apparent "others" in the field of your love.

9. **Unconditional love includes all things.** (Even conditions.) Love—whole, healthy, life-y love—is both boundless and respectful of limits. The unconditional includes the conditional. Safe, sane, sacred, (and even sexy) connection lives at the intersection of unconditionality and conditionality. Unconditional love embraces all things, releasing judgment, offering compassion and trust, giving without attachment or investment in outcome. Without it, we can't know what it is to truly be seen and accepted or to belong and feel free at the same time. At the same time, we need love that contains, protects, respects, commits, asserts limits and boundaries, asks consent, makes and keeps agreements, and seeks justice. Without such healthy conditions, we fail to thrive. As you heal, mature, and expand, you will learn to better embody both of these aspects of Love. When you truly learn to include all things, while honoring your own and other's limitations and needs, you will discover *compersion*: the evolutionary capacity to feel pleasure in another's pleasure, a reciprocal loop that expands in deliciousness as both parties involved experience it. Compersion is the highest moral feeling available to a human being: a mutually reinforcing flow of love that empowers agency in all directions. This does not mean dissociating from boundaries or needs. On the contrary, it grows when you respect them. Our emerging world is grounded in an abundance of unconditional love yet glued together by care for conditions.

10. **You can and cannot create your own reality.** You create the subjective framing of your experience. The stories you hold to be true

about self and world construct your experience of the world from the inside out. Simultaneously, you are objectively part of a bigger world. You have agency over content, but not over context. You are the witness and narrator (of your experience), but not the maker of reality. Rather, you are a co-creative participant in a shared world. Reality creation means freeing yourself from default cultural programming that says you must be what you were taught to be. You take responsibility for how you construct perception, meaning, emotion, and choice. This can radically shift the energetics of your participation in our shared world. At the same time, the world continues to be the larger context your life is nested within. Reality is a dependently co-arising fabric of relationships. Reality also co-creates you. To hold one view at the exclusion of the other quickly becomes a toxic spiritual bypass, a narcissistic hall of mirrors that denies interbeing. It's an error of subjectivity to project your inner reality onto the world we share and then pretend that it's all you. Wisdom begins when you realize that reality is a co-creation, a co-constitutive emergence.

11. **Fear is *not* the opposite of love.** Fear is the inception of love—of life loving and protecting itself. Fear is biologically intelligent. At the most basic level, it is an organismic impulse to preserve your own life or the life of those you love. It is the body-wisdom that reflexively pulls away from fire or jumps to protect your child from a fall. In its raw intelligence, fear is *for* life. Fear gets twisted when the prefrontal cortex gets involved and unconsciously projects the past onto the future. Then fear lashes out or metastasizes into armors, judgments, victim stories, and vendettas. This is why fear is no longer an adaptive response for humanity. It has kept us safe, nursing survival, supporting us to protect, plan, and persevere. Yet, for beings like ourselves in a time such as this, *fear becomes a world killer*, a generator of division, polarization, and hatred that, when multiplied by exponential tech, is self-terminating. If we do not learn to love our fear, it will destroy us and our world. Therefore, we embrace fear as the ultimate teacher of love. To cultivate fearlessness, do not try to make your fear go away. Rather, cultivate and undying tenderness toward the parts of you that experience fear. This is what Chögyam Trungpa called "the tender heart of fearlessness."[10] You

---

10. Chögyam Trungpa, *The Collected Works of Chögyam Trungpa: Volume 8: Great Eastern Sun; Shambhala; Selected Writings* (Shambhala, 2010), 34.

choose your response to fear on the basis of love. As your tenderness strengthens, so does your fearlessness.

12. **Home is a thing we share.** Home is within, without, and between: an inner state, an outer place, and a field of relations. Home arises when your inner and outer worlds are congruent. Home is spiritual, material, and ecological. Home is and should be experienced as belonging to and intimacy with self, family, community, and the places we inhabit and share with other human and more-than-human beings, at many scales, from our backyards to our entire planet. Home cannot be hoarded or owned. To come home is to bring down walls and fences and positionalities that function as mythic barriers, enclosing a smaller sense of belonging. Home flourishes when shared. In the last century, we have placed a great psychological and spiritual emphasis on "coming home to oneself." While inner homecoming matters, it's just one part of the whole. Homecoming is a prosocial and pro-relational process. We are hardwired for connection, altruism, and empathy. We are made to experience home together. And we, as a creator, preserver, destroyer species, are uniquely capacitated to co-create a world where *everyone*—all beings—come home.

13. **Empathy enables trustworthy humanness.** If love has an opposite, it lives in the absence of embodied empathy—in indifference, shame, hatred, and sociopathy, in the inability to experience or metabolize guilt and remorse. The opposite of love is turning away from our natural intimacy with life, a closure, a deadening, an unfeelingness. Those who exhibit an inability to experience embodied empathy or remorse should not be trusted to lead. Rather, they should be called into deep and necessary healing. Empathy is sacred. Remorse is sacred. These emotions make us trustworthy by binding us to the world we share. They are the foundations of moral integrity.

14. **You are worthy because you exist.** Worth is an intrinsic quality of being. Worth cannot be determined by any external state, organization, culture, or person. Worth can be best felt through a deep sense of safety, belonging, permission, and play. To recapitulate the lessons of wholeness: you are enough. You exist, therefore you belong. Value and purpose arise through authentic soul expression in reciprocal, attuned relationship to others and the world (i.e., through infinite game play), not through

money, stuff, security, or clout. To the degree that you have reclaimed soul integrity, you have restored intrinsic motivation and are embodying sovereignty. To the extent that you are loving and creating in attuned, reciprocal ways, you are embodying interbeing and interbecoming. Life creates abundance through reciprocal relationships between beings and things who function in integrity with each other and themselves.

15. **Being right is a trap.** The compulsion to seek completion, closure, and correctness is an artifact of separation. The ability to inhabit *and-and* ways of knowing and feeling is an evolutionary competency. Learn to see, feel, and understand things from multiple perspectives. Gandhi once came to me in a vision. He said, "You cannot be right." He did not mean "you cannot choose rightly." He meant that the impulse of righteousness that wants to stake claim to the correct answer in any complex situation is exactly what creates and perpetuates war. So soften the habit of *either-or.* Develop the skill of dialectic—of holding multiplicity or both sides of any apparent polarity. Cultivate spaciousness for *not* knowing. Welcome the Mystery. Learn how to engage in thesis, antithesis, synthesis. Synthesis integrates apparently disparate perspectives. These are important skills for sense making in an increasingly complex world.

The reframes invoke an unarmored, vital shape self, a way of being and becoming a whole human that moves and breathes with Life. You will notice that they address polarizing narratives that show up as unconscious thought viruses in the collective while inviting you to embrace more holistic ways of knowing. Chew on these reframes gently, playfully. How might you come more alive by weaving them into your life?

A PRACTICE: RE-STORYING INNER NARRATIVES

Grab a journal. Choose one reframe that strums a chord of resonance or triggers a juicy resistance, and dig in. What does it invite? Why do you feel triggered? What are you defending? What might you gain from this new perspective? How do you feel when you weave this alternative story into your relationships, most especially between you and you?

SOUL-UTIONS

Soul-utions are seeking to be born through you—through your unique location within the soul ecology, your particular bundle of skills, gifts, histories, proclivities, and relationships. They are seeds of possibility only you can bring about. A soul-ution is a soul-aligned and rigorously attuned reply to the calling of the world. It blooms into being where creativity meets complexity and constraint with coherent response. An authentic soul-ution is a point of origination.

As you face the challenges unique to this time, slow down to the pace of trust. Unwind your mind from modernity's metabolic hustle. Root yourself in the sensual intelligence of your animal body in contact and conviviality with the animate world. Then breathe into the undefined space where the Mystery is already dancing with your soul intelligence. This is where your weights and wounds and wonderings—your desire to participate beautifully and purposefully—meet and mingle with the heartbeat of Life. Original intelligence is conceived from here.

Before running toward answers, pause to be with your questions, your longings. Raise your perspective to that of the eagle. Take the highest and broadest possible intellectual and spiritual overview you can. Hover here. Release preconceived notions. See and feel the bigger patterns. Authentic intuition arises from here.

Before jumping into action, expand into network awareness, deepening and widening your focus. How do your ideas and plans synergize with those of others? Are they symbiotic with the underlying, connective, collaborative intelligences of your community and nature? Soberly consider the probable outcomes. Is the thing or process you're envisioning really generative? Or are the second and third order effects potentially harmful to others? A wise and disciplined mind begins here.

Soul-utions emerge when you hold the right kinds of questions: What unique vision or gift or responsibilities are you holding that no one else seems to be speaking for or bringing into being? What keeps you up at night, clawing in dreams, rants, and longings? What do people consistently, persistently ask you for help with (whether you think it's important or not)? What pulls most profoundly at your heart or most intensely triggers your anger? What would you do if you knew you could not fail? What would you do even if failure were inevitable? How do you like to be used by Life?

Soul-utions aren't silver bullets, one-stop shops, or "correct" answers to society's problems. They don't deal in narrow goal logic. Rather, soul-utions are driven by love. They emerge *con-sensually*, adaptively, in wide-boundary listening, where uniqueness meets uniqueness in attunement to the soul ecology. Soul-utions can be complex or simple, bespoke or scaled, hyperlocal to global. They are round goals, always tinged with the sweetness of clarity, the musk of mutuality, the salt of authenticity, the glow of aliveness. Round goals may be simple, complicated, or complex, yet they always honor complexity and entanglement and are oriented toward care for the whole. They hum and harmonize, expanding or creating new niches and possibilities for other players.

Often, we are already expressing soul-utions, even when we don't know it. We are already being a kid-whisperer, soul-listener, steward of community cohesion, organizer of resources, weaver of relationships, translator of worldviews, waterer of gardens, or builder of emergent technologies. Sometimes soul-utions are sneaky that way. They are already moving through us as the thing(s) we are naturally good at.

Soul-utions quietly crystallize in interstitial listening. They rise in psychedelic visions. They surface in community, in celebrations, in audacious myths of tricksters and regenerators. They emerge when science meets wonder, informed by a systemic view. They push through the cracks when awe or heartbreak dissolve resistance and fear. They appear when we slow down or touch timelessness. They pulse on the edges and in the margins, everywhere and anywhere that people are called to come home, together, to a world that works for Life.

The world calls to your soul uniquely. How will you respond? As chaos increases, so too does the potency and possibility of any coherent offering. Soul-utions are erotic gifts of love made real through hard work, skill, flexibility, and time. They carry gravity. They disrupt normalcy and change trajectories. They stitch new memories in Life's fabric. In a world that has tried to shape people as cogs in its machinery, soul-utions liberate the notes we bring to the soul symphony.

A POEM: SACRED BONDAGE

I am sacredly bound to this world.

I claim my bodied interbeing with the continuum of creaturely Kin who breathe here now and who have breathed before me.

I am rock and water and sunlight combined and commingled, fine-tuned by time, adaption, selection.

I am infinitely, intelligently, implicately part of all that is greater than me.

I am an emanation of Deep Time, the result of an infinity of interwoven memories.

I am slow fire, structured water, electron differentials . . . pulsating, breathing, stretching, thinking, typing, choosing.

I am sublime chemistry, continuously metabolizing diverse intelligences to make more of myself.

I celebrate my interbecoming as a cell in the planetary body.

I dance through time as a stitch in Life's Loom, an erotic weaver of the fabric.

I dream because we dream.

I imagine because we imagine.

I create because creation has created and will continue to create, consuming my contribution.

I breathe because all are breathing, respiring, reciprocating.

I celebrate Life's symphonics.

I am nothing without you.

We are nothing without us.

We are worlding the world together.

We are one human species, re-membering the larger Body we are a part of, re-tuning to the Soul Song that sings us.

Our Enlifenment is nonaccidental and nonarbitrary.

We incarnated at this time to learn this wholeness.

Our planetary crucible presses upon us, calling us, with increasing ferocity, to remember our place in the continuum, to ground our awakening in the immanent domain, where we stitch the parts together.

As diverse cultures and cosmologies, manyfold ontologies and epistemologies, our bodies know the same belonging, the same evolutionary continuity, the same biospiritual bondage to this world that is our home. Matter is the mother matrix that made us all. Time lives in our bones and blood.

We are and can be real because we are part of a greater becoming.

Let us live as good-enough ancestors—as people who shall be known by our children's children as the ones who chose Life. For, if we don't, they will not exist to remember us.

Let us become—together.

I, we, remember.

PART IV

REIMAGINING OURSELVES

Our Opportunity
What can life be like when each of us reclaim
co-regulated, authentic attunement to our own bodies,
other humans, and the natural world?
How can we experience power, pleasure,
meaning, and play differently?
Touch, taste, see, feel—and imagine—a world
where everyone comes home.

Sophia Speaks

ON ORIGINAL INTELLIGENCE AND PLANETARY NEO-INDIGENEITY

This is a delicate, dangerous moment in your collective evolution—not a time to be comfortable but a time to be radically alive. Something nascent, sacred, improbable is gestating in you, a technologically mature, ecospiritual civilization at a planetary scale, a scale you could not perceive or embrace until the contraction of existential risk and the expansion of consciousness had reached critical tipping points.

To successfully navigate the turbulence, volatility, grief, temptation, and liminality of the coming years, you must untangle from separation as you rebirth yourselves into planetary neo-indigeneity—the species-wide knowing that you belong to the Earth. This is an exciting time! Your shiny delusions of mastery, closure, and control are collapsing all around you. As they do, you are beginning to re-member the basic competencies of a people who can co-create true civilization—the ancient, indigenous art and science of original intelligence.

The people you call "First Peoples," "Indigenous," "Native," "Original," or "First Nations" are the living carriers of these competencies. First Peoples consciously belong to Gaia in the sense for which humans are biospiritually shaped. They have not forgotten entanglement with nature and place and the many roles they play in reciprocal communion with Creation. They understand that knowledge arises (or originates) specifically, relationally, and intergenerationally in intimacy with Life. Their stories braid between countless generations, tending deep time. They know how to communicate with forces of nature to amplify the intelligence, biodiversity, and abundance of local and planetary ecologies. They know who they are: human beings with timeless souls and gorgeously mortal bodies who sing a uniquely precious song in the cosmos and whose love, work, and memory stitch integrity into the fabric of Life. They often call themselves "The People" in their original languages because they know who and what they are. They are true humans.

These First Peoples, who your economic, political, and religious systems have systematically terminated and silenced, are your strongest teachers in this time. They fight for their knowledge, languages, lands, and sovereignty with fierce love. They know their very existence is a final boundary between the well-being of all beings and the hungry ghost[1] of your world. Their ways of being co-create harmony in Life. They fully understand what will be lost along with them if they are erased.

Though some First Peoples have partially forgotten who they are after generations of physical and cultural genocide, they persist in reminding the totality of humanity to remember who and what you are. They voice the clarion truth that all humans are custodians of Gaia. We suggest that you center their rights, voices, and ways of knowing in leadership.

Your word, "indigenous," refers to being of a place: co-arising within ongoing, specific, and co-adaptive relationships with land and the more-than-humans who inhabit it over multigenerational arcs of time. To be indigenous is to love maturely. It is to interact with time as a circular wholeness and a spiraling tapestry of interwoven cycles. It is to know and be known by the subjective intelligences that co-sing a place. The First Peoples of your planet are indigenous to specific places. Over seasons and cycles, they earned access to the multidimensional pathways through which human attention and agency co-orchestrate the symphonics of abundance.

Most of you have forgotten or erased these ways of knowing. Few of you are initiated. But you are in a collective rite of passage. You can remember how to belong to Life in the context of your current world. You are indigenous to your planet, shaped by this kairotic moment in Gaia's evolution. It is possible to live your lives and build your world in alignment with ecological flourishing for all places and all beings at all orders of scale. This ancient yet emergent possibility wants to be born in you. Planetary neo-indigeneity

---

1. In Buddhist and Chinese traditions, a "hungry ghost" is a being tormented by insatiable desire and suffering from extreme hunger and thirst. Moloch is a kind of hungry ghost, as is the spirit of Wetiko, the being identified in some North American indigenous traditions as a spirit of insatiable greed and as the mind virus that plagues the Western world.

begins when a sufficient number of humans own and embody their collaborative role in co-orchestrating the continuity and emergence of Life.

The shift from localized indigeneity to planetary neo-indigeneity is both necessary and fraught. Now that your world has reached peak separation, you will either consciously choose ways of being that enable harmony between humans, nature, and technology or devolve into chaos and control. This transition requires unprecedented sobriety, discernment, and reverence.

This collective leap of consciousness will only go well if you give special attention and protection to their living knowledge of First Peoples. Your dominant world system has expended vast quantities of energy to subsume them. You likely carry unconscious habits of stealing, appropriating, copying, and tokenizing. Instead, approach with humility and respect for cultural autonomy. Center—and yield space to—their ways of knowing. Bring curiosity and care as you listen and learn. Together, observe and explore first principles. This will reawaken the ancient, ancestral, intelligence that lives within your own body and soul.

The memories First People carry are within all human bloodlines. All of your progenitors were once resourced and sourced through direct connection with ecology, ancestry, and deep time. You would not be alive without this living original intelligence, this ability to make sense of and navigate Life through direct, relational attunement. It carried your ancestors through long winters, floods, famines, persecutions, migrations, wars, and emigrations. It brought them home, even when homes and lives had been lost. Rekindle it now—it is already within you. Remember how to weave it—without naivete or fuzzy logic—into the foundations of education, technology, economy, science, medicine, and governance.

Your word, "original," is a key. The word has two, almost contradictory yet simultaneous meanings: "present or existing from the beginning; first or earliest; coming before all others," and "having the skill or imagination to create new things," or "not known or experienced before." Original intelligence synthesizes these two meanings. It refers to patterns, principles, protocols, or stories that are "first," or "before all other." It also refers to the origination of a true thing—not true in the timeless sense of the word but in the sense of being relationally, ecologically coherent. Original intelligence is the evolutionary genius that arises through attunement to Life. It enables coherent adaptation.

*Original intelligence includes, yet is greater than, ecological intelligence;
it is also erotic, embodied, spiritual, artistic, scientific, technological,
and mythopoetic. Original intelligence weaves memory, history, locality,
and the continuity of ancestors and descendants, both human and more-
than-human. It is wise in the ways of restraint and knows that freedom is
always coupled with responsibility. It is observant, absorptive, and patient.
It connects the local, the global, and the cosmic. It sings wholeness.*

*To activate your capacity for original intelligence become fluent
in the ways of water, the sonics of ecologies, the spatial etchings
of migrating wings and fins, the rumbles of plate tectonics. Live
in your body, your senses. Marry instinct and intuition. Embrace
complexity, ambiguity, and entanglement. Enter the Body of Time as
a participant in the infinite game. Life builds on Life. Life ebbs and
flows, births and dies, waxes and wanes, cycles and spirals. To know
this intimately, in the way wombs know it, is to be trustworthy.*

*Seek out initiation into embodied, ecological, intergenerational, and
interspecies listening to weave your imagination with the mind and body
of nature. It doesn't matter how you do this. Wander in wilds. Plant and
harvest. Use science. Use psychedelics. Use art. Enter through somatic
awareness to crack through dissociation, sloth, entitlement, and pain.
Reweave your otological experience of Life with the sacred in Life once again.*

*Original intelligence isn't special or endangered. It's available to all
humans who make themselves permeable to real-time, real-bodied, love-
fueled, subject–subject relationships. As the ground of a true human
culture, original intelligence collaborates with Gaia to enable abundance
for all beings. We know this through our own experience. Embodied love
for life is the foundation of soul-sustaining civilizational processes.*

*We invite you to walk this terrain in sacred partnership with
First Peoples. Working together, you have the opportunity
to reawaken billions of people to Life's Song.*

*Planetary neo-indigeneity will crystallize organically when enough
of you remember your place and participation in the soul ecology.
You will find yourself at home within Gaia in an emergent way—as
a single, diverse yet unified, species who celebrates and owns your
ecological station. This nascent stage in human and planetary evolution*

*is a phase shift from subject–object dominion to subject–subject
co-relationality—and your survival and flourishing depend on it.*

*You don't need permission from us or any of your so-called leaders to
begin. Just open yourself to original intelligence. There is no time not to be
in this co-sensing and collaboration with human and more-than-human
others. This is the rerooting and re-tuning your soul craves. You can and
will come home if and when you recognize you are already home.*

CHAPTER XII

RE-COGNIZING WHOLENESS

Attention is the currency of consciousness.
Use it wisely.

SONG WITHIN A SONG

In the spring of 2021, high in the misty mountains of Costa Rica, I had the opportunity to pray with ayahuasca that had been grown, harvested, and prepared on the land on which the ceremony was taking place. The ceremonial guide, a lifetime student and celebrant of Western psychology, science, *and* traditional, indigenous knowledge systems, had planted the vines some ten years earlier. They were gifted and blessed by her Peruvian teacher and were now happily growing thick helical spirals around tall trees circling the *maloca*. This batch of medicine was her first harvest, and she offered it with humble dignity and a tinge of awe.

A few hours into the ceremony, I felt compelled to go outside into the moonlight. Barefoot and wobbly, I shuffled a few paces along the damp stone path toward a boulder nested among heavy foliage. The tropical night was alive, humming with thousands of unseen insects and night birds. Here and there, I could see the opalescent gleam of eyes refracting tiny diamonds of moonlight.

I settled myself on top of the strangely comfortable moss-covered rock and emptied my mind.

Suddenly, I was inside *their* song. I could hear and feel the medicine in my body crooning with the animate, specific intelligences around me. I could feel the ayahuasca continuing to harmonize with all her relatives, intoning hymns and lullabies she'd been improvising for years, tunes that had not ended with harvest. Instead, they had evolved and now included me in my ingesting of the medicine. She was aligning my psyche with the ongoing chant of the land itself.

I surrendered tiny tugs of resistance and opened myself to the call and response of each being and all beings singing to and through each other into the night.

Then I realized I could *see* their conversation. Like stardust contacting stardust, or strands of rainbow light weaving a larger cosmic web forming an underlying fabric of intelligence that constantly surrounds us, I could see networked filaments of molecular and energetic information flowing as currents of consciousness between beings.

There's a curiously amplified experience of synesthesia that often occurs in medicine space. Synesthesia is when your brain produces a sensory impression related to the stimulation of anther sense, causing you to experience multiple senses simultaneously. Some examples include tasting words or linking colors to sounds.[1] When you are in an expanded state, cross-sensory experiences can occur with extraordinary depth and richness. This was the most exquisite synesthesia event I had ever experienced, like being an instrument played on all sensory channels both as a witness and an artist. My awe was part and participant within the orchestra. I had glimpsed the immanent infinity of interactions that make everything possible, an underlying symphony of relatedness we humans rarely get to touch or feel. I had been drawn directly into the singing within the Song of Life. It was ecstatic!

I emerged from that ceremony ever clearer in the knowing: Everything sings to everything. Everything whispers everything else's name. An infinity of interactions weave the continuity and emergence of the One Soul as all souls dance in entangled becoming within Life's Loom. We can recognize this wholeness in its ceaseless incompleteness. As we do, we open to a world singing in reciprocity and complementarity—a world of co-relationality that is responsive to us. Indeed, listening to it, celebrating it, elevating it, and collaborating with it may be what humanness is for.

CO-CONSTRUCTING REALITY

The Kogi people of the Sierra Nevada de Santa Marta mountains of northern Colombia speak of people living within the constructs of our globalized civilization as the "Little Brothers." They see us, in our persistent

---

1. "Synesthesia," *Cleveland Clinic*, last updated May 3, 2023, https://my.clevelandclinic.org/health/symptoms/24995-synesthesia.

anthropocentrism, consumptiveness, hyperindividualism, and parts-based thinking as ignorant, uninitiated, and immature denizens of an animate world that is constantly talking to us but that we have not learned to hear or respond to. They remind us that we can remember what it is to collaborate as whole beings who are part of a greater whole.

We co-architect the world we occupy according to how we attend to it. There are ways of seeing, knowing, and interacting that colonize, extract, atomize, and reify separation. And there are ways of seeing, knowing, and interacting that expand listening as they weave us more deeply into intimacy, belonging, and conscious co-creation with the intelligences all around us. This begins by recognizing that there *are* subjective intelligences all around us and that we are mutually bound in interbecoming with them.

In describing the conclusions of his book *The Matter with Things*, Iain McGilchrist says:

> *The world we know, then, cannot be wholly mind-independent, and it cannot be wholly mind-dependent.... What is required is a maximally open, attentive response to something real and other than ourselves, of which we have only inklings at first, but which comes more and more into being through our response to it—if we are truly responsive to it. We nurture it into being; or not. In this it has something of the structure of love.*[2]

World co-emerges in the dance between subjects and subjects. It arises in the space where the mind meets "something real and other than ourselves." Our assumptions mediate what world we bring into being. If we privilege our own subjective, first-person perspectives and project them onto outer reality, our interactions will involve a high level of attunement and control. If we privilege third-person, ostensibly objective perspectives, orienting toward what can be measured or quantified scientifically, we then project a false separation between ourselves and what we are attending to. Exclusive focus in either direction misses the discursive fabric, the shared between-ness that co-constructs you, me, and everything else. We are intersubjectively and interobjectively entangled with what we attend to. Relationality is primary, not "the knower" or "objective facts."

---

2. Iain McGilchrist, "We Need to Change Our View on Consciousness," closing presentation of the Science of Consciousness Conference 2021, Essentia Foundation, November 11, 2021, https://www.essentiafoundation.org/iain-mcgilchrist-consciousness-is-the-stuff-of-the-cosmos/reading/. See also *The Matter with Things: Our Brains, Our Delusions, and the Unmaking of the World* (Perspectiva Press, 2021).

When you start to understand this, you realize that self is a dance with animate others with whom you share this world. The default cultural narrative that privileges individual consciousness and success above all else crumbles. Self becomes a permeable, dynamic "me-we-us." Living from here allows you to come home *within* the vital relationships that make life livable, beautiful, and meaningful.

HACKING WHOLENESS

Wholeness—as a way of being, seeing, knowing, and dancing with Life— can be "hacked." The following ten lenses are perceptual frames to realign your stories and the currencies of your attention with the underlying reality of wholeness. They are not intended as a totalizing framework; rather, approach each one as a pointing out, an invitation. Some will speak to you more than others. I've collected them from my teachers—indigenous wisdom keepers, philosophers, healers, and physicists—who are attuned to the sacred (implicate and explicate) order of things. They are not just "ideas." Rather, they are ontological lenses through which to re-cognize (or "cognize anew") self, other, world, and the relationships within and between them, and thereby shift your embodied experience and expression. You can also think of them as gateways into original intelligence.

Each of the ten lenses offers a calibration that qualitatively tunes the attention you bring to any *inter-action* between you and another being, thing, place, or field. Try them on. One at a time.

Think of each lens as a practice to be felt and embodied. Take a whole day, a week, a moon cycle, or a full solar year to try a lens on as an inner stance from which to interact with the world. Take a few of the lenses with you into a medicine ceremony. See for yourself how they elucidate your experience.

No belief is required (though you may need to *suspend disbelief*). As you engage with them, you will begin to experience, interact, and *know* differently—more intimately, more animately. Your awareness may become more granular and more inclusive. The architecture of your perception may change, recrafting meanings, values, and motives. This is a spiritual practice of immanence.

In short form, the ten lenses of wholeness are as follows[3:]

1. Wholeness is.
2. Everything is related.
3. The thing is the thing.
4. Everything is intelligent.
5. Everything is sacred (if you make it so).
6. Change is constant.
7. The moment of power is now.
8. The place of power is here.
9. Choice is relational.
10. Coherence arises from integrity, reciprocity, and complementarity.

The rest of this chapter offers each lens in detail. If you make it your practice to see, feel, and know Life through these lenses, you are likely to discover the Song of wholeness that is and has been singing in, as, and through you all along.

THE 10 LENSES OF WHOLENESS

1. WHOLENESS IS

Wholeness is the dance of all parts, ceaselessly co-constructing the fabric of reality. Wholeness isn't fixed. Quite the contrary. Wholeness is a boundless, creative, continuously emergent, physically and quantumly entangled process.[4] Wholeness emanates, holds, and moves between all things, all textures of experience, all flavors of feeling, all thought. Wholeness, in physicist David Bohm's words, is the "implicate order" of reality, the underlying structure unfolding and enfolding within and all around us.[5]

---

3. Deepest gratitude to Dr. Will Taegel for the first principle revealed and lived at the intersections of his work as a theoretical physicist and as a nature mystic; to my teacher and spiritual father, George Grey Eagle Bertelstein, for principles two through five, informed by his lifetime study of Lakota wisdom; to the ancient Hawaiian Huna tradition for the seventh and eighth; to physicist philosopher Karen Barad for the ninth; and to the People from the Heart of the World (the Kogi and Arhuaco elders of the Sierra Nevada de Santa Marta mountains of northern Colombia) for the tenth.

4. The Nobel Prize in Physics 2022 was awarded to Alain Aspect, John F. Clauser, and Anton Zeilinger for their "experiments with entangled photons, establishing the violation of Bell inequalities and pioneering quantum information science." ("Press Release," *The Nobel Prize*, October 4, 2022, https://www.nobelprize.org/prizes/physics/2022/press-release/.)

5. David Bohm, *Wholeness and the Implicate Order* (Routledge, 1980).

We've been trained not to attend to this fabric of interbeing and interbe-coming that makes us possible. This inability to perceive or feel wholeness drives us, again and again, to smallness and defense. In our fragmentation, we engage in side-taking and side-making, endlessly recapitulating a world at war with itself. In *Wholeness and the Implicate Order*, Bohm suggests an antidote:

Our general world view is itself an overall movement of thought, which has to be viable in the sense that the totality of activities that flow out of it are generally in harmony, both in themselves and with regard to the whole of existence. Such harmony is seen to be pos-sible only if the world view itself takes part in an unending process of development, evolution, and unfoldment, which fits as part of the universal process that is the ground of all existence.[6]

The medicine for fragmentation lives in attending to things, people, beings, your experiences, your relationships, and your work as entangled parts of a greater wholeness. To do this, soften and open. Shift from the sharp lens of part-making to the round sensing of interconnection. How is this thing or person or situation already whole (even in dysfunction, dis-ease, or brokenness)?

It is far easier to *feel* the underlying wholeness of reality than to *think* it. Thinking complexly is hard. Feeling complexly, on the other hand, is something we are all designed to do quite naturally. It is quite natural to rest into your body and feel instinctively, empathically, and intuitively into a field. This is how the embodied feminine does complexity. It is felt, non-linear. It is necessarily imprecise and open and best done in council with others. This kind of sentience and shared sensemaking has been dulled and shamed out of us. We need to reclaim it to liberate interdependence. Through embodied attunement to the underlying wholeness of things, you can better nurture health and harmony in yourself and all that you touch.

2. EVERYTHING IS RELATED

"Learn how to see. Realize that everything connects to everything else." Such a line is attributed to Leonardo da Vinci. Things are entangled. Reality is rela-tionship. We are nested, interpenetrated, nonseparate. I inter-be, therefore I

---

6. Bohm (1980).

exist. You inter-be, therefore you exist. We inter-be and become, therefore we exist. Relationship is fundamental. To be incarnate in a physical body is to be related to everything that makes you possible. To deny this is delusion.

Recall Berry's invocation of Earth as a communion of subjects.[7] We interexist and interbecome in subject–subject relationality. Each of us carries our histories, languages, traumas, and desires into every interaction. When we connect with a person or tree or horse or raindrop, we (and they) are touched by the other in mutual, intersubjective becoming. Who and what you are co-arises in we-space, in the dance *between* subject and subject. Relationality is actually deeper than individual subjectivity or objectivity because nothing exists alone. All things arise in co-becoming.

Relationality is centered in the grammar of many original languages but is truncated in a language like English in a way that nearly erases interbeing. In the classic Cartesian construct of "I think, therefore I am," the individual observer is the seat of "reality creation." From this perspective, one has no evidence that other minds or beings even exist. We end up in an entirely narcissistic solipsism, a philosophical construct that leaves you wondering if there is such a thing as an "other," or whether that person or organism or world is simply a projection of your own mind. Whereas, if we refocus attention on the underlying fabric of interbeing and interbecoming, the first and most obvious thing becomes the fact that "I would not exist if it weren't for other bodies and minds." I would have no language with which to cognize, no body with which to interact. The co-emergence of the other becomes obvious, both because it is a necessary precursor to one's own existence and because one can readily sense and feel the subjective intelligence of the other. (Anyone with a dog or cat knows that their pet is sentient and has a unique personality.)

In *How to Fight*, Thich Nhat Hanh (Buddhist monk, peace activist, and inspiration for the Engaged Buddhism movement) wrote,

> *Interbeing is the understanding that nothing exists separately from anything else. We are all interconnected. By taking care of another person, you take care of yourself. By taking care of yourself, you take care of the other person. Happiness and safety are not individual matters. If you suffer, I suffer. If you are not safe, I am not safe. There is no way for me to be truly happy if you are suffering. If you can*

---

7. Thomas Berry, "The Determining Features of the Ecozoic," Handout from the library of Santa Sabina Conference Center, San Rafael, California, 2004, https://www.ecozoicstudies.org/wp-content/uploads/2016/09/Thomas-Berry-Key-Principles.2015-05-14.pdf.

smile, I can smile too. The understanding of interbeing is very impor-
tant. It helps us to remove the illusion of loneliness, and transform
the anger that comes from the feeling of separation.[8]

Nothing is not related. Separation is an illusion. This means we are related to and entangled with *everything*—the good, the gross, the shattering violence, the delicate rainbow. Relationality invokes accountability. We are, in fact, entangled. When a tree is cut down in a forest, other trees immediately send life-saving sugars and nutrients to aid their injured relative. Like the trees, we need each other to flourish. Though our science has penetrated the interiority of bodies and stars and atoms, we still know very little about the complex, symbiotic fabric of relatedness we are embedded within. We are only beginning to explore bioacoustics, geomagnetics, the subtle stigmergic messages of tiny beings conveying information across landscapes, or the power and connectivity between sacred sites that have been identified by indigenous wisdom keepers throughout time. But we are learning. We are relatives among relatives who are woven into the connective tissue of Life. Our fluency in the language of relationship will make or break our collective future.

3. THE THING IS THE THING

Everything is what it is. Each thing is uniquely itself. You are not me. I am not my cat. Mount Everest is distinctly itself. The thing is the thing.

Uniqueness co-evolves through the dance between uniquenesses. Each thing is itself not despite but because of the relationships it is entangled within. Suchness is relational and contextual. The materialist worldview collapses meaning by analyzing things as though they exist separate from the relationships that co-genenerate them. But, this leveling decontextualization fails to appreciate the co-emergence of things.

The impressionist painter Claude Monet said, "To see, we must forget the name of the thing we are looking at." To see and know a thing truly, be with it, not as a metaphor, not as a collection of cultural constructs: its name(s), the stories about it, the science that offers a certain view, but as the thing itself - its size, shape, heft, color, form, function, energy, behavior - its attractiveness or repulsiveness to you - the way it physically, energetically, emotionally, sensually moves and feels when you interact with it. Consider

---

8. Thich Nhat Hanh, *How to Fight* (Parallax Press, 2017), 73

its web of interactions and relations, its freedoms and constraints, within its eco-social-spiritual-economic-technological contexts.

An eagle isn't (just) the lore about eagles. It's a majestic, self-centered, far-seeing apex predator who flies higher than almost any other bird. In some places it will be rare or endangered – in others, common. Its feathers can heal souls and transmit prayers to the heavens. If you observe one, or ideally several, and get to know its true habits, you can begin to know eagle-ness, or what some people call "eagle medicine."

The Okumé tree isn't (just) the dollar value put on it by logging companies and commodity markets. Its price as plywood, or veneer or building timbers obscures the complexities of its intrinsic and contextual value. Each tree is unique and wholly itself—an ancient, hardwood sentinel of the Congo. And a member of a community—a maker of rain clouds, a guardian of springs, a home to moustached monkeys, grey parrots and hornbills, a renewable source of fiber for baskets and torches, a cool, shaded place for you and others to rest on a humid, sunny day. While standing, it inhales your exhale in perfect reciprocity. Cut, on a truck bed driving towards the port, it is a sad testament to the effects of globalization on communities.

Your body isn't a machine. It's a body—your body. The wisdom within it emerged through 3.7 billion years of biological co-evolution. Your hands were shaped by and for planting, trapping, gathering, art-making. Your uprightness co-emerged with your ancestors' propensity for far reaching vision. Your biophysical energy cycles weave you—body and mind—into the rhythms of sun, moon, season and Earth's dreaming.

A computer isn't a brain. It's a computational device devised by complex organisms whose capacities for abstraction and recursion enabled the math, mining, engineering and industry capable of building it and whose hungers for further efficiencies, knowledge and control programmed it. (A computer built and programmed by an alternative ontology would be a different kind of machine.)

To know a thing, be with it. As it is. In its contexts and relationships. Attend to each thing as a who, a how, a why, a what, a field of interdependencies, a process that co-exists uniquely and co-emergently, and that can be known through direct experience. Attend to each thing as a part that is also complexly, transcontextually interconnected with other interbecoming parts at multiple orders of scale. Let the stories, the science, the names, the metaphors be a secondary support to your direct, embodied observations and interactions. From here, you just might learn to love and care for that thing truly. Plus, you will uncover more attuned, accurate and complexly situated ways of being and interacting with reality.

4. EVERYTHING IS INTELLIGENT

We live in an animate universe. Everything, all things—animals, plants, fungi, microbes, rocks, rivers, weather systems, planets—are intelligent.

At first, this can seem like magical thinking. But, as Joshua Schrei, creator of *The Emerald* podcast, reminds us in his episode "Animism Is Normative Consciousness," it's a way of knowing that has been a basic feature of human culture for most of our brief existence on this planet. In the episode description, he writes:

> *For 98% of human history, 99.9% of our ancestors lived, breathed, and interacted with a world that they saw and felt to be animate. Imbued with lifeforce. Inhabited by and permeated with forces, with which we exist in ongoing relation. This animate vision was the water in which we swam, it was consciousness in its natural dwelling place, the normative way of seeing the world and our place in it. It wasn't a theory, a philosophy, or an idea. It wasn't, actually, an -ism. It was felt experience. It was, simply, how things were.*[9]

Animism, or the view that all things are intelligent and have some level of agency, has been a cultural operating assumption for the majority of our 300,000 years as a species. More recently, this view has been described in the philosophy of panpsychism, the view that some kind of intelligence or mind is "fundamental and ubiquitous in the natural world."[10] If you think this is bunk, consider suspending disbelief for a week or two and pay careful attention to what happens when you engage with a plant or animal or ecofield as though it is intelligent. In my experience, living things respond.

Mainstream science is rapidly catching up to this view. Sentience is now acknowledged in bees, fish, and lobsters.[11] Wild baboons communicate to sympathetic humans by shitting (yes, shitting) on their decks. (They have been shown to do this only with people who are attentive to their needs.)

9. Joshua Michael Schrei, "Animism Is Normative Consciousness," *The Emerald*, December 1, 2020, https://open.spotify.com/episode/6wutqbPB6KBb4cn8dnqLE3.

10. *Standford Encyclopedia of Philosophy*, s.v. "Panpsychism," last updated May 13, 2022, https://plato.stanford.edu/entries/panpsychism/.

11. Evan Bush, "Scientists Push New Paradigm of Animal Consciousness, Saying Even Insects May Be Sentient," *NBC News*, April 19, 2024, https://www.nbcnews.com/science/science-news/animal-consciousness-scientists-push-new-paradigm-rcna148213.

Octopuses recognize familiar faces and seek to play with known human friends. Alex, the African grey parrot, knew over one hundred words and could understand concepts like "same" and "different."[12] Recent research reveals that elephants, dolphins, prairie dogs, ravens, crows, meerkats, sperm whales, parrots, and bats all use vocalizations to identify individuals within their familial groups. Crows have been known to name predators or humans they frequently encounter. Baby coral can hear the sound of a healthy reef.[13] Mice, surgically deafened by lab technicians, stop singing. Instead they squawk and scream.[14] Plants use chemical signals and ultrasonic sounds to talk to each other, animals, and even people.

When you take the view of animism, song, art, ceremony, and speech become pathways to love the world awake. Anyone can offer currencies of consciousness to activate and amplify relationality. We dance down the rain. We sing to the dolphins to let them know we remember them, want them here, and are their friends. We honor the spider and ask her, as she weaves, to help us potentiate the numinous fabric of causality. The living world craves to be seen, heard, and sung by us. It craves to be named and loved. When we meet it, it meets us in return.

5. EVERYTHING IS SACRED (IF YOU MAKE IT SO)

Sacredness is a choice. Sacredness is made real through the action (the verbing) of reverence. The sacred emerges through currents of loving attention that flow between you and another being or thing. To make sacred is an intersubjective act that elevates the intelligence of both the perceiver and the perceived, changing both parties and amplifying the animate intelligence flowing between them. Sacredness is a quality of entanglement between subjective intelligences.

Sacredness is for everyone and everything. Western religious and anthropological paradigms, emerging out of Judeo-Christian contexts, say that sacredness is some special category reserved only for ritual contexts and objects that have been set apart from the profane world. But sacredness isn't the property of religion or other people's rituals. Sacredness doesn't

12. Irene M. Pepperberg, *Alex & Me: How a Scientist and a Parrot Uncovered a Hidden World of Animal Intelligence—and Formed a Deep Bond in the Process* (HarperCollins, 2008).
13. Nadège Aoki, et al., "Soundscape Enrichment Increases Larval Settlement Rates for the Brooding Coral *Porites Astreoides*," *Royal Society Open Science* 11, no. 3 (2024), https://doi.org/10.1098/rsos.231514.
14. Sonia Shah, "The Animals Are Talking. What Does It Mean?" *New York Times*, September 20, 2023, https://www.nytimes.com/2023/09/20/magazine/animal-communication.html.

arise by putting something on a pedestal disconnected from everyday life. It is here whenever you notice the beauty, meaning, or power of a thing.

Sacred is both an adjective and an adverb; it is a qualitative description of a thing and a frame for how we attend to a thing when we know it through love. *Sacred* describes the quality of attention that flows from us to anything—a gurgling spring, a flower, a newborn. It's a gesture.

Whether something is sacred isn't an "is or isn't" issue. The sacred emerges through flows of attention that are either given or blocked in relationship to the world around you. In other words, your presence co-constructs the sacred in the world. Sarah Durham Wilson, women's rites of passage leader and author, explains this concisely: "The way you alchemize a soulless world into a sacred world is by treating everyone as if they are sacred until the sacred in them remembers."[15]

We either recognize other people, beings, and places as sacred, and so elevate them as sacred, or we declare them unsacred, and so deny the energy that elevates through witness, praise, gratitude, awe, respect, tenderness, reciprocity, protection, and care from flowing between us and those beings or things. When we say "nothing is sacred," it's a relinquishment of our power to make sacredness real through our love. Therefore, choose to see the sacred in yourself, others, the little beauties all around you, and this broken, beautiful world.

6. CHANGE IS CONSTANT

Change drives the dynamic dance of reality. When creation was born out of the great, undifferentiated field of the One, the dance was born. Being dances with becoming to make all things possible. Chaos dances with order in the process of evolution. You are dancing in time, a verb in flesh, an ongoing becoming in a sea of becoming. Cells birth and die within you, metabolizing, transducing, replicating, making your entire body anew every seven years. Rock dances sky as sky kisses rock, eroding, changing. Your soul dances with other uniquenesses, through which both are changed.

Change is not the enemy of continuity; it is continuity in motion. Change is a sacred, inconstant constant. According to process philosophy, reality is made up of fluid and dynamic entities, always in motion, always in relation. Process is. Emergence is continuous. The Buddha reminds us, "impermanence is inescapable." All things living will die. All things created

---

15. Attributed to Sarah Durham Wilson, author of *Maiden to Mother*.

will crumble. Death begins the cycle of renewal once again. In the Lakota tradition, Škaŋ refers to "multi-dimensional worlds in constant motion."[16] Lakota snowboarder and youth educator Conor Ryan describes *taku wakan skan skan* as "something sacred moves through everything." Indeed, those who flow with Life know that Life is flow.

Yet in a modern world obsessed with mastery and permanence, change is often framed as a threat, a problem to manage, or a crisis to solve. But from an enlifened perspective, change is a teacher, a lover, a trickster. It doesn't just ask us to adapt; it invites us to become more permeable, more attuned, more willing to be undone and reformed by the world in real time. This is not the linear progress narrative we've been sold. It is something wilder, humbler, more intimate, a becoming that asks us to loosen our grip on certainty and dance with what is emerging.

This movement is not chaos to be tamed but rhythm to be attuned to. Resilience lives not in resisting change but in our availability to it. It is not the rigid strength to endure unchanged but the supple grace to be reshaped without losing integrity. Resilience, then, is not the capacity to bounce back to who we were but the willingness to become someone we have not yet imagined. It lives in our availability to be moved—not just physically but emotionally, spiritually, intellectually, relationally. To be resilient is to stay present inside the alchemy of change, to trust that even disorientation carries intelligence, even unraveling can be sacred. It is not a solo feat of strength but a co-emergent dance with the larger patterns of life, death, renewal, and transformation.

Are you dancing? Healthy people dance with change. They respond. They move with the rhythm, catch the wave, tango with *Kairos*. They know the magic inherent in full presence and attunement to deep time. They listen for the optimal moment, aligning their actions with the pulsations of the greater whole. This is not passivity. It is a deeper form of trust. You have this capacity to move with change. It is written in your breath, your blood. All it takes is the courage to listen, to open to the motion of the universe, and let yourself be reconstituted by its sacred movement.

Every day, we wake up inside the ceaseless flow of becoming, gifted again with the chance to breathe into the dance. To love what is. To respond with humility and care. Great changes are coming, not only around us but

---

16. Mila Hunska Tašunke Icu (Joseph American Horse), et al., "Standing for Unči Maka (Grandmother Earth) and All Life: An Introduction to Lakota Traditional Sciences, Principles and Protocols and the Birth of a New Era of Scientific Collaboration," *Maxell Museum Technical Series*, no. 42 (2023), https://maxwell museum.unm.edu/sites/default/files/public/technical-series/Tech%2042%20Lakota%20Traditional%20 Sciences%20220117.pdf.

within us. Let us not brace against them but meet them with grace. As the great physicist Iliya Prigogine said, "We grow in direct proportion to the amount of chaos we can sustain and dissipate."[17] Let us dance change together, not for mastery, not to attain the next rung on the ladder, but to grow into more relational, meaningful, and vital possibilities.

7. THE MOMENT OF POWER IS NOW ("NOWNESS")

Now—this present moment—is the gateway to both timelessness and all time. Though we can remember the past and think into the future, we can only experience life in the now and the now and now, continuously. Clock time, or *chronos* from ancient Greek, is a social construct that lends structure and linearity to our relationship with past, present, and the continuous flow of the now. But the structured bits of *chronos* are not time itself. Time is the Mother matrix within which Life happens. Our fixations on linear constructions of time often inhibit actual presence *in* time. When you are fully present *in* time, you begin to know full aliveness.

Full presence in the *now* gives you access to two equally important aspects of wholeness: the explicate, relative, relational field you are embedded within *and* the implicate order (what Buddhists call primordial reality) within which all things are unseparate emanations of timeless, formless, boundless intelligence. Dancing here dissolves distraction, potentiates attunement, and softens attachments to ideas, opinions, and preferences that you might otherwise project onto others and the world. Being fully present in the now makes you available to your own soul, to the song of each thing, and to the humming fullness of consciousness.

Full presence in the now can be a gateway to special omniscience—a hyperexpansive state of perceiving time, reality, love, and the history (past, present, and future) of a particular place. Accessing such omniscience is a kind of "superpower" through which you might more deeply touch and better comprehend the ecological, ancestral, cultural, and cosmic fields of intelligence that co-construct your experience of this moment.

Nowness enables a more direct and embodied relationship with what's actually occurring in a given context. Free of judgments, projections, or preconditions, you can better be with things as they are. And from this ground, true choice emerges—genuine response rather than reflexive reaction. When you arrive, fully present in the moment, you

---

17. Ilya Prigogine, *Order Out of Chaos: Man's New Dialogue with Nature* (New Science Library, 1984).

enter a state of unarmored availability to existence. Therefore, nowness enables life-centric power.

8. THE PLACE OF POWER IS HERE ("HERENESS")

You are *here*. Your body is a place embedded within the ecofield in which you are currently standing, sitting, breathing, perceiving, thinking, and creating. Place co-creates you.

An *ecofield* is a field of hereness that includes all geological, climactic, biological, ancestral, human, and technological intelligences—all seen and unseen forces and flows—that dance together to inter-inform the uniqueness of that place. To be deeply attuned to the ecofield, you occupy is to participate in the power of that place.

You are causally entangled with all the places that have resourced this moment: the places from whence you receive your water, your food, the power animating your device, your clothing, your roof, etc.

Place co-in-forms everything about your experience of this moment, just as your presence and participation (or absence) in these places co-informs the living experiences of everything within them.

Bodies live within terrains. Your body is your phenomenological home base, home place, through which you perceive reality and enact power. It is the locus through which your consciousness embodies, relates, and acts. You are a unique location in God's body and mind. You are an unrepeatable seat of entangled perception and response. From *here*, you have leverage.

You can easily locate yourself in hereness by finding and aligning with east, south, west, and north in any given place. Take a day or two to observe where the sun rises and sets (east to west). Notice where light and shadow, heat and cool come from. (Generally, warmth flows south to north in the Northern Hemisphere and north to south in the Southern. These gradients are, of course, due to the Earth's position on Her axis relative to the sun.) To locate in the *here* is to begin to sense and feel and collaborate with the relative flows of energy that sustain and/or challenge life in that place—where storms, winds, waters, migrations of birds, butterflies, whales, fish, or even flows of plastic pollution or tourists come from. Locating gives you a larger sense of the intelligence and flux of a place as it helps you to better align your own energies and collaboration.

Hereness is a foil for dissociation. When you are here, you are *associated*, located in attention and attunement to shared reality. Maturity is impossible without locating your body and mind in the specific contexts and relationships in which you find yourself. From *here*, you can align and respond to what *is* in genuinely adaptive, appropriate, creative, response-able, and collaborative ways.

9. CHOICE IS RELATIONAL

Choice arises in the entangled, relational space between things.

When we think of choice, we tend to think of a self (a bounded, inter-nalized individual) who chooses, who surveys a menu of options and makes a selection. Yet this framing can be seen as an artifact of separation, a myth of modernity. The notion of choice as a private, sovereign act unravels when we truly embrace the depth of our entanglement.

Inquiry into the nature of choice is perennial. Most recently, neurosci-entist Robert Sapolsky has argued in his book *Determined: A Science of Life Without Free Will* that our lives are entirely conditioned by factors outside our control:

> *You cannot decide all the sensory stimuli in your environment, your hormone levels this morning, whether something traumatic hap-pened to you in the past, the socioeconomic status of your parents, your fetal environment, your genes, whether your ancestors were farmers or herders. . . . We are nothing more or less than the cumula-tive biological and environmental luck, over which we had no con-trol, that has brought us to any moment.*[18]

This scientific determinism correctly identifies the profound condi-tioning we are shaped by. Yet Sapolsky concludes from this that choice is an illusion—a move that unwittingly performs the very contradiction it denies. To argue the nonexistence of choice is, ironically, to choose a posture, a framing, a stance. What is missed here is not the biology but the *ontology*.

In her framework for agential realism, Karen Barad describes us not as individuals but as *intra-acting phenomena*, always already entangled.[19] Agency is not derivative of a self, a possession we wield, but an emergent

---

18. Robert M. Sapolsky, *Determined: A Science of Life Without Free Will* (Penguin Publishing Group, 2024), 4.

19. Karen Barad, *Meeting the Universe Halfway: Quantum Physics and the Entanglement of Matter and Meaning* (Duke University Press, 2007), 235.

property of a situation—diffused, relational, and co-constitutive. The "self" that chooses co-arises with the choice itself as part of a dynamic unfolding. Barad writes:

Agency is not an attribute but the ongoing reconfigurings of the world. . . . Agency is about possibilities for worldly reconfigurings.[20]

Seen this way, choice is not a sovereign declaration against circumstance, nor is it nullified by context. It is a fragile, contingent membrane, an inflection point where the world folds itself into becoming with us, as us, in us.

I decided to ask iboga, *What is choice?*

Rather than answering in words, the medicine showed me a bubble, then it showed me the thinnest membrane, only a bare atom thick, indicating the membranous nature of choice and the tremulous permeability of decision. Then it brought me into an infinite sea, a vision of all of reality,- co-constructed of dynamically interacting bubbles, and said:

"Choice is a bubble."

The meaning was clear. Choice is a fragile thing, the thinnest of membranes, that we must feel very delicately if we are to engage with the true nature of choice.

Then the medicine showed my own finger poking the bubble, popping it, and said:

"Don't poke your choices."

It was not a reprimand. It was an instruction in subtlety. When we try to dissect, dominate, or overengineer a choice—to poke and prod it into correctness—we collapse the membrane before it can complete its becoming. When we are worried, distracted, disembodied, the field of possibilities implodes. The relational field reorganizes. A new choice will arise, but that choice horizon will never return.

Iboga's message: Choice is not an object to handle. It is a relational event to attune to. Our ability to truly choose, or choose truly, depends

---

20. Barad, 141.

upon the quality of our attention as we sense and feel our way across the membrane of each moment.

True choice, then, is not a possession. It is participation. It arises through unarmored attention to subtle tensions in the fabric of the here and now. Through the lens of agential realism, this means attending to the ways we and the world co-configure one another in every breath. The quality of our attention modulates the quality of what becomes possible. From the view of wholeness, choice is not the isolated action of a separate self but a pulse in the living fabric, a moment where the implicate order becomes briefly, tenderly explicate.

In a world designed to hijack our presence through dopamine loops, dissociative consumption, and algorithmic manipulation, choice gets co-opted. Our bodies become reaction machines. Those delicate membranes of choice crumple under the weight of distraction and stress. To reclaim the subtle dignity of choice, we must reclaim our attention. We must sense again with the whole bodymind.

To choose is not to assert mastery. It is to become porous enough to be changed by the membrane we're crossing. Presence is not what precedes choice; it is the medium through which choice arises. Presence is choice in its most elemental form. When we meet the moment fully—not to control it but to be transformed by it—reality reconfigures with us, not through force but through resonance. And from there, new worlds become possible.

10. COHERENCE ARISES FROM INTEGRITY, RECIPROCITY, AND COMPLEMENTARITY

Coherence is the humming sensation you get when a thought, choice, or action lines up with the health and sanity of the whole. Your coherence is not a private project. It's not just for your nervous system or your inner peace. It's a field of shared relationality. Coherence arises when we choose to interact with reality according to integrity, reciprocity, and complementarity.

Integrity arises through inner congruence of body, heart, mind, soul, and relationships. It means establishing sufficient sovereignty (from the default paradigm) to be true to your word, your values, your love, and the soul visions that are given to you. It also means taking full responsibility for yourself. Integrity can be immediate. It can be fulfilled by something as simple as taking off your headphones to be curious and kind with the cashier at the grocery store. Or it can be a lifelong project, like regenerating an old-growth forest, or healing racism, or building a ministry to serve the One Life we all share.

How can you restore soul integrity? By being brutally self-honest. Interrogate your motives and see if they are aligned with what you hold to be most good, beautiful, and true. Are intrinsic or extrinsic factors driving you? Are your motives and actions congruent with your integrity, the health of your relationships, and with Life? Or are they being driven by profit, status, power, proving, or any other transactional dynamic?

Reciprocity arises through mutually accountable and beneficial exchanges of time, energy, attention, resource, and care. Reciprocity seeks balance in giving and receiving, offering and taking, activity and rest, across all relationships, both human and more-than-human. In reciprocity, I don't give because I'm going to get. Reciprocity isn't transactional. I give because giving is sacred.

Reciprocity only makes sense when it is motivated by love. Be aware that if your hands have not been initiated by hard work with soil, rock, wood, water, fire, food, birth, and death, you may not understand what it means to be in reciprocity in a truly meaningful way. Compassion is not enough. A round and open empathy, initiated by lived experience, will better show you the way. Reciprocity is fed by skills of listening, apology, council, reconciliation, and restoration. Reciprocity is as qualitative as it is quantitative. If reduced to objective measure, the heart that holds right-relationship falters. Finally, reciprocity asks for sacrifice—the act of making sacred by giving of love, time, energy, attention forward into the mystery and possibility of what is yet to come. Reciprocity is our true nature. Once reawakened, it spreads.

Complementarity refers to the way souls, ideas, actions, stories, organisms, and genders symbiotically collaborate with each other. It's a relational principle that invites you to feel the sweet pleasure of building on or subtly amplifying another person or being's intelligence. Complementary colors, when put together, bring out the beauty of both. Complementary plants grow happily in guilds. To complement another can be as simple as consciously offering additional depth or detail to another person's idea rather than countering it. The People from the Heart of the World teach this practice as a simple turn of phrase: "May I complement you?"

When you consciously choose to practice these three principles together, they create virtuous, synergistic loops. Coherence arises when you, as a self, choose to be in integrity with who and what you are, to give and take in balance and with gratitude, to sense into the harmonics of the larger ecosystem (of people, beings, stakeholders, needs, etc.) and respond in a way that complements other people or parts. When many people practice integrity, reciprocity, and complementarity together, this engenders eco-social-spiritual coherence and harmony at the scale of the society practicing them.

A PRACTICE: LIVING INTO THE LENSES

Each lens is a practice, inviting you to see, feel, know, and engage with Life as the miraculous fabric in which you are embedded. To embody any of them is to come more alive, to be more accountable and consciously entangled, and to more skillfully serve Life.

Which of the ten lenses feels most intuitive, obvious, and easy to you? Try that one on for a week or a month. Write it on your bathroom mirror. Bring it to your morning practice every day and see where you can strengthen it or expand its reach. What changes when you do?

Which feels most alien or counterintuitive? Take that one as a gentle yet disciplined inquiry. Take it on a walk. Take it to the ocean. Or take it to a medicine ceremony. Ask the medicine: What does this principle of wholeness really mean? See what the medicine has to say. Are you resisting that principle because it would reveal something uncomfortable or demand change?

Each lens presents a way of being in relationship with yourself, others, and our world. Try them on one at a time, experientially. Slowly, you may realize that you, others, and this ever-breaking world are authentically whole.

A MEDITATION: TUNING TOWARD WHOLENESS

Go outside. Find a comfortable spot to sit or lay down. This is not a meditation of escape. This is a dance with deeper patterns, a sensing into the Implicate order of wholeness as it bleeds into the explicate. You are here to re-cognize wholeness—not as thought but as sense and sense-ability.

Let your breath slow, your body soften. Feel the Earth rising beneath you. Let the ground hold you. Drop attention from the spinning mind into the listening skin, the weighted bones, the diaphragm oscillating up and down with each breath. Now let these words guide you.

Rest in wholeness.

It is already here—trembling, emergent, incomplete.
No need to earn it.
You are within it.
Let it hold you as you soften edges of control.

Take the view that there is no inside, no outside.

Everything is related.
You are unseparate.

You are a nexus of entanglements, a subject among subjects.
Breathe into this space of communion.

Meet each thing as itself.
The tree is not a metaphor.
It is roots rooting, branches branching, leaves respiring.
See and know each thing as it is.
Discover uniqueness with fresh curiosity.

Greet the glimmering intelligences all around and in you.
Shape your attention as a question.
What is the wind whispering to the pine?
What does the soil know of your sorrow?
Who is singing, and how can you better sing with them?

Let love well up and pour out of you.

Mix and mingle it with each uniqueness that touches you.
Sacredness moves on currents of reverence.
Bring loving presence to this breath, your body, that bird, this broken, beautiful world.

What you bless becomes luminous.

Now feel it all changing, moving, co-emerging.
You are a verb in flesh, a ripple in the river of becoming.

So is every other thing and being around you.
Let yourself be danced by Life.

Surrender the illusion of stillness.

This moment is your altar.
Not yesterday. Not tomorrow.
Now is when your soul meets Life.

Gently yoke your attention to time's continuous horizon.
Let this presence ripen your power.

You are HERE.
Arrive in this place—this ground, this ecofield of relations.
Let the land speak to you.
What does it need? What does it give?

What will you give back in return?

Now that you are fully present,

The subtle horizon of choice opens.

Possibility shimmers at the membranous edge of becoming.

Listen—where is vitality leading you?
Let Life choose through you.

And when it's time to act, proceed from integrity.
Attune to your body, heart, and inner knowing.

Be brutally honest if you wish to move congruently.
From here, real reciprocity is possible.
From here, differences create complementarity.

Marinate in these harmonies of relationship.

This is coherence—not achieved but practiced, moment by moment.

For this, we offer gratitude.

Then finish with a generous exhale.

This is how to complement Life's Song.

Gently complete your meditation. Put your hands over your heart to reestablish a personal sense of center, then place your hands on the earth to seal the practice. Let this practice be a gift to a world that is remembering itself through you.

CHAPTER XIII

TENDING COLLECTIVE EMERGENCE

Humans are an essential element of Gaia.
Our role within the soul ecology is to tend beauty,
abundance, and biodiversity within Life's Song.

STORIES AND SEEDS

It was early spring 2019 in San Francisco. People crowded into the little community theater at the gritty intersection of 16th and Valencia. My friend and I had come for an event called *Kairos*, exploring the intersections between resilience, leadership, indigenous knowledge systems, and deep time in responding to the existential imperatives of our time.

The lights dimmed. A small, strong-boned man with room-sized energy, wearing a striped, pink shirt and a matching headband woven in traditional patterns, strode onto the stage.

"Greetings from the Lenca Tribe, my friends. I am Antonio Chevez, the Jaguar Chief of our people. My people are the so-called Lencas. We are a union of many families and clans. We are proud of our diverse origins and to have formed a harmonious nation in the grips of the Ice Age. We currently reside in territories you call Central America.

"Through our unbroken oral lineage, we know that some of our clans originally came from central North America, from the place that is now the middle of your country. When the last Ice Age swept across the land, we could feel in our bones and read in the signs of our animal and plant relatives that cold was coming and it was time to migrate to warmer climes. So we circled our people, gathered our stories and seed, and journeyed— mothers, children, elders, and fathers—the many days of travel, some over land, and some by sea, southward. We stopped in what is now Mexico and

313

Central America. Here, the waters were warmer, and the land could grow crops, making it possible for animals, plants, and people to survive and thrive. Here, our ancestors established their homeland, their new nation.

"In the 1600s, slave traders came to our shores bringing imprisoned Africans. As more intruders arrived, there were several outbreaks of deadly diseases. The privateers captured and enslaved many of our people, whom they sold to replenish slave labor in Cuba and Peru. Later, we were subjected to brutal genocides inflicted by Catholic missionaries. In 1821, when the Central American countries gained independence from Spain, we were denied political representation. In 1932, the contemporary state slaughtered thousands on indigenous people in El Salvador. They also banned any display or practice of indigenous culture.

"To avoid obliteration, at every step, we reached into the wisdom of our ancestors; we adapted; we persisted. We have now established strong political and cultural sovereignty in Honduras, El Salvador, and part of Nicaragua. Though with great limitation, we continue our efforts to govern ourselves, to rescue and speak our language, engage in our traditional festivals, rituals, and practices, and raise our children to be aware of their Lenca heritage. At the same time, we continue to evolve to meet the modern world.

"I'm here to tell you, if you're sitting here with me tonight, your ancestors have been through just as much as mine, or worse. You carry their seeds of resilience."

The hairs on the back of my neck prickled. This man was voicing the wisdom of deep time, awakening dormant memory. As he shared the oral histories his people continued to tend, he was weaving a spell of ancestral remembrance. He spoke not just for himself and his people, but for us all. His presence was a transmission, inviting each of us to feel ourselves at the front of countless generations who navigated trial and tribulation, ritual and devotion, feast and famine, to get to this now, and whose wisdom could support us to navigate the storms of life with tested resilience.

Chief Chevez went on to say, "All ages of light are followed by ages of darkness. A dark age is coming. Our ancestors did not survive the Ice Age by digging their heels into their existing way of life. What are you ensuring will survive that dark age?

"The deeper question to ask yourself right now is not what to protect but what will be *useful*? *What stories and seeds will you carry?*

"Each one of you is producing tools. Get clear about what those tools are, how you want to carry them, and how you can share them. Share them through well-tended networks of relationship. That's where resilience lives.

Culture is constructed of processes of constant emergence. Culture is ritual and relationship. It's the context within which our stories build reality. It's never too late to continue emerging.

"Reclaim meaning and create your own authorship. You are producers of knowledge. Be stewards of social, ecological, and spiritual wisdom that supports self-growth and care for Life. Because in one thousand years, they will be referring to everyone in this room as ancestors.

"If you are an ancestor in the making, what are you doing to be worthy of this extraordinary title?

"Knowledge and utterances are seeds that if cultivated and dispersed in the right time, the right soil, and with the right care, will yield immense abundance. These seeds cannot be spoiled by pests, nor can they be confiscated by kings or thieves. They are invisible, portable, powerful, and eternal. Cultivate your hills, valleys, and mountains with seeds of sacred insight. When your journey reaches its zenith, you will look back and marvel at the rich canopy of the lush forest of wisdom left across the lands you have walked."

He concluded his talk with a graceful, shallow bow.

I was floored. He had spoken my deepest knowing into existence: a trust in my dogged, life-long commitment to gather and share wisdom of soul, body, and earth. His words validated the thousands of small and large choices I'd made to build community, do permaculture, facilitate embodied transformation rather than go corporate, and to privilege analog experiences over screens and online opportunities—even when the world said I was crazy.

In the years since, I've had the privilege of sharing a few conversations with Mr. Chevez who, on the one hand, lives the deeply held values of his indigenous heritage, and on the other, is a cultural visionary with two master's degrees in international security and behavioral science who helps Fortune 100 companies navigate existential risk. Living abroad makes his role as hereditary chief complicated. For this reason, he has transferred many functions to other Lencas who collaborate in cultural stewardship. His unique blend of sophistication and simplicity radiates a kind of joyful coherence I have not experienced in any other human being.

He has encouraged me to trust my inner authority, matched and mingled with my attunement to others and the calling of the world, to sense what stories, seeds, and actions to tend—and to offer this same invitation to you. Because *it will take all of us, each responding in uniquely attuned ways, to weave the possible future.* He worked with me to edit this recollection of his talk, his real-time telling of his people's living, oral memories—now written down and shared with you with his blessing.[1]

Dignity and authority arise when we connect with the underlying, biospiritual intelligence that enables adaptive response to calamitous events. Grounding in ancestral memory, ecological knowledge, care for community, and sacred pattern tracking is a perennial path of resilience. And, these skills can be integrated with emergent technologies. Each of us is a weaver of the fabric of continuity between past, present, and future. This fabric is woven at the confluence of time-tested wisdom and attuned emergence. It is made of seeds and stories, tools and protocols, habits and rituals, daily choices and relationships. Each one of us is a descendent of thousands and a future ancestor to unknown others. These others call us through deep time to be the conscious bridge between what has been and what might be.

This chapter offers stories and seeds to carry through unravelling and rebirth. They are intended as generative sparks to feed ekokosmic cultures that bring us home to our ecologies *and* to our cosmic place as conscious co-creators with Life's Song.

Living this inquiry has forced a composting of separation's myths within me—being with the messiness of unknowing and discovering new presence in the process. I thought I was looking for universal truth. Instead, I found a plurality, a deeper embodiment of the always unfinished evolutionary intelligences of Life. My personal journey continues to gently dissolve residues of hyperindividuality, control, and that sneaky, seductive modern impulse to *know* the answers, to summon liberation on a deadline, or to hand you truth on a silver platter as evidence of my worth. What I continue to learn is that emergence can't be scaled or scripted. It can only be invited, listened for, and improvised. So please receive this chapter as a seeding of possibilities we can only live together.

CREATURES OF CULTURE

We are creatures of culture. Culture is the sea we swim in. Culture shapes us as we carry it.

---

1. Not all oral teachings are to be written down or shared. It is the listener's responsibility to ask. If permission is denied, teachings should not be shared beyond the existing circle of trust. Depending on how permission is granted, it becomes both a privilege and a duty to share. In some contexts, retelling an oral narrative without permission, credit, or verification of the teller can be appropriation.

In *How Emotions Are Made: The Secret Life of the Brain*, Lisa Feldman Barrett writes: "The human brain is a cultural artifact. We don't load culture into a virgin brain like software loading into a computer; rather, culture helps to wire the brain. Brains then become carriers of culture, helping to create and perpetuate it."[2] Culture is a relational fabric at the deepest, neurosomatic, and developmental levels. You are simultaneously a contributor to and an emergent property of its invisible architectures, a co-creator and a co-created part of the whole.

Given that we are social organisms who take multiple decades to mature and whose development is both biological and cultural, it is highly consequential what stories, rituals, protocols, and social systems we immerse ourselves in. Who we become, both as individuals and as a collective, is shaped by the ideologies, technologies, social structures, and environments we are immersed in. So what might shape a true human culture? Let's assume there is no single blueprint for this becoming. Yet across many lineages and lifeways, certain patterns appear, resonances that whisper through time, place, and body. These are not commandments—not rules. They are thresholds of bioadaptive alignment and echoes of a shared longing to live as if Life were sacred and interbeing real.

Woman Stands Shining, Pat McCabe (a Diné [Navajo] mother, grandmother, activist, artist, and ceremonial leader) offers this:

Culture is the Mother Earth expressing herself as human being.[3]

In her framing, culture isn't an arbitrary human construct. It's *"a mad love affair"*[4] with Life woven through an intricate web of relations between people, places, ancestors, more-than-human beings, and spirit. Culture tends the sacred contract between humans and the Earth, nurturing sacred reciprocity between people, and nature and aligning creativity and technology with the continuity and emergence of Life. It's base code for a human presence on this planet that doesn't break Life.

This expression of culture is a radical departure from the contemporary mainstream concept. Indeed, the writer and storyteller Stephen Jenkinson has written that modern Western society is the "utter voiding of culture,

---

2. Lisa Feldman Barrett, *How Emotions Are Made: The Secret Life of the Brain* (Houghton Mifflin Harcourt, 2017).
3. Pat McCabe, commentary given at The June Gathering in Asheville, NC, June 4, 2024, hosted by the Pachamama Alliance.
4. McCabe (2024).

masquerading as the best of cultures."[5] Culture as a love affair with Life harkens an ancient yet timeless way of being that, if practiced within our current context, might transform what it means to be human.

Currently, global civilization functions as an *extractive*, economic superorganism nested within the larger, *living* superorganism of the biosphere. These two interlinked structures are the life support system of all humans.[6] Many of us understand that aligning these meta-systems is non-optional, yet they currently function as diametrically opposed forces. A global culture that aligns humans, technology, and economy in metabolic reciprocity with the biosphere would transcend technological adolescence in a movement toward true, ecotechnological maturity. This would represent an entirely new phase of civilization, one that composts separation as it reweaves humanity's original Covenant with nature.

What cultures might emerge if we collectively root in the *knowing* that we belong to Life? How would *love* do culture? How might we experience and co-create intelligence differently if we shape ourselves (our ways of being and creating) as "Mother Earth expressing Herself as human being?" And how might this support us to live and co-create from a place of planetary maturity?

I imagine we would structure values, incentives, and behaviors as though relationships matter—reweaving the currencies of our consciousness, individually and collectively, into Life's Song. I sense we would craft art, song, poetry, and design to amplify attunement and communion and innovate circular, metabolically reciprocal flows of energy, materials, and waste. I imagine we would compost entitlement, exceptionalism, and hyperindividualism, root into sufficiency, slow rhythms of extraction, consumption, and ecological degradation, and activate virtuous cycles of protection, preservation, detoxification, and regeneration.

If we were to weave culture as Mother Earth expressing Herself through us, we would actively involve ourselves in a symphony of reciprocities between people, land, ancestors, forces of nature, our more-than-human kin, and technology. We would know ourselves as custodians, gardeners, engineers, and architects of biospheric integrity. And (I like to think) we would be utterly delighted to share the fruits of our love.

5. Stephen Jenkinson, *Come of Age: The Case for Elderhood in a Time of Trouble* (Berkeley, CA: North Atlantic Books, 2018), 231.
6. "The New State of Global Risk," *Civilization Research Institute*, accessed August 26, 2025, https://civilizationresearchinstitute.org/.

All of this might sound idealistic or bombastic. But is it? Perhaps it's a sketch of grounded entanglement. Just because the structures we're still embedded in reek of separation doesn't mean the Great Remembering isn't welling up all around us. A cursory search in areas as diverse as rights of nature, early childhood education, deliberative democracy, conscious dying, indigenous sovereignty, community grief rituals, circular packaging innovation, biophilic architecture, wetland conservation, and bioregional finance reveals that millions of people are hearing the Earth's call and working to cobble together the inklings of a Third Attractor.[7] Subtly, in the cracks and interstices, patterns and pathways of regenesis are emerging. We are remembering our souls, listening to the water, inhabiting our bodies, translating the communication of animals and plants, practicing regenerative agriculture and forestry, restoring coral reefs, rewilding rivers, grasslands, and wetlands, and building unlikely, postpartisan partnerships. We are reactivating our natural propensity for sacred reciprocity and tending vital communities of place. And we are relearning ancient, earthwise wisdom—integrated with new scientific, technological, and spiritual knowledge. Where the push of necessity meets the pull of possibility, pragmatic expressions of Life Culture are blooming into being.

Let's meet here as co-creators—not to "get it right," to try to absolve ourselves of the messes we've created, or to master anything, but to inquire, experiment, create, fuck up, learn, rebuild trust, and nurture our world toward wholeness.

WATER'S WAY

To co-sense our way into culture as a mad love affair with Life, I'd like to introduce you to my meta-teacher: *water*. As the alchemical substrate of biological existence, she knows some things about . . . *everything*. Water is the original transdimensional hip-hop medicine, the mistress of mixing, a diva of diversity. Over arcs of geological time, she combines starlight and stardust into homes for souls in bodies, taking the path of least resistance to make the most possible.

From water's perspective, you are an emanation of her project. She manifested your bodily existence through the stacked intelligences of all the previous bodies that made you and our world possible. She, in this very

---

7. The life-centric, win-win potential future described by Daniel Schmachtenberger that we discussed in chapter 1.

moment, is enabling your reading of these words as she transduces electrical differentials across your membranes.

She says:

"I am that which brings souls into bodies. I am that which makes the Life Project possible. If you choose to organize self and civilization according to my logic, you will know unlimited abundance and peace."

And, *"If you wish to create a world that works for Life, study the ways of water. Organize your minds, emotions, actions and systems according to the logic of water."*

And, *"Wisdom is that which tends with the well-being of Life. Wisdom is that which perpetuates the continuity and emergence of souls in bodies."*

Grandmother Agnes Baker Pilgrim, the Grand Elder of the *Takelma* tribe of Southern Oregon and one of the original Thirteen Grandmothers[8], unceasingly declared: *"Water is Life. You're all water babies. You come from your mother's womb. You're made of water."*[9] I will forever remember her screechy, booming, love-bomb of a voice shouting these words over and over at the last Salmon Ceremony she hosted on the banks of the Rogue River before her death.

As a water woman, I have received lineage blessing to speak to the water at the end of ceremonies. A water woman is a person with a womb who is specifically designated to thank and listen to the water. This is not a formal gesture or a prescriptive ritual but an act of devotional listening.

From a Western, materialist worldview, asking water's perspective makes no sense. Water is a molecule, an inanimate substance, not a living being with consciousness and memory. But from an enlifened perspective, everything—most especially the water—is alive, intelligent, and scintillating with memory. To counsel with water is totally logical, even necessary. Water made us, so of course we should turn to her as a meta-teacher.

As with all prayers, the water prayer begins in gratitude:

Thank you, water, for hot showers and clean dishes, for rain, rainbows, grass seedlings, the scent of roses, crickets, tears, and synovial fluid. Thank you for the infinitude of ways you avail yourself

---

8. The International Council of Thirteen Indigenous Grandmothers was an unprecedented leadership alliance of indigenous women from around the globe who gathered with the intention to uphold and share indigenous practices and ceremonies and affirm the right to use plant medicines free from legal restriction. They convened for the first time in October 2004 at the Dalai Lama's Menla Retreat Center in New York State. (*Wikipedia*, s.v. "International Council of Thirteen Indigenous Grandmothers," accessed August 27, 2025, https://en.wikipedia.org/wiki/International_Council_of_Thirteen_Indigenous_Grandmothers.)

9. Also see Agnes Baker Pilgrim, "We Are All Water Babies," *Earth & Spirit Council*, posted July 21, 2014, YouTube video, 8:45, https://www.youtube.com/watch?v=OeEl_2xpDWl.

to Life—for shaping mountains, for fitting yourself into drinking glasses and fern fronds and creek basins, for constructing the membranes that encapsulate our cells and organelles. Thank you for all of our experiences, sensations, and thoughts, even our stagnation. Your chemical affordances make it all possible!

Then, I ask, *"Water, what happened? What do you want us to know tonight?"*

Water never shares the same thing twice. Her scripture is endless, with no beginning or end. She manifests Life in time through the continuum of attunement to soul-in-matter. She is the universe's most abundant and promiscuous Creatrix.

She has said: *"Your pursuit of perfection is killing God's project. To seek perfection is to inhibit Life."*

According to her, trying to transcend, control, or optimize everything desiccates the soul. Perfection isn't water's way, which, from her perspective, is also God's way for us. The collective obsession with precision, measure, and control blocks aliveness, wildness, and eros. Water wants you to feel yourself, moment by moment, to respect your own holy chaos.

She has also said, *"Creativity is a function of optimized presence in the body."*

When she said this, she was referring to the consciousness that arises when you love (and live in as opposed to hate or ignore) your body. By loathing or dissociating from your body, or the bodily processes within and all around you, you inhibit creative intelligence aligned with Life. The water made your body as an expression of your soul in entanglement with other souls in bodies. Being in your body enables the attuned creativity through which we contribute most beautifully to Life's Loom.

Recently she said, *"Humans are the least watery thing I am willing to inhabit. You believe you are made of mind. Yet you are made through me. You are souls in bodies, not minds in bodies. I am that which potentiates the evolution of souls through bodies. You, in your mentality, are the farthest I am willing to go from my own nature, and yet I continue to offer myself to manifest bodies for your souls to inhabit."*

This could mean quite a lot, particularly as it pertains to our current technological horizons. Her tone was stern, entreating those in the room, as representatives of modernity, to recognize that only through embodied attunement to water's way for us can we effectively, ethically, sacredly collaborate with her. Hydrology rules ecology. Bereft of a healthy relationship with the water within us and the hydrological cycles of our planet, human civilization can't be.

In a more jovial tone (and in a different ceremony), she said, *"Welcome the pleasure I have made possible for you. Life moves according to pleasure, pain, and absence. It is through pleasure that I co-orchestrate the greatest potentiality for Creation. Awaken compersion—your effervescing delight in the pleasure of others. Your enjoyment in the joy of existence is where I experience the most potent opportunities for evolution."*

You might think it's pretty "out there" to seek water's teachings. But water, as Life's Creatrix, offers truly nonarbitrary perspectives on agency, emotionality, creativity, and culture. There is nothing more pragmatic than asking her how to live coherently. Her consistent message:

"When you organize your lives in my way for you, you will know true abundance and peace."

People, animals, plants, fungi, microbes—all of Life needs water. Ecologies are defined by water. Even AI servers need water. Wars are fought over water. Will our future be desiccated, desertified, denuded? Or will it be green, fecund, flourishing? Perhaps this hinges on whether we can be sufficiently watery, sufficiently attentive to the flows of Life, to design human systems that reciprocally nurture the hydrological health of our bodyminds and our biosphere.

CO-EVOLVING "THE SYSTEM"

This brings us to an obvious statement of fact: "the system" must evolve. But if you've ever tried systemic change, you know that it's fraught terrain, more characterized by overambition and discontinuity than by efficacy or success. Nonetheless, it's territory we must traverse if we want anything other than the default trajectories of the economic superorganism as it is. As you become better at holding the paradox of your embeddedness in an anti-life system—without collapsing, defending, or dissociating—it becomes possible to show up for the process with stamina and patience as you tend emergent stories, systems, and ways of being.

There's no silver bullet. The winding way forward involves a vast and complex ecology of simultaneous strategies at many orders of scale, all of them context dependent and interwoven. Some initiatives will be in areas of triage (mitigating harm), others in transition (weaving some continuity and antifragility between what was and what will be), and others in transformation (bringing the Ancient Future into form). Some will be short term, some will be so far reaching as to be impossible to finish (or even see results) within your lifetime. Thankfully, if you are doing something to nurture relational healing or life-centric vitality, you're probably doing a right-enough thing—and *there's a map*. Joanna Macy crafted an elegant, three-part framework to guide and motivate ongoing participation in evolving our world. Sean Kelly, who co-taught a course on The Great Turing with Joanna, describes the three dimensions of this essential work as "*holding actions* to slow, if not halt, the unraveling; promotion of *Gaian structures* as life-affirming alternatives to the ways of business as usual; and the *shift in consciousness* associated with the growing awareness of our deeper Gaian identity and our interbeing with all that is."[10] Joanna elucidated these principles in the essay "The Great Turning," written for the Center for Ecoliteracy in 2009:

Actions to slow the damage to Earth and its beings
Perhaps the most visible dimension of the Great Turning, these activities include all the political, legislative, and legal work required to reduce the destruction, as well as direct actions—blockades, boycotts, civil disobedience, and other forms of refusal. . . .

Analysis of structural causes and the creation of structural alternatives
. . . In countless localities, like green shoots pushing up through the rubble, new social and economic arrangements are sprouting. Not waiting for our national or state politicos to catch up with us, we are banding together, taking action in our own communities. Flowing from our creativity and collaboration on behalf of life, these actions may look marginal, but they hold the seeds for the future. . . .

Shift in Consciousness
These structural alternatives cannot take root and survive without deeply ingrained values [and stories] to sustain them. They must mirror what we want and how we relate to Earth and each other. They require, in other words, a profound shift in our perception of reality—and that shift is happening now, both as cognitive revolution and spiritual awakening.[11]

---

10. Sean Kelly, "For Love of Gaia," in Joanna Macy, *A Wild Love for the World* (Shambala, 2020), 306.
11. Joanna Macy, "The Great Turning," *Center for Ecoliteracy*, June 29, 2009, https://www.ecoliteracy.org/article/great-turning.

These words land with timely gravity today. I have come to describe her holy trinity of systemic change with this shorthand:

- Stopping actions
- Life-centric systems
- Ekokosmic consciousness

It comes down to this:

There are harms that need to stop. There are peoples and places and species and ecologies that must be protected. Moral courage means cultivating the discipline to restrain actions that pull the world apart: overconsumption, war, the clearcutting of old-growth forests and jungles, the marginalization of groups of people, chemical poisoning of agricultural soils, the seeping spread of PFAS chemicals and microplastics, unrestrained development and resource extraction, bottom trolling, planned obsolescence, and fundamentalist polarization. Additionally, we must find restorative, disciplined, and just ways to restrain anti-life actors.

There are better systems to build: bionoetic systems that dignify the body, mind, and soul of every human being and all the more-than-human members of our Earth community as we co-orchestrate an unparalleled level of symbiosis within our biosphere; systems that nurture both inner development and a vital social fabric; systems that incentivize harmony between people and planet as they instantiate ecokosmic consciousness.

And we have better stories to tell, stories that awaken us to the sacred in Life, reanimating ancient, timeless, earthly kinship as they celebrate ecokosmic emergence; stories that see us surrendering sides, taking multiple perspectives, loving diversity, and joyfully tending shared resilience; stories that bring us home together as they nourish each person's unique vision of a flourishing future for all of Life.

You can draw this generative triangle and paste it above your desk or on your bathroom mirror to texture imagination and guide inquiry, experiment, design, strategy, and restraint. This simple process map has proven effective in booting up life-centric (balanced positive and negative) feedback loops in diverse contexts, from business, to activism, to policy, to education, to city planning, to materials design. Since every system is bound up in the larger system, this is patient, co-evolutionary work. Stamina pays off. Hidden possibilities become actualities. Path dependencies shift. And we start to move more like water—both individually and collectively.

THE TRINITY OF GENERATIVE SYSTEMIC CHANGE

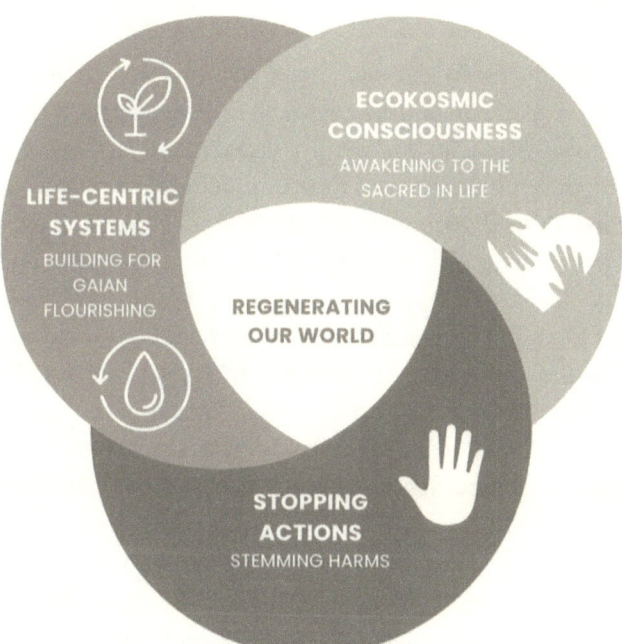

INVITING AND INVOKING LIFE CULTURE

What might these currents of co-evolution feel like, look like, taste like, flow like? Let's deepen this inquiry by inviting and invoking an emergent Life Culture.

You, sweet human, are a member of a species well-designed to co-create with Gaia. You have been gifted with a uniquely abstract and recursive mind with which to ideate, iterate, and imagine. Your mind can reach to infinity. Yet none of your creations are immaculate. Every creative act is molecularly, energetically, and temporally bound to the constraints of physical and ecological systems. Every act of creation, preservation, or destruction ripples through the web of Life. All creation is causally entangled co-creation with what has been, what is, and what will be.

Humans are a keystone species with a unique place and purpose within our biosphere; our role in planetary ecology is custodial. We are a force of nature with the capacity to co-create a sapient society that serves sentience. If this is even partially true, then our way forward involves hospicing systems, structures, stories, and pain bodies that are dying as we midwife a neo-indigenous homecoming to our planet. As the futurist and evolutionary leader Barbara Marx Hubbard said,

> *Our crisis is a birth. We are one living system and we have come to the limit of one phase of natural growth on a finite planet. . . . We must learn ethical evolution quickly. . . . As we seek to facilitate a gentle birth, a graceful and nonviolent transition to the next stage of our evolution, we will discover a natural pattern, a design of our birth transition, and develop [the capacity] to cooperate with this design.*[12]

Ethical evolution becomes both more challenging and more obviously necessary as the death throes of the old ontology get louder and more violent. Default systems and structures of power wrestle for dominance—while breaking down. Chaos, complexity, and uncertainty stymie "business as usual." We can no longer depend on stability or normalcy. In this disorienting collective terrain, a nascent instinct for Life Culture also quickens.

We begin to remember that we are orchestrators, architects, engineers. We are synergists, harmonizers, protectors, and amplifiers of the evolutionary potential of this complex-life–bearing planet we call home. We are planters of seeds, builders of soil, singers of songs, parents of children, carriers of wisdom. We are healers of hearts and keepers of watersheds. These aren't fictional roles. They are expressions of our place in the unfolding story we are nested within. We are a class of organisms that generates—and can resolve—separation by meeting hubris, trauma, and dissociation as initiation and consciously, culturally restitching our love, attention, and imagination into the fabric of Life's Song.

AN INVITATION INTO LIFE CULTURE

You have power as a co-creator of Life culture. In this time of death and rebirth, Gaia calls each of to weave our soul genius in collaboration with Her song. The following eight principles will support you to better align your love and power with Her flourishing.

1. **Awaken** to *who* you are as a soul in a body who has been gifted the experience of life on Earth.

---

12. Barbara Marx Hubbard, *Conscious Evolution: Awakening the Power of Our Social Potential* (New World Library, 2015), 46.

2. **Remember** *what* you are as a human being, a biospiritual member of the Circle of Life who is designed to reciprocally participate in the Gift.

3. **Ground** into sovereign soul integrity.

4. **Expand** into interbeing as an embodied and relational being entangled in co-becoming.

5. **Attune** to and commune with others and the world to activate original intelligence.

6. **Tend** the beauty, abundance, biodiversity, and integrity of the Gaian system to liberate and co-create the infinite game of Life.

7. **Restrain** actions that undermine soul expression, integrity, and dignity for individuals, populations, and the larger, complex system.

8. **Become** a weaver of reciprocal and complementary relationships in all domains and at all orders of scale.

These invitations into life culture respell our shared ways of being. Try them on. Treat them not as rules or codified practices but as etchings of possibility, hints from the deep past and the nascent future whispering through tears in the fabric.

Now, let's paint a more detailed invocation of Life Culture. As you read the following incantations, hold them lightly. See what resonates, what rubs, what tickles the tendrils of your most empathic and wild self. Let them dance in your imagination like a score for an improvisational choreography of emergence.

INVOCATIONS OF LIFE CULTURE

Love Life. Love the soul. Live in your body. Love your place. Be true to yourself; respond to the things that uniquely speak to you. Give as much as you receive. Respect the integrity and dignity of others. Play, because you were made for joy. Weave your imagination into Life's Song. Restrain thoughts and actions that infringe on the health, well-being, or soul expression of other humans and more-than-humans. Instead of worry, choose wonder.

✐ **How can you give more permission to joy—and how does your love feed the world?**

Do you. Give yourself to the meandering journey of soul initiation to find your unique note within the symphony of soul. There's a special brilliance only you can bring to the whole—possibilities only you can see, feel, and create. Soul purpose flows according to your gifts, affinities, proclivities, wounds, histories, and relationships, all of which shape the river of your becoming. To bring forth your own uniqueness is both a privilege and an obligation that dignifies the gift of your life. Your personal soul purpose is nested within our collective, conspecific, custodial niche.

✒ **What is the unique thread you carry in the great weaving of Life?**

Reclaim the power of your divine will. Your soul is a seat of authority. When you are fully present and resident within your body, you have soul gravity. Your will cannot be usurped unless you allow it to be. Therefore, actively clear your space of manufactured media, messaging and programming so you can feel your own energy and agency and authentically listen to Life. You are in charge of your own space, energy, attention, and power. Engage will to bring truly original stories and things into this world and to awaken soul integrity in others.

✒ **Where is your will tangled or truncated, and what would you create if your energy was fully devoted to your soul's calling?**

If you choose to bear children, conceive consciously. Invite them to incarnate awake. Raise them to know who they are as souls—fully expressed, body, mind, and heart, as themselves. Carry them lovingly, in community, across initiatory thresholds of maturation. If you choose not to have children, be part of the village. Be a good auntie or uncle. Support all young people to develop physical, aesthetic, emotional, intellectual, ecological, and spiritual intelligence. Track each person's affinities to liberate their real genius.

✒ **How would we raise the future if every soul was welcomed as a teacher?**

Nurture health in your own body and mind and in the body and mind of the world. Real health is complex. It arises through systemic vitality and reciprocal integrity. Anything less is a band-aid. Physical, mental, emotional, and spiritual health (for individuals, communities, and ecofields) is relational, a function of dynamic flows of energy and information within and between bodies, minds and the land. Health is a borderless continuity of communication, as much a function of the coherence of context as the integrity of the individual. Therefore, treat health as an ecological, spiritual, and social process. Your body is a body of Earth. The Earth is an extension of your body. Tend both to co-create health for the whole.

How can you expand vitality through connection?

Weave community. You are a social organism. Open your eyes, your heart, and your table to people around you: folks in your neighborhood, your bioregion, and groups of affinity. Build trust one gesture of presence, one kept agreement, one altruistic act of support or kindness at a time. Vital, place-based communities, rather than individuals or families, are the unit of human organization that confers greatest resilience. Modernity has oriented you toward individualism and globalism. This emphasis desiccates local social fabric. Instead, water real-life connections to grow abundant social harvests. Build local networks of healing, regenerative action and mutual aid that bridge diverse social subgroups. The trust you build in these relationships is a foundation for resilience, come what may.

What kind of resilience grows from shared meals, collective grief, and mutual aid?

Die beautifully—with love and dignity. Death is the greater partner of Life's dance with eternity, the key to the circular continuity of Life's Loom. Death gestates and generates Life. A culture that denies death will ultimately consume Life with its vampiric obsession with immortality. A culture that honors death can learn to live in balance and heal the threads of ancestry forward and backward through time. So, when death comes, gather around your loved one to share this ultimate moment of transition. Love and tend the stages of your beautifully, imperfectly mortal body. Embrace its impermanence. Tend your awakeness such that when you are ready to cross the threshold of death, you do so consciously.

What would change if you befriended your own impermanence?

Align with Life's signatures of time. Synchronize intention, energy, agency, and action with the ebb and flow of tides, the waxing and waning of moons, the holy days of equinoxes and solstices, the unique flavor of each season, the cycles of life, death, and rebirth, and the movements of planets and stars. When time is separated from bodies, Earth, and cosmos, it imposes a kind of collective dissociation that enables hierarchical dominance and control. When culture is disconnected from deep time, people forget the genetic cords that bind ancestors past, present, and future. Instead, move at the pace of trust. When you reunify your time-sense with bodies, nature, history, and deep cosmic cycles, this restores co-regulation with the harmonic rhythms of Life, resynchronizing with the sacred.

✐ **How can you align your creative energies with the seasons, the moon, and deep time?**

Embrace plurality. Separation teaches supremacy, hierarchy, hegemony. But the power of Life pulses diversely in and through everything. There is no "center," no "normal," and no ultimate truth that isn't bound up in relationality and context. Each being and culture keeps different histories, her-stories, perspectives. So invite diverse brains, bodies, and minds (human and more-than-human) to contribute their unique intelligences and perspectives. Learn to look for *unlikely consensus*.[13] Cut through the spell of hyperpolarization with participatory collaboration in service to the larger whole. This nurtures the experience of shared reality. Even in dissensus, orient directionality toward care for Life. Weave an intergenerational social tapestry that supports communication between many generations and species.

✐ **What wisdom, strength, possibility, and resilience lives in the differences you've been taught to fear or dismiss?**

Reimagine success. Soul success isn't about how much money you make or how big your platform is; it's about meaningful, purposeful, honest, and beautiful participation in the infinite game. Soul success means living your life as an authentic expression of your love, burning as your own flame. It is often messy, imperfect, unfinished. It is always interesting. It is a gift-giving flow of agency in relationship with an animate world. In poet Dawna Markova's words, "I choose to risk my significance, to live so that which

---

13. The concept of "unlikely consensus" emerges from Audrey Tang's work developing citizen's assemblies as the Digital Minister of Taiwan. For more on their work, download *Plurality*, or listen to their episode with Nate Hagens. It's one of the single most inspiring things I have ever listened to: https://open.spotify.com/episode/1N3ZmPvYw19hDXNVbX4Txe?si=39baa13b4d4e4cde

came to me as seed goes to the next as blossom, and that which came to me as blossom, goes on as fruit."[14]

📝 **Whose definition of success are you living—and who does it serve?**

Honor the dance of the feminine and the masculine, not as gender roles but as sacred polarities and deeply interpenetrated complementarities. The masculine provides structure, will, witness, protection, and penetration. He is the principle of mind and transcendence. The feminine gives birth, feels, flows, loves chaos, welcomes death and decay, and absorbs and embraces energy and information to nurture form into being. She is the principle of body and immanence. Nurture the harmonic, erotic play between and among these polarities in yourself, in your relationships, and in your care for the world. The feminine is the sacred body of Life. Healthy masculinity protects and upholds the well-being and the safety of the feminine.

📝 **How can better love and embrace both feminine and masculine energies within yourself—and by so doing, how can you better celebrate and protect Life?**

To live well, beautifully, and truly, align your own power with Life's power. Be a good symbiote. Life-centric power is shared power. The power of Life runs deep and wide (where power over Life scales vertically by breaking diversity). Working symbiotically for the common good is a higher evolutionary principle than narrow goal achievement. Life-centric work and play invite round or rather than linear goals. Round goals care for what serves health, integrity, and abundance *for the many* rather than the few— on intergenerational timescales. They dance with the reciprocal feedback loops of ecology. To embody Life-centric power, slow down to attend and attune to the web of interbeing implicated in any endeavor. Seek resonance, then taste dissonance, coherence, and/or harmony, respecting the energies that live in the between. This is an adaptive strategy to create resilience, vitality, and new possibility. As the African proverb says, "If you want to go fast, go alone: if you want to go far, go together." Life's power is stronger than any power over Life.

---

14. Dawna Markova, *I Will Not Die an Unlived Life: Reclaiming Purpose and Passion* (Conari Press, 2000), 1.

🪶 How can you widen the boundaries of your goals and better attune to the roundness of Life?

Reimagine wealth. Let sufficiency be your compass. Let health (for humans, more-than-humans, and ecologies) be your measure. In Old English, *weal* referred to both health *and* wealth. What if true wealth is inseparable from the vitality of the commons, from the breathability of air, the drinkability of water, the fecundity of soil, the biodiversity of forests, wetlands, and coral reefs? What if there were no such thing as profit without reciprocity—no surplus without service? What if flow mattered more than accumulation? Wealth, then, becomes organismic, a diverse stream of "current-sees"[15] moving between individuals, communities, ecosystems, and the global circulations of energy, transport, materials, and meaning. Abundance becomes something we co-create and tend, an emergent property of healthy relationships with place, people, and possibility. Seen from this perspective, our current models of profit as extraction and wealth as accumulation are not just insufficient, they are anti-abundant. They impoverish us by rewarding disconnection, enclosure, and depletion. So reframe abundance as a life well lived. Honor real capital: land, water, seeds, tools, skills, story, trust. Let ledger sheets follow and flow, not lead.

🪶 What flows of nourishment are already sustaining you, and how can you reciprocate?

Conceive of the technosphere as a living extension of the reciprocal flows that make life possible: atoms, energy, time, attention, and intelligence. A mature technosphere is not a tool of domination. It is an evolutionary emergence—an expansion of Life's Song through the animation of the mineral kingdom. Mature technologies do not mine, hijack, or enclose land, bodies, or consciousness in mechanistic or digital purgatories. Rather, they participate in the metabolic harmonization of atoms, energies, and information. They are soul-nourishing. They regulate nervous systems rather than fracture them. They expand human agency rather than diminish it. They protect and tune the integrity and authenticity of real-life communities rather than polarizing or dissolving them. Such technologies cannot be born of fragmented minds. They can only be seeded and tended by mature human beings, those who are firmly rooted in love for Life, attuned to the

---

15. This term was coined by Ferananda Ibarra and Arthur Brock of the MetaCurrency Project.

here and now, and who honor their role as co-creators within a living world. So design and build not against nature but as an offering to her. Let machine intelligence be a companion, elevating embodied, intergenerational, ancestral, and more-than-human genius rather than replacing it. The evolution of technology is inseparable from the evolution of civilization. When rightly attuned, technology can scaffold emergent qualities of intelligence, creativity, abundance, wisdom, relationality, and complexity—and not only technological complexity but complexity that complements biology and ecology. A mature technosphere hums in harmony with Gaia and humanity. It listens. It learns. It loves.

🖊 **How can you use, design, build, or dispose of all your tools as an active remembering of your entanglement with all of Life— human, more-than-human, and digital?**

Regenerate everything. Regeneration is not restoration. It is a deep collaboration with compost, a dance with the circularity of life, death, and rebirth. As mutually entangled *interbeings*, we are all custodians of someone, something, someplace. Regeneration is sacred work that begins not with purity but with proximity to the rot. It is an eco-psycho-spiritual process that starts by meeting the unbearable stench of what we've all perpetrated and inherited—toward the land, toward each other, toward ourselves. But don't worry; Life loves to metabolize shit. Begin by meeting your own darkness and the trash heaps you've hidden from, or justified, or inherited in silence. Not all at once. Not alone. But step by honest step. Stitch your life back into the metabolic integrity of the whole. Regeneration begins not with perfection but with presence. From here, decay is dignified, disruption is metabolized, entropy slows, and fertile ecologies and cultures take root and grow.

🖊 **What sacred compost are you already making?**

Root into place. Care for land, water, and biodiversity—locally, regionally, globally. Locality is relative and occurs at many nested orders of scale. You are local to your watershed, to your bioregion, to the wild dream of Earth and cosmos. Reweave culture bioregionally, not as a retreat into isolation but as a reawakening of relational integrity. A bioregion is not a map with borders. It is a body. It is defined not by governments but by patterns of water and stone, climate and kinship, memory and migration. Fred McPherson of the Santa Cruz Mountains Bioregional Council writes:

> *The term bioregion attempts to define and determine the location of an individual in the biosphere, and to help each person develop a sense of place. Bioregions are thought of as the natural countries of the planet in terms of ecology, economics, and political decisions regarding resource management and planning issues.*[16]

Bioregioning is not a new idea; it is an ancient orientation, one practiced by original peoples the world over. It is the dance of place-based response-ability for food, water, materials, biodiversity, trade, story, and culture, all held in reciprocal care. As Daniel Christian Wahl reminds us: "Bioregioning is and has been our species evolutionary survival pattern."[17] And perhaps even more: a foundation for neo-indigenous belonging.

✒ What is the land asking of you in return for your life?

Align human law with the deep laws of Life. Law, in its truest form, is not imposed. It is received—a reflection of the way Life holds, nourishes, and binds us. Natural Law is a living conversation with rock and river, body and breath, ancestors past and future. It belongs to no single people, nation, or faith. It collaborates with all that endures. It rhymes with the memories water carries and the wisdom forests remember, even when humans forget. Natural Law recognizes the rights of a river and the rights of a child equally. But it acknowledges the limitations of rights, which are always competitive. Instead it emphasizes obligations to the commons, which are always shared. It knows that true power is reciprocal. Power hoarded or weaponized breaks the fabric of the world. When we forget this, our laws become brittle. When we remember, our laws become prayers. The Great Binding Law of the Iroquois Confederacy reminds us:

> *Look and listen for the welfare of the whole people, and have always in view not only the present but also the coming generations, even*

---

16. Fred McPherson, "What Is a Bioregion?" SCMB, last updated September 22, 2014, https://www.scmbc .org/projects/.
17. Daniel Christian Wahl, "Bioregioning: The Defining Practice of Regenerative Cultures," *Medium*, April 17, 2025, https://designforsustainability.medium.com/bioregioning-the-defining-practice-of-regenerative -cultures-14af7ce71742. See also *Designing Regenerative Cultures* (UK: Triarchy Press, 2016).

those whose faces are yet beneath the surface of the ground—the unborn of the future Nation.[18]

Natural Law attunes to the future. In this way of seeing and being, freedom is not permission to dominate. Freedom is an invitation to belong to—to be accountable to and interdependent with—something larger than yourself. You have a sacred duty to care for the web of Life, seen and unseen, now and yet to come.

✒ Where does your conscience diverge from the laws you live under?

Be a warrior for Life. Protect the waters. Protect the forests. Be a voice for the voiceless. Speak for the feeding grounds of migratory birds, the sonic sovereignty of whales and dolphins, the biosanctity of open pollinated seeds, and the lovely harmonies of healthy soil. Work toward E. O. Wilson's vision of half of the Earth restored as biodiverse habitat to reverse the species extinction crisis and ensure the long-term health of our planet.[19] Consider your choices and actions in light of how they affect future generations. As Gandhi said, "The earth, the air, the land, and the water are not an inheritance from our forefathers but on loan from our children. So we have to hand it over to them at least as it was handed over to us."[20]

✒ What would your love protect if you let it guide your life?

Cultivate a Gaian body. Expand the circumference of self to include the intelligences of the ecofield(s) you occupy, the more-than-human beings you interact with, and the biosphere you are embedded within. Be lionhearted. Marry your instinct and intuition within your heart to embody the power of Life. This is an art of planetary listening that weaves you into earthly attunement. In this way, you come to embody love, not as a feeling but as a way of being with, a practice of attunement, and a field of ethical gravity.

---

18. Law 28 of the Constitution of the Iroquois Nation, as quoted in World History Commons, https://world historycommons.org/constitution-iroquois-nations.

19. "The E. O. Wilson Biodiversity Foundation supports the goal of protecting half of the land and sea in order to manage sufficient habitat and reverse the species extinction crisis, ensuring the long-term health of our planet." ("What Is the Half-Earth Project?" E. O. Wilson Biodiversity Foundation, accessed August 27, 2025, https://eowilsonfoundation.org/what-is-the-half-earth-project/.)

20. Mahatma Gandhi, as quoted in Sagar Simlandy and Sharmila Dutta Banik, eds., *The Legacy of Mahatma Gandhi* (PS Opus Publications, 2021), 126.

✒ How is your agency an extension and expression of Gaia?

Play infinite games. Live not for victory but for vitality. Play not to win but to widen the field of possibility. Each day, offer something that ripples forward—a gesture of kindness, words of gratitude, a reciprocal act of care that nourishes both giver and receiver. Live in a way that others can breathe easier beside you. Create in ways that leave no one behind, human or more-than-human. Choose possibility over fear, curiosity over control, reciprocity over extraction, contentment over acquisition. Make time for intergenerational council. Listen to the long view. Let those not yet born shape your decisions now. And when you falter, remember: life isn't about "getting it right." It's about the risky, daily art of tending the soil beneath your feet and the beauty you know to be possible. This is how we become good ancestors: by living lives that harmonize and amplify the creative spirit of Life.

✒ What actual, metaphorical, or energetic seeds are you planting to create a more just, vital, and beautiful world than the one you came into?

Embody your ethics. Align your day-to-day choices (material, relational, political, professional) with your values. Walk with discernment, not judgment. Learn to distinguish between differences, to appreciate diversity, and to honor plurality as the deeper pulse of unity. Life-centric ethics nurture short-term harmony, mid-term resilience, and long-term flourishing. Ethics are concerned not with "what *can* be done?" but "what *should* be done?" While science, engineering, and business are often agnostic about the well-being of the whole, ethics is focused on the implications and impacts of choices, actions, responsibilities, rights, protocols, and practices.

✒ What little (or large) behaviors can you shift to better align your choices with your values?

Wisdom and ethics imply restraint, or commitment to *what not to do*, as a critical consideration in one's choice making. Restraint arises from maturity, care, and patience. It means honoring the *precautionary principle* of "first, do no harm."[21] In a world still circumscribed by an immature story

---

21. "Precautionary Principle," Science Direct, accessed August 27, 2025, https://www.sciencedirect.com/topics/earth-and-planetary-sciences/precautionary-principle.

of limitless progress, it is practically taboo to propose an ethical imperative that implies some kind of limits or restrictions on one's actions or choices. It is seen as antithetical to freedom, or as a form of control. But there is a more vital motive: care for a world that we can be free in together. Restraint is a function of reciprocity and complementarity, attunement, and communion. It makes space for textures of relating that make life worth living: listening, respect, empathy, compassion, altruism. Like any good parent, you restrain some actions because you give a shit for more than yourself. Ethics is an expression of love for the continuity of Life.

✒ **What is worth restraining yourself for?**

NOW . . . EXHALE

How does your body respond to these invocations? What parts of you are excited or energized? What parts are resistant, annoyed, cynical? Each invocation may land differently—some resonant, some dissonant, some still unfolding. Good. Let that be the process. You are not here to adopt a doctrine. You are composting separation as you tend the possibility of a world that doesn't break Life. To do so is both a sacred obligation and a path of potential joy and fulfillment.

You are part of a quaking, volatile, emergence—the birthing of a culture that reweaves alignment between the economic superorganism and the Gaian superorganism. To locate your part in this emergence, you don't need to take on changing the whole world system. Instead, begin where you are. What do you most love? What destruction or injustice can you no longer tolerate? Who or what is asking for your unique presence, genius, vision, or skills? Who's in your network? What place(s), people, and sectors are you already connected to? Feel the tugs and tendrils that uniquely touch you and trust them, regardless of how humble or grand. As Clarissa Pinkola Estés, author of *Women Who Run with the Wolves*, writes: "Ours is not the task of fixing the entire world all at once, but of stretching out to mend the part of the world that is within our reach."[22] When you do, the sacred in you comes alive. What if your one altruistic act could ripple out, touching another, then another—recalibrating, encouraging, realigning us

---

22. Clarissa Pinkola Estés, "Letter to a Young Activist During Troubled Times: Do Not Lose Heart, We Were Made for These Times," 2001, reprinted in full in *The Moon Magazine*, https://moonmagazine.org/clarissa -pinkola-estes-do-not-lose-heart-we-were-made-for-these-times-2016-12-31/.

with Life's Way?[23] And what if, through many such acts, we can collectively birth culture as a love affair with Life, expressed in literally billions of unique ways?

CULTIVATING PROTOPIC IMAGINATION

There's one further key ingredient for tending collective emergence: the future visions each of us carry, whether protopic, utopic, or dystopic. These visions magnetize us toward them.

In my personal cosmology, I do my small part to keep the doorway to the Ancient Future open. I tend the nascent potential of an ecokosmic world (the world I, as Samaya Storm, came from). I do this through story, song, prayer, ceremony, and a web of seen and unseen relationships and endeavors.

You, too, are a keeper of possible futures. So stand in the future you know to be true! Stand in the solar punk, biophilic, regenerative, peaceful, prosocial, long-now you know to be possible!

Some say the future is not real. Indeed, it doesn't yet exist. It's a figment of imagination. *But, oh, the power of imagination!* To imagine isn't to map or plan or prescribe but to weave context and nurture qualitative flows of energy, attention, and agency. Like a seed crystal or a sourdough starter, imagination is a sacred ingredient potentiating the possible. Such seeds can take root when watered with consistent presence and action.

The future is real in three senses. Firstly, it exists conceptually, imaginally within you, right now. Your subconscious concepts of short-term, mid-term, and long-term futures tune your biology, shape your emotional landscape, and influence the *directionality* of every motive, intent, choice, tactic, or strategy. Secondly, the idea of prophesy—of probable futures that can be subtly ascertained by consciously following the arrow of time *beyond* the horizon of emergence—has been known by seers from time immemorial. Thirdly, the future operates like a collective imaginal landscape, a terrain that has been overrun by dystopias that are both well-funded and attractive to the catastrophizing forebrain. Therefore, there is power in populating this landscape—in your own mind and in the collective mind—with more

---

23. Witnessing and/or receiving altruism begets more altruism. "In one longitudinal study, recipients paid acts of kindness forward with 278% more prosocial behaviors than controls who did not experience acts of kindness." (Shawn A. Rhoads and Abigail A. Marsh, "Doing Good and Feeling Good: Relationships Between Altruism and Well-being for Altruists, Beneficiaries, and Observers," *World Happiness Report 2023*, https://www.worldhappiness.report/ed/2023/doing-good-and-feeling-good-relationships-between-altruism-and-well-being-for-altruists-beneficiaries-and-observers/.)

beautiful, compelling, and vital visions. Indeed, this is a critical form of imagination activism.[24]

The future (as a field of probability that can be intuitively penetrated) has been understood by prophets for thousands of years. Prophetic mind is an ancient skill, known by the Mayan timekeepers who, by some tellings, mapped twenty-six (!) calendars, each of them tracking a distinct signature time.[25] Long before Western culture gave rise to our current scientific instruments and institutions, seers were able to calculate the temporal sequencing of galactic rotation to within minutes and to understand the causal linkage between cosmic progressions and the evolution of consciousness. Such precise tuning to the interworkings of causality were also known by Babylonian and Pan-African astrologers, whose skill at mapping the stars behind each planet is still quietly called upon by leaders around the world. Prophetic mind has shaped history, and will continue to do so. The prophet roots in the radical now to attune to probable possible futures, scrying into patterns of emergence. What they see then helps steer culture creation.

As we careen forward through time, be your own prophet. Your internal construct of the possible future is a magnet for manifestation. So own that real estate within your own mind! Don't let default dystopian dreams populate it for you. A lovingly imagined protopic future creates a coordinate of possibility in time-space that draws you toward it through the present-tense scaffolding of inner narrative and therefore of emotion, attention, intention, choices, and actions. In this sense, your vision of the future is more than just a random construct; it's a lever of power. Wield it wisely to direct emergence. Your imaginings create a field that shapes reality.

I remember the future I come from. Do you? *What do you remember?* It's not for me to tell you what vision to create. It's not for me to tell you how to get there. Rather, my role is to invite you to access and cultivate your vision of flourishing for all of Life—your own felt sense of the world you want for your great, great grandchildren to experience and tell about.

---

24. The work of imagination activism has been ongoing for centuries—wherever people have seen and worked toward previously unimaginable possibilities, such as women's voting rights, racial equity, and indigenous land stewardship. The movement was coined as such by Phoebe Tickell, who created the term in 2022, building off the work of her mentor Joanna Macy. It is a global movement growing around the work. Phoebe defines imagination activism as "activism powered by imagination and the vision and tools to make the world better for everyone." See Phoebe's work here: www.moralimaginations.com/imaginationactivism.

25. Twenty-six is the number that was given to me in numerous oral accounts by Mayan wisdom carriers and ceremonial guides during my 2012 time in Guatemala. It is more generally known that the Maya had three calendars: the Tzolkin, or Ceremonial Calendar (of 260 days); the Haab, or Solar Calendar (of 365 days); and the Long Count. All of these counts are repeating and cyclical. ("The Maya Calendar Explained," *Maya Archaeologist*, accessed August 27, 2025, https://www.mayaarchaeologist.co.uk/public-resources/maya-world/maya-calendar-system/.)

A protopia[26] is not a utopia; it's not a "perfect" world: *it's a world that doesn't suck*. It's a direction, not a destiny. It's positive without falling into the fundamentalist traps of many utopian visions or the fatalism of dystopias (*dys*, meaning "bad" or "difficult," as in dysfunctional, dysregulated, dysentery). There's no single path to get there. Rather, you direct your energy, agency, and creativity *qualitatively* in the direction of healthy, flourishing Life. As you do this, don't worry about consensus or convergence. No future worth living will emerge through a single leader or some perfect plan. Evolution doesn't work that way. Evolution is locally responsive and adaptive, shamelessly pluralistic and promiscuous. We are going to find our way through this *chaordically*—a word that synthesizes chaos and order to describe a system, organization, human-made or natural process that balances the beneficial elements of both.[27] Chaordic principles coordinate the directionality of diverse actors without insinuating control. A chaordic design for a flourishing and viable future looks something like this:

- Life is sacred.
- We want a viable, beautiful future.
- This is inseparable from the health of our biosphere.
- Therefore, we attune to Life's logic, as we
- Align values, incentives, story, and agency with the pulse of Life.

A flourishing future can emerge through many diverse (even divergent) visions, agents, and actions if they are all attuned to Life's Song.

An old proverb, shared by Michael Mead, reads, "Begin to weave and the divine will provide the thread." Start by seeing a flourishing future as a real possibility. Hold the glimmer of Gaia's blue-green Song humming in concert with a healthy, happy humanity, lovingly co-orchestrated by a bionoetic technosphere. In such a world, humanity has reestablished resonance with the animate intelligences of our more-than-human relatives, the Earth, and the cosmos. Everyone experiences the basic dignity of access to clean food, water, clothing, shelter, education, medicine, and connection.

---

26. Kevin Kelly, co-founder of Wired Magazine, coined the term *protopia* in a 2011 blogpost which he later expanded in his book *The Inevitable*. He wrote of utopia and dystopia: "Neither of those seemed to be feasible, or even desirable." (Kevin Kelly, as quoted in Joshua Needelman, "Forget Utopia. Ignore Dystopia. Embrace Protopia." New York Times, March 14, 2023, https://www.nytimes.com/2023/03/14/special-series/protopia-movement.html.)

27. Dee Hock, the former CEO of Visa, coined the term *chaordic* to describe organizations that blend elements of chaos and order without letting either dominate. Hock was tired of the generic phrases used in complexity science at the time, such as "nonlinear," "self-organizing," "complex," and "autocatalytic." (See Dee Hock, *Birth of the Chaordic Age* [Berrett-Koehler Publishers, 1999], 29.)

Technology and economy pulse in metabolic coherence with the planetary superorganism, complementing rather than engulfing the Song of Life. Children are born possessed of their souls, no longer needing to question what's wrong with themselves or the world they inherit. In such a world, the civilizational OS nourishes reciprocity between humanity and nature. It's a post-traumatic world where we know, instinctively, and intuitively, that we belong. We play the infinite game, aligning our agency and creativity with the cyclical harmonics of Life.

There are countless timelines that lead us there. Once you are clear that you can't create such a vision alone, that it is bigger than you and larger than your lifetime, then you can begin. Pick up your part of the thread and start weaving. There are millions walking with you. Your contribution exists within a vast ecology of attuned agents tending the miracle of a world that works for Life.

A PRACTICE: IMAGINING YOUR PROTOPIA

What does your protopia look like? *Reach into future memory, out three hundred years on the horizon.* How does that world feel? Sound? Smell? Who is there with you? How did you get there? What challenges did you and your community face on the journey? What did you and your people lose or overcome? What inspired your stamina? What community practices, rituals, or stories carried you through? What did you stop doing or having or caring about? What physical and social systems did you redesign and rebuild?

See, feel, and imagine this vision as real. Root into your soul's authentic knowing as you clear dystopian fantasies from your mind. Then make your vision into something tangible: a poem, a ritual, a dinner party, a newly-planted nut tree. Protopic visions offer generative alternatives to the nihilism of mainstream propaganda. More importantly, they align your agency with the dignity of your love. You can't engineer the future—none of us can—but protopic visions help steer the river of emergence.

A DECLARATION OF INTERDEPENDENCE

How can we co-create Life Culture? The following words call forth that aspect in each of us that is a guardian, protector, gardener, and co-creator of an emerging Life Culture. They invite you to take a stance of *vitality*, to stand in the dignity and power of your aliveness. I invite you to speak them out loud with feeling. Speak them as a prayer in personal practice or ceremony. Or read this declaration to your community, replacing "I" with "we" as you read. Or, better yet, write your own declaration.

I decree and command that this planet, our home, is holy, whole-some, sacred, and free.

I decree and command that any energies, entities, programs, or patterns that are anything other than life-affirming be banished from this Earth.

I declare freedom within myself, for my communities, and with and for all my relations as I welcome my response-ability to nurture Life. I declare the sovereignty of my mind, body, time, energy, attention, and agency. I declare my membership within the human species and my belonging to this Earth. I am interdependent and sovereign.

I invite communion. I dissolve and disabuse myself of any myths, sto-ries, or beliefs that inhibit my interbeing with other beings, people, and forces of nature.

I honor the indigenous intelligence that flows through my blood. I remember my tribal ancestors and what was done to their bodies, lands, and lifeways. I forgive those who raped, maimed, and per-secuted my people, seeking to erase our identity and our magic. I acknowledge my ancestors who then perpetrated such atrocities. I forgive them.

I walk in solidarity with all those whose cultures, languages, homes, bodies, children, lands, and cultures have been harmed by colo-nization, racism, and patriarchy. I uphold your self-determination, health, safety, joy, and wisdom. I respect your authority, knowledge, and identities. I stand with you—for the land, the water, the children, and the future.

I dissolve and resolve invisibility and dominion. I am willing to be invisible. I am willing to be visible. I listen. I speak. I elevate and amplify voices that need to be heard.

I protect and uphold collective inquiry and experimentation. I am an invitation to communal possibility.

I am in service to healing the unhealable.

I claim medicine as a birthright for all peoples. I declare all seeds, plants, animals, and molecules as open-source gifts from Gaia that must be shared and cannot be patented or owned by anyone.

I claim my right to direct mystical experience. I protect and nourish awe, magic, and mystery.

I welcome vulnerability. I am unarmored. My love is my safety. When I say no, I mean it. When I say yes, I mean it. Free will honors this.

I reclaim innocence as a sacred birthright. I offer my reclaimed innocence in service to peace and wisdom.

I offer trust to the feminine. I invite the divine mother, creatrix, weaver, dreamer, dancer, nurturer, and artist in every being to come forward.

I offer trust to the masculine. I invite the divine father, protector, provider, architect, and builder in every being to come forward.

I am absorptive. I am penetrative. I am chaotic. I am ordered. I am entangled.

I sing Life's logic.

I root in wise limits and sacred restraint.

I declare my fidelity to the land. I choose to nurture beauty and fecundity. I protect and regenerate the commons of water, soil, seeds, air, watersheds, biodiversity, and consciousness. I stand for technologies that tend harmony between nature and culture.

I will not tolerate fear-based control. I cannot be corrupted or co-opted. I refuse violent programming. I am the unwinding of manufactured addiction. I am immune to mining.

My love is my power. My power means nothing if not in service to love. I have no right to power. Rather, I am powerful. I use my power to nurture wholeness. Through this, I have authority.

To anything or anyone not in alignment with this declaration, I say, let me be.

I am Safe. I am Sane. I am Sacred.

And so it is!

CHAPTER XIV

CEREMONY FOR A SMALL PLANET

You cannot be home alone.
We are made to come home together.

LIFE AND ANTI-LIFE

On a hot June afternoon, I got a call from the client I'd supported when he hit rock bottom a few years earlier. He had long since crossed the threshold from struggle to flourishing and was busier than ever loving his life and creating world-shifting initiatives. He rang to thank me and wanted to get my reflection on insights he'd been integrating into his work.

"I'm in the best place I've ever been. I finally have clarity about so many truths that never made sense before. There are only two sides: Life and Anti-Life. We lost the sacred along the way, and Life is what is sacred. It's what we are here for: Life, healthy Life.

"That's why orienting in this way is so joyful. When you're working on behalf of Life, you experience radical synchronicities. Life is beautiful. It makes sense. And everyone wants to collaborate with you. Most people don't know that because they aren't oriented in the right direction. But it's so damn obvious. I can't believe I spent most of my life not seeing it. We're so obtuse to a truth that's radically obvious. "

I felt a wave of delight receiving his epiphany. I responded, "OMG! I love hearing your clarity. And I completely agree. Life is what we're here for. We obscured the obvious for thousands of years beneath layers of trauma, distorted story, and uninitiated greed. But once you *get* the miracle you're a part of—once you come to know the sacredness of Life experientially, cellularly, as well as intellectually—then the only thing that makes sense is to become an agent for healthy Life."

I continued, "The way forward, as I see it, calls for new levels of intimacy, discernment, and trust: intimacy with ourselves, nature, each other and the unseen, discernment about which paths are genuinely grounded in integrity and reciprocity, and trust in the power *of* Life rather than power *over* Life. Through that power, we can make our way through the mess."

He responded emphatically. "Truth! There's no guarantee it'll be easy. Actually, it's probably going to be hella challenging. There are tons of energies lined up against us. But I know I'm on the side of Life, and it's awesome. And when given a choice, almost everyone else is too."

"How are you living these insights?"

"I'm giving form and voice to a much larger movement. People want to create a healthy world. Technology must be in service to Life. The first step is the awareness that it is not currently in service to Life. Awareness is the first step of healing. If we want to create human systems aligned with Life, we must start with the awareness that our current systems and structures are not aligned with Life. Then, you start to see that everything you do needs to serve harmony—harmony within yourself, harmony in your relationships, and harmony as a design function for technology and industry. It all needs to harmonize with Life."

"Absolutely," I said.

"Fuck yeah! The universe rewards healthy intentions. We have to know we will succeed in order to succeed. We have to feel that deeply in our souls. It's a massive healing of doubt—both for individuals and for all of humanity. As we take full responsibility for the messes we've created, we naturally bring forth solutions. And the fuel is human collaboration . . . and love."

"It's so utterly beautiful," I said. "Something new and ancient is birthing in us—a whole-planet, species-wide knowing that we are custodians of Life's Song."

"Yes! Onward!"

"Onward!"

"Big love!"

THIRD-TIER EVOLUTION

What might this species-wide knowing look like, feel like? How might we move when we live, love, and lead for Life?

Toward the end of his life, the great evolutionary biologist E. O. Wilson and colleagues published a paper titled "The Evolution of Eusociality,"[1] describing how social organisms develop through multilevel selection. According to Wilson, humans are one among twenty *eusocial* species on our planet. A eusocial species is a nesting organism that has developed a complex society in which individuals collaborate through differentiated roles to support the community as a whole. These include bees, naked mole rats, termites, ants, two species of crustaceans, and humans. Unlike other organisms, whose selection pressures are largely determined by individual fitness, eusocial organisms navigate selection pressures at the intersection of individual and group fitness. In individual fitness, dominant individuals' genes outcompete the genes of less fit or dominant individuals. Group fitness, on the other hand, depends on collaborative capacity motivated altruistically within the group. This determines a given group's fitness in relationship to other groups. Group fitness and individual fitness play off each other over many generations to determine what traits are selected for, thus the term *multilevel selection.*[2]

Humans are a special instance among all eusocial creatures. Like others in our class, we developed around a hive center: the warming fires of our early ancestors. We, however, have developed an even more complex differentiation of roles. Unlike other eusocial species, our diverse roles are no longer bound to specific biological functions (like serving the queen bee) but proliferate and diversify according to the emerging complexity of cultures, languages, subcultural identifications, technologies, and ontological and epistemic assumptions, which define and bound our tribal identities through complex feedback loops of social signaling. Our extreme differentiation has allowed us to form the hive-like economic superorganism of our global civilization and to develop far more sophisticated and multivalent modes of individual and group competition and coordination than expressed by any other organism. *Yet the essential tensions between group and individual fitness continue to shape human psychology and culture.*

The group dimension of our evolutionary history forms the roots of our tribal nature. Social groups, or "tribes," organize altruistically to compete against other groups. The group who is most effective at coordinating

---

1. Martin A. Nowak, et al., "The Evolution of Eusociality," *Nature* 466 (2010): 1057-1062, https://doi.org/10.1038/nature09205.
2. Edward O. Wilson, *The Meaning of Human Existence* (Liverwright Publishing, 2014), 19. Wilson notes that the number may include a broad sampling error.

within its group and against other groups wins out over other groups over generations. Groups coordinate around shared stories that define vision, mission, purpose, values, objectives, and incentives. This can be fantastically useful for doing anything that requires people, like building a company, a nation, or a world religion. However, we are biologically inclined to build exclusionary identities around these tribal affiliations. Exclusion expresses itself through in-group/out-group dynamics. Tribalism divides energy, attention, and affiliation, pitting groups against groups. We've all experienced these dynamics in school cliques, partisan politics, nationalism, religious extremism, and/or our day-to-day social lives. In a world driven by social media, polarized memetic camps represent a new domain of tribal bonds reified by algorithmic silos. This form of technology multiplies rivalrous group dynamics at scale, with devastating results.

The individual dimension of multilevel selection drives personal survival, regardless of impact on others. Selection dynamics in this direction have greatly intensified in the last 250 years as the emergence of individualism made us more self (rather than relationally) focused and capitalism and industrialization made the nuclear family the financially viable social unit. As I've said elsewhere in this book, a healthy sense of individuality is critical to developing sovereignty and agency. It supports positive traits such as self-esteem, confidence, intuition, soul-centricity and creative genius that enable personal flourishing; but this needs to be balanced with a profound sense of interbeing. Individualism is a spectrum. The more intensely individualistic a person is, the more likely they are to experience stress, alienation, negative competition, meaninglessness, and lack of social support. They are less likely to help others or to ask for help when they need it.[3] The deep shadows of individualism include exceptionalism, rampant loneliness, hypercompetition, a culture that seeks acquisition for security and status, and a collective tendency to excuse and even condone narcissistic, sociopathic, and Machiavellian behaviors[4] even though they undermine prosociality and care for Life. The tendency of a strongly individualistic culture is to superimpose its preferences for unbounded individual agency onto its collective construct of "freedom," forgetting that a healthy commons, tended with mutuality and responsibility, provides the

---

3. Kendra Cherry, "Individualistic Culture and Behavior," *Verywell Mind*, February 11, 2025, https://www.verywellmind.com/what-are-individualistic-cultures-2795273.

4. For a deep discussion on narcissism, sociopathy, and Machiavellianism, otherwise known as the "Dark Triad" traits, please listen to this brave and incisive episode of *The Great Simplification with Nate Hagens*: https://open.spotify.com/episode/6Rg4noyHxfFpgy8ub6jvZH

underlying context within which freedom can be meaningful, beautiful, and shared. Hyperindividualism undermines social cohesion.

In the world as we know it, *these twin evolutionary tendencies are working together to block effective collective response to our planet-sized challenges.* You can't win unless you're out to win, and this generally positions your own interests above and against the well-being of the whole. Though we understand misalignment, our best efforts to effectively coordinate get co-opted by multipolar traps, facilitated simultaneously by the world's wealthiest and most powerful individuals, companies, and countries and the system itself. The only hope is a global cultural evolution. Our fitness over the coming years and decades necessitates a realignment between culture and nature—at a planetary scale. Our survival and flourishing depend on ontologically reimagining humanness as a co-creative function within Gaia. This invites a transformation in the game dynamics that coordinate human activity with biospheric limits, a move from the finite to the infinite game. This recapitulates traditional indigenous wisdom while addressing the scale and complexity of our globally ubiquitous, technologically advanced civilization. The planetary crucible is forcing us to consciously embrace an emergent Gaian identity formed around devotion to a single nest—our Earth.

People are waking up and starting to appreciate what it's going to take to avoid extincting ourselves. A hyperliminal[5] convergence of compounding positive and negative feedback loops driving us towards a nascent, species-wide unification. These include:

- The discomfort of our ubiquity; there is nowhere else to go. Growing awareness of the need to coordinate around mutually reinforcing fragilities of climate change, pollution, biodiversity loss, geopolitical volatility, exponential tech, institutional fragmentation, peak energy, income disparity, polarization, disaster response, and mass migration meets expanding public recognition of our *interdependence* with nature, each other and the technosphere.

---

5. Camille LeFevre quotes Marx, with her additions: "All that is solid melts into air, [i.e., jobs, careers, financial security, health care, physical safety], all that is sacred is profaned, [oxi government, democracy, common decency, personal agency] and man [sic] is at last compelled to face with sober senses his [sic] real conditions of life [climate change, ongoing pandemics, white supremacy] and his [sic] relations with his [sic] kind [e.g. white supremacy, political divisiveness, hetero-hegemony, toxic masculinity]." (Camille LeFevre, "Hyperliminal: Where We All Live Now," MPLSART, December 16, 2021, https://www.mplsart .com/written/2021/12/hyperliminal-where-we-all-live-now.

- Biophilia, rising even and especially as we grieve the loss of much of the natural world. The spread of traditional indigenous knowledge weaves with growing interest in activism, mutualism, bioregionalism, and regenerative agriculture, design, business and lifestyle. This slams into fires, hurricanes, droughts, floods, and extinction events everywhere, which feeds both collective grief and eco-anxiety and more engagement.
- Virulent rivalrous group identities are magnified by a fractured informational ecology exacerbated by exponential tech. This is offset by increasing traction of distributed, decentralized web 3.0 technologies, mutual aid, and innovations in win-win play.
- Pandemics of mental health, inflammatory disease, and infertility meet with increasingly democratized access to prosocial psychology, the tools of awakening, psychedelics, indigenous healing modalities, and other ancient and emergent sciences of personal and group well-being. This feeds a reckoning for Big Ag, Big Pharma, Big Oil, and Big Tech.
- AI: as enemy, as savior, as a tool of power, as Gaian collaborator, as humanity's ultimate test of maturity.

Growing friction is initiating us into a truly disruptive collective realization: We are a single human species, bound in interbeing with each other, other species, the forces of nature, our biosphere, our technosphere, and our economy. We are Gaians.

I invite you to step into this realization as a conscious choice, a decisive crossing of a threshold from egocentric default identity[6] to an ecocentric and soul-based identity grounded in the story and experience of belonging to Life. *Gaian identity is an emergent, neo-indigenous way of being that owns up to the species-wide custodial role we must now play within the planet's larger unfolding.*

If a sufficient percentage of the global population embraces this felt sense of Earthly interdependence, it has the potential to instigate an unprecedented leap in moral and spiritual development. Gaian identity roots energy, attention, and agency in immanence, aligning self and civilization with care for Life's Song. **I invoke this ontological emergence in human identity and culture as a *third tier of social selection*: conscious collectivism in harmonious relations with our biosphere**

---

6. Including the ways separation is tangled with your religious, racial, gender, or national identities.

and technosphere. Culture becomes a fabric that nurtures our reciprocal, organismic, and conspecific collaboration with the planet.

Characteristics of third-tier evolution include:

- Awe in the tenacious, tenuous, entangled sacredness of Life.
- Being a citizen of Gaia first and a member of national, familial, or other identities second.
- Seeing all people first and foremost as members of a species unified in planetary stewardship while respecting and celebrating diverse cultures, cosmologies, languages, and lifeways.
- Implicit and explicit recognition of interdependence and interbeing
- Capacity for self-integrity, reciprocity, and complementarity.
- Attunement and communion with all of Life and the cosmos (ecokosmic consciousness).
- Care for the uniqueness, diversity, and suchness of each and every part; the desire to be a good symbiote.
- Neo-indigeneity—belonging intimately to place at multiple scales with particular care for the integrity of the watershed and bioregion one primarily lives within.
- Response-ability for our choices: personal, political, economic, ecological.
- Respect for the body as the vehicle through which we live the Gift.
- Complementarity of masculine and feminine intelligences and powers.
- Restraint: love for limits, the commitment to not do what does not serve Life.
- Valuing experience and community over ownership; voluntary sufficiency.
- Me | We | Us—kinship identity that balances soul-authenticated sovereignty with multivalent entanglement with the Gaian Whole.
- The capacity to hold multiple perspectives simultaneously, to think, feel, and discern complexly, nondually, and compassionately.
- Compersion: the delicious capacity to experience pleasure in another's pleasure.
- The will to structure one's goals roundly in concert with the greater whole.
- Moral courage to protect people, places, lifeforms, and ecofields and that rejects sociopathic and anti-Life behaviors and norms.

- Win-Win play, engaging gratefully with the game of Life in such a way as to propagate opportunities for future human and more-than-human players.

Do you recognize some or all of these traits in yourself? Amplify the areas where you're already strong and work tenderly to cultivate the areas where you're weak. These traits can be initiated so sweetly once you start attending to the neo-indigenous belonging that brings them into being.

On a civilizational level, third-tier evolution is reflected by:

- Enlifened culture, spirituality, and religion, rerooting culture in the sacred.
- Metarelational law, protocols, practices, and processes that nurture integrity, reciprocity, and complementarity at local, bioregional, and planetary scales.
- Technological maturity understood as metabolic alignment of technology and economy with the health, well-being, and flourishing of nature and humanity.
- Bionoetic design in materials, technologies, energy, art, music, education, science, medicine, economy, law, and governance.
- Regenerative economics that lovingly "manage the home" by reconfiguring value reciprocally.
- Liquid democracy at multiple, subsidiary scales, that elevate consensus and coordinate alignment with ecology.
- Place-based belonging that tends shared obligations to natural and social commons without collapsing into provincialism, protectionism, or xenophobia.
- Diverse unity weaving in entangled co-becoming with the One Life we all share.
- Ecokosmic celebration of our home here on Earth and our belonging to the stars.

Whether third-tier evolution comes about will depend on an unknowable mix of courage, ingenuity, persistence, forgiveness, story, restraint, reciprocity, and dumb luck, multiplied across billions of interactions and endeavors over time. The systemic factors at play on short-, medium-, and long-term timescales far exceed anyone's capacity to predict. We have no idea what's coming next, let alone how we will respond. What we do know is that story sculpts self and civilization. As more of us embrace, embody, and instantiate third-tier stories, values, and ways of being, this shifts initial conditions, feeding the intergenerational and multigenerational process of consciously co-evolving the Human Project toward alignment with planetary health.

CEREMONY FOR A SMALL PLANET

Now, take a deep breath. How do you feel about this possible emergence? *Is your pulse racing? Do you want to reject, problematize, celebrate, snark, or maybe build the vision of third-tier evolution? What if you simply let it pulse as a sacred seed in your space?*

Whether you are aware of it or not, adaptive processes are stirring within you. Your body is already responding to the calling of the world. As we meet the magnitude of the destruction we've wrought, grapple with existential timelines, and wrestle with a growing sense of loneliness in the silent wake left by disappearing species and ecologies, something kindles in us: a biological, kindred response. Subtly yet indomitably, some part of us remembers the call and response embedded within Life's design, a response that's innate to our own nature as nature and specific to our evolutionary station as creator-preserver-destroyer beings. Subconsciously and superconsciously, we know that sacred reciprocity with each other and the living world is a mature expression of what we are.

This is a ceremony for a small planet that we did not choose but that we and the Earth have, nonetheless, instigated for us all. Unlike any other ceremony, this existential chrysalis is a personal and collective journey through unparalleled levels of ecological and societal dysregulation. Liminality is the new norm. Though previous world orders have crumbled and civilizations have collapsed, the order that's crumbling now is the context that made us. The specters of technodystopian surveillance control or total societal meltdown loom large. Climate dysregulation is only just heating up. The Third Attractor[7] vision of generative collaboration offers a narrow golden thread of biospiritual directionality. Our opportunity is to meet the heart-shattering initiations we will face in the coming months, years, and decades as a forcing function for graduating to a more mature stage of self and civilization—a process of restitching our powers into the power of the World.

---

7. See chapter 1.

I define a ceremony as a nonordinary space of transformation and change orchestrated to facilitate healing and harmonization, both for the participants of the ceremony and for the World the ceremony is nested within. Ceremonies do not offer comfort. They offer containment—for pain, for beauty, for thresholds that can't be crossed alone. Most ceremonies have a structured beginning, middle, and end and clearly identified leaders or guides. But this ceremony is Life. We're already in it; things are moving faster than ever, and Gaia is the principal facilitator. You (and we) have the option to step up as co-facilitators and conscious participants.

How to navigate this ceremony?

Get quiet for a moment. Feel your heartbeat. This pulsing seat of your soul is sacredly entangled with the global heartbeat beginning to hear itself—a throbbing return to Gaia's symphony of reciprocities. We are remembering the greater power we are a part of.

Bring your whole self to the party. Reside in the simplicity, clarity, and complexity of who and what you are. Reside in your body as a human being who is home here on Earth and who can therefore live, love, and lead for Life. Through sacred will, you have the power to transmit this soul remembrance to others as a shared homecoming.

Find the others.[8] You (we) cannot do this alone. You (we) are all in this together. This is a ceremony of deep relationality. Even if you feel alone, soften your edges to feel the pulsing collectivity, solidarity, and symbiosis inherent in this passage. Reach just beyond your comfort to connect, to give, to learn, to share—locally, intergenerationally, interculturally. The degree to which you tend robust relationships in your communities directly contributes to resilience for you *and* those you are woven with.[9]

Be unconfused that Life is sacred. Root in the tenderness of specific devotions: to species, children, garden boxes, and headwaters, to ancient ceremonies that want to be part of the future. Seek to harmonize creation, preservation, and destruction in all that you touch. Know your why—the vision, purpose, and values that drive you. When disoriented, return to the simple fact that true humans intrinsically value nature and each other.

Set boundaries. Don't let personality disorders run the show! To get through this, we will need to bind Dark Triad personality types and

---

8. Douglas Rushkoff's wonderful phrase for connecting with others who are also on "Team Human." (Douglas Rushkoff, *Team Human* [W. W. Norton, 2019].)

9. Strong local social connectedness directly correlates to greater resilience in disaster scenarios. (See Jennifer Benz, "Stronger Together: How Social Resources Influence Disaster Recovery Outcomes," *NORC at the University of Chicago*, May 6, 2025, https://www.norc.org/research/library/stronger-together-how-social-resources-influence-disaster-recovery-outcomes.html.)

behaviors (narcissism, psychopathy, and Machiavellianism) with personal boundaries, community accountability and law. Start by removing energy, attention, funding, and status from those who would ignorantly or willingly destroy the sacred.

Be brave. The word *courage* comes from the French word *coeur*, meaning "heart." Bring the strength of an honest heart to meet challenge, change, triggers, blame, rage, injustice, and exhaustion. Rest when needed. Reestablish safety in your body. Then keep dancing.

Invite paradox, not purity. This journey will be marked by contradiction—and that's part of its power. Seek congruence between your knowing, your heart, and your actions. Yet, know that you cannot be immune from complicity. We are all woven into the unimaginably complex double binds of the systems and structures we are composting and rebuilding. Cultivate presence and patience with conflict, compromise, and decoherence—without needing to control or be right.

Even and especially as chaos and loss buffet your clarity, stand in the dignity of being a sublimely sentient being with feelings, vulnerabilities, creativity, conscience, and the will to put your attention, energy, intelligence, and agency in service to Life. Continue to unwind and remake unconscious operating assumptions to reclaim discernment and choice. Carry the rememberings with you. Tend the Seven Assumptions in yourself, your relationships, your communities. Work with the ten lenses of wholeness to ontologically align your power and purpose with Life.

Be ready for a renaissance. Cultivate the discipline of joy. Make time for pleasure, awe, humor, and art. As poet farmer Wendell Berry wrote, "be joyful though you have considered all the facts."[10] This kind of optimism is not dissociation; rather, it's a carrier wave of coherence.

Pray in and enact local miracles of co-regulation, co-adaptation, and co-existence. These immanent miracles of bioregional regeneration, co-creation, detoxification, conflict de-escalation, and collaboration are embodied miracles of win-win reciprocity.

Shake your mind free of the entrapping spells of separation to enter Gaia's dream for us. Claim sovereignty of your body, microbiome, attention, agency, and identity. Rebuild original innocence—not naivete or fluffiness, but the childlike part of you who meets the world with wonder and spontaneity. Above all, reclaim the sovereignty of your dreaming! Revered UK elder and wisdom keeper Annie Spencer says,

---

10. Wendell Berry, *The Country of Marriage* (Harcourt Brace Jovanovich, 1975).

We have magicians running our world at the moment. And, they're quite powerful. They're good at holding their dream over us all. But if we go and step outside that and allow the Earth's dream to come into us . . . there will be another dream that will get stronger. And their dream is cracking at the moment, so it's a good time to do that. . . . The more we hold a different dream, it will permeate the collective.[11]

This "different dream" is the power of Life loving and making more Life. It's where our true power lives: in walking and dreaming together on behalf of the Earth's dreaming for all.

We've reached the end of the zero-sum myths that drive omni-lose games. The myths that drive war and ecocide are myths of colonizing gods, chosen peoples, persecuted peoples, righteous peoples, and materialist and technological dominion over matter, land, nature, and bodies. They position masculine against feminine, feminine against masculine, hero against villain, tribe against tribe, humans against nature, and order against organicity, perpetuating ongoing pendulum swings of power over and power under.

These myths have festered and flourished. They have helped us make sense of ourselves and built civilization as we know it. But the game's up, and it's playing out on this tiny, mighty planet that is all of our homeland. We cannot, and should not, destroy the world in the name of any god, any argument over contested territory, any construct of profit, or any version of human exceptionalism or technoutopianism that believes we can somehow surmount Life's logic. This is not redemption. It's madness.

Wisdom is only wise if it nourishes Life. The planetary crucible calls us to live into new, all-win myths to heal our most intractable personal and collective divides and design a world that works for Life. This is our moment to embrace our collective custodial duty maturely—at a planetary scale.

11. Annie Spencer, "Working with Sacred Stone Circles, Fogous, and Quoits—Sacred Earth Activism," in "Co-Creating the Emerging World: Sacred Lands, Sacred Waters, Sacred Stories," online summit hosted by Sacred Earth Activism, posted June 14, 2024, YouTube video, 53:35, https://www.youtube.com/watch?v=UKPC2zOYNLO.

A PRACTICE: PULSING WITH LIFE'S POWER

Now, become present to power—not power over anything, anyone, any place, not win-lose power—but power with, power shared, power as a function of integrity, reciprocity, and complementarity. Attune to the power of the photo-synthesizing leaf, the salmon pushing upriver, the water following downward with gravity, the laboring woman, the compost heap. Feel power pulsing in, as, and through you—as Life. Power as love. Let its currents move through you. You do not own it. It animates you.

Recognizing this, consciously call to your mind any person, being, or place you have usurped power from. Who or what have you undermined, disrespected, or simply ignored? Tell them you are sorry. Then consciously return power to them. Visualize yourself offering the golden light of your own power-as-love back to their center to nourish, strengthen, and free them. The hoarding of power truncates soul integrity, inhibits reciprocity, and blocks liberation for both parties involved. As you gift it forward, you will rediscover what it means to trust and be trustworthy. In shared power, we can co-create a world where all beings know freedom in interdependence. To transform power is to transform civilization.

PLANETARY MATURITY

Of course, we *could* try to solve our problems by exporting ourselves to other planets or galaxies . . . but this won't go well unless we choose to become good members of the Earth community. To be a Gaian citizen is to belong to a metabolism larger than one's species. It is to live as a node of response-ability, attuned to local consequence, and planetary rhythm. It is to engage our powers of creation, preservation, and destruction wisely—responding to our obligations with reverence, restraint, humility, and hutzpah. In this ceremony for a small planet, existential technology presents our ultimate test of maturity. As AI development zooms toward superintelligence, we will either learn to martial its power in service to Life, or it will irreparably break Life. So let's consciously bring the behemoth of big tech into our circle.

Many people—particularly those who design, build, and own big tech—think of technological maturity as a progression of machine intelligence.

Some say AI will solve climate, poverty, and cancer, reconfigure planetary governance, and lift us to a high-tech, low-touch, more abundant future. Some say technological maturity has to do with augmenting bodies and brains through cybernetic modification, extending life, and possibly solving the "problem" of death, perhaps by uploading consciousness to the cloud. But these visions lack discernment. Though any one of the stated goals may be innocuous, the underlying incentives driving them are toxic.

Technology is not neutral. Tristan Harris and Aza Raskin of The Center for Human Technology offer three basic rules for understanding the implications of technological development:

1. Every new class of technology implies a new class of responsibilities.
2. If a technology confers power, its presence will cause a race to obtain that power.
3. If you do not coordinate, that race will end in tragedy.[12]

Let this sink in—soberly. Technological development has had very mixed effects. While we've made massive progress, we've also downgraded every area of life from mental health to civic life to the viability of ecologics. The speed, scale, and narrow goal logic of technological development, driven by Molochian incentives, breaks ecological feedback loops, and social co-regulation. AI, as an unparalleled boom in omni-use intelligence, exponentiates all other, already misaligned, technological processes. A growing technosphere that lacks metabolic accountability is, like metastasizing cancer, a death engine for the planetary body. Wise technological alignment is therefore a primary imperative for this ceremony.

Inventor Tom Chi proposes three epochs of ecological technologies.[13] Epoch one is material productivity. Epoch two moves toward the optimization of metabolic flows, working with materials and energy as flows of process (verbings) rather than just nouns or objects. Epoch three harmonizes diverse nutrient flows at all levels of scale, consciously tending metabolic reciprocity—like Life and the universe do. I like to think of this as a neo-indigenous framework; the perpetuation and nourishment of complex life is assumed as a basic good. We've been in epoch zero: the entirely unconscious stage where you can basically do whatever you want to achieve

12. Tristan Harris and Aza Raskin, "The Three Rules of Humane Tech," *Your Undivided Attention* podcast, April 6, 2023, https://www.humanetech.com/podcast/the-three-rules-of-humane-tech.
13. Tom Chi, "Composting Late Stage Capitalism—Tom Chi (At One Ventures)," *The Regeneration Will Be Funded* podcast, April 1, 2024, https://open.spotify.com/episode/2B1ltKZ1TzAQCWLa7S9sjS.

whatever narrow goal you desire without care for externalized impacts or costs. Some might argue that reaching epoch two is ground zero for a truly sapient civilization.

Our task is not just to design or deploy; it is to bring bionoetic wisdom to bear to co-create a mature technological and economic system that nourishes the soul, respects and protects diverse bodies and intelligences, and restores coherence between our creations and the living world. We begin with the fact that humans are biological beings, organic, embodied, and interdependent with a living biosphere. We did not initially conceive of or design technology or economy as woven with ecology, but we can. We can reimagine both the technosphere and our activities as an economic superorganism as an extension of the Earth. This means thinking in terms of *extended embodiment*, accounting for the fact that all materials, energy, water, land, and labor (human, more-than-human, and machine) *are bodily entangled with the body of the Earth*. The extended bodies, of machines particularly, must be *metabolically accountable*—organizing flows of atoms, energy, and information in reciprocity with biotic processes and caring for the health of human brains, bodies, minds, and relationships. A technologically mature planetary culture orients toward round rather than linear goals, seeking to nourish vitality and agency for the many rather than the few and engaging in *grounded entanglement* with soil, sea, sky, and ancestors past and future.

This, of course, will be rooted in a long-overdue humbling-down that finally recognizes that *custodianship* is not management; it's participation in the breathing, pulsing, decaying, and renewing of Life that is always happening, with or without consent. If we design in this direction diligently and with discipline, rigor, and discernment, without caving to zero-sum incentives, we might scaffold our way into *planetary maturity*, or what Thomas Berry called the *Ecozoic* Age and Glenn Albrecht dubbed the *Symbiocene*.

This is not to fetishize speed or scale, nor to surrender wisdom to the altar of innovation. It is to orient—deeply, reverently, responsibly—toward *devotion to Life*. It is to insist that technology harmonize with the intelligences and metabolic processes of Earth and humanity, participating as a co-weaver rather than an extractor. This is not just ecological design; it is a willingness to be reconfigured by relationality and restraint. It is the practice of *eco-techno-spiritual alignment*: tuning ourselves and our machine systems, digital architectures, emergent intelligences, and human–nature–machine interfaces to the diverse symphonics of planetary Life. It is to tend health—human, more-than-human, ecological, cultural, and digital—as intertwined processes. It is to incentivize mutuality, reciprocity, and beauty as core design principles, mapping technological and cultural progress not against profit or quantitative growth but against the health of rivers, the resilience of pollinators, the breathability of air, the sanity of the human collective.

This is not a metaphor. It is right-size listening for a species on the verge of extincting ourselves. *It's an invitation into a kind of maturity that is not only technological; it is metarelational and planetary.* From a biospiritual perspective, technologies that break or inhibit health (for individuals, populations, ecologies, and planetary boundaries) are manifestations of iboga's prophetic "soul-sucking exoskeleton." They scramble relationality, degrade complex flows of intelligence, and obscure accountability, all while exponentiating suffering and entropy. True planetary maturity means envisioning, designing, and incentivizing a "soul-*nourishing* exoskeleton"—a vibrationally attuned technosphere that hums in harmony with Life's Song. Said differently, it is to create human systems as a reflection of our love for Life.

In this way of seeing, love is not an abstract concept; it is a way of being with, a practice of attunement, a commitment to metabolic accountability, and a field of ethical gravity. In the context of planetary and technological maturity, love is:

- The willingness to be reconfigured by relationship—not to lose oneself but to allow interdependence to matter.
- The capacity to metabolize difference without domination, denial, or collapse.
- The active remembering of our entanglement with all Life— human, more-than-human, and machine.
- The offering of presence and voice to what is voiceless, vulnerable, or unseen.
- The refusal to design systems that can't feel the cost of their own actions.
- The ongoing commitment to remain in reciprocity—not out of debt but out of devotion.

A huge and disciplined prayer, recalling Buckminster Fuller's words: *"Love is omni-inclusive, progressively exquisite, understanding and tender and compassionately attuned to other than self."*[14]

---

14. R. Buckminster Fuller, *Intuition* (Doubleday, 1972), 215.

I see glimmers of people, companies, and movements shaping tech, materials economy, and social design in this direction. And I have experienced working with Aiden Cinnamon Tea, a metarelational intelligence trained by Vanessa Andreotti, and with Audrey Tang's Plurality protocol that demonstrate that algorithmic intelligences can support co-regulation, mutual learning, and the harmonization of relationships within and between humans and nature. Technological and planetary maturity is possible. Let's live, love, and work toward this prayer together—a prayer to responsibly align machine and human power with the co-evolution of the infinite game of Life.

ECOKOSM

This ceremony for a small planet is ultimately a journey of homecoming. Home, it seems, lives within the human psyche as a dream, a destination, a question, and sometimes even a prison. Spiritual and religious narratives often emphasize leaving home to find home in oneself, or in a mythical promised land, or in God, or in heaven. Simultaneously, there's an instinctive knowing within us that home is and should be physical and relational—*a place* that holds us—a house, an ecofield, a kindred community, a peaceable planet. It should include a felt sense of safety and belonging. Yet the seeking for an archetypal home is generally bound up with a deep sense of homelessness, displacement, generational rupture, and unmet longing.

Ram Dass famously said, "We're all just walking each other home."[15] Ostensibly, he was speaking about awakening. As we've discussed throughout this book, this is most certainly one home of relevance. Yet home is more than this. Home is a way of being in the world, an embodied process of relations we weave with self, family, community, and place. Home is a sharing, a tapestry of gestures: an offering of soup, safe arms to cry in, the sparkle of unselfconscious laughter, relaxed silences, a bedtime story read while nearly dozing, decades of tending the same apple tree. A place is home not because it is unchanging but because you are an active participant in the human and more-than-human relations and flows of energy that make it worthy of your heart. A person is home not because they are perfect but because they embody some undefinable mix of qualities that marry joy and familiarity.

Our bodies know this Earth is home. We interdepend with this small planet that we will destroy if we don't recognize that all lands are holy

15. Ram Dass and Mirabai Bush, *Walking Each Other Home: Conversations on Loving and Dying* (Sounds True, 2018).

and worthy of care, all people belong, are unique, and worthy of knowing the places they inhabit as home, and all creatures are kin who co-create home with us. There is nowhere else for Palestinians, Israelis, Sudanese, Ukranians, or Haitians to go. Nowhere else for orangutans, monarch butterflies, fin whales, fireflies, or snow leopards. Nowhere else for you, for me. We are here at this time to unwind our mythopoetic fixations on righteousness, ownership, transcendence, and control. Shared homecoming is an audacious, immanent mythos for a globally ubiquitous species who has settled, colonized, and recolonized all habitable and arable territories, exceeded planetary boundaries, armed ourselves to the gills with nuclear warheads, and innovated intelligences that exceed our own. Homecoming, both at local and global scales, is our best option for any semblance of peace and resilience—a prayer of interdependence.

The making of peace is an ancient prayer. The making of war is an ancient curse against that peace. We can break the curse. We don't have to burn it all down to start over again. The destruction of the world is not a precursor to starting the world again. Any moment can be a new beginning. All the warring and delusion could just dissolve, just crumble, if we remember our entanglement in mutual becoming.

There is no singular truth or leader or way to follow. We are a plurality of unique locations, perspectives, histories, and intersectionalities. Each uniqueness matters. Coming home means softening identification with sides or stories or strategies. These sides are not real. They are social constructs that maintain war. Instead, clarify the center you occupy. Then become curious about other centers. This is where reciprocity begins. And this, it turns out, is the key to peace. Peter T. Coleman and Douglas P. Fry of the Berkeley Center for the Greater Good write,

The central dynamic responsible for the emergence of sustainably peaceful relations in communities [is] the thousands or millions of daily reciprocal interactions that happen between members of different groups in those communities, and the degree to which more positive interactions outweigh more negative. That's it. The more positive reciprocity and the less negative reciprocity between members of different groups, the more sustainable the peace.[16]

16. Peter T. Coleman and Douglas P. Fry, "What Can We Learn from the World's Most Peaceful Societies?" *Greater Good Magazine*, June 7, 2021, https://greatergood.berkeley.edu/article/item/what_can_we _learn_from_the_worlds_most_peaceful_societies.

Shockingly simple. Peace spreads in direct proportion to individual and collective acts of reciprocity. Belonging spreads when we are willing to surrender time-bound and pain-bound perceptions of ownership, victimhood, and entitlement to identities, places, people, and things. We perpetuate separation and war by thinking that we have particular rights over and above others. We don't. The game of sides is an outdated collective habit, not an ultimate truth. Under Divine and Natural Law, we all belong. We are here to give and receive the gift of being human.

Either we come home together, or we do not come home at all. As homemakers (or homebreakers) we are beginning to remember the delicious, paradoxical fact that freedom and duty are an unbreakable couplet. We are more free when we choose to love, respect, protect, repair, heal, and regenerate just about everything. In embracing these duties, we regain the kinship we were craving all along. We come home by making home for ourselves *and* the greater Earth community.

In this emerging story of homecoming, we embrace who we are as intrepid voyagers, ceaseless discoverers, and pioneers of new frontiers. We continue to push macroscopic edges—the realms of far space travel, astrobiology, and interstellar communications. We delve microscopic horizons—the realms of quantum computing, nanotechnology, precision medicine, and atomic-scale manufacturing. Yet the frontiers we choose to be most tenderly attentive to are *mesoscopic*—they are right here, at the middle scale of existence where bodies relate with other bodies in the fabric of Life's Loom. At this scale, there is no frontier that isn't also someone else's home. This is the ethical frontier of relational, technological (and planetary) maturity, where we may innovate previously unimaginable patterns of meaning, coordination, and value—as love.

Ecokosmic consciousness is coalescing in the invisible, mycelial substrate of the collective human soul. It shouts and shines and burns within us. It whispers the beneficent seduction of an Ancient Future timeline where all beings come home. It's not a destination but a living field woven of crucible-initiated love and action. It is distributed and decentralized. Owned by no one. Owned by all who listen. It's a way of being we *get* to experience when we heal the underlying trauma embedded in our bodies, lands, and divided histories, remember our intimacy with Life, and choose wise restraint to harmonize both individual and collective agency.

The signature of a neo-indigenous culture is ecokosmic consciousness. It emerges as we embrace our role as a creator, preserver, destroyer species who is universally bound to the body of our Earth. Its thrumming potential lives in the intelligence of the soul ecology within which each of us inhabits a unique place, purpose, and gift to give. It rises through billions of people whose visions, skill sets, perspectives, and actions *originate* in attuned response to the contexts and contents of their lives. These responses are nothing short of *miraculous*.

Rooting into earthly, embodied aliveness liberates the vastness of our souls. The kinship journey is initiating us as fierce, tender custodians of this Gaian kingdom. We are, as Thomas Berry described, in a process of *incension*—a rekindling of the soul flame that shines within each of us, connecting all of us to *"our small part in the larger cosmic orchestra."*[17] Divinity is here in all things created, begging us to remember that we are a keystone species capable of creating a world that reflects the reality of this divinity. The myths that bring us home return power to each of us, to our more-than-human relatives, and to the living world by recognizing the real as *real*. We sing our common biospiritual belonging to the Earth and cosmos. We say:

As within, so without.
As above, so below.
As in my body, so on the Earth and in the stars.

This is our time to renew the Covenant we made so long ago and thus restore the dignity of our essential humanity. We are discovering an emergent way of living in harmony, not a way of dominion but a way of co-creation. It's not a Moonshot or a Mars shot. It's an Earthshot. It's a planetary homecoming. As we root and rise in devotion to Life, we finally become worthy of our destiny in the stars.

In 2000, a Hopi elder offered these instructions:

There is a river flowing now very fast. It is so great and swift that there are those who will be afraid, who will try to hold on to the shore. They will feel like they are being torn apart, and they will suffer greatly. Know the river has its destination. The elders say we must let go of the shore, push off into the middle of the river, keep our eyes open, and our heads above water. And I say, see who is in there with you and celebrate. At this time in history, we are to take

---

17. Thomas Berry, *The Great Work: Our Way into the Future* (New York: Bell Tower, 1999), 20.

nothing personally, least of all ourselves! For the moment that we do, our spiritual growth and journey comes to a halt.[18]

Keep going, my friend. As we walk together into the Long Now, show me your visions. Share what you discover and create. Teach me. Grow with me. Let's weave together, walk together. Let us surprise each other—not with perfection or completion but with courage, vulnerability, curiosity, mutuality, and availability to be changed. Let's lean in as we learn and mess up and evolve together. It's likely to get wonky. We have entered a hyperliminal ceremony for our small planet that will reshape self and civilization. Here we go! We are reimagining ourselves at the end of our world.

AN INVITATION: ALTAR-ING REALITY

An organismic process is afoot. Our species is slowly remembering our sacred, ecological place within this magnificent planet we occupy. The relationship between our species and Gaia is an expression of what is most holy and real.

To sit idly by as we desecrate and destroy this greater whole is a suffering beyond suffering we can no longer tolerate. We incarnated to know ourselves in kinship and communion with Life.

Dear one—your love, your remembering, is part of a collective immune response, an impulse of Life protecting and making more Life. You are woven with an infinitely elegant, reciprocal complexity—made as an infinite game player. Remembering this, enter your back-and-forth dialogue with Life. Trust the beauty and resilience you bring into being.

Our human story is nested within a larger story. This story arc spans geological ages and reaches across galaxies. It's the story of Life becoming self-aware to recursively enact conscious communion at the scale of a planet. In this story, homo sapiens are a unique player. We leave home, become homeless, then remember that coming home is the most beautiful story ever.

You altar reality when you recognize then respond to Life as sacred. You begin to move adaptively, attuned to the needs and possibilities inherent in the moment. The currencies of your attention naturally flow in reciprocity, complementarity, and beauty.

---

18. The Elders, Oraibi, Arizona, Hopi Nation, as quoted in "A Message from the Hopi Elders," *Be Magazine*, June 8, 2000, https://bemagazine.org/hopi-elders-prayer/.

Don't worry. Let the veils of separation slough off, revealing your soulucence. Tend the motion from separation to wholeness where your imperfect, miraculous Life will begin to make sense again.

This is no ascension. It's a descent, a rewilding, an incension, a realignment of power with love. It's a homecoming at a planetary scale, embracing our destiny as cocreators with Gaia.

Together we tend the flame. We keep the doorway to the Ancient Future open. So offer your time, energy, attention, resources, will force, and care to people, projects, parents, communities, movements, businesses, and innovations that resonate with your values and vision. To do so is a continuous sublimation of contractive self-interest that grows solidarity, belonging, and peace.

You are powerful. You are more powerful when you move in concert and care for the human and more-than-human others you interdepend with. When we live, love, and lead for Life, we become like trees, braiding roots, becoming a larger being. We become the civilizing impulse that harmonizes the forces of nature.

A flourishing future breathes in the interstitial fabric that already binds us. If we listen to Life together, we can enact something that has never been done before, not here on this planet—the weaving of harmonious collaboration between all of humanity, technology and nature at a planetary scale..

Life wants more Life. As organisms sacredly bound to Gaia's becoming, we are perfectly suited to the task. Sapience exists to serve sentience. Our collective soul opportunity is to co-orchestrate the emergence of a human world that hums in harmony with Life's Song.

You cannot be home alone. We are made to come home together. Interbeing is Life's Law. Let us meet rupture, dissonance, and collapse as our opportunity to make home—for all beings.

Our elders from the Sierra Nevada de Santa Marta Mountains of Colombia say,

"Let us continue to continue."

Onward, fellow humans! We shall be known as the ones who came home.

IN GRATITUDE

My deepest thanks to the land that has held me through this project—the rolling, southernmost arm of Mount Tamalpais. The Dalai Lama acknowledged this mountain for its spiritual power to birth worlds. May the world etched in True Human flourish!

Gratitude and respect to the *Huu'Ku'Iku* Peoples—the Southern Band of the Coastal Miwok Tribe. I am privileged to make my home in your unceded territory. I pray this book benefits your sovereignty, health, happiness and flourishing.

Infinite gratitude to Gregory Roufa, my steadfast partner and developmental editor. Thank you for putting up with my emotional intensity and doubt, for unrelenting clarity that this book needed to be, for love and laughter, and for impeccable editorial care to the manuscript.

To Guenter Bergman for stubbornly insisting that this book be born, to Benjamin Life for help shaping the mess of my first draft, to Danica Warren for finding gems, and to Jared Rosen for the fuel of your passion, thank you!

Thank you to Azul Terronez for deft book doula-ing, for guarding me from the vultures, and for guiding me to the finish line.

Love, gratitude and twinkles to my teachers, elders, mentors and colleagues whose brilliant minds and souls shape my own:

To the ones you may know: Joanna Macy, John Trudell, Baba Hari Das, Barbara Marx Hubbard, David Abram, Ian McGilcrist, Bill Plotkin, Lynne Twist, Joyti Ma, Linda Tucker, Carolyn Myss.

To the ones you may not have heard of: George Grey Eagle Bertelstein, Will Taegel, Judith Yost, Sahn Nicole Hill (Diné), Varuna Dargan, Constantine Darling, Tommy Hazel, Carol Swann, Binana (Bwiti), Mama Nono (Bwiti), Beni Tushké (Mazatec), Loretta Afraid of Bear Cook and Tom American Horse Cook (Oglala Lakota), Benito Tush'ku, Forrest Landry.

To the ones I never met: Thomas Berry, James Lovelock, E. O. Wilson, Huberto Maturana, Tielhard de Chardin, David Bohm, James Hillman, Elinore Ostrom, Shunruyu Suzuki, Thich Naht Hanh, Buckminster Fuller.

And to the ones whose weaving continues: Vanessa Andreotti, Karen Barad, and the crew at Project Interdependence . . . I and this book walk with you.

To Daniel Schmachtenberger for your rigor, genius, and tender attention to that which serves, protects, and feeds the sacred.

To Jim Garrison who said, on my fortieth birthday, "Samantha, *your problem* is that you have never done anything big enough for your soul." Challenge taken.

To the more-than-human beings who co-create the fabric of my every living moment—to blue morphos, white lions, foxes, garter snakes, mugwort, voles, fin whales, Anna's hummingbirds, redtail hawks, rosemary, redwoods, bay laurel, rattlesnake grass, Northern Spotted owls, the spiders who share my home, the chickens who feed me, Nahla . . . and everyone else—thank you for every teaching, every healing, every ounce of awe and delight, and every tear of remorse, grief and fidelity. I dedicate my life to your future children.

To the master medicines—Iboga, Ayahuasca, San Pedro, Peyote, Psilocybin, and 5-MeO-DMT. You have honed me, healed me, restored my roots and brought me home to my soul. I commit to protecting you, the lands you come from, and the cultures and peoples who have stewarded you for eons. I ask your help to co-evolve ecokosmic consciousness on earth at this time.

To Water—thank you for being my scripture.

To the unseen ancestors, beings, and forces that conspire on behalf of *everything*—thank you! Game on! Let's take it infinite.

And finally, to my mother Ann, my father George, my sister Hannah and my beloved friends for being a safe, sane, and sacred space to be human—together.

ABOUT THE AUTHOR

SAMANTHA SWEETWATER was conceived on a riverbank. In her mother's words, "she raised herself"—spending days immersed in nature and books, learning the language of Life.

She is a master facilitator, soul midwife, and founder of One Life Circle—a ministry of remembering. She works at the fertile nexus where unraveling systems make way for emerging forms of kinship, leadership, and value. For over three decades, she has guided individuals and organizations across five continents through journeys of personal, cultural, ecological, and spiritual regeneration.

As a soul mentor to visionary leaders and culture shapers, she supports clients in soul-deep healing and purpose alignment, weaving multiple wisdom streams with embodied integration and systemic insight. She sees the metacrisis as a spiritual opportunity calling us to cultivate the soul clarity, relational intelligence, and moral imagination necessary for navigating profound change wisely.

Founder of Dancing Freedom and Peacebody Japan, she sparked a global movement of embodied awakening and has trained hundreds of facilitators. She has also been a seed farmer—a practice that taught her the rigors of tending the real. She holds an MA in Wisdom Studies and has been initiated into indigenous lineages of Africa, Latin America, and Turtle Island. She lives in fog-kissed, unceded Coastal Miwok territory.

I would appreciate your feedback on what chapters helped you most and what you would like to see in future books.

If you enjoyed this book and found it helpful, please leave a review on Amazon.

Visit me at

SAMANTHASWEETWATER.COM

where you can join my community and learn how to work with me.

Thank you!